True Stories

of

Old Houston

and

Houstonians

WITH

A Thumbnail
History
of
The City of
Houston, Texas

From Its Founding in 1836 to the Year 1912

By Dr. S. O. Young

Copano Bay Press

2020

A Thumbnail History *first published in June 1912 under the same title by Rein & Sons Company of Houston*

True Stories *first published in June 1913 under the same title by Oscar Springer, Publisher, of Galveston*

ISBN: 978-1-941324-34-9

True Stories

of

OLD HOUSTON
&
HOUSTONIANS

TABLE OF CONTENTS

WHISKEY, WOMEN AND SONG

CRITTERS (NATURAL AND SUPERNATURAL)

FIGHTING HOUSTON MEN, IN WAR AND IN PEACE

Publisher's Note

This new edition of *True Stories of Old Houston and Houstonians* appears here as it was originally written, with all of Dr. Young's original stories intact. The only modifications consist of minor ones that occur during the usual editing process. A few spellings were corrected here and there; some punctuation was updated. The stories have been loosely grouped according to subject matter so that the reader might find what he or she is looking for more readily.

Reading these stories requires that the reader recall that what passed for "political correctness" in Dr. Young's day was vastly different than the modified speech habits that we employ today under the same guise. There most certainly are words this book that may be deemed offensive to some if not mindfully taken in the context of the period in which they were written. However, I am of the view that, for better or for worse, history is history. It illustrates where we've been and shines a critical spotlight on where we are at the moment. Racial views and cultural vernacular are a part of that history. It can't and shouldn't be modified or edited away, nor has it been in this book.

Michelle M. Haas, Managing Editor
Seven Palms - Rockport, Texas

An Introduction

by Mark Pusateri

I first encountered *True Stories of Old Houston and Houstonians* in the Houston Public Library's Texas Room about fifteen years ago. As a native Houstonian, I was delighted to read Houston's history as it was lived, not just a distillation of facts and dates. I read it cover to cover and decided I had to have my own copy. Due to the rarity of the book and my meager budget, the search took almost five years.

Who was S. O. Young? How is it he knew so many stories from Houston's early years? Why, in 1913, did he compile them into a book at his own expense?

Samuel Oliver Young, Jr. (1848-1926) was born just two months after the death of his father in the midst one of Houston's many Yellow Fever epidemics. He grew up among San Jacinto veterans and the prominent citizens of early Houston. His mother reared him in the home of her father, Nathan Fuller, one of Houston's early mayors. Young served in the Civil War, enlisting while he was still a teen, in the Bayou City Guards (Company A, Fifth Texas Infantry), a unit of Hood's Texas Brigade.

His mother seems to have been set on making him a carbon copy of his father, giving him the same name and pushing him to become a physician. Young dutifully practiced that profession from 1870 until her death in 1882. At that time he abandoned medicine to become a newspaperman. He founded the newspaper which, after many mergers became the *Houston Post*. In 1885, he sold his interest in the paper and moved to Galveston to write for the *Galveston News*.

Some readers will already know S. O. Young from his account of the 1900 Galveston Storm which is detailed in Erik Larson's book, *Isaac's Storm*. He was still a Galveston resident in 1900, working as Secretary of the Galveston Cotton Exchange. Dr. Young was determined to ride out the storm in his home. The storm destroyed the house sending him surfing across the island on his front door.

Then, as now, native Houstonians were a rare breed. Dr. Young was in his mid-sixties when he began telling these tales in the *Chronicle*. In his lifetime Houston had grown from a town of 2,400 people to a city of 80,000. Nostalgia literally means, "a longing to go home," and Dr. Young was clearly indulging his own nostalgic impulse, attempting to preserve the way of life he had known and loved. His pen was certainly capable of doing that, but in order for there to be market, a demand must also exist. There was indeed a demand, and not only from old-timers, but also from newcomers wanting to know something of the city they had adopted.

Dr. Young's stories of boyhood in Houston read like something out of *Tom Sawyer*. They take place in the 1850s and here the natural environment looms large. With a population of only about 3,500 souls, Houston was lush and unspoiled. Artesian springs could be found in what is now Downtown. Adventure lurked around every corner and it was nothing less than a boy's paradise.

The greatest number of stories, however, take place during the period from 1870 to 1885. These stories are set in a town busily growing from about 9,000 inhabitants to 23,000. Here we are presented with a Houston of mud streets, thriving saloons, and flamboyant gamblers. We get an insider's view of Reconstructionist military rule, political feuds and even rigged elections. Dr. Young treats us to the eccentricities of early Houstonians, their habits of speech, modes of dress, their schemes, their passions and pastimes.

J. Frank Dobie said in his introduction to *Coronado's Children*, "These tales are not creations of mine. They belong to the soil and to the people of the soil." Likewise, these stories were not created by S. O. Young. They belong to Houston and Houstonians, of the past, of the present and of generations yet to come.

A Word in Advance

These stories owe their being largely to chance. The whole series was unintentionally begun. I wrote an article for the Houston Chronicle, giving the correct version of something that occurred in Houston forty years ago, an inaccurate account of which had appeared in one of the newspapers. Managing Editor Gillespi liked my story so much that he asked me to write others of the same kind. I agreed to do so, thinking that I could probably find material for half a dozen stories. After I got started, each subject suggested another and so it has gone on, until now, the half dozen has grown into the hundreds, with the end not yet in sight.

So many people have written to me asking that I print the stories in book form, that I have determined to do so, and have selected those found here as being, in my opinion, the best. These letters have come from all parts of the state and from several Eastern and Northern states. Then too, people are constantly writing to the Chronicle asking for back numbers containing the stories, showing the demand for them.

I have enjoyed writing these stories, for each one has brought back some pleasant memory, and I hope that all those into whose hands this little book may fall, will enjoy reading them.

THE AUTHOR

IN THE BEGINNING...

I suppose it must have been published many times, but if so it has escaped my notice until the other day. I refer to the original advertisement of the town of Houston by the Allen Bros. The following is the document in full, which appeared originally in the *Telegraph*, published at that time at Columbia, on the Brazos River:

★ ★ ★

"THE TOWN OF HOUSTON"

Situated at the head of navigation on the west bank of Buffalo Bayou, is now for the first time brought to public notice, because, until now, the proprietors were not ready to offer to the public, with the advantages of capital and improvements.

The town of Houston is located at a point on the river which must ever command the trade of the largest and richest portions of Texas. By reference to the map it will be seen that the trade of San Jacinto, Spring Creek, New Kentucky, and the Brazos, above and below Fort Bend, must necessarily come to this place, and will at this time warrant the employment of at least $1,000,000 of capital, and when the rich lands of this country shall be settled a trade will flow to it, making it, beyond all doubt, the great commercial emporium of Texas.

The town of Houston is distant 15 miles from the Brazos, 30 miles a little north of east from San Felipe, 60 miles from Washington, 40 miles from Lake Creek, 30 miles southwest from New Kentucky and 15 miles by water and 8 miles by land above Harrisburg.

Tidewater runs to this place and the lowest depth of water is about six feet. Vessels from New York and New Orleans can sail without obstacle to this place, and steamboats of the largest class can run down to Galveston in eight or ten hours in all seasons of the year.

It is but a few hours sail down the bay, where one can make excursions of pleasure and enjoy the luxuries of fish, fowl, oysters and sea-bathing.

Galveston harbor, being the only one in which vessels drawing a large draft of water can navigate, must necessarily render the island the great naval and commercial depot of the country.

The town of Houston must be the place where arms, ammunition and provisions for the government will be stored, because, situated in the very heart of the country, it combines security and means of easy distribution, and a national armory will no doubt very soon be at this point.

There is no place in Texas more healthy, having an abundance of excellent spring water and enjoying the sea breeze in all its freshness.

No place in Texas possesses so many advantages for building, having fine ash, cedar and oak in inexhaustible quantities, also the tall and beautiful magnolia grows in abundance. In the vicinity are fine quarries of stone.

Nature seems to have designated this place for the future seat of government. It is handsome and beautifully elevated, salubrious and well-watered and is now in the very center of population and will be so for a long time to come.

It combines two important advantages—a communication with the coast and with foreign countries and with different portions of the republic. As the country shall improve, railroads will become in use and will be extended from this point to the Brazos and up the same, and also from this up to the headwaters of the San Jacinto, embracing that rich country, and in a few years the whole trade of the upper Brazos will make its way into Galveston Bay through this channel.

Preparations are making to erect a water sawmill, and a large public house for accommodation will soon be opened. Steamboats now run in this river and will, in a short time, commence running regularly to the island. The proprietors offer lots for sale at moderate terms to those who desire to improve them and invite the public to examine for themselves.

(*Signed*)   A. C. Allen for
                                          A. C. & J. K. Allen
                                          August 30, 1836

That old document is as fine a piece of advertising as any turned out by the "artists" of today. It has one great merit, that of truthfulness, for whether intentionally or not the Allens told almost the literal truth in every line they wrote, for all that they forecast has come true a thousandfold.

I was glad to come across that old advertisement for it settles two stories that have been told so often that everybody has grown to believe them to be true. No doubt, impressed by the fulfillment of so many prophecies made by the Allens, some writers have deemed it safe to add a little to them, and have allowed their imaginations somewhat free play. An instance of this is the story that when they were laying out the streets and blocks for Houston, one of the Allens placed his pencil on "Railroad Street" and remarked that the future railroad would have its start right there. Unfortunately for this story, there was no Railroad Street laid out by the Allens, and the street that now bears that name was not created until over 20 years after the Allens laid out their town. Their city was bounded on the north by Buffalo Bayou. All the territory north of the bayou was densely wooded and they paid no attention to it. Now, since Railroad Street is on the north side of the bayou and got its name from the railroads that run over it, it is quite evident that the Allens could have had nothing to do with naming it when the city was laid out.

Another story destroyed by that advertisement is the one about Mrs. A. C. Allen naming the town. She may have named it and if she ever said she did I know she did, but not in the way the story goes. Following is the story: While the Texas congress was in session, the Allen brothers were trying to find a suitable name for their city. One of them consulted his sister, Mrs. A. C. Allen, who without hesitation said: "Name it Sam Houston." She also offered to write to General Houston, who was then at Columbia and ask his permission to name the town after him. She wrote the letter and a few days later received a letter from him in which he said, "Leave off the 'Sam' and call it 'Houston'."

The fatal point for that story is the fact that the Texas congress, which the story says President Houston was attending, did not convene at Columbia until October 3, 1836, while the Allen brothers were advertising the sale of town lots in the "Town of Houston" on August 30, or over a month previous to any possible date for the story.

★ ★ ★

HOUSTON'S POLICE FORCE

Even after Houston had received a charter and had a regularly elected city marshal (now called the chief of police), police matters were more or less in the hands of the sheriff. There was never any jealousy, conflict of authority or anything of that sort. The question was a simple one. If the sheriff happened to be present, he acted and the same was true of the marshal. No questions were asked by the absent one or his friends, and everything moved along smoothly.

The office of city marshal and market master were combined at first, and Captain Newt Smith, veteran of San Jacinto, had the distinction of being the first city marshal of Houston. He was a small man, but a very game and determined one, and never had the least trouble in enforcing his authority, because the evildoers knew that to resist him meant disaster to themselves, so they submitted gracefully. He served until 1844, when he voluntarily retired to private life and was succeeded by a namesake, Captain Billy Smith.

The old records do not contain anything that gives evidence of Captain Billy having had anything except an easy, quiet time during the five years of his incumbency.

Captain Billy was succeeded by Captain Bob Boyce, who was very much such a man as the first marshal, Captain Newt Smith. Captain Boyce was rather too aggressive, perhaps, quick-tempered and willing to go more than half-way to meet trouble. He was a regular gamecock, and after his true character as a fighter became known he had little difficulty in asserting his authority. Captain Boyce held office for about twelve years, and though he had numerous chances he never had to actually kill anyone.

Either in 1860 or 1861 I. C. Lord was elected city marshal after a rather heated and exciting campaign. Had Mr. Lord known what he would encounter beforehand, it is doubtful if he would not have quit the race before he started it. His term of office extended through the four years of the war and through three or four years after the war, during the beginning of the Reconstruction period. The latter part of his incumbency was never dull nor unexciting for a moment. There was always something doing night and day.

That is no wonder at when it is remembered that Houston at that time had something of rather worse than a mixed population. There were returned Confederate soldiers out of employment, tough Federal soldiers, gamblers, cut-throats, thugs and bad men of every description, while, worse than all else combined, there were thousands of newly-freed, ignorant and idle negroes who were completely under the control of designing carpetbaggers, who were constantly putting them up to do something to enrage the white men. Slung-shooting and highway robberies were almost nightly occurrences, and each man carried his life in his own hands and knew it.

To contend with conditions such as these, Marshal Lord had only four or five policemen, who were expected to look after the whole city night and day. However, there was one thing that saved the officers much trouble. Each citizen knew that he was expected to take care of himself, and did so. Perhaps the presence of Davis' regiment here did more to cause trouble than anything else. This was the notorious Federal regiment commanded by E. J. Davis, future Reconstruction governor of the State. It was called a "Texas regiment," and was made up of deserters from the Confederate army, Mexicans, negroes, thugs and a generally undesirable element of society. They had not made camp here a week before robberies and knockdowns began to occur.

Eventually there were dead soldiers found once or twice each week on the back streets, and as these dead soldiers had handkerchiefs tied over their faces and slung-shots tied to their wrists, it was not difficult to guess how they had died. No one ever knew the details of their taking off, for the surviving actors were not anxious to brag about their share in it, since it was an easy thing for the Federal authorities to claim that the affair was a murder pure and simple, and that the robbery features had been introduced by the slayer, after the death, in order to make it appear justifiable. There was practically martial law here then, and to get in the hands of the Federal military authorities was a very serious matter.

To show how severe the military authorities were, the following instance is given: One of the Houston policemen was shot at by a drunken Federal soldier, whom the policeman tried to arrest for trying to kick in the door of a millinery establishment on Main Street. To protect himself, the policeman was forced to shoot the soldier. He did not kill him, but he might as well have, for he was arrested, thrown in the guardhouse and had a terrible time before he was released. Finally, after several of the lawbreakers had been killed by the citizens, they concluded that the business was too unhealthy and quit it.

But the marshal and police force had troubles of their own in the way of keeping the disorderly negroes in line. There were, as already stated, a number of trifling, irresponsible white politicians here who were constantly stirring the negroes up and causing them to make bad breaks. They organized what was called "The Loyal Legion," a secret political party, composed mainly of carpetbag white men and trifling negroes. The white men always kept in the background but they shoved the negroes forward, with the result that when any killing was necessary, a negro furnished the victim.

One morning in the early seventies, a negro preacher and fifty or more negroes went to the city jail with the announced intention of taking a negro out of jail and lynching him, because he was a democratic negro and because he had shot another negro who had tried to assassinate him the night before. Marshal Lord attempted to argue with them, but the preacher put an end to all talk by slipping up behind the marshal and trying to blow his brains out. Fortunately, someone managed to knock the pistol aside and the marshal escaped with no further damage than the loss of his hair on one side of his head.

Alex Erichson and Martin Ravell, two of the marshal's force, were there and without hesitation opened fire on the negroes, who attempted to rush the marshal. There was a quick volley and when the smoke cleared away there were several dead negroes on the ground. The preacher escaped for a moment, but was killed by Erichson but a few minutes after. This incident is given here just to show what a strenuous time the police force had in those days.

In 1868 Governor Davis turned Marshal Lord out of office and appointed Captain A. K. Taylor marshal. Captain Taylor, as all old Houstonians know, was an elegant gentleman. He took possession of the office, but within a few weeks he became so disgusted with his surroundings that he sent in his resignation and retired to private life. The situation was too tough for him.

The governor then appointed Captain M. S. Davis to the place. He was a former army officer and a fair man, so he soon made friends with the people and never had serious trouble during his tenure of office.

The Democrats secured control of the state in the November election in 1873 and the charter of Houston was amended in January, 1874, to give the governor the authority to appoint all city officials, an authority he used at once by kicking out all the Republicans and appointing representative men to the offices.

By a singular oversight, no provision was made in the new charter for a city marshal. That complicated things for a while, but the problem was solved by Major S. S. Ashe, who was sheriff at that time. He made Henry Thompson nominally city marshal and gave him twelve or more deputy sheriffs to act as policemen until the defect in the charter could be remedied. When everything was put in shape an election was held and Henry Thompson was elected city marshal and made one of the best the city ever had.

It must not be supposed that the Democrats getting in power settled the negro question, or that Marshal Thompson and his officers had an easy time. On the contrary, their defeat appeared to make the negroes worse than ever, though they worked more secretly and acted more undercover.

After Marshal Thompson retired, Alex Erichson was elected and held office for a year or two. Erichson was one of the coolest and bravest men that ever lived. He was absolutely fearless, but he had one fatal defect. He had too much personality to make a perfect officer. By that is meant that he could never realize that he was an officer first and Alex Erichson next. If a drunken prisoner swore at him he took the thing as a personal insult and resented it as such. This defect in his character led to a bloody encounter between him and a prominent gambler, in which both came near losing their lives. He kept perfect discipline and was absolutely honest, so that on the whole he made a good officer, far above the average, if not a perfect one.

After Erichson retired there were rapid and frequent changes in the office of city marshal. Among those who filled the office were John Morris, who was killed some years ago. He was a regular bulldog kind of a fellow. He carried things with a strong hand, would stand no interference and did just what he pleased. He was game all the way through, and would go out of his way to get into a difficulty rather than try to avoid one. He was a good officer, though, and made a fine marshal. He was succeeded by Gus Railey, who in turn was succeeded by Charley Wichman.

Over in the police office on Preston and Caroline is a book, yellow with age and dingy with dirt and dust. This old book is marked on its cover, "Time Book." Its first entry is dated 1882 and is made up of a record of the police department of that time. Charles Wichman was the "chief of police," for the title had been changed from "marshal;" W. Glass was deputy chief. W. H. Smith and F. W. McCutchin were the day force, while B. F. Archer, Jack White, James Daily and Nat Davis were the night force. It is believed that not one of the men named in the foregoing is alive today. It is regrettable that the keepers of this old book saw fit to abbreviate all the entries instead of filling out the items, were content to make only the briefest mention of facts that contained material for most interesting stories.

Under date March 17, 1882, is recorded: "Officer Richard Snow killed in the Fifth ward." That is all. No mention is made of who killed him nor of why.

On November 1, 1885, an entry chronicles the appointment of the first mounted officers. They were J. E. Jemison and George Penticost. The entry refers to them as "cow catchers."

On February 8, 1886, the following entry is made: "Henry Williams killed by Kyle Terry at Market square."

W. W. Glass resigned February 19, 1886. J. Fitzgerald was clerk June 1, 1886. Alex Erichson was again chief of police in 1892 and B. W. McCarthy was clerk at the same time. James H. Pruett was chief and A. R. Anderson deputy in 1894.

"March 14, 1891, J. E. Fenn was killed by Henry McGee." Under date of September 17, 1893, is recorded the accidental killing of Officer Pat Walsh, who dropped his pistol when getting off a streetcar. It discharged and inflicted a fatal wound on the officer.

One of the greatest tragedies that has ever occurred in police circles here is discussed with a mere statement of facts, under date July 28, 1901. W. A. Weiss, an officer was shot and killed by J. T. Vaughn who was, in turn, shot and killed by another officer a few minutes later. This case created immense excitement at the time.

So far as excitement is concerned, this case was overshadowed by one that is recorded in the old book under date December 11, 1901. As usual only a few lines, giving merely a statement of facts, is the record. Sid Preacher shot and killed J. C. James, a policeman, with a shotgun. After killing James, Preacher whirled and killed Policeman Herman Youngst. Just as Preacher started to go away, another policeman arrived on the scene and shot Preacher dead.

These extracts illustrate the fact that the pathway of the peace officer is not strewn with roses by any means. Of course, it is not necessary to review the history of the department during recent years, for all are familiar with it.

★ ★ ★

HOW THE RAILROADS CAME

The first spade ever stuck in the earth for the construction of a railroad in Texas was at Harrisburg away back yonder, as early as 1840. That was for the construction of the Harrisburg & Brazos Railroad, a line that was never built, at least not under that name.

Some grading was done, some ties were placed, but no iron was ever laid and the enterprise was abandoned soon after it began. For 11 years the people of Harrisburg and Houston talked railroad, but they seemed to have wasted all their energy in talk, for they did nothing else.

However, in 1851, the line now known as the Galveston, Harrisburg & San Antonio was actually begun at Harrisburg, and construction was pushed so vigorously that in nine years 80 miles of road was actually constructed. In this day of rapid transportation, when all the material for railroad construction can be obtained almost at a moment's notice, it seems strange to hear that it took nine years to build a crudely constructed line 80 miles.

That was rather rapid work for the early days, for all the material, except for ties, had to be brought in sailing ships from Boston, New York or other ports on the Atlantic, unloaded at Galveston and then brought up the bayou in steamboats.

There were many difficulties to be overcome in the way of transportation and equally great challenges in obtaining money or credit to pay for construction. Just as the Harrisburg road got under good headway, the Houston & Texas Central got into the game. The first shovel of dirt for this road was thrown by that great railroad genius, Paul Bremond, in 1853. When he threw up that dirt he turned up more trouble for himself than generally falls to the lot of one man.

Of course, he did not know this, but I am convinced that had he known, he would have made not the slightest change in his plans. His faith in himself and his confidence in his ability to accomplish whatever he started out to do were absolutely sublime. When it came to energy, he had any engine on his road faded to a standstill. He was a wonderful man, and he did not hesitate, at times, to attempt the apparently impossible. When his first contractor got cold feet and threw up his job, Mr. Bremond promptly undertook to carry out the contract to build the road himself. There is where his troubles began.

The company had money enough to build two miles of road and to buy an engine. Then the unlooked-for and unprovided-for element of credit bobbed up and scared all the other stockholders, except Mr. Bremond, off the track.

He stayed and went straight ahead as if he had millions behind him. He had faith, the kind that is spelled with a big 'F', but the difficulty was to pay off several hundred clamoring Irishmen with some of his faith. He did not actually perform that miracle, but he came as near doing so as anybody could. He was a very honest and square man himself and the Irishmen, while they cursed and hunted for him everywhere, knew that they would be paid eventually. They made life a burden for him, however. Of course, he hid out as much as possible and was not given to parading up and down Main Street in those days, but while this modesty on his part saved him some trouble, it did not save him all the time and he had some remarkable experiences.

On one occasion several hundred of the Irishmen went in a body to his residence. They yelled and hooted and made lots of noise, but finally contented themselves with tearing down his fence and carrying away the pieces. Finally they got tired of making demonstrations against him and, entering into the spirit of the game, they backed him up and went to work.

Mr. Bremond knew that when the road reached Hempstead, it would begin to earn money, so he turned all his great energy towards constructing it to that point as rapidly as possible. It took him five years of the hardest work any man ever had, but he accomplished it in 1858, and at once entered on a period of comparative ease. It was a wonderful performance and not one man in 10,000 could have done it.

In two years more the road was completed to Millican and, the war coming on, it stuck there. In the meantime the Buffalo Bayou & Brazos Railroad had built into Houston. It used to come down San Jacinto Street and had an engine house and turntable at the foot of that street, right where the bridge is now. It had a long wooden depot at Polk Avenue and San Jacinto Street where all the cars stopped, but the locomotive would come down to San Jacinto to turn round and go into the engine house.

A lot of New Yorkers backed Abe Gentry up and he began the construction of a road to New Orleans. This road had money and credit too, and while it began construction later than the Houston & Texas Central and the Buffalo Bayou & Brazos roads, when the war broke out it had as much line constructed as either of them, and had trains running to Orange.

I don't suppose there ever were such railroads as those leading out of Houston became by the second and third years of the war. Schedules and time-tables became farces. The trains came and went as they could, and spent almost as much time off the tracks as they did on them. I remember on one occasion pulling out of Columbia on the Buffalo Bayou & Brazos road, at the same time that a company of cavalry left there for Houston.

During the whole day we were never out of sight of that company. Sometimes we would be ahead and sometimes they would lead. It was see-saw all day, for it took from early in the morning until dark to make the trip of 50 miles. Finally, just at dark, we reached Brays Bayou and lost sight of the company there. They had entered the woods, ahead of us.

Before the close of the war all the railroads except the Houston & Texas Central and the Galveston, Houston & Henderson had gone out of commission and had ceased to run at all. In some way these two roads were kept in such condition that they could be used, but that was all. Using them was not a safe thing by any means. They crept along so slowly that while wrecks were so frequent as to attract no attention, it was a rare thing for anyone to get killed or even hurt.

If full justice were done, the name of Mr. Bremond would be perpetuated by the Houston & Texas Central road. It is true there is one of the principal towns on the line named after him. It is true he received loyal support and assistance from W. R. Baker, W. M. Rice, William Van Alstyne, William J. Hutchins, Cornelius Ennis and others, but theirs was money help and soon gave out. The real credit for building the road belongs to Paul Bremond, for he did what others could or would not do. He pulled off his coat and went in the trenches and, figuratively, on the firing line of railroad construction in Texas.

I do not know what the reason for doing so was, but in those days the builders of locomotives always put immense smokestacks on them. The smokestacks were funnel-shaped and several feet in circumference at the top. The locomotives burned wood and every few miles there were big stacks of cordwood piled alongside the track.

There was no such thing as spark-arresters and every time the fireman put fresh wood in the box the passengers got the full benefit of the sparks, cinders and smoke. It beat travelling by stage, however, and as the people knew nothing of oilburners, spark-arresters or Pullman cars, everybody was content.

The old-time fireman earned every dollar that was coming to him, for he had to keep busy all the time. It was not child's play to have to keep steam up with only wood for fuel. Then too, it took more steam to keep an engine going at that time, for the engineer was using his whistle 10 times as often as he uses it now.

There were no fences along the right-of-way and, as there were thousands of cattle on the prairies and woods where the road ran, the track was generally filled with them every few miles. As soon as the trains would get out of the city limits, the whistle would begin tooting and this was kept up almost without cessation. Of course, a great many cattle were killed and this led to bitter warfare between the cattlemen and the railroads.

Wrecks and attempted wrecks were frequent, for there was no lack of men who, to get revenge on the railroad company by destroying its property, were willing to run the risk of destroying the lives of innocent passengers. The first wreck of this kind that ever occurred in Texas was on the Houston &Texas Central, near where the water tank is, about 12 miles from Houston. Some scoundrel drove spikes between the ends of the rails and wrecked the train. No one was killed, but Mr. Bremond, who was on the train, received quite serious injuries and was laid up for repairs for several days.

It is a pity some historian of that day did not keep a record of the ups and downs of the lives of the early railroad builders. It would make interesting reading today. It would show, as the Frenchman said, "more downs as ups," for their progress was marked by more temporary failures than by successes.

★ ★ ★

Good Old Steamboat Days

In one respect Houston has deteriorated woefully in the last forty or fifty years. Commerce has ruined Buffalo Bayou, from an artistic point of view, though it has made it a thousand times more valuable and important in every other way. In the "good old days," when the fine steamboats were in evidence, it was a delight and pleasure to make a trip down the bayou.

The old bayou was not what it has become since. It was narrow, but it was deep; its water was clear and beautiful and its banks were overhung with trees which were vine-clad, and, while they impeded navigation, they added greatly to the beauty of the stream. Then the steamboats they had in those days! They were beauties—veritable floating palaces. The Mississippi might have had larger boats, but there was none finer or more elegantly finished than our bayou boats.

The trip from Houston to Harrisburg was rather difficult, because of the twisting and winding of the bayou and also because of overhanging trees. After passing Harrisburg, the bayou broadened and then it was simply delightful. They served but one meal on the boats—supper, or as we would call it today, dinner—at about 7 o'clock. It was a meal long to be remembered, for it was composed of every delicacy obtainable and was justly famed throughout the country. Travelers wrote about it and everybody enjoyed it.

The very early boats were not so famed. They were rather primitive in every way, but after 1850 the bayou boats began to put on style and there was none finer anywhere.

There were no railroads in Texas in those early days and all the commerce with the outside world was done over Buffalo Bayou. The cabins of the steamboats were fixed luxuriously for the passengers, but the lower deck and every other available inch of space was given over to freight. The principal cargoes down the bayou consisted of cotton and hides, while the return cargoes were dry goods, plantation supplies and such things.

The modern compressed bale of cotton was unknown at that time, and the bales of cotton were huge, unwieldy things that took up much space. It was surprising to see how many of these one of those steamboats could get on board. They were piled on top of each other until they reached up to the hurricane deck. Of course the danger of fire was very great, but, while one or two boats actually burned, probably none of the fires was ever traced to cotton becoming ignited.

There were several serious tragedies on the bayou, for one or two boats blew up with disastrous effect. There were some narrow escapes from storms in Galveston Bay, too. History is not certain about the name of the boat, but it was the *Palmer* or *Farmer*, that blew up and caught on fire in the bay in about 1853. If one could get into the old Episcopal Cemetery at the foot of Dallas Avenue, this could be ascertained. In the lot of Dr. Evans in that graveyard is a small monument erected to the memory of a negro man whose remains lie buried there with those of the members of the doctor's family.

This negro lost his life when the steamboat was wrecked, while, after having saved some lives, he was making heroic efforts to save others. The writer went out to the cemetery the other day for the express purpose of looking for that monument, but found it in such a disgraceful condition, overrun with weeds, and, as one of the park employees said, with snakes, too, that the search was abandoned.

After the war two or three magnificent boats were bought by Captain Sterret in Cincinnati, brought down the river and over the gulf to Galveston and put in the bayou trade. That gulf trip was a ticklish affair for the least rough weather would have swamped the boats. The trips were made immediately after a norther, when the gulf was as quiet as a mill pond. One of those boats was especially fine and was named the *T. M. Bagby*, after T. M. Bagby, one of the most prominent citizens of Houston. This boat had a calliope, but it was very seldom used, possibly because no one knew how to play it.

Two of the fine boats that were brought here around the breaking out of the war deserve more than passing mention because of the distinguished service they rendered the Confederate forces at the Battle of Galveston. These were the *Neptune* and *Bayou City*. They were fitted out as gunboats, having breast works of cotton bales. Each carried a big gun and a number of armed men. They made the attack on the Federal fleet while the land forces attacked on the land side.

Both boats headed for the *Harriet Lane*, the largest of the vessels. The *Neptune* was sunk by a shell from one of the Federal gunboats but the *Bayou City* rammed and disabled the *Harriet Lane* and finally captured her. It was a most desperate undertaking, and though it was successful simply because of its audacity, it would have failed a thousand times had it been tried over. How either of the frail boats escaped utter annihilation is a mystery.

Those good old steamboat days have gone, and gone forever, for now the bayou has been widened and deepened and oceangoing ships run where the palatial steamboats once floated. Of course the present is greater and grander than the past, but one cannot keep from sighing for the old days, when there was real pleasure in traveling and less breakneck haste and hurry.

★ ★ ★

HOUSTON'S FIRST MARKET MAN

Not long ago I was talking to Colonel Phil Fall and one or two old-timers, when one of the gentlemen asked me if I could remember when the first market house was built. As that famous old house was erected several years before I was born I denied all remembrance of its beginning, but told him that I remembered the man who had the first marketplace in Houston and I do, too. He was a Frenchman named Rouseau.

Originally there were two Rouseau brothers. They had a big tent which was located on Preston Avenue between Stude's coffeehouse and Milam Street. Of course, Stude's Place was not there then, but the Rouseau tent was on the lot west of where it now stands. Market Square was vacant then and was used as a wagon yard by those who brought country produce to Houston and by ox wagons from the interior of the state, which was at that time over on the Brazos, up about Washington County and over toward the Trinity. Texas was sparsely settled, but Houston was then as now its commercial and business center.

The Rouseaus were wide-awake and progressive and their tented market was profitable. They made too much money, in fact, for their prosperity attracted fatal attention and one night when one of the brothers returned to the tent after a temporary absence he found the other one dead with his throat cut and all the money in the place gone. Thieves had murdered him, ransacked the place and had gone, leaving no trace behind them, and the mystery has never been solved to this day.

The elder brother, though doubly stricken by the loss of his brother and all his money, did not give up, but continued the business until the city, early in the 1840s, erected the old wooden market house and drove him out of business. Then he erected a one-story frame house on the site of his tent and opened a little grocery store.

I can remember the old man well by two things. One was his pretty daughter, who was named Charlotte, and the other was a large parrot that he had that had a habit of swearing in French. Charlotte had charge of the store and was always there as was the parrot, who sat upon its perch near the center of the store. The old man was very seldom seen in the front room, or in the store proper, but remained nearly all the time in the back room, where he could be heard grumbling and growling about one thing or another. All the boys in town were afraid of him, though for what reason I am unable to say.

That was 15 or 18 years after his tent experience and he must have been rather an old man when I first knew him. He was considered to be wealthy then and was prosperous. He was not destined to have a peaceful life, however. His early days in Houston as already noted, were marked by a tragedy and another blighted his latter days here. For no known reason one night Charlotte ended her life with poison. Her death was as great a mystery as the murder of the brother had been. There was apparently no reason for her action. She had beauty, riches, a kind father (for the old man almost worshiped her) and everything to make her happy. The old man could not stand it. He sold his store and business for what he could get for them, closed up all his affairs and left Houston forever. Some said he went back to France; others that he went to California.

★ ★ ★

IN THE GRAND OLD TIMES

One gets in the habit of speaking of "the good old times," without ever stopping to think what those "good old times" really were. Distance lends enchantment, and only the pleasures are remembered, while the discomforts are either forgotten or ignored. Things today are so vastly better and superior in every way that instead of pining for the good old times one actually wonders how one could have put up with all the discomforts and inconveniences of former days.

I remember when the first streetcar service was established in Houston and what a great thing it was considered. There was one little car drawn by a diminutive mule, that had a sleigh bell attached to its neck to let people know he was coming. There were no conductors. Passengers went up to the front of the car and deposited fares in a box, under the watchful eye of the driver. No one could get into that box except the man at headquarters, for it was locked with a padlock and only he had a key. At fixed hours he would take out the fares deposited in the box and then lock it again. The service was just barely better than walking, though frequently not so expeditious, for from time to time the car would jump the track and it would take some time for the driver and passengers to get it on again. When a wreck occurred it was expected that every male passenger would get out and work like a section hand to help matters along. The cars were so small and so light that the driver felt safe against long delays if he had two or three men among his passengers.

Now, about the time those streetcars made their appearance in Houston there was a kind of anti-corporation feeling all over the state that caused the streetcar drivers and the conductors of the big railroads to make predatory war on the various companies they served. "Knocking down" became one of the fine arts and the company that got a fair proportion of its passenger earnings at the end of the year considered itself fortunate. This is no joke; it is an actual fact, and the cause for it was a mistake that the railroads made in assuming that every one of its conductors was a thief and setting spies to watch them. The conductors resented that action on the part of the railroads and went in to get the benefits of being dishonest since the roads assumed they were. Honest men were classed as rascals by the roads and they became rascals.

There were no gates, ticket punching or things of that kind in those days. If there was the least trouble about the matter the passenger did not go to the ticket office at all, but got on the train and paid the conductor. But the whole thing came to an abrupt termination through the mistake of a green hand who was put on a run in place of a regular conductor who had been taken suddenly ill just as his train was about to pull out. That was on the northern division of one of the big roads running out of Houston. The conductors on that division had "gotten together" and agreed on what proportion of the fares they would give to the railroad when their run was over and they made their report.

When the regular conductor had taken sick he did not have time to instruct his subordinate, a baggagemaster from the south division, or to warn others. So the baggagemaster went through the whole run without any of the other conductors knowing he was there. He went to the division superintendent's office, made his report and turned over about $600 in cash. Now, according to the rules adopted by the regular conductors, the railroad should have received only about $150 for that run. The superintendent asked many questions and when he found that there had been no convention, picnic or anything of that kind and that it was just an ordinary run, he reported the matter to the president of the road by wire, and within an hour or two every conductor on that division was out of a job.

Of course, the streetcar drivers had no picnic like the big conductors did, but they managed to hold up their end of the line pretty well. In place of nickels, the streetcar companies issued tickets, and these passed everywhere just as actual nickels or five-cent pieces would do. Once I was on the old fairgrounds car when several railroad men were in the car. One of them, a long-legged fellow they called Judge, went forward and was soon busily engaged in a conversation with the driver. One of the others said, "I'll bet Judge is telling that fellow to rob that box." We slipped up closer where we could hear the conversation and sure enough he was.

Here was what he was saying: "Catch a young grasshopper and tie a thread round his wings, leaving the legs free. Then lower him carefully into the box. The minute he touches bottom he will grab onto everything in his reach and you can't shake him loose. Then all you got to do is to haul him out, clean his feet and drop him back again. You can empty that box of every ticket in it in a few minutes."

I never had a chance to find out if the driver followed his advice or not, but I suspect he did, for I noticed he kept a good lookout on each side of his track after that, evidently fearing that some fool grasshopper might come out of the grass and attempt to cross the track.

Now when I began to write this I intended to point out that in the "good old times," it took as long to go from Preston Avenue to the fairgrounds and return on the old mule car, as it takes to go from here to Galveston on the Interurban. There were several other points I wanted to make, all going to show what humbugs the "good old times" are, but I got switched off on the north end conductors and the Judge's grasshopper and have used up all my space talking about them, so I will have to postpone my comparisons until some other time.

SOME CHARACTERS &
THEIR MISADVENTURES

★ ★ ★

A PRESS CLUB EVENING

The Houston Press Club is rather a remarkable aggregation, more so than even the members themselves realize. Seated around a table in the reading room a few evenings ago was a representative of Grant's Army of the Potomac, another of Lee's Army of Northern Virginia, two men who had served through the South African war, one with the Boers and the other with the English, a Philippine veteran and one or two others, whose claim to fame rested on the fact that they had seen much of the world, having been wanderers and adventure seekers. On the whole, these last were the most interesting members of the group.

The talk drifted from the Potomac to Ladysmith, from Cuba to the Philippines, drifted about over Central and South America and finally cast anchor in the magazine offices and theatres, where newspaper men generally come to rest. There was a guest present who, I have since heard, held a clinical position in the advertising department of a New York newspaper some years ago. At the proper time he seized the central position in the talk and soon had everybody "backed off the boards."

"I saw Jack London last month," he said. "In fact, I was with him for several weeks—went over to Salt Lake City from San Francisco with him. He is writing a new book—best one he ever wrote. Jack is a bird—easiest thing in the world for him to write. On the train something happened that reminded him of a story. He got out his pad, scribbled off a couple of thousand words, put it in an envelope and mailed it on the train. About a week after we arrived in Salt Lake there came a letter from the Saturday Evening Post, containing a check for $1000 and asking for more."

"Do you ever write fiction?" I asked him. I knew that he dealt in it, but I wanted to know if he ever sold any of it.

"Sure thing," he replied. "Make my living writing stories. Have never had one sent back yet. Got $75 for the first one I ever sent in and it was only about 700 words. Happened to hit 'em the first time and have been hitting 'em ever since."

"Yes, sir," chimed in the voice of the Boer veteran. "I was there. I had a big store on the outskirts of Johannesburg, and was doing good business when the war began. I was trying to sell out so as to join the army when a company of English cavalry come along. I had a big warehouse filled with hay. The officer in command belonged to the quartermaster department and was out searching for provender. He offered me a good price for the hay. I accepted his offer and he paid cash. He left, going South. About an hour later another party of English came along. The officer in command was a young lieutenant who was very pompous and dignified. He recognized me as a native, and, rightfully, concluded that I was a rebel. He saw the hay and fearing that it would fall in the hands of the Boers if left there, ordered it burned. I told him that an English captain had bought it and that it belonged to his own people, but he would not listen to me. He ordered me to stand aside and set fire to the hay much to my secret delight. I lost $30,000, got wounded three times and suffered greatly during the war, but that fellow burning hay compensated me for everything I went through. Every time I think of it I feel better."

"Before Teddy butted into their game those Panama chaps used to be 'some soon' on revolutions," chimed in the deep bass voice of the ex-telegraph operator, former newspaper man and ex-gentlemanly tramp. "The first day I got down there they pulled off two, one in the morning and one in the afternoon. I was taking a drink when I heard some shots fired up the street. The barkeep went crazy in a minute, uttering the Spanish equivalent for 'Give me liberty or give me death.' He seized an old hoss pistol, leaped the counter and tore up the street. I followed him to the door, but when I saw about 50 ragged, dirty-looking fellows coming down the street, shooting old-fashioned muzzle-loading shotguns and muskets, right and left, I went out of the back door, swam the river and quit the revolution right there. In a couple of hours the revolution was over and the new government had been established. I determined to return to town. But just as I got to the bridge another revolution broke out, only a block away. It was a revolution to overthrow the revolution that had taken place in the morning. I went under the bridge and lay there until it was over. Then I crawled out and left town for good."

"Why," said one of two gentlemen who had been comparing notes on Arizona, New Mexico and Mexico, "that mine you speak of is nothing. Six years ago a party of five of us left New Orleans for Mexico. I got sick and had to turn back. The other four went on and a month after they got there discovered a rich gold mine. The ore assayed more than $1000 to the ton.

They got the German consul interested with the result that they sold the mine to a German syndicate for $4,000,000 in gold. The syndicate put up fine machinery and went to work, but in a week the ore played out. It was only a 'pocket'."

Now, one can judge from these fragments of conversation just what an interesting place the Houston Press Club is. As a matter of fact there may not be a successful author or playwright in the crowd, but that does not bar claims nor assertions, and if there are no really successful writers there should be for there is plenty of raw material on hand, and one has only to keep one's ears open to get everything necessary for the making of a short story, book or drama right from first hand.

The Press Club is a great institution and its members are great, too—if you let them tell it.

★ ★ ★

SJOLANDER A HERO

It has been my good fortune to have known several writers of note, among them one or two poets. Strange to say these latter have always been those whose friendship I valued. I say strange, because it is really so, for aside from their personality we have nothing in common. My taste is so depraved that I think that the fellow who raves in verse over a sunset, or a moonlit night, is heading towards the nearest asylum, and if he is not he should be pointed that way. I confess that I enjoy the jingling verses, telling of breakfast foods and fine soaps, that one sees in the streetcars, much more than I do the poems that others rave over.

Among my poet friends is Sjolander, the sailor poet. He and I have been intimate friends for about 30 years, and it is a fact that I feel proud of. I have enjoyed his stories, skipped his poetry and admired the man thoroughly and honestly. But for his extreme modesty he would be one of the most talked of men of today. He persists in keeping in the background, however, and there is no way of lugging him to the front.

Despite our intimacy I never knew, until the other day, that Sjolander was a hero, a genuine one, too. It came out accidentally. We were talking about the sea, as we always do when we get together, and I mentioned a wreck that occurred just off Galveston in the early eighties. It was before the jetties were built and Galveston Island terminated at Fort Point. The inner bar was located just beyond where the quarantine station is now located, and beyond that was the Gulf of Mexico. The outer bar was further out and was one of the worst on the gulf coast. During ordinary rough weather the bar was so rough that it was considered unsafe for a vessel to attempt to cross it.

It was either in '83 or '84 that a terrible storm occurred off Galveston. The wind came from the southeast, and piled up the breakers mountain high. During the night there was a fearful blow, and at daylight next morning it was discovered that a large ship had gone down and that her crew were clinging to the masts. She was located a mile or two off shore and was right in the midst of the breakers that would soon wash the men from their perilous position if it did not destroy the masts altogether. There was no life saving station equipped with proper boats or anything of that kind. The men had to be rescued though. The Morgan steamer, *Josephine*, was in port and got up steam to go out. She reached a point not far from the outer bar and met such huge breakers that she was forced to abandon the attempt and turned back to her place at the wharf.

When it was found that the *Josephine* would not, or could not go to the rescue, one of the bar pilots leaped in a small sailboat and called for volunteers, saying that he would save those men or share their fate. Nine men sprang in the boat at once, among them my poet, Sjolander. That crew of ten braved the fearful bar, passed it, went to the stranded vessel and after hours of heartbreaking work succeeded in rescuing every one of the men clinging in the masts. The return trip, in the little overloaded vessel, was far more dangerous than the outward trip. The captain was a fine sailor, knew just what to do and had the men to do it, so they made the trip safely and got back to the wharf without the loss of a single man.

Now, I knew about that wreck and of the heroic rescue, but I did not know that Sjolander was one of the heroes. The other day he referred to it casually, mentioning it only in telling me of his introduction to Texas, he having arrived on an inward bound vessel only a day or two before. When I asked him if he knew of the danger before he started he laughed at the question and said that he knew as well as an experienced sailor could know how slim the chances were for success. "But I would have gone anywhere that any other man would have gone at that time. I was not desperate or anything of that kind, but I was young and felt my oats. I felt at that time that I could do anything that any other man could do, and since I realized that something must be done quickly to save those men, I jumped in that boat with no thought of anything else than the fact that we were going to save them."

Strange to say, the *Galveston News* gave only a brief account of the daring rescue and passed it off as if it had been only an ordinary, everyday occurrence. It was really a gallant thing; one that only those familiar with the dangers of the sea can appreciate at its full value. Had it been during these latter days when so many mock heroes are getting Carnegie medals every one of those ten heroes would have been decorated, far more to the point, they would have honored the medals by accepting them instead of the medals honoring them. Of all the ten, I believe only Sjolander is alive. I have always had a warm place in my heart for him, but after I heard his story he advanced several points in my estimation, if that be possible. The next time he comes to town I am going to get a full list of those gallant men and publish it so as to do their memory some tardy justice.

★ ★ ★

A CORNER IN TURKEYS

All old citizens remember John Collins. He was one of Houston's merchant princes. It would be more fitting to describe him as a merchant king, for that was what he was. He was the king of Houston retail grocers, made more money, spent more money and gave away more money than any other five grocerymen in the city combined. He left a fair estate when he died, but had he been possessed of less heart and a little legitimate greed he might have died an unusually wealthy man.

Thanksgiving and Christmas, days when the turkey seemingly becomes the national bird, and the Cuero turkey trot, make me think of Mr. Collins, for at one time he and some turkeys caused a lot of amusement among his intimate friends. He had a large two-story brick store at Travis Street and Preston Avenue, the corner now occupied by Sauter's place. It was the best corner in the city, since Preston Avenue was then the greatest business thoroughfare in all of Texas, for all the business done with the interior came over Long Bridge at the foot of Preston. The corner also had the advantage of facing Market Square. Most anyone located there would have done a good business but Mr. Collins, being something out of the ordinary as a business man, did an immense one.

He had lots of what is now called the initiative and was always doing the unexpected. On one occasion he got up a corner on empty bottles, a trick none tried before nor since his day. That was outside his regular business, but he was too active to permit of his confining himself to his grocery trade.

Since his day, ambitious men have tried to corner the cotton and wheat markets. Some have done so and others have failed. Those who succeeded risked millions and paid for success with health and nerves. Before these ambitious ones appeared, Mr. Collins entered the field, created a corner, carried it through successfully and quit the game a double winner.

In the late fifties Mr. Collins, a few weeks before Christmas, conceived the idea of cornering the turkey market. Next to his store was a vacant lot. He put up a rough board fence around it and put the turkeys in the enclosure.

He bought all he could get hold of and a week before Christmas he had by actual count 400 turkeys. In and around Houston there was not a turkey for sale that Mr. Collins did not own. The corner was complete.

Then the unexpected happened. Mr. Collins calculated his profits, but he did not calculate the power of bad boys to procure trouble. On the very night that he went to bed congratulating himself on the success of his scheme, some of those bad boys cut the straps on his turkey pen gate and the next morning the pen was empty. Every turkey there had departed for parts unknown.

For a moment Mr. Collins was in despair, and then an inspiration seized him. He put out a board offering fifty cents for each of his turkeys returned to him. He had handbills scattered all over the city making the same offer. In an hour after the appearance of the handbills, boys with turkeys began to arrive. White boys, negro boys, Mexican boys and all kinds of boys arrived with turkeys and by night the pen was pretty full again. The next day the turkey arrivals continued. Mr. Collins was kept busy paying out fifty-cent pieces. Then the pen got overcrowded, which was not the case before, so Mr. Collins made an investigation and found on examination of his book that he had paid out $300 and that he had 200 turkeys more than he had before the boys cut the gate.

It was all true, for the boys had scoured the city and county and brought in every turkey they could find. He had his own and everybody else's turkeys, and his corner was an absolute cinch.

★ ★ ★

HOW HAMP COOK WAS ROBBED

I have told this story once before, but it is so good that I venture to tell it again, for it was several years ago and I am sure but few of the readers of the *Chronicle* have ever seen or heard of it.

In 1884 we were running a daily paper called the *Houston Chronicle*. We did not have any money, but we were all willing workers and what we lacked in cash we made up for in enthusiasm and style. As a matter of fact we had more style than anything else. We had an editor-in-chief and a managing editor, an exchange editor, a telegraph editor and a city editor. For a short while we had a sporting editor also, but he got drunk one night, raised a rough house in Bell's honky-tonk, got thrown out and, making directly for the *Chronicle* office, wrote up the place in the most lurid style. He slipped it upstairs to the printers and left town, leaving me to face Bell the next day when he had blood in his eyes. Bell's dive deserved all it got, but I did not want the *Chronicle's* readers to see such language used in its columns as the drunken sporting editor put there.

But back to my story. Colonel Hamp Cook was city editor and, of course, he had a local staff. The staff consisted of one man, a bright chap who had one fatal defect—he could never get past a barroom if he chanced to see anyone he knew on the inside. However, as he "toted" his liquor well, Hamp never had much trouble with him, and as he never gave him anything but routine work to do, he managed very well. Dud Bryan was the Houston representative of the *Galveston News* at that time and covered the local field most thoroughly. He kept Hamp and his "staff" on the jump all the time.

One cold winter night, between 9 and 10 o'clock, a big fire broke out in the Fifth Ward. Hamp gave his "staff" some hurried instructions and rushed to the fire. About an hour after he left, a friendly policeman came in and reported that an unknown dead man had been found in a deserted house away out in the Third Ward. The body had no head, it having been cut off and carried away. It was a fine story, but the best part of it was that the fire in the Fifth ward was still blazing and we knew Dud Bryan would be detained there too long to give him a chance to get the murder story for the *News* the next morning. It was the chance of a lifetime for a big scoop on the *News*.

I sent the "staff" hot-footed after the murder story and sat down at his desk to write up the local news from Hamp's notes. Twelve o'clock struck.

The fire had been put out, but Hamp had not returned, nor had the "staff." I knew it would take some time for Hamp to get back, for it was a long way to the Fifth Ward at that time, the only bridge across the bayou being the old iron bridge at the foot of Milam Street. One o'clock, no Hamp, no staff, but the foreman, importuning me for "copy." I gave him a handful of reprint and quieted him momentarily. Two o'clock! The foreman sending down every few minutes for "copy." I fed him whole batches of newspaper clippings to keep him quiet. Then, much to my relief, Hamp Cook showed up, but I had to take a good look at him before I recognized him. He was one living, moving mass of mud from the top of his head to the toes of his shoes.

How he ever managed to get to the office with that load of mud on him was a mystery. He told his story briefly. He had been waylaid and robbed on the other side of the bayou. The highwayman had knocked him down and then had rolled him over and over in the mud, searching for money. Finally, he found 35 cents, which he took and departed.

We stood Hamp up by the stove, and the printers' devil, who had come down after "copy" and who had remained to hear Hamp's story, took the coal shovel and began to spade the mud off of him. Just then the door burst open and in came the foreman, with blood in his eyes. The "devil" thought he was after him and hastened to explain.

"Oh, Mr. Cook was knocked down and robbed," he exclaimed.

"Damn Mr. Cook!" shouted the foreman. "I am looking for that —— who put a bag of paste in my chair. Look at me. I sat down on it!"

We took the foreman down in the pressroom to wash him off with a hose and we found the "staff" lying on a pile of newspapers, dead to the world. He had never gotten further than the Rice Hotel bar, where he met some of his friends, who treated so liberally that evening that his good "toting" qualities were taxed beyond their capacity and he had fallen.

Cook was game, though. He sat down and wrote a fine account of the fire and then wrote up the robbery. He spread himself on this and made an interesting and exciting story of it, too. But he made a fatal blunder. In closing the article, he stated that while the robbers got 35 cents, they overlooked a $5 bill he had in the watch pocket of his pants. That ruined him. The next evening Uncle Dan McGary of the *Age* reproduced his story under the heading, "The Champion Liar of the Season," and went on to say that Hamp, being false in one thing, must be false in all, and that the whole story was a fake, because everybody knew that he never had as much as $5 at one time in his whole life. He accused Hamp of trying to put on style in trying to speak of a watch pocket and then of lying about having a $5 bill in it. The state papers copied Uncle Dan's version of the affair and within a week one could not tell from their comments whether Hamp robbed the robbers or they had robbed him. The whole thing got dreadfully mixed, all because Hamp made the mistake of putting that last line at the end of the story. No doubt he referred to that $5 bill for the purpose of making the robbers feel bad because they overlooked it, but it proved a boomerang and came back on his head.

Of course the *Chronicle* did not scoop the *News* with the murder story, but we all had a strenuous time trying to do so.

★ ★ ★

MRS. BURKHART AND THE BOYS

Not so long ago one of my legal friends asked me to go with him to locate a fence that was built long ago along Preston Avenue to the bayou, near the bridge. The question to be determined was whether there had been a fence there or not and if there had been, where it was located.

That visit brought back more amusing memories than any other locality could have possibly done. The property under dispute was formerly owned by Mrs. Burkhart. She owned the whole block on the bayou between Prairie and Preston, fronting Smith Street. She had no more idea of riparian rights than she had of the constitution and by-laws of the Fiji Islands, and when she built her fences she covered all the land and as much of the bayou as she could. Having erected her stronghold, she stood ever ready to defend it against intruders. Dickens' old lady who carried on relentless war against donkeys was not a drop in the bucket as a warrior compared to Mrs. Burkhart conducting her private war against the boys. There were some nice fishing holes inside the enclosure and there were lots of nice mustang and winter grapes along the banks of the bayou. These tempted the boys, but by the time they were getting their first fish out of the water or reaching for the grapes Mrs. Burkhart would loom up armed with bricks and bones and open fire on the intruder or intruders. I don't think she ever caught a boy so I can't say what she would have done had she taken a prisoner. The boys never gave her a chance to show her hand in that way, for on the arrival of the first piece of brick or bone a hasty retreat was beaten.

About the nearest she ever came, to capturing a prisoner was in the case of Dick Fuller. It was "popgun time" and chinaberries were in great demand. Near the Prairie side of the block there was a large chinaberry tree that extended over into the street. One day Dick got up in this tree, gathered a number of bunches of berries and began picking them into his hat. He wanted to get a hatful so as to have a big supply. He became so absorbed in his work that he forgot all about Mrs. Burkhart and she crept up under him without his knowing anything about her warlike intentions. Dick was sitting on a limb with his feet resting on another and was very comfortable and well content.

While he was sitting there he began to feel the waistband of his trousers tighten mysteriously and on attempting to move found he could not. He looked down and was horrified to see, directly under him, Mrs. Burkhart, who had made him a prisoner in a novel way. She had taken a long pole she used to prop up her clothes line with. This had two nails driven in the end of it. She had reached up and succeeded in entangling those nails in the seat of Dick's trousers. When she saw that Dick had discovered her she threw aside all disguise and went at the entangling work in real earnest. Dick tugged and squirmed and Mrs. Burkhart twisted and twisted. It was terribly humiliating to be captured by a woman and captured by the seat of his pants, too, but Dick's mind was not on the disgrace, humiliation or anything of that kind, but was on how to make his escape. Dick pulled and pulled and Mrs. B. twisted and twisted, trying to secure an indestructible hold, so between the two they managed to overdo the thing and, the seat of the pants being human (if I can say such a thing about the seat of pants), they gave way and Dick was free.

When she saw that her tail-hold had broken she grew desperate and made strenuous efforts to punch him out of the tree with the pole. He saw only one avenue of escape. He rushed out as far as could on the limb and made a dive into the street. He did not ask her for the part of his wardrobe she flaunted at the end of the pole in his face, but turned tail and fled. He managed to save his hat, but lost all his berries, of course.

Now, looking back after all these years, I am inclined to believe that Mrs. Burkhart actually enjoyed having the boys intrude on her premises because of the fun it afforded her in running them off. She looked like a fiend when she had Dick Fuller hooked up that time, but I am willing to bet she enjoyed a good laugh all to herself when she began untangling the seat of his pants from the nails at the end of her pole. She made it a point never to recognize a boy on the street or to take the slightest notice that he was on the face of the earth; but let him crawl over her fence and all that was changed and he found himself the center of the most ardent and heartfelt attention. There was no ignoring him then.

★ ★ ★

NOT DOWN ON THE PROGRAMME

Whatever may be said of Houston's quiet Christmas, the same does not apply to New Year's Eve, the death of the old year. Houston fairly stood up on its hind legs and welcomed the new year in the most royal manner. There was noise enough to make up for the deficit for Christmas and then have some left over. I did not see any of it, for I did not venture away from the Press Club, where a number of us welcomed the new year in an orderly manner.

That noise, the firecrackers, pistol shooting and everything else, showed me that there was some love of fun left in the old place yet and made me like it all the more. It was much after the way we used to celebrate and for the first time I began to feel as if I were at home. One terrible explosion had a good effect on me, for it carried me back instantly to so many years ago that I am not going to say how many.

There is a good story involved in that explosion, too, and I am going to tell it, although it is on Sinclair, and he may not like to have it told. The reader must remember that we were all much younger and that W. R. Sinclair was very far from being the staid and dignified editor that he is today.

The newspaper boys and the police stood in with each other much closer then than they do today. The "force" was not large, but it was lively. Alex Erichson was chief and Bill Glass was deputy chief. Alex was serious and took but little stock in fun and jokes, but Bill Glass made up for all the chief's defects in that way.

There was a good sprinkling of railroad men who ran with the gang also, and it was the neglect of one of these that gave rise to the following incident, which is absolutely true.

A conductor who "ran with the gang" got married during Christmas week and on New Year's Eve gave a dance at his residence down in Frostown, as that part of the city where the gas works was located was called. His house was a small one and presumably for that reason he failed to invite any of the "boys" to the dance.

Bill Glass and Sinclair, or "Sin," as he was called, understood well enough that no slight had been intended, but they pretended to be greatly outraged and worked on the others until they were ready to do anything that Glass and Sinclair suggested. These two thought of every possible way of getting even with the conductor and at last hit upon the following novel plan, which would not only accomplish their purpose, but at the same time let the whole town know that they were on their job.

Near midnight they got the boys together near the courthouse and shared their plans. There were several pieces of field artillery, six-pounders, that had been accumulated by the Federal army of occupation and left on courthouse square, to be shipped North. These guns were all dismounted and were lying on the ground.

The two conspirators selected one of the cleanest, found that the vent was open and that it was in good firing condition. Bill Glass had a quantity of gunpowder and they stood the gun on end while he poured about a hatful of it into the gun and then rammed a newspaper down on it with a long stick. It was a crude loading, but it was enough to make a noise. Having loaded the cannon, they got some heavy sticks, or rather poles, and half a dozen fellows vied with each other for the honor of acting as pallbearers. The weather was outrageous and the mud was knee-deep everywhere, but that made no difference.

They marched down to the conductor's residence, opened his front gate and proceeded to plant their gun on the sidewalk. They got the proper elevation by propping up the muzzle of the gun with pickets, bricks and anything they could find, and when they got through the piece was well placed, aiming exactly at the doorknob of the front door.

It was a very cold night and all the doors were closed tight. The gang could hear the music and the revelry going on inside and chuckled to think what a surprise they were going to give the revelers. Having planted their gun properly, they inserted a friction primer, attached a long rope to it, hitched the rope to the front doorknob, so that simply opening the door would fire the cannon, and then they hid out to await developments. They waited and waited, but no one came to the door. Finally Sinclair determined to wait no longer, so he slipped up to the door, intending to knock on it and get out of the way before anyone answered the knock. His idea was good, but it miscarried. Just as he reached the door and extended his hand to knock some one jerked the door open.

The surprise was a success in more ways than the boys had calculated. The cannon went off with a roar that woke up all the old people in Houston who had gone to sleep, and when it did so it shot Sinclair clean into the hall and halfway through the back door. It came near wrecking the house itself. Every pane of glass and every dish in the house was smashed to pieces. The worst part was that Sinclair had been shot right into the enemy's hands and had no earthly excuse for being there.

The conductor was so frightened that he did not know what to do. In the confusion, Sinclair managed to escape. When he got outside he found that every one of his conspirators had deserted him. They all thought that Sinclair and everybody in the house had been blown to pieces, so they took to their heels. Sinclair trudged through the mud to town.

His hair was singed off and his clothes torn into bits. In fact, he was as much of a wreck as the house was. About 2 o'clock in the morning the conductor showed up at police headquarters and reported the outrage to Deputy Chief Bill Glass, who listened patiently and made the most strenuous promises that he would investigate the thing and punish the guilty persons.

By next morning Sinclair, who had thought over the thing, wrote an indignant letter to the conductor, charging him with having attempted to take his life. He said that he had called to pass the usual congratulations, having found the house lighted and everybody up, and that just as he knocked on the door the conductor had exploded a concealed mine on him and had come near killing him.

Sin took the offensive from the start and won out. It was not so difficult to do, either, for it was against reason to believe that a man would fix up such a thing and then voluntarily get right in front of it himself.

Bill Glass investigated, got clues and abandoned them. He finally gave up and informed the conductor that he was unable to solve the mystery. The old cannon lay out on the sidewalk in front of the conductor's house for a long time and was finally taken by the Federal authorities. The conductor had been in the Federal army and, as the gun was a Confederate cannon, no doubt that New Year's night was not the first time it had been fired at him.

Just imagine the deputy chief under Chief Noble engaging in anything like that today. The thing is scarcely thinkable.

★ ★ ★

COLONEL CY S. OBERLY

In the early 1880s there were a lot of first-class newspaper men in Houston. The *Galveston News* had a very large circulation here and generally kept two or three men in their Houston branch office. Then there were two or three pretty good local papers here and all these had good men on them. There were good reporters, bad reporters and a good sprinkling of amateur reporters. Among all the distinguished ones there was one who stood out prominently as both a good newspaper man, fine writer and gentleman, Colonel Cy S. Oberly. All those who were so fortunate as to know the colonel will agree with me in saying that he was a man and gentleman from the crown of his head to the sole of his foot.

The colonel was more of an author than a newspaperman. He was a good writer, but not a good news gatherer, though he never got left in the shuffle, for the other boys always looked out for his interest. He wrote books, poems and newspaper verses and paid more attention to the trimmings than to the serious things of life. He had been a Texas Ranger and had served on the Rio Grande for about three years, so he had a rich fund of personal experience to draw on for his books, which were about Mexican outlaws and wild Indians.

They used to tell an amusing story on the Col. Oberly, but always when they were certain he was absent. He had just issued one of his thrilling frontier stories and all his friends in Memphis, where he was living, were reading and praising it. There was an old printer working on the morning paper who was considered the best critic in the country, for no other reason in the world than that he said he was himself. He criticized everything from the Bible down. All newspaper men will recognize him, for there was never a newspaper office that did not have among its printers one of this type. They are as necessary to a composing room as the printers' devil and the dirty towel. One morning Colonel Oberly was taking an ice cream soda and discussing his last novel with the barkeep, when the latter said: "Colonel, here comes old —. Hide behind the counter. I will ask him about your book, and then you can get his real opinion, which I know will be nattering to you."

The colonel thought it a good idea and hopped behind the counter. When the critic came in and had his whiskey set out in front of him the barkeep asked him, casually, if he had read Colonel Oberly's last novel.

"Yes," growled the old printer, "and he stole every line of it from Ned Buntline."

"You liar!" He rose from behind the counter with the ice pick in his hand and took after the critic. It was a hot chase. The critic got away, but lost his drink. There were two shocked and surprised individuals that morning. Colonel Oberly expected to hear all kinds of praise for his book and got the opposite, while the old printer expected to condemn the book in a breath and take his drink in peace.

Colonel Oberly had one great virtue. Whatever he wrote for a newspaper he held himself responsible for and never sought to hide behind the management or any of the higher editors. I will never forget the advice he gave me when I was made managing editor of the *Galveston News*.

"Now," said he, "you will be called on to pass on many things that affect character and interests. It is a big responsibility and I want to tell you the easiest way to meet it. When you strike anything questionable, read it over carefully and then go out and take a walk, thinking it over. When you get back, read it again and then ask yourself, 'Am I willing to fight for this in case a row is made?' If you can't answer in the affirmative throw the stuff in the wastebasket. There is a world of wisdom in that advice.

What made me think of Colonel Oberly this morning was seeing in the papers where the printers were preparing their burial place in such an elegant way. The colonel's name was mentioned among those buried in Glenwood Cemetery. He died suddenly, I think, in 1886. It was awful weather in February and it had been raining for weeks. Houston was a sea of mud and after getting off the few paved streets navigation was impossible. The road to Glenwood was impassable and it was necessary to use the streetcars for the funeral. The coffin was taken over to the Central Depot and there transferred to a streetcar drawn by mules. Other cars took the places of carriages and thus the first and probably the last streetcar funeral in Houston took place.

★ ★ ★

HATED NEGROES AND LOVED MULES

Poor old Tom Delaney! Had the yellow fever spared him in 1867 he would have left a lasting impression on Houston, for he had much about his make-up that would make men remember him. Tom was an ex-Yankee soldier, who came to Galveston with the army of occupation and was mustered out of the service there. He then came to Houston and rented the old stable and lots on the corner of Smith and Prairie, owned by Dr. Evans, and now occupied by the big brick building of the Model Laundry. Tom had a little money which he had saved and he invested in one or two horses and one or two mules and began some kind of contract work.

Delaney had one or two marked peculiarities. One was his intense love for dumb animals and the other his intense hatred for negroes. In his estimation, a mule was far ahead of a negro and anyone could get a fight out of him at a moment's notice by merely suggesting that he had fought in the Yankee army to free the negroes. He claimed that he had fought for the old flag and that the negro got free through accident and not through intention and that if the ex-Yankee soldiers could have their way every negro would be put back in slavery right off. This, by the way, was the way nine-tenths of the ex-Federal soldiers talked, so Tom was not peculiar to so great a degree in that respect.

Tom's love for his horses and mules was sublime. He was a "muletarian" and "horsetarian" of the highest order. Everybody knows that, having such feelings, Tom was bound to have lots of trouble with his mixture of negro drivers and mules. He was in hot water all the time and were it not for the fact that he was built on the giant plan and able to use his fists with almost as much force as his mules could use their heels, he would never have been able to manage his negroes.

Tom had to employ negroes, for at that time white men did not care to work for ex-soldiers as mule drivers. It was a case of pure necessity. He hired the negroes but got satisfaction by knocking them about whenever he found them out in any rascality. One fixed and iron-bound rule was that the drivers should not ill-treat the horses and mules. Now anybody who knows a negro and a mule knows how absurd that rule was. A mule expects to be mauled and ill-treated by a negro and a negro could no more get work out of a mule by treating him as if he were a Sunday school scholar than he could fly. Tom had several fights before he found out the truth of this and the negroes found out that he was in dead earnest in enforcing his rules.

The climax was reached, however, not through any ill treatment or anything of that kind, but, strange to say, through the efforts of one of the negro drivers to beautify one of the horses he was driving. This horse had a rather long tail, and probably it was because the horse switched this long tail in his face and not for the purpose of making the horse more attractive, as the negro claimed, that the latter determined to cut it off. Whatever the cause that led to this act, the fact remains that when Tom came in his lot one hot Saturday evening he found his horse with a much abbreviated tail and the fly season just under good headway.

Tom looked at the poor horse wagging his patch of tail and then exploded. It is no use to quote his language, for the *Chronicle* would not publish what he said. He ended by informing the negro that unless he had that tail back on the horse by Monday morning he was going to hear something drop. The idea of growing a new tail on a horse in so short a time was so absurd that the negro thought Tom was joking and would never think of the thing again. He was so sure that this was true that, instead of throwing up his job and keeping out of Tom's way, as he would have done had he been wise, he showed up bright and early Monday morning prepared to take his team out. Just as he was ready to drive away Tom showed up. He carefully examined the horse's tail, just as if he expected to find it grown out again and, discovering that it was still in a nubbin' state, without a word he made a lunge at the negro's head with his big fist. The negro was too quick for him, however, and dodged to the other side of the wagon. Unfortunately for the negro, when he dodged he got between the wagon and a high board fence and was thus penned up, with no way out except through or over Tom, who took up a position closing the way out.

The negro became desperate and tried to argue with Tom, but that did no good. Tom advanced slowly but surely until he got within easy striking distance, and then he lammed loose with his fist. The negro lowered his head and received the blow on the top of it, thus rendering the blow harmless. The negro was thoroughly desperate by this time, so when Tom hit him he straightened up and aimed a kick at Tom's belly with all the strength he had in him. Now Tom had on what in these days would be called a "sweater." It was a big woolen shirt, loosely fitting, that came down well on his waist and was worn outside his pants. Tom dodged in his turn. The negro's foot flew up, caught the lower edge of the shirt in front and peeled it upward clear over Tom's head, just like skinning a piece of sausage. Tom was rendered absolutely helpless in a moment and could neither see nor use his arms, which were bound fast by the shirt. Before he could extricate himself the negro rushed past him and attempted to get over the high board fence. There was a big post in the yard and the negro took refuge on top of this. He was perched up there, about 20 feet from the ground, when Tom succeeded in getting untangled. He took a look at the negro and started across the street to get his gun. The other negroes shouted to the one up the post warning him of Tom's intention. I don't know that there is any truth in the story, but the other negroes told it as true for a long time, that when the negro found Tom had gone after a gun he came down the post so quickly that the friction set his pants on fire. He made a dive at the fence, knocked off two or three boards, and when Tom came back with his gun he found his victim gone.

★ ★ ★

INTERVIEWING AN OLD-TIMER

During some years of active newspaper work, I have had, of course, some funny experiences, but I had one the other day that beat anything with which I had ever come in contact. I wanted some special information and sought one of my old-time friends to obtain it from him. Before I could ask a question, he asked me one and that set him going. He asked me who was the editor of a certain paper published in Houston, and when I told him, truthfully, that I had never heard of the paper, he launched out as follows:

"You are like Sarah Bernhardt. When someone asked her about Mrs. Potter, she said, 'Mrs. Pottair. I don't know there is an actress by such name as Pottair.' That was her way of ignoring all competitors. I'll tell you a good story about Sarah. You know what a great actress she is, but to my mind there used to be better than she in the French companies in New Orleans. Ah, those were fine days! I was in the telegraph business then. There was no Western Union then. It was the Washington and National, or something of that kind. Old Thompson was manager and he allowed us to send private messages as much and as often as we pleased. Old Thompson was a thoroughbred. He built the lines to Natchez and then he built the Red River line. Speaking of Red River, reminds me of a certain class of fools who you hear speaking of the 'Rio Grande River.' Wouldn't that jar you! They don't know that 'Rio' means river. It's like a fellow I heard talking about having 'the la grippe.' There's another who don't know that 'la' means 'the' in French. But one thing gets on my nerves more than anything. That is the new word they have made to fix on a driver of an automobile, 'chauffeur.'"

Here I ventured to suggest that it was not a new word, but an old one, and meant a stoker, fireman, or something like that, but he would not listen to me, but went on.

"They don't even know how to pronounce the word. Some say 'showfer,' some say 'chawfer,' while the proper way to say it is 'shaw-fer,' sorter lengthening out the 'fer' part. Do you catch it?

"I pride myself on my French, for I learned it first from old Loui du Ples in New Orleans. There was a man for your money. As polite as a basket of chips, but always looking out for a fight, and never so happy as when he found one. I saw him clean out a barroom in New Orleans one night. I say barroom, but they call them 'coffee houses' over there. I don't know why, for they never sell coffee in them. Loui always had half a dozen duels on hand after he had had his fun. Those duels in New Orleans are the same as the French duels. They go out and poke at each other with little swords that look like knitting needles, long drawn out. Finally one will stick the other through the skin of his arm and their honor is satisfied. Then they embrace and go off somewhere to eat a good breakfast.

"One night a little Frenchman came in our office to send a telegram and got sassy about it. Old man Thompson called him down and started to kick him out of the door, but the chap was too quick for him and got away. In half an hour two young men, who said they were their friend's 'witnesses,' brought Thompson a challenge. The old man accepted it at once and told the 'witnesses' that since he was challenged he had the right to choose weapons and that he would take double-barrel shotguns, loaded with buckshot and fight at ten paces. The 'witnesses' left and we never saw any of them after that. The old man used to say that if his terms had been accepted he would have been the one to leave.

"I did see a sure enough duel over there, though. It was fought between a man named Williams and another named Sydnor. This Sydnor—I'll tell you about it—was a big planter. He owned one of the largest plantations in Mississippi. He was fine folk, too. He married a Guafney and one of his brothers was talked of for the Senate at once. He raised long staple cotton, which, you know, is the best in the world. I have often wondered why they don't try to raise more of it in Texas. There are lots of things the Texas farmers could raise if they would only realize that they can do so. Texas is certainly a great state. I have been living here for over 40 years and the longer I stay here the prouder I grow of the state.

"By the way, I started to tell you a good joke. What was it about? Do you know?"

I did know that it was about Sarah Bernhardt and I also knew that he had started to tell me about a real duel he had witnessed, but I had too much sense to refresh his memory, and made my escape. I realized that I had not gotten the information I wanted, but I concluded it was best to give that up and seek elsewhere, and thus escape having to listen to a condensed, though rather disjointed history of someone's life.

The foregoing perhaps reads as if it were prepared for the occasion. It is an absolutely correct report of what occurred and I have a good witness who will testify that it is correct. The worst part about it was that it was told very slowly and consumed nearly an hour in the telling.

★ ★ ★

AN ALL-ROUND NEWSPAPERMAN

I once heard a public speaker, who got his quotations mixed, declare in the most dramatic manner: "A rolling stone is the noblest work of God." If that be true then Wm. E. Sinclair has about as much nobility about him as one man can stand, for he has rolled a great deal during the 30 years I have known him. He has rolled from Houston to Dallas, from Dallas to Galveston, from Galveston to St. Louis and then back to Texas and begun his endless chain of rolling all over again. He is here in Houston now and says he is going to buy a home and settle down for good. I think he believes he is going to do so, too, but I do not.

"Sin," as the boys love to call him, is well-qualified to lead any life he chooses and to see as much of the world as he cares to see, and that too, on the easiest terms, for there is no better newspaperman in the country than he. One great advantage he has over most newspapermen is the fact that he is as fine a printer as newspaper writer. If there is no opening in the "brainery," he turns to the mechanical department, for he is as much at home in one as in the other.

Twenty-five years ago Sinclair was considered to be the best telegraph editor in Texas. At that time the position of telegraph editor was one of the most difficult and responsible on a newspaper. It is hard to realize that today "copy" comes in typewritten on a clean white paper, with no abbreviations and all that has to be done is to read it, put on a suitable head, and send it to the composing room. In that day it was different. The copy was on flimsy tissue paper and was in skeleton form. Every word, not absolutely necessary to make sense, was left out and a dispatch of, say a column, frequently came in half that space and the telegraph editor had to fill in, straighten out and make it read sense. Sometimes the abbreviation was carried to such an extreme that it was difficult to make any sense out of the dispatch at all. Here is where Sinclair shone, for he could take a condensed story, rewrite it and turn out better copy than the original writer had produced.

Sinclair was also a good reporter and all-'round man in the editorial room and, as he was always on deck and could be relied on, he was very useful. You notice that I speak of him in the past tense. I do that in deference to his announcement that he is going to quit and settle down, which, as I have said, I do not believe.

In 1884, Sinclair and I were running the *Houston Morning Chronicle*. He was foreman of the composing room. He was then and is now an intense Democrat. When the dispatch came saying that Cleveland was elected president, it was about 2 o'clock in the morning. Sinclair had come down after something and was in the editorial room. I showed him the dispatch. He seized my hat and broke for the market house, where the fire bell was located. Climbing the ladder that led to the tower where the bell was, he seized the rope and in a few moments had the whole town aroused. Captain Jack White, who was chief of police, could see no fire and concluded that a drunken or crazy man had gotten hold of the bell, and went up to investigate. When he got up there he found Sinclair.

"What are you doing with that bell? There's no fire anywhere," he said. "You come with me." So saying, he grabbed Sinclair by the collar.

"Hold up, Captain," said Sin. "Cleveland is elected."

"Is he?" said the captain. "Give me that rope," and the two took hold and woke the town up some more. By the time they reached the sidewalk, after tiring themselves out, the whole town was in an uproar, for the news had spread and everybody was rejoicing. The captain invited Sin over to have a "snifter" and as they were taking it he looked at Sin and said, "Sinclair, if you have got the jimmies and have spread a false report, I'm going to lock you up in jail if it takes me a year to catch you." The news seemed to good to be true.

During the whole thirty years I have known Sinclair I have never heard of his doing a small or mean thing. I am sure ex-Mayor John Browne will not say the same thing, for he holds different views and, perhaps, has reason for doing so. Some years ago Sinclair, while on the *Post*, got up his famous goat races. He had the whole town goat mad. Mayor Browne met him on the street one day and told him he would give him some goats if he would come after or send for them. Sinclair thanked him, and going to his office he put the following in the *Post*:

"NOTICE"

> Any boy in Houston who wants a fine goat for nothing can get one by calling at Mayor Browne's residence this morning. As there are only a few goats, it will be first come, first served. The first boy there gets the pick.

The next morning Mayor Browne thought every boy in Houston had gone crazy. His yard was full of boys, the street was full and they kept coming. When he could get away he went gunning for Sinclair, but Sin hid out until the mayor's wrath had died down a bit.

If Sinclair would only settle down, write his memoirs and tell of his journalistic experiences, it would make a most interesting book. He has seen both the tragic and humorous side of newspaper life and can tell his story well.

To meet the quiet, affable gentleman that he is for the first time, one would never suspect that so youthful a man could be one of the oldest and most competent newspapermen in Texas, and yet Sinclair is all of that. I believe he has filled every position on a newspaper, from printer's devil to editor-in-chief, except that of society editor. I would not swear, however, that he has not tried his hand at that, too, on the sly.

★ ★ ★

EARLY HOUSTON DOCTORS

As old Uncle Remus used to say to the Little Boy when he began one of his stories, "This ain't no tale." It is merely writing down some memories that came to me the other day when Judge J. K. P. Gillaspie allowed me to look over an old court record that belonged to Judge Andrews, one of Houston's early justices of the peace. The record is for the year 1859, and aside from the memories evoked by reading the names of those who had business in the court, it has no great value. There is the usual number of disorderly conducts, breaches of the peace and suits for small debts. One feature that stands out prominently is the number of suits filed against delinquent patients by the doctors of that day.

Now in reading over those old names I find something entirely foreign to the court and its record connected with nearly every one of them. The personality of the actors appears vividly before me, and when I read that Dr. W. H. Howard is suing Mr. Blank for $25 for medical attention I do not think of the suit at all, but of Dr. Howard and of his ways and doings. The doctor was one of the leading physicians of Houston, for years. He was a man of profound learning and one of the best equipped physicians of his day. His great and leading characteristics were absolute loyalty to his friends and his detestation of shams and frauds. He had the courage of his convictions and was always willing to back up his opinions. He was a large man, had injured his knee, making it stiff, so he always carried a heavy walking stick. His size and that stick generally combined to bring him out winner in every combat he entered.

It may be said here that only strangers ever tackled the doctor, for his combative nature was too well understood by those who knew him to allow them to make the mistake of riling him. Personally, I never saw the doctor in but one engagement, but that was a good one and might have been a record one were it not for our interference.

Of course, it was with another doctor and occurred during a consultation of physicians over a case of supposed yellow fever. That was an occasion that afforded lots of amusement outside the fight. Yellow fever was dreaded by everybody and by none more than by the merchants, because it put a stop to all business, of course. The old citizens, or "yellow fever nurses" as they styled themselves, took about as much dish in an investigation of the kind that we were making as the doctors themselves. Dr. Howard was contending that the case was a genuine one, but one of the doctors, who had a vast amount of book knowledge about yellow fever and no practical knowledge at all, was contending that there was a doubt. That led to the fight, finally, but before it started a funny thing occurred.

One of the old and eminently respected citizens butted right in the sick man's room and reappeared in a few moments with his head thrown back, sniffing briskly. "That's no yellow fever," he declared, positively.

"The hell you say," said Dr. Howard. "How can you tell so easily?"

"Why, by the smell, of course. Come in here and take a sniff and you can tell it yourself."

"I'm no hound dog to go 'round sniffing for yellow fever," the doctor retorted, hotly. They had some words, and the doctor ended by telling him he not only knew nothing about the case, but that he doubted if he had sense enough to give a sick man a glass of water.

"Why, doctor, you are certainly not in earnest in making such a statement as that," said the gentleman. The doctor told him that he certainly was and asked him how he would do it. "I would get a clean goblet, go to the cistern, pump the water a long time until it was cool, then I would place my left hand under the man's pillow, raise his head gently and give him the water."

Here the doctor broke in: "I knew you would do some fool thing like that when I asked you. Your goblet, with its long stem and broad base, would spill all the water out of the glass before a drop of it reached the patient's mouth."

Then Dr. Howard turned his back on the citizen and renewed the discussion that ended in the fight. I may say here that the patient was on Dr. Howard's side, for soon he began to throw up black vomit and after his death the autopsy revealed a genuine case of yellow fever.

The doctor was loyalty itself and would wade through fire in the interest of a friend. He, Dr. W. D. Robinson, Dr. L. A. Bryan, Dr. George McDonnel and I were very intimate friends. We all had offices, of course, but Conlief's drug store was headquarters and a general loafing place. Conlief had a number of slates with our names painted on them hung on the wall near the front door. Anyone wanting one of us would leave his order on the slates. One hot summer day Dr. Bryan and I were sitting near the door when Dr. Howard drove up in his buggy. He called to Dr. Bryan and asked him to look and see if there was anything on his slate. Dr. Bryan did look and then answered in the affirmative. Dr. Howard commenced getting out of the buggy to come in and read it, when it occurred to him that Dr. Bryan could do it for him. He was halfway out, but halted and asked Dr. Bryan to read it.

"I can't do that," answered the doctor.

"Why not?" asked Dr. Howard.

"Because it is nothing but a fly," said Dr. Bryan. Dr. Howard climbed back in his buggy and drove away in deep silence.

Here, on another page of this old book, I find where Dr. W. D. Robinson was suing some fellow. The chap must have been a hard case to drive Dr. Robinson to do anything of that kind, for a better hearted, more generous and charitable man never lived than he. He was the "family physician" of Houston for many many years, and was the friend and confidant of more people than any priest who ever lived here. He was a very handsome man, warm hearted and generous, and was beloved by everybody. His practice was very large and he did more charity practice than any two or three doctors in the city. He told me a funny story once that will bear repeating.

He said that when he first came to Houston he had but little experience as a doctor and was very modest and retiring. On one occasion he attended a Mexican circus that was performing here. One of the actors fell from a high bar and sustained serious injuries. A call was made for a doctor. Robinson kept his seat hoping that some other doctor was present and would take the case. None did so, and he finally got up and went forward. He said the man was stunned, so he got out his pocket case and prepared to bleed him right there. Just as he was about ready he heard a voice asking him what he was going to do. He looked around and saw Dr. Ashbel Smith, whom someone had sent for.

"I am going to bleed him," said Dr. Robinson.

"Did anyone hear you say you were going to do that?" Dr. Smith asked.

"Well, it is the wrong thing to do," he whispered, "but if anyone heard you, go ahead and bleed him, even if it kills him." Dr. Robinson bled the patient and it did not kill him after all.

Now, as a fine accompaniment to the suits of these two doctors I find one filed by Mr. Pannell, the great undertaker, of whom I have spoken before. The suit is evidently for money due him for putting away some of the doctors' work, as he used to say. Old Man Pannell was a great character. On one occasion the doctors got up a big hunt over on the San Jacinto. They asked Pannell to go, but he would not consent until he secured the promise of every doctor in the city to go. Everyone promised, but at the last moment

Pannell showed up and announced that he could not go, because Dr. Robinson had a case and he knew his services would be needed before he could get back. An investigation revealed the fact that Dr. Robinson did have a case, so he and Pannell were left behind.

Now I don't know that one word of all this will be interesting to the readers of the *Chronicle*. All of it is interesting to me, though, and I think some of it will interest some of the older people who knew all the people I have mentioned. When Judge Andrews was making those formal entries in this little leatherbound book he little dreamed to what use they would be put to half a century after they were written. They have served the purpose today of carrying me back to a day when some of the greatest men of Houston tread the boards, and the experience has been very pleasant.

★ ★ ★

Indians in Houston

Only the real old old-timers can remember the days when Houston had free "Wild West" shows—the days when the Indians were here. There was a tribe living near Houston in the early days and they used to come to town quite often. They brought venison, bear meat and other game and also brought skins and pelts. In 1836 there was a trading post down near the bayou, where the residence of Mr. Horace Taylor was located afterward, but in 1850 and for a few years later the Indians had no particular place at which to trade. Generally they did most of their trading with John Kennedy and Cornelius Ennis. Mr. Kennedy got most of the trade, however, because his whiskey was the strongest, perhaps, and then, too, old Mingo, the chief, was a great friend of Mr. Kennedy, whom he considered a great man.

Those Indians would come in town like lambs but would go away like raging lions. They would come in looking like a lot of dirty vagabonds, but a few drinks of whiskey would transform them into veritable warriors and wild west acrobats. Their capers and antics were amusing and everybody turned out to see them.

On one occasion Mr. Ennis presented Mingo, the chief, with a dilapidated buggy and harness. Mingo at once hitched his war horse, a little mustang pony, to the buggy and the pony resented the indignity, of course. There were all kinds of antics cut up before the pony could be brought to enter into the spirit of the game, but Mingo persevered and finally conquered. Then he proceeded to get drunk, or, more properly speaking, proceeded to keep drunk, to celebrate his added glory. He drove all over town and would not leave his buggy even to get a drink. He drew the line on going home and stayed two days to celebrate. I remember those Indians well, for all my life I have been afraid of Indians, of the tame ones as much as the wild ones. They generally had their knives and guns with them, and I was not alone in being afraid of them.

I was talking to ex-Mayor Lord, who is also an ex-officer of many kinds, the other day about those Indians, and he told me that while he was city marshal, or something of that kind, some of the Indians got drunk and one big fellow got very bad. He had a big bottle of whiskey. Mr. Lord said he did not care to tackle a drunken Indian because he did not know anything about Indians, and he did not care to have any of his men tackle them either. Still he recognized the fact that the Indian had to be arrested and locked up.

Finally he hit upon a plan. He had one of his friends grabbed the bottle of whiskey from the Indian and ran into the old calaboose with it. He knew the Indian would follow the whiskey. The plan worked all right. The Indian ran into the lockup, the decoy duck slipped out and then Mr. Lord locked the door.

There was another tribe further up on the San Jacinto who used to come to Houston also. I can remember a gang of them bringing a big buffalo, which they had captured or stolen somewhere, and hauling it about market square. Perhaps it would be more truthful to say that the buffalo hauled the Indians about the square, for that is what it did. They had two hair lariats around his horns and guided him when he was not guiding them. I don't know what they ever did with the buffalo, for all I can remember is seeing the fun.

Now, one would suppose that having a lot of drunken Indians about would be a great nuisance, and I suppose it was at times, but as a rule they were a source of much fun and amusement. It is really a pity that "high life" was unknown at that time, for its possibilities for extracting strenuous action from those Indian ponies would have been most welcome by the funmakers. As it was, turpentine had to do duty, and many a drunken Indian found his horse prepared to share his wildness and activity when he staggered out of a saloon or a back room of a grocery, all through the kind attention of some unknown gentlemen who had invested their money in turpentine to help the play along. Fortunately there was only soft mud for the Indians to fall on, so no damage was ever done. The Indians died off rapidly and finally a few survivors were moved to the Indian Territory, north of Red River.

The old chief Mingo was really an Indian gentleman. He would get drunk, of course, just as any and every other Indian will, but that was his only fault. He spoke rather good English and was liked by the citizens of Houston with whom he came in contact. I think he died before his tribe moved away, but I am not certain.

★ ★ ★

JIMMY DAW

Jimmy Daw has been dead and buried for forty years, but, if I were a Spiritualist, I would swear that he has been around me for the last three nights. I have not thought of him for about forty years and yet he was not a man to be soon or easily forgotten. Two or three nights ago I woke up thinking of Jimmy and he has been with me ever since. Perhaps he has gotten hold of a *Chronicle* and has seen where I have been writing about some of the old boys and wants to come in for his share. Anyway, I am going to pretend that I believe that and gratify him. However, he is entitled to a place in the *Chronicle* on his merits, as Captain William Christian, Mr. A. B. Nibbs, Mr. I. C. Lord, Henry Thompson, Colonel Phil Fall or any of the real old-timers will bear witness.

When Mr. William R. Baker was county clerk, or something of that sort, in the very early 1850s, Jimmy was his chief clerk and right-hand bower. He was devoted to Mr. Baker and thought there was no man on earth like him. He was a man of some education, good manners, and, while he knew nothing of "sonatas," "movements," "positions" and all those kind of things violinists love to talk about, he was quite an accomplished fiddler and made delightful music. I remember him first on account of his fiddle and next, in after years, by the strange philosophy he developed and the strange theories he fathered. He was always a bit of a character and in his old age he developed into a most pronounced and highly entertaining one. He lived out near the old graveyard, not far from Hangsman Grove, and I used to go out there to hear him talk. Mr. Baker took care of him in his old age, so he was quite comfortable and had nothing else to do but think and talk. One of his pet theories was that the world had been ruined by education.

"It makes me mad to hear the preachers talking about hell," he said one day. "There ain't no hell. It's all education; that's what it is. You take the lowest form of life, the jellyfish or the earthworms. They don't know anything; they float or squirm around, picking up what they want to eat as they go. They don't know anything, they don't have to work or do anything but eat, sleep and enjoy themselves. That's heaven. Now, come a little higher—to the birds and small animals. They know something and they have to pay for it, too, for they have to rustle for a living. That's sorter between heaven and purgatory. Next, we come to horses, cows and animals that have got more sense, and they have to work and toil for everything they get. The smarter they are, the more is expected from them. That's purgatory. Now, come to man. He knows everything, and the result is that he is in hell all the time. The more a fellow knows the worse off he is and the more you educate him the more hell you fix up for him."

All my life I have been fond of "characters," inordinately so, I fear, and in Jimmy Daw I found a most entertaining one. He had a great contempt for history and historians and swore that all the stories about Napoleon and Julius Caesar and George Washington had been fixed up by sharp Yankees to work off on the people, just as the wooden nutmegs were fixed up.

"Why," said he, "it stands to reason that those things are fixed up. Even a hundred years is a long time for a man to remember anything. I know that for a fact, for once when I was a boy I walked five miles to see a man who was a hundred years old and all he could tell me was something about a bear hunt. He didn't know anything about George Washington and if George Washington had have been a sure enough man and had done all the big things history says he did, don't you know this old fellow would have re-membered all about George instead of about that bear?"

Jimmy had some original ideas about astronomy and held with the an-cients that the earth is the center of the universe and that the sun, moon and stars revolve around it. He admitted that the earth is round, but claimed that it is round rather like a bowl and not like a ball, and that it is surrounded with a wall of ice to retain the water and that the land floats about in the water.

When I asked him about ships sailing around the earth he said all such tales were lies hatched up by historians; that if anybody claimed to have gone around the earth they lied, for they had simply gone off somewhere and hidden out and then come back with their story. "It stands to reason," he would say, "that if anybody got off on the far edge of the ice, they would have slipped off into nowhere and never come back again."

I think it was in 1872 that I saw him last. Then I was out of town for several weeks, and when I returned I learned that he had died during my absence. He was quite a queer character but as faithful and true as any living being could be. He never in his whole life injured anyone and, though the peculiarities I have mentioned developed late in life, even as a comparatively young man he made few friends. He kept to himself, and his violin seemed to afford him all the company he desired. Mr. Baker and I went to see him often, but I do not remember ever meeting anyone else there.

★ ★ ★

MIKE CONNOLY'S ESCAPE

A jealous "bad man" with a six-shooter and a modest and retiring philosopher, when thrown together suddenly, are apt to produce complications either tragic or ludicrous. Some years ago such a mixture was made here in Houston, and caused more laughter than all the funny papers combined have produced since.

Mike Connoly, poet, philosopher, expert telegrapher, electrician and all-'round newspaperman, is too well known to need other introduction than the mention of his name. It is true he has confused the situation somewhat, since leaving Houston and going to Memphis, by becoming a colonel and changing the spelling of his name. He is today Colonel Mique Connoly, though that is the only change in him; he is the same old Mike.

In the early eighties Mike was chief electrician for the Western Union Telegraph Company, the office of which company was located on the second floor of the Fox building, corner of Main and Preston.

His duties requiring him to be up at night, he had to sleep during the day and therefore sought a room as far away from the business center as possible, so as to avoid noise. After much search, he obtained what he wanted—a room in a cottage situated down in Frostown, which was the name given that part of Houston down where the gas works is now located. This cottage was owned by a real "bad man," a killer, who was intensely jealous of his wife. Just why he should have been jealous of her no one could understand, for she was as ugly as a brush fence. But he was jealous and took no pains to conceal the fact.

It was late in July when Mike got located, and everything moved along smoothly until about the middle of August. One very hot Sunday night Mike, who was off duty, repaired to his room and retired early. Unfortunately, that same Sunday night the bad man's wife concluded to visit her mother over in the Fifth Ward and the bad man himself concluded to get drunk. That combination was hard to beat, and, as a matter of fact, it was not beaten.

The bad man arrived home about midnight, and, finding no wife in his room, he instituted a search. Of course, he suspected Mike at once. Going to Mike's door and finding it locked he tried to kick it open. That got Mike out of bed in a hurry. The man, finding he could not kick the door open, drew his pistol and shot the lock off. But Mike was too quick for him.

Before he could get the door open Mike was out of the window, out in the street and was well on his way to the banks of the bayou. The man entered the room, shot under the bed and into the wardrobe, but by that time Mike had buried himself in the weeds on the bank of the bayou and was beginning to realize what a fix he was in. He was safe, but he was clad only in a thin summer undershirt that reached scarcely to his hips. Aside from that undershirt he had not a stitch of clothes on and he was barefooted. The moon was full and the night was almost as bright as day. Such a thing as returning to his room for his clothing never entered his head. If he could only get to some friend's house he knew he could get some clothes, but how to get anywhere at all was the problem.

Finally he crept along the bank of the bayou until he reached the foot of Main Street, and then began working his way up that highway. His progress was slow, because he had to hide in doorways and behind barrels and boxes every time he saw anyone coming. At last he reached the Fox building, long after midnight, skipped up the steps and appeared before the astonished, lone night operator.

Mike explained the situation and persuaded the operator to lend him his clothes so he could get out and rustle some for himself. Mike, as everybody knows, is long and lank, while the operator was somewhat squatty. Mike had to have clothes, however, so he forced himself into the borrowed ones and started out to find others. Unfortunately, he had a desire to refresh the inner man, so he headed for the old Capitol bar, where he knew the barkeep. In the bar he met a number of his friends and had to tell the story of his escape and take a drink so often that he forgot all about the naked operator he had left in the office and went to bed in the hotel, oblivious to everything. He slept until midday, and when he awoke he realized what he had done. He got other clothes and hurried to the office, to find a half crazy operator, two-thirds suffocated, hiding himself in the battery room.

Mike was a long time squaring himself with the operator. He never attempted to have the bad man square himself at all. He sent a drayman for his trunk and sought other quarters.

★ ★ ★

UNCLE DAN AND CAPTAIN FAULKNER

The other day I was talking with a lot of old printers when one of them recalled an incident that had escaped my memory completely. I have said once or twice, in speaking of Uncle Dan McGary, that there was but one man on earth to whom Uncle Dan would tip his hat. That man was Captain Andy Faulkner, who had commanded Uncle Dan's company during the war. The old fellow knew the great worth of the captain and knew that he was a man under all circumstances and conditions and he always paid the captain the utmost deference when in his presence. Of course the captain thought much of Uncle Dan and was constantly doing something for him. He liked him but that did not prevent his playing a practical joke on Uncle Dan that nearly drove him crazy for awhile.

Dud Bryan, Frank Small, Uncle Dan and several others of the Bohemian Club went to Austin one winter while the Legislature was in session. There was some bill affecting the railroads being discussed and there were also several representatives, of the railroads in Austin. Among the latter were Captain Faulkner and Major Waldo, representing the Houston & Texas Central road. The newspaper boys and the railroad men were together for a few days and then the newspaper representatives returned home.

An exception was Uncle Dan, who could not be found when the party got ready to leave. Captain Faulkner said he would look out for him and ship him down on the next day's train. The truth was that Uncle Dan was out with some friends he had found in Austin and was painting the town a vivid red. Finally his friends fell by the roadside and about midnight he found himself alone somewhere, he did not know where. He made an effort to get to the hotel where Captain Faulkner was, nominally stopping, but ran against a policeman on the way. Acting just as he always did at home, he ordered the officer to get out of his way and let him pass. The policeman did not know him from a side of bacon, and, judging from his personal appearance that he was a drunken tramp, he promptly arrested him and started for the station house with him. That sort of brought Uncle Dan to his senses and he began to explain who he was and to offer proof of the truth of what he said if the policeman would take him to the hotel where his friends, Faulkner and Waldo, were staying. The policeman did not believe one word of the story, but finally concluded to stop at the hotel, as he had to pass it on the way to the station.

Captain Faulkner and Major Waldo were having a last cigar before retiring, when a bell boy announced that a policeman with a tramp in tow wanted to see them for a moment. They guessed at once who the tramp was and told the boy to bring the policeman and his prisoner in their parlor. In came Uncle Dan, looking as bright and happy at the prospect of release as possible. As soon as the policeman opened his mouth to explain, Uncle Dan cut him short and addressed Captain Faulkner himself.

"You see, Captain," he said, "this man has made a mistake and pinched me. Tell him who I am and send him on his way."

"Tell him who you are?" asked the captain, looking Uncle Dan straight in the face without batting an eye. "I never saw you before. Take him out of here officer, and lock him up."

Uncle Dan could scarcely believe his own ears. He was too far gone to realize that he was being made the victim of a joke and he concluded that either the captain or he himself had gone stark mad.

The policeman chuckled, and grabbing Uncle Dan by the collar, commenced dragging him out of the room. The poor old fellow was too surprised and indignant to say a word until he got nearly to the door when he concluded to make a last stand and a last appeal. Captain Faulkner waived him away and pretended to be intensely indignant that a creature looking like Uncle Dan should dare to claim to be a friend of his. "Take him out of here and take him in a hurry, too," he said to the officer. "I am surprised that an officer of any intelligence should listen to such a story as he has been telling you. Take him away and lock him up."

Then the captain turned his back on the officer and his prisoner and pretended to resume his conversation with Major Waldo. So soon as the door was closed they fell over in convulsive laughter, for either of them would have paid good money for a chance to play such a trick on Uncle Dan. Half an hour later they sent a note to the chief of police to release Uncle Dan and tell him to come to their hotel at once. They waited in vain for him, for he caught the next freight train out of Austin and the next time either of them saw him was weeks later when he showed up on Main Street in Houston. He was so indignant that he threatened to write both of them up in the *Age*, but Captain Faulkner threatened to give a full account of Dan's Austin experience to Dud Bryan for use in the *Galveston News* and that scared Uncle Dan off.

★ ★ ★

MAKING A BEGGAR

Seeing the street beggars the other day reminded me that I have on my own conscience the crime of having inflicted on the community one of these gentry. My doing so made me very unpopular with the public. I have often thought how very easily the people were to be taken in by the fraud I helped to create. Instead of being allowed to impose on the public, he should have been arrested by the police, furnished with a wooden leg and put to work.

He had absolutely no excuse for being a burden on the public, but he was one and a very successful one, too. His history is somewhat amusing as well as instructive, so I will give it here.

Soon after I had graduated in medicine and was still eager to show my skill as a surgeon, there came to Houston a big negro from somewhere up the state. He was the most trifling specimen of humanity I ever saw, though I must say he was smart, in a tricky kind of way. His history was that since his leg was stiff he could not navigate well. He used crutches and got about very well except that his leg, which stuck out like a rudder, interfered with his movements somewhat.

About a month after he arrived in Houston he was taken sick with fever and was sent to the hospital by the city authorities. After he got well, Dr. Connell and I persuaded him to let us take his leg off. We had to use strong arguments with him, but finally overcame his objections. The operation was "a beautiful one" from our point of view and resulted in making his fortune.

We had told him that after his leg was off he could get a wooden one and then could get all the work he wanted. That was just exactly the thing he did not want. He had much higher finance in view than the paltry sums he could accumulate with a wooden leg and work. So soon as we discharged him from the hospital he took to a sunny side of the street and became a professional beggar, just as hundreds have done since his day.

He had the most deceptive face I ever saw. He could put on an expression of woebegoneness that would pull dimes out of the pockets of skinflints. His voice was plaintive and many gave to him feeling that they were doing a real charity, whereas they were only helping to foster a fraud. He always pulled off his hat and bowed low whenever Dr. Connell or I passed him, though he never had the gall to ask us for a donation. He looked on us as his benefactors, for he knew we had set him up in a lucrative business.

Had he saved his money and invested it he might have become a wealthy man. All great men have some pet weakness, however, and our great one loved whiskey too well. For a year or two he never drank while on duty, but then, growing bold because of his great prosperity, he kept a little flask in his pocket and took sly sips from it. The whiskey upset his judgment and he became saucy and irritable, so much so that the public lost confidence in him and began to look on him as a nuisance rather than as an object of charity. All of this, of course, was fatal to his "career" and much more.

One day he took too many drinks, got drunk and abused some white ladies who had refused to give him anything. They complained to the police and he was arrested and locked up. Then the unlooked-for and unsuspected happened.

So soon as the news of his arrest spread among his friends, negro women began to arrive at the city jail to find out why their husband had been locked up. Wife after wife came and before long there were six wives anxious to get him out of jail. Each one asserted that she had "done been had dat man for two years."

An investigation revealed the fact that he had old Brigham Young "skinned to a finish." They were only negro marriages, however, for no preacher or justice of the peace had officiated at any of them. Several of the wives fought among themselves and were locked up also. Then the recorder's court took a hand.

The man was fined and given a jail sentence. He promptly paid his fine and left the city. He went to Galveston, but was run out at once by the police there and I have never seen nor heard of him since.

★ ★ ★

CAPTAIN ANDY FAULKNER

Everybody remembers Captain Andy Faulkner, for he has been dead for such a few number of years that maybe some of the new-issue Houstonians remember him. He was a man not easily forgotten, for his individuality was such as to stamp itself indelibly on any community. He was for many years general passenger agent of the Houston & Texas Central Railroad. His love for and devotion to that road was sublime. You could say mean things about the captain, behind his back, and there was a chance for you to escape the consequences of your indiscretion. The chance was very remote, but still there was a chance, for the captain might forget it before he caught you.

If you said anything mean about the Houston & Texas Central, however, you were doomed, for the captain took no chances about forgetting; he had it penciled in black and white. He had all the Texas newspapers sent to his office, and had a clerk who did nothing but read those papers and clip out every line that made reference to the railroad and paste it in a big scrapbook he kept for that purpose. This book was properly indexed, so the captain had no trouble to turn to the record of any particular paper at once. When an editor applied for a pass the captain looked over what he had said about his road during the year, and if there was anything against the road in the book, the pass was refused and the editor was referred to his own paper, such and such a date, for the reasons for the refusal.

Captain Faulkner and Colonel Bill Sterrett were warm personal friends to the day of the captain's death, but professedly they were at daggers' points and if Colonel Sterrett wanted to reach any point on the Houston & Texas Central road, he had either to dig up his cold cash for a ticket or walk. The colonel had so far forgotten himself as to refer to the captain's road as "the angel maker" because of the frequent and fatal wrecks that were taking place on it. That settled him. Captain Faulkner placed him on his blacklist in boxcar letters and kept him there. Colonel Sterrett got no more favors, nor did he ask for any. He practically kept his reference to the Houston & Texas Central as "the angel makers" as standing matter and ran it in nearly every issue of the paper.

One or two papers were silly enough to copy Colonel Sterrett's remarks and make some up of their own. They also went on the blacklist. Colonel Nat Q. Henderson was among the erring ones. He was living in Georgetown, but happened to be in Austin and wanted to come to Houston, so he wrote to Captain Faulkner asking for a pass. The captain looked up his record and found that it was generally good and that Henderson had sinned but slightly. But Faulkner wanted to punish him, so he sent him a pass "good from Austin to Hempstead and return." Colonel Henderson glanced at the pass and, without reading it, boarded the train for Houston. He did not discover the trick until he got to Hempstead and the conductor refused to let him come farther without a ticket or pass. There was a wait at Hempstead for the main line train, so Colonel Henderson persuaded the conductor that Captain Faulkner had made an error and had written Hempstead instead of Houston, as he should have done. He got the conductor to telegraph to the captain for instructions on what to do. The answer came back: "Make Henderson pay fare or put him off." He paid and came to Houston, in no good humor, however.

I did not set out to tell of Capt. Faulkner as a railroad man. What I wanted to speak of was his innate gift as a storyteller. He had a fine sense of humor and was one of the best talkers I ever knew. In 1883 nearly every Sunday night, Tobe Mitchell, Colonel O. T. Holt, Colonel Sy Oberly and I would sit out in front of the Capitol Hotel, now the Rice, and listen to Captain Faulkner talk for hours. He was always full of good, clean, healthy stories and told them in the most charming manner. I remember a number of very funny ones he told, but about the best was one he used to tell on himself.

He said he was in one of the fashionable barrooms in Austin with a number of friends one evening when he noticed two rather seedy-looking fellows eyeing each other keenly. Finally one advanced to the other and said:

"Was you at the battle of Gettysburg?" The other seedy fellow said that he was. "When you rebs drove the Pennsylvania troops back, going to Little Round Top, did you pick a wounded Yankee boy up and put him behind some rocks?" The other fellow became much agitated and said he did. "I was the boy you picked up and I knew you as soon as I saw you come in and have been trying to place you."

With that, they fell into each other's arms and embraced warmly, after which they shook hands over and over. Finally, each dug down in his pocket but found nothing. "If I had any money with me," said the Yankee, "we shore would have a drink over this."

The captain said it was all very touching. He had been a soldier himself and knew what such meetings as this meant, so he slipped the Confederate a dollar and told him to treat his friend. The other gentlemen who had witnessed this scene were also touched and became deeply interested and insisted on buying an unlimited number of drinks for the two old war horses, with the result being that the two got so drunk and boisterous that the saloon man had to put them out.

The captain said that a month or two later he was in Dallas and went into a saloon to get a drink. There was a crowd near the bar and as he entered, he heard a familiar voice say, "Was you at the battle of Gettysburg?"

He looked and saw the two old "heroes" go through the same scene he witnessed in Austin. He realized that they were two old bums who invented this plan for getting free whiskey from a sympathetic crowd. It worked, too, just as it had done in Austin, and no doubt worked in every place they visited.

I think Captain Faulkner was the only man "Uncle" Dan McGary ever took off his hat to. Uncle Dan knew him in the highest regard and esteem because he knew him. He had served in the captain's company during the war. The captain also had a warm place in his heart for Uncle Dan. He said Uncle Dan was one of the best soldiers he had and one who could always be depended on. He told a story of an old fellow who was a Union sympathizer and who refused to sell anything to the Confederate soldiers. The old fellow had lots of corn but would not give or sell any of it to the Confederates and, as he was a fiery old chap and backed his refusal with a double-barrelled shotgun, there were only two things to do: kill him or give up all hope of getting corn. One day Captain Faulkner told Uncle Dan to take a wagon and go over and buy a load of corn from this old fellow. He gave him the money to pay for it and told him to avoid all trouble, but to get the corn if possible. After a very short time Uncle Dan came back with the corn and the money, too.

"He didn't raise any objection when I commenced loading up the wagon," said Uncle Dan. Captain Faulkner inquired as to how he accomplished this.

"Well as soon as he showed up with his gun, I took that as a declaration of war and I pied him right then and there. I knew I would have to do it before our interview closed, so I didn't waste any time, but plugged him and argued the matter with myself afterward."

★ ★ ★

DR. MCBRIDE AND COL. CHARLEY MARTIN

Who among the oldtime newspapermen does not remember Dr. McBride? There was a yellow journalist that would make some of the yellow of today look like pure white. The doctor simply lived thirty years too soon. Had he been of today he could have commanded his own salary, and Hearst would have gone down on his knees to get him on any of his papers.

He was the Texas representative of the *St. Louis Globe-Democrat*, which made a special feature of crimes in Texas. They could not have gotten a better man than he, for he had absolute genius in handling such matters. He could take an ordinary item, such as an exchange of shots between gentlemen, which would be dismissed with a few paragraphs today and turn out a couple of columns of as sensational and readable stuff as anyone could wish to see. The doctor got to be a monomaniac on the subject of crime. He thought of nothing else, and with him no other item had even the flavor of news. Tell him that a syndicate was going to build a million dollar hotel and the chances were that he would forget it before he had gone a block, but tell him that a negro bootblack had used a razor on a competitor and he would run all over town to get the details, or the hints for details to be supplied. I met him one afternoon and he was in great good humor.

"The old town is waking up," he said. "Things are beginning to boom. Why, I got a suicide and a murder this afternoon and I haven't had two such good items in a long time." That remark alone will show you what kind of a reporter he was.

Frequently the doctor furnished some of the sensations himself, for he published the news as he found it, painted and exaggerated, of course. No one was spared, and, of course, he was frequently in hot water. On one occasion there was a woman with a bullwhip waiting on one corner, a banker with a six-shooter on another and a policeman with a club further down the street, all waiting for the doctor, because he had written them up in the *Globe-Democrat*. The doctor, totally oblivious to the fact that there was so much war fixed for him, just at that very time, was engaged in a knock-down and drag-out with little Quick, a reporter on the *Age*, not two blocks from where his friends were waiting for him. The trouble between the doctor and Quick had no connection with the St. Louis paper, but it surely saved the doctor a lot of trouble that morning. The woman and the banker did catch him afterward, but they'd had time to cool off and were not so enthusiastic as they would have been while the grievance was fresh on their minds.

When I was about six years old a German stabbed his wife in the street. The injured woman was taken into my grandfather's house and died in his dining room. The German was convicted and sent to the penitentiary for life. Thirty years afterward he was pardoned. One of the newspapers mentioned the location of the murder and also mentioned the fact that the woman died in my grandfather's house. Dr. McBride hunted me up at once. I told him all I knew, which was simply the fact that she was stabbed and brought into the house and died a few minutes afterward. That was enough for him. He got three columns of as magnificent reading matter out of it as you ever saw. Uncle Dick Westcott was running the *Age* at that time and was perfectly familiar with all the details of the crime. He went for the doctor hot-footed and heaped ridicule and scorn on his head, but he might as well have poured water on a duck's back. The doctor was simply incorrigible.

Another great character of that same time was Col. Charley Martin, city editor on the *Telegram*. He was of a different type, and he had nothing sensational or startling about him. He was a good newspaperman and a dignified gentleman. He was a scrapper from way back, which made for his success. In those days there were no convenient managing editors to stand sponsor for everything in the paper, so every reporter had to fight for his own items. Charley soon established a reputation and after that he had clear sailing. His whole career might have been one of dignity and success to the end but for an accident.

One chilly night, after a hard day's work, the colonel sought relaxation and a warm place to sit at the theatre. Milt Noble was playing "Phoenix" at Perkins Hall. Since the house was full, the manager gave the colonel a box all to himself. He watched the play for a few minutes, then being wearily went to sleep in the comfortable seat. He was snoring away peacefully, when a noise on the stage brought him to and he opened his eyes on the famous fire scene. He did not know for a moment where he was. All he knew was that the house was on fire, and yelling "Fire! Fire!" at the top of his voice, he leaped out of the box onto the stage. The audience thought it was part of the play and applauded loudly, but Charley knew better. He slipped out of a side door and left town the next morning before the story got out. He went to Dallas and did not come back to Houston for ten years.

★ ★ ★

JIM AND SHORTY

My first meeting and acquaintance with those kings of Bohemian printers, if there are any such things, "Shorty" Parish and Jim Baker, dates from the summer of 1880. I had just begun newspaper work and was in the editorial room of the *Post* late one night when Shorty and Jim came in. They were pretty well-loaded and were in the best of humor.

"So you are going to run a newspaper," said Shorty. "You are making a big mistake. There's nothing in it. Quit it while you've got time. It eats up more money than anything in the world. A newspaper is the only thing that ever beat the devil and that is the only good thing I ever heard about one of them. Yes, I'll tell you how it was. A man sold his soul to the devil for all the money he could spend, the devil to produce every Saturday night. That man sure had a good time. He spent money for everything he could think of, but the devil always had the cash on Saturday night. The man built railroads, ship canals, erected big dams and went into every big thing he could hear of, but the devil always promptly paid the bills. The man got desperate, for the time was drawing near for him to settle with the devil. One day he established a newspaper, just as you and Gail Johnson are doing. The first and second payments were made promptly by the devil, but the old chap began to look blue. In a few months the devil asked for a little extension of time and at the end of the next week he gave up the job altogether and tore up the contract. Now that's a true story and you better take warning from it." Shorty then asked for what he called "brain food," which was his name for newspapers, and taking a large bundle of exchanges, he waddled away in company with Jim Baker.

These were the two most distinguished members of the "bummers" crowd that ever graced Houston, Galveston and other Texas cities, where there was any printing to be done. They were fine printers, regular experts, but they worked only spasmodically, and when they were forced to do so by stern necessity. There were no type-setting machines in those days. The old fashioned printer set type by hand. Both Jim and Shorty were good members of the union and could always get at least a day or two's work in any union office and that was all either of them wanted.

Shorty was in constant trouble with the barkeepers. He would show up frequently minus a hat or coat, which articles of wearing apparel had been ruthlessly seized by some irate saloon man in liquidation of his bar bill. About 1882, Shorty went to Galveston and Major Lowe performed the miracle of sobering him up. Then the most wonderful things occurred. Shorty turned out to be exquisite, a regular dude. He broke out in broadcloth, patent leather boots, stovepipe hat, kid gloves and gold-headed cane. He was sober so long that he was made foreman of the *News* composing room. It was really a treat to see him walk down Tremont or Market Street. He was a good looking little fellow and for about a year was the envy of the men and the admiration of the ladies.

One night he was tempted and fell. His glory departed like a summer cloud, just faded away, and the old bum printer was in full swing before the end of the week. Shorty never attempted to regain a new foothold, but went down with flying colors, the colors he had chosen. He went to the *News* office and got an armful of "brain food" one afternoon and about 9 o'clock that night some one going to his room found him sitting in his chair with his glasses on, a newspaper spread out on his knee, stone dead.

Jim Baker was somewhat different from Shorty. He never, for one thing, ever quit drinking voluntarily. When he quit there was a cause, other than moral. He had a voice that would have been worth a fortune for an ambitious tragedian. It was a grand voice and when he would repeat a poem or some extract from one of Bob Ingersoll's speeches, it was worth listening to. He was a great schemer and could get a quart of whiskey where Shorty could not get a drink.

One of the amusing things I remember about him was once when he tried to work the Rev. Mr. Clemens, rector of Christ Church. Mr. Clemens was one of the best and most tender-hearted men and was always eager to respond to an appeal for assistance. He was in the *Post* editorial room one night when Jim rushed in with the request for a half dollar, saying that he was hungry and had not eaten for two days. Mr. Clemens listened to his tale of woe and then, taking him by the arm, hurried him down to a restaurant and told the man to give Jim the biggest supper he could fix up. Mr. Clemens took a seat to see Jim enjoy the meal. It was brought, but Jim could not eat a mouthful of it. He made a clean breast to Mr. Clemens and never tried to impose on that gentleman again for drinks. Mr. Clemens forgave him his deception and gave him an order for a night's lodging at a nearby boarding house. Jim actually needed the bed, so he took the order. Instead of going to the place at once, he got drunk and went there about midnight. He had gotten an idea in his head that he owned the place by that time, so when he descended on the boarding place, he did so like a whirlwind and kicked up such a row that the police were called in and they locked him up. Poor fellow. He, too, is dead and gone. He died in Dallas several years ago, keeping up his record and beating Shorty to the grave.

★ ★ ★

BILLY TOOLE

All the old-time printers and newspapermen remember little Billy Toole. There was never but one Billy and there will never be another. The time and place were just right and Billy fitted in just as a setting does in a ring. In the strict business of commercial life today Billy would be an impossibility, but in the late 70s and early 80s things were the reverse of what they are today and Billy was enabled to flourish in all his glory.

As a matter of fact, Billy was a real and genuine Bohemian. He was the real article in every sense of the word. He was a skilled printer in the days when type was set by hand and skill actually counted for something. He had a brilliant imagination and was fond of writing blood and thunder stories, some of which would have done credit to Ned Buntline. The only defect about Billy's stories was that he never completed any of them. He would leave the hero or heroine in the most blood-curdling situation, and without taking the trouble to get him or her out, would lay aside his manuscript and start in on another story, the scene of which would perhaps be on the other side of the world. Billy almost completed one story, which had such merit that Professor Girardeau urged him to complete and publish it, but he never did.

Billy was little but he was loud. No Spanish gamecock was ever more eager for battle than he on any pretext or excuse. It is a remarkable statement to make, nevertheless it is true, Billy rarely went to war and met with defeat. In some way he always managed to come out winner. The only time he suffered absolute defeat was when he bucked against John Barleycorn. He would try that game, too, being a genuine Bohemian, but he met the fate of all those brave but unwise people who enter the unequal fight.

Billy figured as the star actor in one of the most laughable shooting affairs that ever occurred on Main Street, and by way of parenthesis it may be said here that he had the sympathy and backing of every man in town, when all the facts were learned.

Billy, after "looking on the wine that was red" went wandering into the Ironclad gambling house on Main and Congress. He did not like something that was said or done and expressed his opinion of the whole crowd of gamblers from the proprietor down. For this offense he was promptly handed over to the official bouncer, who was a great, big, strapping fellow. The man was a brute and, though he could have taken Billy up with one hand and carried him downstairs like a baby, he proceeded to handle him in the most brutal and outrageous manner. He slugged and beat him and then, grabbing him by the lapels of his coat, he butted him in the face. Then he carried him down and deposited him on the sidewalk.

Billy was pretty nearly dead by this point, but he was so angry it put life and energy enough in him to enable him to go off and borrow a six-shooter. Unfortunately the only pistol he could get was an old army pistol that was large, heavy and hard to handle. Billy took the gun nonetheless and went back to get his man. He stood on the corner and waited. Before long the brute showed up, and, not knowing Billy's intentions, advanced on him as though he were going to attack him again. Then Billy pulled out his artillery and the fellow turned and fled. Billy fired one shot and took after the man. The gun was so heavy he had to hold it up with both hands. Billy would run up close to the man, stop, cock his pistol and, holding it with both hands, would fire at him. It was strictly a running fight that extended from Congress to Preston, clearing the sidewalk of everybody except Billy and his victim.

I am not certain, but I think Billy hit his man once or twice. I am certain of one thing, though: Billy came in for general condemnation for being so bad a shot and not having killed the brute the first shot out of the box. The only extenuating circumstance was that Billy claimed the gun was so heavy he could not handle it with any degree of satisfaction and that he had done his best and could have done no more under the circumstances.

Billy was quite fond of practical jokes, and on one occasion he came very near ruining a fine oration by one of Houston's most brilliant lawyers by asking a question and making a foolish remark at just the wrong time. The occasion was a lecture or rather oration on the tariff question, the object of which was to explain what the tariff really was. The oration was in the opera house and since the great power of the speaker was well-known to all, the affair was made into something of a society event and the house was crowded with ladies. Billy was there in all his glory, seated away back in the gallery. The speaker had nearly completed his address when Billy stood up and called out, "May I ask you a question, major?"

The major recognized him and answered, "Certainly, Mr. Toole."

"Did I understand you to say that the tariff was a tax on everybody, though so concealed that its presence is not recognized by all?"

"That is correct in substance," said the major.

"All right, major," said Toole. "That puts the drinks on you. It's all I wanted to know," and he went out of the hall.

The interruption and the irrelevant reply of Billy so upset the major that he forgot "where he was at" and made a halting and stumbling close of an address that had started off brilliantly and been, to the time of Billy's interruption, one of the best efforts of his life. For many days after that Billy kept his eye skinned for the major and always succeeded in seeing him first. He knew it would not do to meet the major until he cooled off.

I have often wondered how Billy managed to die a natural death, for, according to all chances and probabilities, he should have been killed a dozen times. He did more to be killed for than nine-tenths of those who were actually killed. Not long ago I read of a fellow out in a West Texas town who armed himself with a piece of lead pipe and strolled down the street, slugging every man whose looks he did not like. When I read that my thoughts reverted to Billy Toole, for that was his method of doing business, barring the lead pipe, of course.

★ ★ ★

A HEARSE, A BOY AND A BUM

Once or twice I have spoken of Old Man Pannell, the "old man" being used as a term of affection, for everybody loved him. He was one of the characters of the early days; was the only undertaker, or as it was called then, "sexton," here, and no self-respecting citizen felt that he was properly buried unless the old man had done the job.

Mr. Pannell was full of fun and enjoyed a joke as well as the next man, but he concealed that fact as much as possible, put on a woebegone expression to accord with his calling and, before his death, had become the typical professional burier. From time to time his love for fun would crop out, but he never permitted such a breach of ethics while on duty. A pauper was buried in Potters Field with as much solemnity as was the merchant in the great cemetery. Of course, the pauper did not ride in the fine hearse afforded the merchant. Alternate transportation was provided.

Mr. Pannell had an old fashioned black hearse drawn by a little gray mare, which was used for second and third class funerals. He insisted, however, on having order and dignity and the little gray mare walked as quietly to and from the cemetery in front of the little black hearse with no carriages following, as did the black steeds drawing the grand hearse at the head of a procession of carriages and buggies.

As I say, Mr. Pannell had the old black hearse, and the little gray mare and he had something more. He had a boy whom he had raised, named Rick Nolan. Rick was a typical boy, thought less, hair-brained and ready to engage in anything that gave promise of fun, as all real boys are. Rick was placed in command of the pauper hearse and the little gray mare, and he had not officiated at many "plantings" before he discovered that the little gray mare should have been on a race track rather than before a hearse.

Potters Field was then located on the banks of the bayou beyond the San Felipe graveyard, and as that was way out in the country the San Felipe Road gave Rick as fine a race track for developing the speed of his gray mare as the heart could wish for. He would go out quietly enough but would come back at a 2:40 clip, racing everything in sight until he reached Main Street, when he would slow down and creep along as quiet as a mouse.

Rick might have continued his sport indefinitely but for an accident. During the fall of 1866, a tough and wild-looking old "bum" and the cholera struck Houston. The bum might have remained in obscurity, but not so the cholera. It was something new. The people knew all about yellow fever and after the first panic among the tenderfeet, the situation was accepted and everything ran along as usual. They knew nothing of cholera, however, and its advent produced a genuine and lasting panic. Every man was afraid of his neighbor and friend whom he regarded as the carrier of the fatal germs. Stories of miraculous cures, of apparently well men falling dead, of apparently dead men coming to life and all such things became current and everybody believed them.

Now just when this nervous tension was greatest Rick was called on to bury a negro out in the Potters Field. He performed his duty and started back. Just as he reached San Felipe Road he encountered the bum mentioned above. The bum asked for a ride to town, but as that was almost a capital offense in Mr. Pannell's eyes, Rick wisely refused.

Then the bum offered him ten cents to take him to town. Rick was tempted and fell, but he insisted that the bum get inside the hearse and lie down so no one could see him, and that he get out when Main Street was reached. The bum agreed and got in. Rick drove along quietly until within a few blocks of Main Street. Then he concluded to give his passenger a touch of high life. He gathered up his reins and hit the mare a sharp lash with the whip. That settled it and in a moment Rick realized that he had overplayed his hand. The mare took the bit between her teeth and bolted.

Main Street was reached in a jiffy and people along that highway were horrified to see an apparently crazy mare dashing toward town, having in tow a dilapidated hearse containing a "dead" man who was making frantic efforts to escape. The door of the hearse was latched on the outside so the bum could not open it, but he was doing his best to do so. Everybody who saw the thing concluded that the hearse panic was due entirely to the revival of the dead man and that Rick was trying to get away in his terror.

Down Main Street the frightful rush came. When a point was reached about half way between Texas Avenue and Prairie, the tramp in desperation, kicked the door open and tumbled out, doing some excellent grand and lofty tumbling after striking the ground. He picked himself up and started for the sidewalk, but his appearance had inaugurated a new and genuine panic. Everybody fled from him. People rushed into shops and stores and barricaded the doors. Saloons were closed and he could not get within a hundred yards of those who failed to get in a place of safety.

Since it was daylight, the ghost element was lacking, but the bum was regarded as a dead cholera victim and therefore as a perfect walking magazine of cholera germs. Some even went so far as to want to shoot him and have Nolan take him back and bury him sure enough. Finally the truth leaked out. Nolan was fired by Mr. Pannell and the people were so relieved to find that the bum was not what they thought he was that everybody joined in the laugh.

★ ★ ★

NEGRO FIREMEN DURING THE WAR

In 1863 every able-bodied man in Houston who was anything of a man at all had gone in the army. Houston's fine volunteer fire department existed only in name, for all the young men comprising it had promptly volunteered at the first call. There were only the old men and boys left and as these were poor material from which to make active firemen, the situation was rather grave. There was a good hook and ladder outfit, that of Hook and Ladder Company No. 1, and two fire machines—I came near saying engines, but they were not. They were the old-fashioned machines that had a pump somewhere in the middle, worked by two side arms having at their ends long bars, which were worked up and down by from ten to fifteen men on each side. Doubtless many readers of the *Chronicle* have seen pictures of these old fire fighting machines, which exist now nowhere else except in pictures. But there was no one here to work even these old machines, so it was finally determined to detail a number of negroes to act as firemen under white officers. The negroes made splendid firemen and enjoyed it so much that it was feared by some of the timid citizens that the negroes would start fires just for the fun and pleasure of putting them out.

It was a pleasure to watch the negro firemen at a fire. They threw their whole souls into the work and seemed never to grow weary, although it was the hardest kind of work and frequently lasted for two or three hours without stop or rest. Nominally they were under the control of white men, but actually, after they got their pumps going and their streams of water well directed, they were under their own control, so far as running those handlebars was concerned. A little whiskey handed around in a bucket and drunk out of a tin cup without water was all-sufficient to keep them on the go under a full head of steam for hours. They sang, of course, for a real negro can do nothing that requires rapid action without singing, and they composed their own words and, I suspect, their own tunes, too.

I remember a big fire that occurred down by where the gas works now are, in 1863. Quite a number of small houses were burned. Of course, with the present day fire department the fire would never have extended beyond the first house, but at that time whenever a house caught fire, if there was one near it, it was pretty apt to go, too. Anyway, four or five went that time, one after the other, the negroes fighting the fire like demons, and singing like angels, for they do sing sweetly. One of my grandfather's negroes, John Cook, better known to every body as "Big John," because of his great size, was choir leader. He would sing a verse alone and then other negroes would take up the refrain. I heard the song so often that I remember the tune and one of the verses. I can't give you the air, but I can give the verse, which was as follows:

> If I had a wife and she wouldn't dress fine,
> Whiskey, oh whiskey!
> I'd leave this world and climb a pine.
> Whiskey, oh my whiskey!

Big John, who had a powerful voice would sing, "If I had a wife who wouldn't dress fine." The crowd would join in with the refrain. It was fine. There were about fifty verses, but the one I give is all that I remember. The air was very musical and the words fitted well to the beat of the handlebars, so that the work of handling them became a real pleasure instead of hard work, as it would have been without the singing. It was something like going to a good concert to attend a fire in those days.

I don't know that there is such a thing as a negro fire company in existence today anywhere in the United States, but if there is, it can't, with modern fire fighting apparatus, be anything like the old negro company that Houston had during the war.

★ ★ ★

JACK AND JIM MARTIN

Houston has produced many men who have made names for themselves in civil, military and naval life and others still, who, while they never attained success in financial, commercial, military or naval circles, still, by their marked individuality so impressed themselves on the early history of Houston that it is impossible to speak of youthful Houston without recalling them.

Two of the latter kind were the Martin brothers, Jack and Jim. They were of a type seldom seen now. They were gamblers and absolutely honest men. I don't suppose either ever took the shade of an unfair advantage over an opponent nor would they have a man in their employ who was even suspected of being crooked. As Jack used to explain, "Cheating don't pay in the long run. If a gambler can't win out with the advantage of having the percentage of the game in his favor and the other advantage of making the other fellow do all the guessing, he better quit."

Both Jack and Jim had the respect and confidence of the businessmen of Houston and though they never pretended to be anything more than what they were—professional gamblers, their word was good without other security for any amount of money within reason with such men as B. A. Sheppard, T. W. House, Sr., Paul Bremond, Wm. J. Hutchins or any of the big merchants or bankers of those days.

Jack was relatively taciturn. I say relatively, because had it not been for Jim, Jack might have been considered an ordinarily talkative man. However, Jim was such a conversationalist, told such interesting and instructive stories, and had had so broad an experience which gave an inexhaustible fund from which to draw, that Jack always seemed to be something of a clam when Jim was around.

The Martin brothers had a fine establishment on the second floor of a building about two stores north of where Sweeney's Jewelry store now stands on Main Street, between Prairie Avenue and Preston Avenue, and their rooms were always well filled by planters, interior merchants and others who came to Houston to sell their cotton and sugar. These gentlemen were always willing and glad to take a whirl at faro to pass away the time and hear Jim talk.

With all his good nature, his talkativeness and apparent indifference to the serious affairs of life, there was one subject which had for Jim the greatest interest and that was the future life. It was a subject he considered too sacred for indiscriminate discussion and he never talked about it in a crowd. When alone with someone whom he thought could appreciate his views, he would unbosom himself.

"You see," said he to me one evening, "it's this way. We don't know anything about it. I don't believe in the preacher's hell, where they burn you in brimstone, and I don't believe in these men and women who tip tables and go off into trances and tell you the future is the very reverse of what the preachers say. That whipsaws me, of course. I lose both ways and I end where I started."

"Well," said I, "why don't you give it up and quit thinking about it?"

"I would," said he, "but for two things. One happened to me and the other to Jack." I knew there was a good story coming, so I remained silent and waited for the details.

"What happened to me was a plenty, too, for I actually died and went to hell, so I know there is a hell. That part's settled in my mind, almost. You are too young to more than barely remember that there was a big yellow fever epidemic in Houston in 1852. It was a hummer and as it was the first one since 1847 when so many people died, there were lots of newcomers here who had never had the fever and it seemed like everybody in town was down with it and either dead or dying. About the fourth or fifth week it got me and I grew sicker and sicker until finally I did not know anything at all until suddenly I came to my senses for a moment and realized I was dying sure enough.

"The next thing I knew I was dead and could hear my women folks crying and going on. Then everything became black and silent and when I came to I was in a great big hall with a big throne at one end of it. The hall was crowded, but there was window which the throne was facing. On each side of it the sheep and goats were lined up. They had me on the goat side. On the throne was a big man with a long white beard who had a long shepherd's crook in his hand. He looked like the picture of Moses I had seen, so I concluded it was him. Whoever he was, he had full charge and went on sorting the sheep and goats with his crook as fast as they came in.

"Now, I didn't like being among the goats, so I slipped across among the sheep, but it didn't do any good, for I scarcely got across when Moses, or whoever he was, reached out and caught me round the neck with his crook and put me back with the goats. I tried it again, but he roped me with his crook without even looking around at me. I waited a moment and sneaked over again. This time he caught me before I got clean over and twisted my neck when he shoved me back. It made me mad and I blurted out, 'Damn it, sir, don't do that.'

"In a second old Moses changed. He looked vicious and, instead of pushing me clear back among the goats, he gave his crook a sudden flirt and threw me clear through the roof out into space. I thought I never would land anywhere. Finally I saw solid earth under me and when I got nearer it I saw a little hole in the ground like one of those doodle holes the boys stick straws in and catch doodles. I was heading straight for that hole, and the next minute I hit it, head on, and went through like a flash. The squeeze through the hole broke my fall, and the next moment I landed safely in a beautiful garden. It was a fine place. I stood up and looked round. There were horse races going on and big crowds of ladies and gentlemen were attending them. Right out under the trees were faro banks, roulette tables and every kind of gambling, and everybody seemed to have plenty of money. There were beautiful women and elegantly dressed men, and waiters passing round with all kinds of drinks.

"Finally an elegantly dressed gentleman, wearing a stovepipe hat, came up and, calling me by name, welcomed me to hell. 'You don't tell me this is hell,' I said.

"'Yes,' said the devil. 'This is it. How do you like it?'

"'God Almighty, man,' said I, but the devil popped his hand over my mouth before I could finish my sentence.

"'Don't use that name down here, Jim,' he said.

"Then he took me everywhere and showed me what a fine place he had. I was beginning to feel thankful to old Moses for throwing me out of his sorting shop, but just then we came to a big flat rock. It was so hot it looked blue. The devil did not say a word, but I knew right off that I had to pull my shoes off and get on that rock. 'Look here, old man,' I said to the devil. 'Can't we just cut this part of the performance out? You know what a good friend of yours I've been.'

"'Yes, Jim,' said he. 'I know you have always worked for me and I feel grateful to you for it, but I can't help you now. It's the rule and nobody can break a rule in hell. Why, the whole place would fall to pieces if I broke a rule or allowed one to be broken.'

"I saw there was no way out of it, so I pulled off my shoes and mounted the rock. When I did so I heard my mother say, 'Keep rubbing.' Then I came to and found that the women were rubbing my hands and feet with pepper and mustard to keep up circulation. I got well, but could not handle anything or walk for a week or two because of blistered hands and feet."

"Now, you see, I know all about hell, because I've been there and have seen it. The other thing happened to Jack. Jack and Lige McGowan were great friends. They were over on the old White Oak bridge one moonlight night and got to talking about the hereafter. Jack said a man was the same as a tree, and that when he was dead he was dead, and that was all there was about it. Lige didn't know so much about that. So, after arguing awhile, they agreed that the first one that died should come back to the survivor and tell him all about it, or as much as he could. They shook hands in agreement.

"About a month after that Jack had been dealing faro until late. The game broke up about 3 o'clock and everybody except Jack and another man went home. It was a hot summer night and the moon was full. Jack and the other man concluded to lie down on a big table and sleep there instead of going home. Jack says the other man dropped off to sleep as soon as he lay down, but that he was lying there, wide awake, looking out of the big window which he was facing. All on a sudden he saw Lige McGowan come walking across Main Street, right up in the air. Jack grabbed the other fellow and tried to wake him but failed. Lige walked straight to the window, stepped in, hopped down on the floor and came right up to Jack.

"'Jack,' said Lige, 'are you awake? I've come to tell you there is a hereafter, though it is not as good nor as bad as you might hope for. There is an after-life and you can improve it by what you do here.' Saying this, Lige vanished and then the fellow whom Jack was pulling on all the time waked up. Jack described how Lige was dressed and told the whole story. He said Lige had on a big blue military coat, with brass buttons down the front.

"The next day we hunted for Lige, but no one knew where he was. Two or three days later a man came in from the Brazos and brought news that Lige had died out there. Strangely, Lige had shown up at a house crazy with fever and had lost nearly all his clothes in some way. When they got ready to bury him the only thing they had to put on him was an old blue military coat with brass buttons, the same as he wore when he came to see Jack.

"When Jack heard about the coat, he knew he had absolutely seen Lige and I had hard work keeping him from going right off and joining the church. We had a big game and were making lots of money, and if Jack had joined the church it would have completely ruined us."

Poor old Jim, and Jack, too, have long ago turned over their boxes and cashed all chips, but when they quit the game for good they took with them the respect of all who knew them for they died as they lived, "square men."

★ ★ ★

Col. Geo. Baylor

The other morning I woke up thinking about the old Indian trading post that was formerly located down at the foot of Preston Avenue. From the old post my mind wandered off to Indians in general and I remembered a story about them that my friend, Colonel George Baylor, once told me. It is a good story, too.

His brother, General John R. Baylor, was governor of New Mexico and Arizona, and had the Indians pretty well in hand, particularly those he had on the reservation he had established where he made his headquarters. Colonel Baylor was temporarily with his brother. The two brothers had a negro servant with them, who was afraid as death of the Indians at first, until he found that they would not molest him, and then, nigger-like, he got to showing off before them and resenting their calling him "Buffalo," which they did because his head was kinky like the head of a buffalo. Before long the negro got it in his head that there was no harm in an Indian and that "Marse John had done subdued 'em." Then he took advantage of the situation and began to run off and spend days in the woods, for he was one of the "runaway" kind of negroes. Both General Baylor and Colonel Baylor warned him that he was likely to be caught by some Indians who did not know him and that if that happened he would be a gone coon. He said nothing, but he evidently thought their warning was simply to try to scare him and paid no attention to it.

Finally he ran away and was gone for several days. General Baylor concluded to give him a lesson that would cure him for all time. He called one or two chiefs in his office and asked them to take a body of their followers, go out and catch the negro and give him a good scare. The Indians were tickled to death at the idea of having such fun and entered into the scheme eagerly. They put on their war paint, armed themselves with their knives and tomahawks and set out to find the negro. They caught him, about five miles away, asleep under a tree. They tied and gagged him and then held a big war dance all around and over him. He was scared half to death before they got half through their dance, but his fear was as nothing compared to that he felt when they jerked him to his feet and bound him to a tree with a rope. They whooped and danced and began piling leaves and brush over him, as though they were preparing to burn him. When they stood him against the tree they took the ropes from his legs and merely had one rope around his neck to hold him to the tree. He could kick all he pleased and he did a lot of it, trying to keep them from piling the brush and leaves on him.

Then the chiefs changed the program. They got their young men to form a line and throw tomahawks at the negro, the object being to see who could come nearest his head without hitting him. Finally, when they had him about dead with fright, one of the Indians, intentionally, threw a tomahawk and cut the rope that bound the negro to the tree. He realized that he was free and bolted. The Indians let him get a good start and then, raising awful whoops and yells, they took after him. He made a bee-line for home with what he thought was a whole tribe of bloodthirsty Indians at his heels.

Colonel Baylor said they could hear the Indians yelling for two miles away and they knew they had the negro headed for home. He says when the negro finally showed up his eyes were popped out and twisted so that they were back of his head. The negro tore through the camp and made for a little shanty he occupied. He rushed in and slammed the door, which was immediately broken open by the Indians, who rushed in on him.

Then the fun commenced in earnest. The negro became perfectly frantic with fear and fought like a fiend. An Indian knows nothing about fighting with his fists, so the negro had everything his own way. The colonel says the Indians were knocked here and there and pummeled terribly, but took every thing good-naturedly. They did not get the least angry but fought on until the shanty was wrecked and fell down on the combatants. Then the negro, finding himself in the open air once more, got on his feet and knocking Indians right and left cleared a passage and made for the river, half a mile away. When he reached the river he dived off a high embankment, where there was a big whirlpool, and came near drowning before some Mexicans roped him and pulled him safely to shore.

The colonel said there were at least a dozen Indians with black eyes and bloody noses, but not an angry Indian in the whole bunch. They seemed to have enjoyed every moment of the chase. So far as the negro was concerned, he was cured and could scarcely be induced to go near an Indian in the camp, let alone out in the woods, which he feared was full of them.

During that conversation, the colonel told me another interesting story about a fight he had with the Comanche Indians when he was captain of a Ranger company. He said he was certain that he had killed the last Comanche Indian killed in Texas. His company had had a fight with a band of them and was following them. He had a very fast horse and got far ahead of his men, following three Indians. The trail they were on dipped down into a dry gully and when he saw that the Indians did not ride out on the other side, he said he knew what they were doing just the same as though he could see them. They had gotten on one side of the trail and intended on shooting him as he rode down the gully. Instead of doing that he turned to one side and came up behind them. They were close together, ready to shoot him the moment he appeared. He got right close to them and fired both barrels of his shotgun, loaded with buck shot, killing all three of them. The others of the gang got away, but that was the last raid the Comanches ever made, therefore Colonel Baylor says he is certain that he killed the last of the tribe that was killed in Texas.

★ ★ ★

FISHING IN THE BAYOU

Saturday afternoon I saw two or three little negroes coming across the Preston Avenue bridge, and each one had a small string of very small perch. They told me that they had been fishing way above Glenwood Cemetery, in Buffalo Bayou. The sight of those fish carried me back many years, for when I was a boy, fishing was one of the greatest delights of my life. There were plenty of fish here, too, and both Buffalo Bayou and White Oak Bayou were famous fishing places. I believe, on the whole, that White Oak was the best fishing stream, though both were good. There were perch, goggle-eyes, as we called them; sun-perch, gasper-gou, catfish, suckers and last, but not least, thousands of buffalo.

There was more fun in catching buffaloes than in catching anything else, though after we had caught them they were so full of bones no one could eat them. We never fished for the table, however, so the eating feature cut no figure with us. The method of catching them was simple. We would buy some fish berries at the drug store, mash them up carefully and then mix them with cornmeal and cotton, so as to form balls about the size of a marble. We would boil these in a pot and then dry them out thoroughly. After we had prepared our fish balls we would get in a boat and row along slowly, throwing the balls in all the deep holes. In about half an hour we would return over the same course and then we would find the fish on a regular spree. The berries would make them so drunk that they would flop around on top of the water and would actually try to climb up the banks of the bayou. All we had to do was to row along and pick them up. I believe it has been made against the law to fish in that way now, though I don't see why, since the fish will get over their drunk in a little while and will be as live and active as ever. Very few of them that we came in contact with ever had a chance to reform or get sober either, for we had an idea that the fish had to be cleaned at once, otherwise they would poison anyone who ate them.

Saturdays were always busy days for the boy fishermen. We made up parties, and, starting early in the morning, we covered every famous place for miles around Houston. There was not a deep hole, a sunken log or other place where fish congregate that was not known to us. We took lunch with us and made a day of it, returning long after sundown.

We had lots of fun in every way, for something funny was bound to happen before the day ended. Once Joe Harris, Charley Harris, Dick Fuller, Will Palmer and Andrew Hutchison were fishing in a big hole up on White Oak Bayou. The current had dug out both banks of the stream, making it very wide as well as very deep. Joe went up the bayou and crossed over to the opposite side, to try his luck there. The bank was very steep, right down to the water's edge, but he managed to secure a foothold and commenced fishing. We were all very quiet, for it was against the rules to talk while fishing, so we could hear even the faintest sound in the woods for some distance. After a while we heard a frog squeaking off in the distance behind Joe Harris.

"Squeak, squeak." It came oftener and apparently was coming nearer. Joe made some remark about the frog, when a good-sized fish got on his line and he began to play him, all of us forgetting our rules and shouting out directions to him what to do. Right in the midst of our excitement that frog put in a personal appearance. He reached the top of the high bank immediately behind and over Joe, and seeing the bayou so near, he made a desperate leap and landed safely in the water.

The next moment the haste of the frog was explained, for a great big snake that looked like a show snake in a circus, he was so big and ugly, came tearing over the bank. The snake was going so fast in its efforts to catch the frog that it was over the side of the bank and coming right down on Joe before it saw him. The snake made a desperate effort to stop or turn aside, but it was all in vain, for he came down, writhing and twisting, and would have certainly collided with Joe, had the latter given him a chance to do so. As it was, Joe was too quick for the snake, for before it reached him, he threw aside his fishing pole, went head foremost into the bayou and the next instant was on our side. We could never decide whether Joe or the snake was more scared. Joe really got some advantage out of the snake's interruption, for it enabled him to lie for the balance of the day about the size of that fish he had on his line when the snake broke in.

There must have been thousands of black bass in the bayous at that time, but no one suspected it because no one knew how to fish for them. A few years ago Dick Fuller devised a plan, or rather found suitable bait for them and since then has caught hundreds of them above Shepherd's dam. The fact that Dick can catch black bass is no argument that anybody else can catch them, for he can come as near catching fish on dry land where there are no fish, as anything. As the negro says: "Mr. Dick shore is a fishin' man."

Speaking of Shepherd's dam reminds me of a little natural history I learned some years ago. When the waterworks built the first dam across the bayou near their plant, there was a broad sandy bar formed just below the dam. One day I took a crab net and scooped along the bottom to try to catch some small fish for bait. When I took the net up I found in it one or two small flounders. I made several dips and caught several more. It was evident that they had come up with the tide and had been stopped by the dam. I never knew until then that flounders bred in fresh water. I never heard of a large flounder being caught in the bayou, so they evidently return to the bay or gulf before they attain any size.

But then Buffalo Bayou is full of surprises. Some years ago Dave McNally, who lived not far from the bayou, discovered a porpoise down about the foot of Louisiana Street. It was a real sea porpoise, too. Dave notified Albert Erichson of his discovery and Albert went down and shot it. When it was shot it was about at the foot of Smith Street. They pulled it out of the water and exhibited it as long as they could, which was until the health officer threatened to get after them for keeping a nuisance on hand. Then they got a big pot and made oil out of the porpoise and made a lot of it, too. I don't think a whale has ever come up the bayou, but I would not be surprised to hear that one had.

★ ★ ★

OLD SWIMMING HOLES

If ever a place has been absolutely ruined and sent to the eternal bow-wows by modern improvement and expansion, that place is Houston, as judged from a boy's point of view. Huge buildings of stone and brick, paved streets, factories and shops of all kinds are fine for the grown-ups, but they are not conducive to that unalloyed happiness the old-time boys enjoyed. I don't know how the modern boy gets any enjoyment out of life. If he wants to learn to swim he gets lessons in a tank. If he wants to go fishing he has to take a train and go elsewhere. If he wants to go out in the woods to gather wildflowers for his sweetheart or get some sweet gum he has to go miles in an automobile. To indulge in any of these delightful sports, this modern boy has to prepare as if he were going on a long railway journey.

Not content with expanding out all over the old hunting and fishing places, thus wiping them off the map, modern Houston has gone a step further and absolutely ruined the bayou. Looking at the dirty, grease-covered bayou of today, one would never think that at one time it was one of the prettiest streams in Texas; that its water was clean and limpid, covered with water lilies and filled with fish and crabs, and that its banks were grassy and overgrown with wildflowers.

"Going in swimming" was then one of the greatest delights of the Houston boys and from about the middle of April until late in the fall the swimming holes were generally well filled from morning til night. There were some favorite swimming holes, but I venture to say that 99 per cent of the boys learned to swim in "Stockbridges," down at the foot of Texas Avenue. This was a famous place. The water at no point was more than four feet deep, while the bottom was pure white sand. It was a great watering place for draymen and teamsters and was also used as a ford for teams to cross from one side of the bayou to the other. As a rule, only the little boys used Stockbridges, for it was considered beneath the dignity of a boy who could swim to go in there. It was a kind of kindergarten swimming hole.

About two blocks below Stockbridges, near the foot of Prairie Avenue, was "Evans hole." There were large trees on each side of the bayou, which cast a good shade over the water, thus making it a delightful place at all hours of the day. Evans hole had a hard, sandy bottom, was free from snags and, while quite deep in the middle, was shallow on each side.

Further down the bayou, at the foot of Smith Street, was "The Sycamores." This was a very deep hole, having a large sycamore tree leaning far over it, from which the boys were accustomed to dive. Being so deep, with steep banks and no shallow water, The Sycamores was used only by the boys who, I may say, were in the junior class of swimmers. I have seen some fine fights and funny things down at The Sycamores, but one that, while funny enough, came near ending disastrously, I will never forget.

Jim Blake, afterward Dr. James Blake who died a few years ago, came down to the swimming hole one afternoon, bringing two immense Mexican gourds. Each was corked tightly and had a piece of rope tied round its middle. When asked what he was going to do, Jim informed us that he was going to show us how to walk on water. He pulled off his clothes and was ready for action, for bathing suits were unknown at that time. He carefully tied the gourds, one to each ankle, and without the slightest hesitation crawled out on the sycamore overhanging the water and let himself down. He had a good start, all right, for the distance was just sufficient to submerge the gourds so they would bear his weight.

We looked on admiringly and then Jim turned loose his hold on the tree. There was a terrible splash and Jim's head and body disappeared but his feet remained in sight. You should have seen how those gourds whirled and moved about. We were all so scared we did not know what to do. In the struggles to get his head where his feet were Jim drifted out toward the middle of the bayou. So far as we were concerned Jim would have drowned right there had he not managed to catch hold of one of the ropes up by the side of his feet. He coughed, spluttered and threw up water like a walrus, but he kept his head above water and began abusing us for not helping him.

Seeing that he was safe and in no immediate danger of drowning the boys returned his abuse with interest and guyed him about walking on water, calling on him to walk out. Finally one of the big boys swam out and towed him to shore. He was mad with himself and mad with us too and his temper was not cooled the least bit when after getting rid of his gourds he started to dress and found that someone had tied his shirt, coat and pants in hard knots. He sat there, "chawed bacon," as the process of untying the knots with the teeth was called, and swore he was going to whip us individually and collectively, as soon as he got dressed. As he was big and strong we thought discretion the better part of valor so by the time he got his knots untied we were dressed and gone and he was all alone in his glory.

The next great swimming hole was the "Arsenal," at the foot of La Branch Street. It got its name from the fact that in early days there was a fort and arsenal there, though both had disappeared long before my time. The Arsenal was very wide and very deep and only the best swimmers ever went in there. It was strictly a big boys' place and they, knowing the danger, took good care to drive all small boys and poor swimmers away. The big boys vied with each other in diving, swimming and other aquatic feats. One of the great diving feats was to crawl into the water on one side, disappear, swim along the bottom and come out on the other side of the bayou. I have seen this attempted by hundreds of boys, but remember only one who could accomplish it with ease. His name was John Hale. He was an expert swimmer and while still a boy jumped off one of the bayou steamboats and saved the life of a negro man who had either fallen or been knocked off the boat.

When I think of those happy, carefree days I have a sincere pity for the modern Houston boy who goes bathing in a concrete tank, hunting and fishing in an automobile and what is worse than all, has to put on a bathing suit when he goes swimming. Times have degenerated awfully and Houston and Buffalo Bayou have led in the degeneracy.

★ ★ ★

TWO FAMOUS CHARACTERS

There were two characters in Houston in the early days about whom I would like some information and I hope that if this is seen by any old-timer he will supply the missing links. I remember them both and remember the name of one, but can't recall the name of the other.

One was named Egerly and he was a man-about-town kind of fellow. If he had any profession or calling no one knew it and if he had lived in modern Houston instead of primitive Houston he would have been classed as a bum. He was no bum, though, but was a man of education and some refinement, and evidently had means which enabled him to loaf, which he did in a lordly manner. He boarded at the old Hogan House, which occupied the half block opposite the north side of market square, and his favorite loafing place was at the ten-pin alley adjoining a saloon that stood on the corner of Main and Franklin Avenue, opposite the present First National Bank.

Egerly was very dignified and spoke with great deliberation as if weighing every word he uttered. No matter how drunk he got he never relaxed his dignity nor his deliberation of speech. All this earned for him a nickname and he was known to everybody as "Exact Egerly." If the stories told on him were true he well deserved the name, for it was said that even in taking his drinks he would always pour out just the right quantity he wanted. If by chance he poured out too much, he would pour it back in the bottle and never drink until he had the exact amount. Then, too, he would generally have the exact change to pay for the drinks when he drank alone or set 'em up for others. Of course, some of the stories told on him were exaggerations or entire fabrications, but many were true, and I think it is safe to say that he well deserved his name. I don't know anything about his barroom manners, for I never saw him take a drink, but I recall one instance of his exaction of speech which came near ending in a fight.

At that time there was a lawyer here named Tompkins. He was a brilliant man and, in spite of his rather wild habits, stood pretty near the head of the bar. After the termination of some hard-fought case in court he would seek relaxation at the faro table. He had some disease which had made his bones chalky and consequently very brittle. One night he attempted to pick up a piece of money from the faro table and in doing so he broke two of his fingers. The next morning Egerly and some others were standing on Main Street when Captain Bob Boyce came up.

"Did you hear about Tompkins breaking two of his fingers last night trying to pick up a silver dollar?" he asked.

"Captain," said Egerly, with his usual deliberation, "you are entirely mistaken, it was not a silver dollar."

"Well, what in hell was it?" asked the captain, who was high tempered and quick to take offense. "What was it? Did he try to pick up the check-rack, the layout or what was it he tried to do?"

"It was not a silver dollar at all," said Egerly. "I was a witness to the whole affair. It was a five-franc piece."

Then Captain Boyce lost his temper completely. "That makes a hell of a difference!" he shouted. "Whether it was a dollar or 95 cents he tried to pick up, cuts a heap of importance. Egerly, you are a damned fool." That was too much, and Egerly stripped for action at once, but friends got between them and prevented a fight.

I remember Egerly being in Houston up to the beginning of the war. No doubt he was in the army. Anyway, he disappeared and though I have often thought of him I haven't seen him since. I hope some old-timer whose memory is better than mine may know and tell some further facts about him.

The other man, whose name I forget, was the most curious specimen of humanity I ever saw and was of a type which has become impossible and therefore extinct today. He was the opposite of Egerly in every way, for he had no education or refinement and was simply a bum and nothing else. Strange to say, he was popular and everybody knew and liked him. He was born with a flat place on his head where the bump of reverence is located, according to the phrenologists, and he placed the highest and the lowest in the land on the same footing. To him William M. Rice was "Billy;" Mr. Bremond was "Paul;" Mr. Shepherd was "Ben," and so on down the line. That, however, might be construed as simply a bad case of gall and impertinence, but he had other qualities that distinguished him above his fellow citizens.

He was the most reckless man I ever saw, and was constantly doing things that would have killed anybody else. But he seemed to have a charmed life and always pulled through safely. One night in the old Houston House bar down on Franklin Avenue, he provoked a gentleman who had just landed from the steamboat from Galveston and who was an entire stranger to him, to such an extent that the gentleman took out his bowie knife and nearly severed his head from his body. They laid him out on the floor and the doctors came in, looked him over and gave him half an hour to live. At the end of the half hour he was still alive, so they hauled him off to a room somewhere. He was laid up for a long time but finally got well. Now I will tell you of his recklessness.

In those days the steamboats would come to near the foot of Main Street and discharge their cargoes. The bayou was not quite wide enough for them to turn, so they had to go up a little further, back into White Oak Bayou, then haul the bow around and thus head downstream again. During this performance it was necessary to attach a line to a big cypress stump that stood on the bank of the bayou some distance beyond the mouth of White Oak Bayou, so as to hold the bow of the boat in proper position while backing into White Oak, and then to use a tree further downstream when turning 'round, so as to head downstream.

In time the big stump became greatly worn and finally almost useless, so it was determined to remove it and substitute a post. It occupied the exact spot where the best leverage could be obtained, so its removal was absolutely necessary. It was not easy to do, so after much cutting and digging it was decided to blow it up with gunpowder. Holes were bored in the stump and filled with powder, and a fuse was attached. About twenty-five pounds of powder were used and as a big explosion was expected, everybody ran for cover when the fuse was lighted. The fuse sparkled a bit and then apparently went out. A minute later little puffs of smoke showed it was still burning.

The crowd was on tiptoe of expectancy, looking momentarily for the big explosion, when they were horrified to see this man I speak of come out of some coffee bean weeds that grew on the bank further up stream and walk direct to the stump. People shouted to him to go back but he paid no attention and calmly advanced, puffing a big cigar. He went to the stump and, finding that the fuse had really gone out, he lighted it with his cigar and stood there while it sputtered and went out again. Then he picked up the fuse, examined it and threw it into the bayou. Kneeling down, he raked the loose powder into a train and coolly touched it off with his cigar. There was a terrible explosion and everything in the vicinity of the stump was hidden from view by smoke. When it cleared away the chap was flat on the ground, entirely unhurt. How he escaped being killed or seriously injured was a miracle.

Now, if any of the old-timers, and there are lots of them in Houston, more than I ever dreamed of, remember these two men and their queer doings they can give the *Chronicle* some very interesting reading matter.

★ ★ ★

A Big Newspaper Scoop

All old citizens and newspapermen remember the big *Post* published in Houston in 1883. It was the biggest and best paper ever published in the South up to that time and a good-sized fortune was spent in keeping it going during the year of its existence. Hardenbrook was general manager and looked after the business end, while Tobe Mitchell was managing editor. Both were wide awake newspaper men, Hardenbrook being graduated from the New York newspapers, while Mitchell had been for years one of McCullough's assistants on the *Globe-Democrat* of St. Louis. Judge J. W. Johnson spent a lot of money wrecking the *Post*, which he owned, in a futile attempt to beat John Ireland, the Democratic nominee for governor, with Wash. Jones, who ran as an independent. He concluded that running a newspaper was not his forte, so he sold the paper to a number of Houston capitalists, headed by Mr. W. R. Baker. These gentlemen knew absolutely nothing about newspapers, but they knew that Houston and Texas needed a first class Democratic paper, so they determined to risk their money in trying to establish that paper. *The Galveston News* had secured a strong foothold in Houston, so it was recognized that the *Post* must be made superior to the *News* in every way if it hoped to gain ground and drive out the *News*.

Hardenbrook was given all the money he asked for to look after business matters and Tobe Mitchell was allowed to spend money freely in gathering news. Both knew how to spend money and the result was that the *Post* soon took first place among the papers of the South and compared favorably with those published anywhere.

Tobe Mitchell had a splendid staff, one that it would be hard to beat anywhere. He paid large salaries and was enabled to get the very best newspaper talent, not only in Texas, but from other states. Tobe was an enthusiastic and untiring worker himself and had the happy faculty of creating enthusiasm in others, and he could get more hard work out of the men without having them feel that he was doing so than any other managing editor I have ever met. He was quick to appreciate good work and equally quick to condemn anything that was careless or slipshod. At that time there was no literary syndicate that furnished columns or pages of ready-made articles for Sunday editions. We had to make our own Sunday editions and every man on the paper that had talent in that direction became a space writer for the Sunday paper. There, were short stories, special articles, poetry and sketches of various kinds and, on the whole, the Sunday edition was quite a creditable affair.

The *Post* was noted for one thing—the rapid changes that took place on the staff. It was strictly the survival of the fittest, for Mitchell would fire at a moment's notice any man on the paper who showed that he could not keep step with the others. I remember an occasion when he came very near firing every man on the local staff, including the city editor himself. There was a young man on the staff named Sherman who came from no one knew where. He was quiet, unobstrusive and a fair worker.

At times Sherman was dreamy and appeared to be under the influence of some drug, and he was supposed by the other members of the staff to "hit the pipe," which was a new thing in Houston at that time. He did his work well, however, and we were greatly surprised one night when he came out of Mitchell's room about 8 o'clock and told us that he had been fired. He took his hat and left and we thought nothing more of the matter.

We were somewhat surprised about midnight to see Sherman come in with a big roll of manuscript in his hand and go into Mitchell's office. He stayed in there for half an hour and when he came out, instead of leaving he went over to his old desk and seated himself. Then Mitchell came out and lit into the local staff and city editor. He said all kinds of things to them. I have forgotten just what he did say, but I remember his telling them that Sherman was the only genuine newspaper man in the crowd and that he was the only one who could tell a piece of news from last year's almanac. Then the facts came out.

Sherman had gotten hold of a big news item, had worked it up all alone and had not only scooped the *News*, but had scooped the local staff of the *Post* as well. Sherman, after he had been fired that evening, had gone over in the Fifth Ward for some purpose. On his return about 10 o'clock he had crossed the bayou at Milam Street bridge and had come up Milam Street. There was an Irish boarding house and barroom on Milam Street near Congress run by a man named Flyn. Sherman stopped there to get a drink and while there learned that there was a man upstairs in one of the rooms who had taken poison and that a doctor was working on him then. Sherman at once went up to investigate and what he found was plenty, for the man proved to be none other than Major Robinett, an engineer in the United States army, who for some unknown cause had sought this out-of-the-way place and had poisoned himself.

As a matter of fact Sherman did not know at first what a big news item he had unearthed. The simple fact that a distinguished army officer had attempted to kill himself in a low Irish boarding house was good enough for him and he worked it up for all it was worth. But when the fact became known in the office, Sherman found that he was a regular hero as a news gatherer, for he had truly unearthed a big item of great local interest and value.

This Major Robinett was the same engineer who had constructed Fort Robinett, near Corinth, Miss., which bore his name, and it was against the fort that the Second Texas Infantry Regiment under command of the gallant Rogers, had been hurled when instead of a regiment a half dozen brigades should have been sent. A great blunder had been made, the Second Texas had been nearly annihilated and Balaclava had been surpassed when that fatal charge had ended and that was all. The Second Texas was made up largely from Houston and nearby points, so the local interest in the item is apparent. The pressman on the *Post* was Captain Birtwhistle, a Federal veteran, who had served with Major Robinett in the Mississippi campaign and remembered the major well. Captain Birtwhistle was in Fort Robinett when the fatal charge of the Second Texas was made. The captain came to the editorial room and he and I, the only two who knew anything about it, completed Sherman's article. When we were finished, Tobe Mitchell closed everything off the front page and next morning the *Post* had a magnificent scoop over everybody and everything.

Sherman was reinstated in his old position, of course, but a few weeks later he quit voluntarily and left town, and I have never heard of him since. A few months later the *Post* quit also and the staff was scattered to the four winds. Some went to New York, others to Chicago, New Orleans, St. Louis and other places. Mitchell went back to the *Globe-Democrat* at St. Louis and died there a few years ago.

MUD, COURTHOUSES AND CANNON:
HOUSTON LANDMARKS

★ ★ ★

HANGSMAN GROVE

It is an historical fact that at the first session of court held in Harrisburg County, as Harris was then called, two men were found guilty of murder and sentenced to death. It is stated that those two men were hanged immediately because the jail was uncomfortably cold and the kind-hearted judge did not want the prisoners to suffer unduly.

The court sentence is true, no doubt, but the story about the jail being too uncomfortable must be taken with a large pinch of salt, since there was no jail to be uncomfortable. The first jail was not built for at least two years after the date of that incident. By the way, that first jail was a curiosity. It had neither windows nor doors. It was simply a one-story log house with a flat roof. On its top was a trap door. This was raised, a ladder was lowered and the prisoner went down into the jail. Then the ladder was withdrawn, the trap closed, and the prisoner was left to meditate on his sins.

The first legal hanging in Houston, about which old citizens know, took place many years after the date of the reported hangings. It was that of a man named Hyde. He had waylaid and murdered a man and had then left the state and gone to Louisiana or Mississippi. Someone recognized him there and reported the fact to the authorities here. Proper papers were made out and Hyde was arrested and brought back. That was in 1853, and the hanging took place in what was afterwards known as Hangsman Grove just on the southeast corner of the old cemetery out of the San Felipe Road. At that time and for many years after, that place was way out in the country, but is now thickly settled, with blocks of houses far beyond it.

Captain Thom. Hogan was sheriff of Harris County at the time and was so nervous and excited that he stood on the trap with the condemned man and was about to cut the rope that held it in position, but was dragged off before he could do so.

The next execution to take place out there was that of a negro named Johnson, in 1868, followed about two years later by the execution of another negro named Johnson. I witnessed both of these and at the last one I learned something that has done me more good and helped me to have faith in my fellow man than anything that has ever occurred to me. I suppose every reader of these lines has heard one or more honorable man get on the witness stand in court and swear to something that was not true. Such swearing is not confined to any one class and the very best men, men of the highest integrity, have been guilty of it. The majority of people put them down as willful liars and let it go at that, without attempting to go further. Not so with me. I have faith in them and know that they are telling what they think is true. The reason for my feeling that way is explained by this incidence. When the last negro was hanged, I was standing where I could see him plainly. I saw the hangsman adjust the rope about his neck and fit the knot under his left ear. I was on the right side. The negro wore a white shirt with a big, turned-down collar. When the drop fell I saw the rope peel back the black skin for about an inch, leaving the white flesh exposed for a moment. Then several large drops of black-looking blood formed on the wound, slowly trickled down and fell on the white collar.

After the negro was cut down I went with the doctor to the old pest house on the bank of the bayou to see the postmortem examination he was going to make. Of course the first thing I looked for was the wound on the neck, but, to my amazement, I found none. The skin was unbroken, not even scratched. The truth is that I had simply seen something that I expected to see, without knowing that I expected to see it. I was greatly excited, but was not conscious that I was so. Ever since then when I have heard absurd and palpably false statements made in court, by reputable men, I have felt that those making them were telling the truth, or at least what they thought was the truth. I know that if occasion had arisen, and I had not have seen the negro's body after it had been cut down, I would have willingly staked my life betting that the rope had cut his neck exactly, as I thought it had. Those two Johnsons were the last men executed at Hangsman Grove, for after that, all executions took place in the jail or jail yard. The general idea is that many men were hanged out there, but as a matter of fact only three executions took place there. That of Hyde and the two negroes.

★ ★ ★

BIG GULLIES IN HOUSTON

About the first thing that the Houston & Texas Central Railroad had to do when that road was begun, was to build a long trestlework over an immense gully that lay between the present Grand Central Depot and the old city graveyard. That gully began about on Houston Avenue and ran parallel with the track for a block or two and then turned to the northeast and extended to White Oak Bayou. It has since been almost completely filled, though traces of it still remain.

In the early days Houston was remarkable for its numerous large gullies. There was one great one that took up rather more than the lower end of Caroline Street. It was narrower after reaching Congress Avenue, and gradually narrowed until it completely disappeared between Prairie and Texas Avenues. There were two big bridges crossing the gully, one on Franklin and the other on Congress Avenue. Those were the two principal streets used at that time, very few people living south of Texas Avenue.

But the king gully of all was the one on Rusk Avenue. This began on Smith Street and before it had gone a block it was almost a block wide. It became much wider as it neared the bayou and really got so broad that it was two or three blocks wide. Both this and the Caroline Street one have been filled up and now one would never know that they had existed.

One of the famous gullies was that between Texas and Prairie Avenues. It began on Milam Street about in the middle of the block and ran down to the bayou. Unlike the other gullies, this one appeared to have been quite ancient, for its banks were covered with vegetation and free from fresh erosions. Near where the gully passed Smith Street there was a very large spring overhung by a large oak tree. I can close my eyes now and see that spring and the little school of minnows that were always swimming about in it. I walked down that way a few days ago and found an immense brick building on a paved street, 40 feet above where that beautiful spring was. I found not a trace of the gully, it having been filled up and converted into building lots, all now covered with houses.

There used to be quite a large gully running from Preston Avenue to the bayou. My earliest recollection of this gully is of the spring that was at its head, near the southeast corner of Preston and Louisiana Street. As I recall it this spring was not much for beauty, though it was large enough to cause a standing mudhole on Louisiana Street. Going from Preston towards the bayou this gully widened rapidly and was quite an obstruction to travel by the time it reached Congress Avenue. It too has been filled and today not a trace of it remains.

Now, of all the mean and disagreeable gullies that ever existed anywhere, the big one on Rusk Avenue took the cake. It was caving constantly and its banks and sides were sticky, red clay. When it rained, this gully was a place to be avoided. At each street crossing there was a plank near the bottom of the gully to enable persons who had to cross to escape the water in the bottom of the gully. The descent was perilous and ascent equally so. Everybody that had any sense went around the head of the gully, but there were lots of people who preferred to risk the gully to taking the walk. Of course, none of the boys had any sense. As a rule they were barefooted and did not care much whether they got muddy or not. I remember one evening when a German "pardner" of mine and I got caught by darkness on the other side of that gully. We had been out on the San Felipe Road, had stayed too long and were making shortcuts for home. I can look back now and see that we did not gain much by our shortcuts, but then we thought we did and that counted at the time.

Finally we came to this big gully. I wanted to go around its head, but my friend did not agree. He announced that he was a goat when it came to going down a muddy gully and told me to watch him and then I would see how easy it was to do. I watched alright and he found it much easier to go down than he had anticipated. About the third step he took, his heels flew up and he started down with a rush. Just before he reached the narrow plank near the bottom, he succeeded in stopping himself, but the halt was only for a moment, for the next thing he did was to go head foremost into the mud and water at the bottom. I could not see him very distinctly because of the darkness, but you bet I could hear him, and he was not making a Sunday school address, either. Now the funny part of the whole thing was that having been whirled and twisted about so much, he lost his bearings and when he started to crawl out of the gully, he crawled out on the same side that he went in. He would dig his hands and feet in the slippery clay and yell for me to come on, saying that if I did not hurry up he was going to leave me. He was angry, anyway, but when he finally reached the top and saw me standing there and realized what he had done, he nearly had a fit. I wanted to get home and had no time for a fight, so I refrained from saying anything to him about being a goat. I knew it would make him supremely happy if I gave him the least excuse for starting a war. Finally I started off to head the gully and he followed, bringing along with him a surprisingly large quantity of clay and mud, for which he had no use on earth.

I don't know that there is a single gully left in the city limits, and there should be none, for of all the useless things on earth they are the chief.

★ ★ ★

THE FAMOUS TWIN SISTERS

There is an old story about two fond parents who were watching the passing of a military company, in the ranks of which their son was marching. "Look at that," said the mother. "Our boy is the only one in the whole company who is keeping step."

This story has recurred to me several times lately and I will tell you why. Two or three years ago there was a great deal of talk about the famous "Twin Sisters," the two cannon used with such good results by the Texans at San Jacinto. One report was that they were buried somewhere near Harrisburg; another was that they were thrown in Galveston Bay, between the island and Virginia Point, and another story located them in the National Museum at Washington. All these stories spoke of the Twin Sisters as iron pieces. Some gentlemen made extensive excavations near Harrisburg, where they were said to be buried, but the search was fruitless. Obviously it was impossible to search Galveston Bay, but the Washington story could be investigated and I did so, with the result that I am informed by those in authority that there were no such cannon either in the museum or anywhere else in Washington.

Aside from the historical interest in the subject I was attracted to it by the fact that when I was a boy there were two brass cannon, six-pounders, known as the Twin Sisters, that stood for many years on the northwest side of Market Square. They were beautiful guns and each bore this inscription, engraved just in front of the vent: "Presented to the Republic of Texas by the Ladies of Cincinnati."

These guns seemed to be under no particular care and the boys pulled them about, sighted them and mowed down whole imaginary armies of Mexicans and Indians and played with them to their hearts' content without let or hindrance. To the boys of that day the Twin Sisters were as familiar objects on Market Square as are Dick Dowling's monument and the fountain to those of the present day. These guns were used by a Confederate battery during the war, but in 1871 or 1872 I saw one of them near the land office in Austin and read the inscription on it. Being so familiar with the subject, I was a bit amazed when I saw the Twin Sisters referred to as iron pieces and as having plates screwed on their sides stating that they were presented to the Republic of Texas by General Chambers. Up to that time I was sure that I was the only man in the company who was keeping step and that all the others were wrong. Then I read Governor Frank Lubbock's *Memoirs* and when I found there an account of the iron guns known as the Twin Sisters being turned over to Texas by Louisiana during or after the war, I began to wonder if I had not best catch step with the others.

That two guns known as the Twin Sisters were used by the Texans at San Jacinto is a matter of history, but whether those guns were the iron pieces presented by General Chambers is the question, for now there can be no doubt that there were four guns in existence instead of two. Thus instead of settling the question it becomes more involved for all four are not only lost, but when, if ever, they may chance to be found, it will have to be determined whether they are genuine or not. That the Twin Sisters that were so long on Market Square were brass pieces I know beyond doubt, and the fact can be proven by Colonel W. M. Stafford of Galveston, Mr. I. C. Lord, Mr. Owen Cochran and Mr. Henry Thompson of Houston and no doubt by others who were raised in Houston, whose names escape me now.

When our war broke out these cannon were turned over to some Confederate company, but I know nothing of their history during the war. I do remember the last time they, or rather one of them, was fired before the war. It was in 1860, when Sam Houston was elected governor. Because of his pronounced Union views many of his former friends opposed him and he had a hard fight. When the news of his election was received, his friends got the Twin Sisters with the intention of firing a salute in honor of his victory. The guns were taken to a grassy hill, corner of Fannin and Commerce Streets. One gun was fired and a bag of powder was rammed down the other, but when they started to prime the piece they found some one had spiked it. They rushed to the other gun, but found it spiked also. That broke up the salute, of course, but it was a fitting thing that the last time one of the Twin Sisters spoke in time of peace should have been in honor of the hero of San Jacinto.

In early days there were a great many survivors of San Jacinto living in or near Houston and San Jacinto Day, April 21, was always celebrated in great style. The Twin Sisters were taken down to the corner of Commerce Street and a salute was fired, after which the town was literally turned over to the heroes of San Jacinto. I remember well one of the most conspicuous of them. He was Tierwester, an old Frenchman. At the battle of San Jacinto he had a powderhorn slung to his neck. This powderhorn was a cow's horn scraped very thin and had a wooden plug at the large end and a small plug at the little end of the horn. During the battle a Mexican bullet struck this horn and entered through one side, but did not have enough force to go out of the other. Tierwester never removed the ball, but on San Jacinto Day he came to the reunion wearing this horn round his neck and the drunker he got the louder he told the story and rattled the bullet. He was a great character and lived and died in what was then known as Frostown, not far from the Hutchins residence, now the center of Houston almost.

But these San Jacinto celebrations were not always fun alone. Tragedy cropped up occasionally. I remember one which occurred when I was a little boy. The Twin Sisters had been taken out, as usual, for the salute. A man named Tom Ewing took charge of the big end of the gun and volunteered to hold his thumb on the vent hole, a necessary precaution to keep the gun from exploding after it became heated. Mr. Warren Stansbury performed the duty of loading the piece. The salute was about half over and Stansbury was ramming home a charge when the gun became so hot that Ewing, thoughtlessly, took his thumb from the vent. Instantly the piece was discharged and Stansbury's arm was so badly mutilated by the rammer that amputation was necessary. He recovered and lived several years afterward.

Of course all has been done that can be done to locate the Twin Sisters, but there is one question that can be and should be settled: Which Twin Sisters were used at San Jacinto? Those presented by the ladies of Cincinnati or those by General Chambers? As a native Texan, I had the greatest respect and reverence for the brass pieces of market square and I would like to know if I have been worshipping false gods all these years. I know nothing of the Chambers iron cannon, but if they should be proven to be the real San Jacinto cannon I am willing to transfer my homage and allegiance to them.

★ ★ ★
Constitution Bend

I don't blame outsiders very much for laughing at Houston's ship channel when they receive their only impression of what the channel is from the end of it that lies within the city limits. If I did not know that a short streetcar ride would land me on the banks of the real channel, very wide and very deep—a waterway that by easy engineering can be made a second Manchester Canal—I suppose that I would be tempted to laugh too. The bayou at the foot of Main Street is not of such proportions to suggest great confidence, nor is its greasy, dirty and sluggish water such as to inspire much respect.

As the city has grown the bayou has shrunk. The bed has gradually filled up with debris, washed from the streets, and the bayou has become much smaller. In former years Buffalo Bayou was really an attractive stream. Its water was clear, its banks were grassy and full of wildflowers, and on the whole it was a beautiful stream. I can remember when all that part of the Fifth Ward that comes down to the point where White Oak and Buffalo Bayou meet was a dense forest and a great picnic ground. A steamboat or barge would be swung across the bayou and the picnickers would cross on it as a bridge. The bayou was very deep, too, with a natural depth at the foot of Main Street of from fifteen to eighteen feet. I don't know how deep it is now, but it can not be very deep anywhere along there, owing to the sand and mud that has filled it up.

Some miles below Houston there used to be a big bend in the bayou called Constitution Bend. At this point the bayou is very deep and wide. I can remember when I was a child trying to find out why it was called "Constitution" Bend. I do not remember having found anyone who knew. Lately I discovered the reason, or rather, a possible explanation.

In 1838 Mr. John K. Allen gave the captain of the steamer *Constitution* $1000 to bring his boat to the foot of Main Street. The *Constitution* was an oceangoing vessel that plied between Galveston and New Orleans. She had a terrible time getting from Harrisburg to Houston and after she got here she could not turn around, but had to back down to a big bend below the city. There is no record of her having made a second trip, but it is evident that she gave her name to the bend. Constitution Bend has been eliminated by a cut-off channel dredged in recent years.

The *Laura* and the *Yellowstone*, the two steamers that had been in the trade for about a year prior, were small affairs and could turn with ease. Had the *Constitution* been on to the trick developed later by the steamboat men she could have turned also. The thing was very simple and easily accomplished. The bow of the boat was tied to the bank beyond the mouth of White Oak Bayou and then the stern was backed into that bayou, the bow hauled down stream, and there you were, as nice a turn as possible. In later years much larger boats than the *Constitution* came to Houston regularly and none of them ever had the slightest trouble in turning.

The *Laura*, under Captain Griffin, was the first boat that ever came up the bayou to Houston. She arrived at the foot of Main Street January 22, 1837, and it took her two days to get from Harrisburg to Houston. Not long after the *Laura's* exploit the *Yellowstone*, under Captain West, arrived here, coming through the West Bay at Galveston, from Quintana.

However, the largest oceangoing steamer that has ever been to the foot of Main Street was a blockade runner. I don't remember her name. She came up here during the spring of 1863 and anchored at the foot of Main Street, but afterward dropped down and discharged her cargo of war munitions near the foot of San Jacinto Street. There was a big flood in the Bayou and, since the water was very high, she had no trouble either in coming or getting away. It is possible that Captain Bill Flagg knows something about this steamer, for he was in the Confederate navy and had much to do with blockaders and blockade running during the war.

It is not going to be so very long now before real, bona fide oceangoing vessels will be running regularly to the foot of Main Street, and it is well to put these pioneer steamers on record for the use of future historians.

★ ★ ★

HISTORICAL SPOTS

Putting that tablet on the Rice Hotel building to designate the point where the capitol of the Republic of Texas once stood was a good idea, but there are one or two other points whose historical memories also should be preserved. One of the chief of these is the Preston Street bridge, for where it stands once stood the pioneer bridge of Houston, over which passed the commerce of Texas. Until 1842 there was no bridge across Buffalo Bayou. There was little or no need for one, for north of Houston there was only scant settlement and what travel was done was mainly to and from the west over the San Felipe Road, which passed to the west of the bayou. The stray farmer or traveler from the north or east had either to go around the head of the bayou or use Stockbridge ford at the foot of Texas Avenue. But in the early 40s it became evident that a bridge was absolutely necessary, because Montgomery, Washington and Grimes Counties were settling up rapidly and the farmers desired some speedier means of getting to the "city."

The city built the bridge at the foot of Preston Street and it stood for a number of years, until swept away by a big rise in the bayou. When it was replaced a longer, higher and stronger bridge was built, and this was known as the Long Bridge. It stood for years and was the only means of communication between Houston and the rapidly growing interior. Over it passed the cotton, hides, corn and all farm products that were brought here to be marketed and all goods for the interior purchased in Houston, were taken back over this bridge.

Farmers and merchants from as far north as Waco came to Houston to sell their produce and to purchase their goods. Both for the sake of company and for mutual protection they traveled in companies of four or five, and it was no unusual thing to see a row of wagons, each drawn by from eight to sixteen oxen, crossing Long Bridge. Then, too, Main Street and Market Square would present a strange sight when crowded with oxen and ox wagons. It used to be a hard pull from the end of the bridge on this side to Louisiana Street. Preston Street has been cut down and graded since then, but in the early days it was uphill from the bridge to Louisiana Street, and it was all deep white sand. It was a regular sandhill and a big wagon loaded with several bales of cotton had need of all the oxen obtainable to get through safely. I have seen teams doubled up more than once and two or three trips made to get the wagons through.

Of course, from over on the Brazos the wagons came in over the San Felipe Road, but the great bulk of the commerce of Texas passed over the Preston Street bridge. All the cotton raised in Texas at that time was brought to Houston and sold here and all the goods consumed in the interior were bought here. The cotton crops in those days were small affairs as compared with those of today, hence it was possible for the Houston merchants to finance the whole crop. Of course the fact that very little cash was paid out, the cotton being traded for both goods and cash, rendered it possible for even a small merchant to do a big business and in this way the foundations were laid for some of the big fortunes many of the Houstonians made.

In those days a favorite sport among the boys was sledding. The sleds were made by rounding off the ends of two pieces of plank, to serve as runners, and then joining them together by nailing a stout piece in front and a broad piece behind to serve as a seat. A long rope was attached to the front end and the whole thing was ready for use. When an ox wagon came along we would slip up behind it, pass the rope around the rear axle, or whatever it is called, and then drawing it far enough back so as to be able to sit on the sled and hold the loose end, we would mount the sled and ride to our heart's content, or until the driver discovered us. If he showed hostile intentions, all we would have to do was to turn loose the end of the rope, grab our sled and get away. It was lots of fun then, but looking back on it now, I can see that there was lots of hard work about it, too.

But I have wandered from the point I wanted to make, that of showing how appropriate it would be for the Cotton Exchange, the Board of Trade, Chamber of Commerce, or all of these organizations, to take steps to mark appropriately the point where the commerce of the State of Texas passed, long before the days of railroads.

★ ★ ★

FAMOUS FOR MUD

I saw some workmen repairing the pavement on Main Street the other day and it occurred to me what a vast difference there is between the streets of today and those of thirty years ago. At that time Houston was justly famed for its mud. There was considerable traffic on Main, Preston, Congress and other streets in the business part of town and also on some of the side streets, and as there were no pavements, when it rained everything fairly bogged down. The mud, too, was not the milk and water slush we have today, but was the genuine old-fashioned thing and was so outrageous that the Houstonians actually got to be proud of it, just as the old gunfighters were proud of their wicked records.

Every winter was bad, but that of 1879-80 carried off the prize for outrageousness. About the middle of October it commenced to rain and kept it up until the middle of November. The "oldest citizen" and the weather prophet showed up and announced that it would rain for forty days and nights. It then commenced anew just as though it had never even sprinkled before that. The forty-first and fifty-first days were worse than any that had preceded and it began to look as if it were never going to stop raining.

Weather such as that would be pretty bad today, so one can imagine what it was then with no paved streets nor sidewalks. Drays, buggies, wagons and other vehicles bogged down on the business streets and were left there to be dug out later when they could be moved without fear of having them bog down on the next block. Finally it got so bad that only the most imperative necessity would make people venture out in a carriage or buggy. One or two public hacks would get out occasionally, but it cost about as much to ride in one of these for, say a mile, as it would cost today to go to New Orleans.

Right in the middle of all this magnificent weather, the Z. Z. Club concluded to give its annual ball. Giving the ball was easy enough, but getting the ladies there and home again with out drowning them or smothering them in mud was another thing. I am not certain, but I believe it was Chief Coyle who solved the problem. He sent for Theodore, the most responsible hack driver in Houston, and consulted with him.

The two together evolved a plan that worked like a charm. Chief Coyle prepared a list of the young ladies and their escorts and had all the young gentlemen meet at Gray's Hall early in the evening. About 7 o'clock Theodore came 'round from Preston Avenue driving six yoke of oxen hitched to an omnibus. He got the omnibus from Westheimer's stable, but where he got the oxen I never did know. Theodore had the list of the young ladies and had mapped out his route. The young men boarded the omnibus and the procession started. One by one the young ladies were picked up and within an hour or two everybody was safely in the ballroom. Everybody enjoyed the ride as much as the ball and it was a perfect success in every way. Theodore is still living in Houston and is as proud of that ox team drive today as he ever was. He is about the only hack driver who ever took ladies and gentlemen to a ball in a vehicle drawn by oxen.

But everything was not quite as novel and enjoyable as that drive was. Dr. Charley Owens, who had charge of the City Hospital, located on McKinney Avenue and Austin Street, was called out of the city and got me to take charge of the institution during his absence. One evening a messenger from the H. & T. C. railway office brought a note asking that a surgeon meet the incoming train with a carriage to take charge of a man who had broken his leg. There were no ambulances in those days. I got Jim Slavin's hack but could not get Jim to drive it, as he was sick.

I met the train and got the injured man in the hack, fixed up as comfortable as possible, and we started for the hospital. Everything went smoothly until we were crossing Academy Square. Here the front wheels went into a deep hole and the sudden lurch threw the driver off on top of the horses and he bounded off in the mud. He scared the horses so badly that they bolted and went out Rusk Avenue like skyrockets. Fortunately the poor fellow with the broken leg fainted at the first dash out of the box, so he was spared a lot of pain and suffering. The hack was up in the air one moment and several feet down in the mud the next. Those horses must have been almost scared to death to keep up the pace they did. Finally after going about four blocks the mud conquered and they stopped.

I was wondering what I should do and was preparing to get out and try to drive the hack to the hospital, when the driver showed up. He beat anything I ever saw. He did not look like a human being at all. I could scarcely tell that he was a man at all, he was so disguised in mud. How he carried the load he had on him was a mystery. There was nothing broken, so he got on the box and we drove back to the hospital. I am willing to bet that the man with the broken leg never forgot that ride. I don't think the driver ever did and I know I never will.

★ ★ ★

HOUSTON'S FOUR BRICK COURTHOUSES

I was much interested in a discussion that took place yesterday afternoon between an old citizen and a county official, relative to the courthouse history of Harris County. The old citizen contended that the present magnificent building is the fourth brick courthouse that has been erected on that block. The county official said that there had been only three and he could prove it by the county records.

Now if this county official be correct, then the county records are radically wrong, for this is the fourth brick building that has been erected there. Long before my day, and in fact before the day of anyone except the very, very old settlers, there used to be a frame building on the northwest corner of the square, which was the original courthouse, while the jail was another frame building on the southeast corner. In the early 1840s these buildings were torn down and a small two-story brick courthouse was erected in the middle of the block. The jail was located at the north end of the market building, which was a long frame house extending across the middle of the block from Preston Avenue to Congress Avenue on Market Square.

Courthouse Square was a great place then, and if I may borrow from the geography I will say it was bounded on the north by the residence of Wm. M. Rice and a frame post office; on the south by the residences of Peter Sampson and E. W. Taylor; on the east by Peter Gable's brewery and the residence of Cornelius Ennis, and on the west by the residences of Judge Peter Gray and John Brashear and a number of law offices. Messrs. Tankersley, Palmer, Hamblen, Manley, Riley and others whose names escape me were among the old time lawyers who had offices there.

I remember this old, first brick courthouse well, for it seemed a magnificent building then, though I suppose it could have been placed in a space about the size of one of the present courtrooms in the building of today. There were no blinds on the windows and common calico curtains were used instead. As a kid I went through the lower halls, but do not remember having ever ventured to the second floor. I do remember the staircase and the cistern that was built under the building in which a man was drowned. All the neighbors got water from the courthouse cistern in that day. This water got to tasting and smelling bad and finally an investigation revealed the dead body in the cistern. I don't know whether the man jumped in the cistern or whether he fell in, but I do know that he gave those courthouse square residents cause to remember him for some time.

Another thing I remember about that old building was a long rope that was coiled up under the steps. Doubtless this rope was used for ordinary purposes, but we boys always looked on it with the most profound awe and respect for it was a notorious fact among us that more than a dozen men had been hanged with it and that the sheriff kept it in a convenient place, always ready for instant use.

A year or two before the war that old building became so cracked and decayed that it was torn down and another larger brick building was erected, this time on the north side of the square, facing Congress Avenue. This building had a basement and two stories placed on that making it practically a three story building. This building was scarcely finished when the war broke out and during the war the basement was used as a guardhouse and later converted into a receiving prison for Federals, who were captured at Galveston, Sabine Pass and other points.

The real prison was located just this side of Hempstead on the Houston & Texas Central Railway, not far from Col. Jarad Groce's residence, now used as a colored state school. We used the basement of the courthouse to lock the Yankees in during the war, but after the war, during reconstruction days, they turned the tables and locked us up in the same place, whenever they could find the slightest excuse for doing so. Major De Gress was provost marshal and ran things to suit himself, which he could do with impunity, seeing as he had the army of occupation at his back. Still on the whole he did what most any stickler for military methods would have done in his place, for he had rather desperate people to contend with and some very few tough citizens as well.

Finally this old courthouse outlived its usefulness and it was decided to tear it down and erect a new one on the same site. This was in the early 80s. There was a great deal of opposition to the new courthouse, and this opposition was hardly confined to the taxpayers. The county commissioners were by no means unanimous in its favor. They fought among themselves and finally the question became a matter of debate in the newspapers. I remember it well and you will see later why I do.

Colonel Hamp Cook was the Houston representative of the *Galveston News* and he wrote so much and wrote so well that it was not long before both he and the *News* became factors in the fight. The discussions became somewhat bitter and were verging rapidly on the coffee and pistol stage when Colonel Cook learned that one of the commissioners had taken the warpath and was out for his scalp. The colonel came to me and told me of his trouble and ended by borrowing a fine Colt six-shooter with which to down the warlike commissioner on sight.

I did not see Colonel Cook for a week or ten days and I never did see my pistol again. I heard afterward that the two had met on the street and adjourned to Japhet's saloon to talk it over. They stayed so long that when they came out neither had a very clear idea of what had occurred except that they had sworn to be lifelong friends. Neither could remember what had become of my pistol. The colonel offered me a brand new one, but I refused, being more than satisfied at the peaceful solution of the question.

After awhile all obstacles were overcome and the old courthouse was torn down and the new one erected. That one stood there until lately torn down to make place for the present magnificent building.

This briefly is a history of the Harris County courthouse and from this, it is evident that the present courthouse is the fourth brick building erected on that square, whether the county records show such to be the case or not.

GAMES FOLKS PLAY:
POLITICS, GAMBLING AND OTHER SORDID MISCELLANY

★ ★ ★

KU KLUX DAYS

In 1868, Reconstruction was on in full blast all over Texas, and Houston, being so prominent a central point both in commercial and political matters, came in for a large share of shame and outrage. The "black belt" over on the Brazos being so near, it was an easy thing for the scalawags and carpetbaggers to bring negro voters by the hundred whenever a so-called election was held. There was no registration required and all that was necessary was to have a red or blue ticket or a white one with a big flag painted on it, so that the ignorant negro could tell what ticket to vote, and the Republican leaders were assured of success in advance. Governor A. J. Davis had appointed the negro state guard a special police, and had suspended habeas corpus and given these negroes the right to make arrests on their own judgment without writ or any legal process whatever. Not content with this, the scalawags and carpetbaggers went even further in their effort to put the negro above the white man. They organized the Union League, an organization formed for the sole purpose of controlling the ignorant negro votes and boosting the worthless white men, who were out for everything in sight, into office.

There was only one voting place for the whole county and city at first—the courthouse—but later this was changed and the country people were allowed to vote in their own precincts. Everybody in Houston, though, had to vote at the courthouse and this was done because it enabled the Republicans to control things to suit themselves. It is almost incredible the power the scalawags had over the negroes. They owned and controlled them like so many dumb animals and voted them, not in blocks, but as a solid unit.

With so many imported negro votes in the field, the white men found themselves in a hopeless minority, but be it said to their honor and glory, they did their duty as voters and citizens, and under difficulties that were at times almost insurmountable.

In order to reach the voting place each voter had to get in line and keep his place, too. If he stepped aside even for a moment, unless he were a negro he forfeited his place and was forced to take a new one at the end of the line and begin all over again. Long before the polls opened there were hundreds of negroes and as many white men as could get there in line. This line was often one or two blocks long and two men abreast. Only two men were admitted to the polls at once so the voting was long, drawn out and tedious. Extending from the courthouse down to the room where the voting took place was a double line of Federal soldiers with fixed bayonets, and every free American citizen, black or white, had to pass between a line of bayonets to express his will at the ballot box.

Republican strikers and henchmen were continually passing along the line of voters and were swelling the Republican majority by slipping belated negroes into the line ahead of the white men. It was a great outrage but it worked all the same and gave the Republican managers absolute control of everything. Of course, the voting time was limited, which enabled them to shut out the white vote in part if not in whole. The negroes in the advance voted leisurely, consuming as much time as possible, thus holding back the line. When a white man showed up he was put through a sharp questioning; his right to vote was contested and every obstacle possible was placed in his way. Finally he was either allowed to vote or was thrown out, and the negroes behind him were allowed to vote rapidly in order to make up lost time. I have known of old citizens, holding their places in the line for hours and then losing their votes by having the polls close on them promptly at 6 o'clock, or just about the time the white voters reached the polls.

Now, conditions such as these were enough to drive men crazy and irresponsible, but yet, strange to say, there was very little rioting or bloodshed. Most of the lawlessness came from the other side. Davis' state guard, all negroes, did more to overthrow the Republicans and scalawags than all the other causes combined. This was in two ways. The outrages committed by the negro policemen enraged the whites and the punishment meted out by the whites terrified the negroes and their worthless backers, causing them to become less open and aggressive in their diabolical work.

It is really hard to believe at this later day the outrages perpetrated by the negro state guards. By the authority given them by Governor Davis they were supreme and above all local authority. They arrested whomever they pleased. Little things like making a complaint or securing a warrant for an arrest cut no figure at all. They generally went in bunches of four or five and were heavily armed. It was no unusual thing for them to stop good citizens on the streets or county roads, cross-examine them in the most insolent manner and then curse them, using the vilest language in an effort to make the citizens do something to give them an excuse for killing them. They did kill a great many men in various parts of the state, but as the only witnesses to these killings were themselves, they never had the least trouble.

Things were in this shape when the climax came. Three or four of these negro police were in Brenham sitting on a bench in the public square. A highly respected citizen and merchant by the name of Ledbetter started across the square from his store to go to the post office. He passed some distance from the negroes and being hard of hearing, did not hear them when they called to him and demanded to know where he was going. They jumped up and ordered him to halt. Still not hearing them he continued on his way. He had taken only a few steps when he fell dead, riddled by bullets from the negroes' guns and pistols. The murder was so cold-blooded and unprovoked that the whole community rose in arms. The negroes made their escape, but the black flag had been raised and from that moment Davis' state guards were doomed to dogs' deaths wherever found. None of them was ever arrested for anything they had done, because when they were found they were wiped out. They were placed in the same class with snakes, wolves and other undesirable things and the average white man thought no more of killing one of them than he could have thought of killing a snake. I don't know whether it was true or not but it was currently reported and believed, that after the murder of Ledbetter not a single member of Davis' negro state guards, originally about 80 strong, ever died a natural death.

This change of front on the part of the white men had a salutary effect on the negroes. They became less bold and open, but the carpetbaggers and scalawags maintained their hold on them through great political organizations.

The time was now ripe for an organized effort on the part of the whites and that fact was recognized. One afternoon I was seated in front of the old Capitol Hotel, where the Rice Hotel now stands, in company with Colonel Jones, a young lawyer who had made quite a reputation as a Confederate officer and soldier; Major Crank, Captain Charley Evans and one or two others. After a desultory conversation Colonel Jones asked me abruptly if I believed in white man supremacy. Of course my answer was in the affirmative. He then asked if I was willing to take part in a movement to insure white supremacy. I told him I was. He then told me that a movement was on foot to organize the white men and he wanted me to join the organization. I agreed and on the following Tuesday night I was initiated in the Texas Ku

Klux, though it was known by a different name. I was the first man initiated, my number being eleven. There were ten charter members, Colonel Jones being No. 1, Captain Evans No. 2, Major Clark No. 3 and I forget the others, but I do remember that the late General C. C. Beavens was No. 10, but since he was a strict Catholic and the priest objected to his belonging to a secret society, he never took part in the organization. Aside from the advantage gained by making the order as mysterious as possible I could never see reason for any secrecy, for it was an absolutely lawful association, and its members were sworn to do all in their power to maintain the supremacy of the white man by lawful means and to restore law and order.

We picked our men and in less than a month we had over 300 members in Houston and the order had extended to nearby towns. In a month or two the order had gone all over Texas, and had thousands of members. The idea of profound mystery was carried out in every way. Members were known only by numbers, and no written record was ever made or kept. When investigations were necessary or when any outside work was to be done no one ever knew who was chosen to do the work except the general and those who were chosen. Of course the negroes, loyal leagues and carpetbaggers became greatly excited when they discovered the existence of our organization and they made every effort to find out something about us. That they could not do because there was absolutely nothing to find out.

I belonged to the order from the day of its organization until it was dissolved and I never knew of an unlawful act done by it, nor of one done by some overzealous or silly member that was not promptly rebuked. The order accomplished its object the very moment it was organized, for its mere existence, surrounded as it were with so much mystery, struck terror to the negro heart and caused their white backers to pause and take notice. During a small riot and threatened uprising of the negroes one Sunday morning, the old market bell was tolled in a peculiar way by some unknown person. Within a few minutes several hundred men armed with shot guns and pistols suddenly appeared on Main Street and the negroes and their white friends disappeared as suddenly. But, as Kipling says, that is another story, and as it is rather an interesting one, I shall reserve it for another time.

★ ★ ★

A Sure Thing

All the old Houstonians surely must remember Mr. Frank Le Mott. He was born in New York, though he claims to be from the old Huguenot family of that name, who originally settled in South Carolina. Frank is very proud of the blue blood in his veins and claims that he is the only black sheep in the family. He also claims that he was a black sheep for but a short time, and he is perfectly correct in saying that, as for many years past he has been as staid and circumspect as any Presbyterian deacon could be.

When Colonel Abe Gentry was building the Texas & New Orleans Railroad, he went to New York and met Frank, then a mere boy. He liked him so well that he induced him to come to Houston with him, took him into his home and made him one of his family. It was not long after his arrival here when the war broke out. Frank took the side of the South and when Captain Ike Stafford raised his cavalry company the first raised in Houston, to go down on the Rio Grande, Frank joined it. He served four years in the Confederate army, and was with Baylor, Ford and all of the others in West Texas, New Mexico and Arizona.

When the war closed, Frank found himself without home or employment and, what was worse, he had formed peculiar tastes that had made him a wanderer and largely an adventurer. His career as a soldier had coincided with that particularly formative stage in his young life and stamped itself squarely on his character. Owing to what he'd experienced during the war, he could no longer stand the humdrum routine of everyday civil life. He wanted excitement and since he could no longer get that from a war, he took the next best thing and became a gambler. I would not make mention of this at all were it not for the fact that he reformed many years ago and is now and has been for half a generation one of the most reputable and highly esteemed citizens of Galveston.

He is a superb raconteur, has had some wonderful experiences over the course of his life, and it is a great treat to hear him relate some of his adventures. His stories are all good, but one is always inclined to think the story he is presently telling surely must be the best of all. When he gets deeply interested in what he is recounting, he is apt to lapse into the gambler's habit of speaking of everything in the present tense. Here is one of what I consider to be his best stories. He and I were talking about "sure things" one day, and he shared the following:

"Don't you fool yourself. There are no such things as sure things. I know, because I have had experience with them. Why, once I had such a 'sure thing' it was too dead to skin. The funny part about it is that it worked perfectly, too, but I didn't press my luck working it but that one time.

"I'm over in Gonzales, where there is a big horse race meeting going on. There are lots of cowmen there, and they all have big money and they bet it free, too. The first night I got there I went against faro bank and dropped my roll. That didn't bother me much, because I knew I could get a stake from some of the boys next day. I went to my room and got to thinking about the races. Everybody was betting so free and easy that I saw a good killing could be made if I could hatch up a scheme. Before long a plan suggested itself to me. The Devil helped me, and before I went to bed I had one of the 'surest-sure things' that any sport ever got his claws onto.

"The next morning I tapped one of the boys for a stake. He was not very strong, having only $80, but he split that with me. It was not much, but I was satisfied, for my 'sure thing' was so good that all I wanted was to get my first bet down and it would work itself after that.

"I got out to the racetrack early so as to size up the crowd. There was a big bunch of red-hot sports there and they were all howling to get their money down on a big horse that was a favorite at 2 to 1. I didn't make any bets, but just walked around looking for the right man to help me out. Finally I found him. He was a long, lanky fellow and had only one arm. I took him off on one side and interrogated him.

"'Sawmill or gin?' said I, pointing to his absent arm.

"'Army,' says he.

"'Infantry or cavalry?' says I.

"'Infantry,' says he.

"'Then you ought to be able to walk like hell,' said I.

"'I can,' said he.

"I saw that he was a man of few words and decided to trust him. Then I unfolded my plan to him. It was simple. I would make a bet and he would hold stakes. He would then slip the money back to me and I would bet it all again. When the horses got started good, he was to slip out over the hill and meet me next day in Seguin and we would divide up.

"He agreed and I went out to slaughter 'em. I saw a sport waving a big bunch of bills he wanted to get down on the 4-year-old that was the favorite at 2 to 1. I took him promptly, he putting up $80 against my $40. I remarked that I was a stranger and looked around for somebody to hold the stakes. 'Here's the right man,' I said. 'He hasn't got but one arm and we can spot him easily.' The sport agrees and the one-armed man gets the money and then slips it back to me and I puts the $120 against $250 another sport is howling to get rid of, and my one-armed man holds stakes again.

"I don't know how many times I bet that roll. Finally the sports conclude from my betting so freely that I know something against the 4-year-old and I can't get any more bets. Then I force things and give odds against him— anything to get action on my money. Before the race started I had the whole bunch bet to a standstill. Finally the race started. Everybody is watching the horses except me. I'm watching my one-armed man, and I don't breathe easy until I see his head disappear over the hill. Of course I'm prepared to help the gang raise hell over the stakeholder getting away with the money, but there ain't any hell raised. A little flea-bitten gray mare, ridden by a nigger, comes under the wire a length ahead of the 4-year-old.

"I'm crazy. I've bankrupted West Texas, and I break over the hill after my one-armed man. But I don't find him, for he sure tells the truth when he says he can walk like hell. I search the county for him that evening, but I don't find him. The next day I go over to Seguin, but he ain't there. I wait there two days, but he never did show up, and he must be going yet, for I have never seen him since his head went over the hill. That's the surest thing I ever had, and you see a plumb outsider got away with all its fruit.

"There are two things that have worried me ever since. One is trying to figure how much money I beat those sports out of, and the other is how anybody could have acted as dishonest as that one-armed man did."

★ ★ ★

A COMPANY OF GAMBLERS

Everybody knows how scarce Confederate soldiers were in the South toward the latter part of 1863. As some wit expressed it, Jefferson Davis had robbed the cradle and the grave and was almost tempted to call out the cavalry. It is needless to say that the wit belonged to some other branch of service than cavalry. Texas was the only Southern state on whose soil the federal troops had not succeeded in making a permanent foothold. The naval and military forces had been driven off by Magruder at Galveston; the invading force of Banks had been defeated at Sabine Pass by Dick Dowling, and Banks' Red River campaign had resulted only in making large, though involuntary, contribution of food, clothing and ammunition to the Confederates who opposed him.

And yet with all this pressing need for men at the front there were hundreds upon hundreds of able-bodied men in Houston, the headquarters of General Magruder who commanded the Trans-Mississippi department. There were blockade runners, cotton exporters and hundreds of others who, on one pretext or another, secured immunity from military service. Then, too, there were scores of gamblers. How these latter escaped the conscript officers no one knew, but they did and they lived on the fat of the land, too.

At that time there was an old gentleman, a distinguished criminal lawyer, living in Houston. He was eager to go to the front and had almost evaded his friends and succeeded in doing so on one or two occasions. Of course, being a criminal lawyer who almost invariably won his cases, he was vastly popular with the gambling fraternity and it was principally they who raised such a strenuous objection to his risking his valuable life on the field of battle.

One night the judge had an inspiration. He hatched a plan by which he could not only get to the front himself, but could take all his troublesome friends too. He would organize an independent cavalry company, make every man furnish his own equipment and would thus be in position to choose his own men. He knew that no others than the gamblers could stand the expense, so he determined to get his recruits from among them only.

The next morning he called at General Magruder's headquarters, outlined his scheme and, of course, readily received the authority to carry out his plan. The judge knew how futile it would be to appeal to the gamblers on grounds of patriotism, and he did not try to do so. He sent for two or three of the leaders and told them that he had just left Magruder's headquarters and that an order would be issued in a day or two revoking all exemptions from military service and all special privileges. He pointed out to them that since they would have to go in the army anyway, they might as well go of their own accord and thus be able to choose the branch of service they would prefer to belong to. He then told them that he had secured from Magruder authority to raise an independent cavalry company; that he, the judge, would be captain, but that the men could elect all the other officers and that Magruder had promised to confirm them. The plan was instantly endorsed and before night about 80 men were enrolled, officers were elected and the work of securing equipment was begun.

The only delay was occasioned by their inability to secure things fine enough. The best and showiest horses and bridles and silver and gold mounted six-shooters were secured and within a week everything was in readiness.

As already stated, there were no Federals in Texas at that time. So after this fine company was organized it had everything requisite for a brilliant victory except the enemy to win it from. In this dilemma they took Horace Greeley's advice and went West. Their first halt was at Velasco, where they saw two or three Federal gunboats lying off the mouth of the river, hoping to pick up blockade runners. There was nothing to be done there, so they moved on and finally reached Matagorda Bay. Here they halted to rest for awhile and it was here that they had the time of their lives.

Their camp was about four miles from the gulf in a live oak grove and they rode out every day over the prairie and down to the water front. A favorite excursion was far out on a peninsula that extended obliquely into the gulf. Occasionally a Federal gunboat would pass, always too far out to notice them, but it made them feel better to know that there were enemies about even if they were so far away.

One day the company concluded to have a big oyster roast out on the peninsula. So early in the morning they rode out to its end, where the grass was most plentiful, hobbled their horses, returned to the oyster bed and began operations. The oysters were on the bay side, so their backs were to the gulf and the view in that direction was further obstructed by high grass and shell banks. Some of them waded in the water and threw out the oysters, while others built fires or dug trenches in which to roast them. It was a hot and sultry day, and as they took their time, it was fully 10 o'clock before the feast was ready. A few black clouds had piled up in the west and thunder was to be expected, but the clap that came fairly drove every thought of oysters from their minds and nearly paralyzed them. It struck about half way between them and the main land, and pieces of it bounded off and went kicking up the water of the bay every three or four hundred yards for over a mile. They sprang up the bank as one man, and saw to their horror a Federal gunboat about a mile off shore and realized that they were about to receive their baptism of fire. Their first thought was to make for their horses, but a glance in that direction told them that the attempt was useless, for there before their eyes was a boatful of bluecoats nearing shore rapidly. Their plight was pitiful, for as every old soldier knows, bombshells frighten an infantryman, the rattle of minie balls among the spokes of his guns scares an artilleryman, while if you get a cavalryman away from his horse any and everything scares him.

To say that they hesitated would be a gross exaggeration and wholly incorrect. There was no hesitation. They faced the mainland and fled, their valorous captain fulfilling the promise he had made at their organization by working far in the lead. The Federals behind them had now landed, and being within long range, opened fire with their muskets, while the gunboat sent a six or twelve-pound shell over their heads every few minutes. Their pace was fearful from the first, but it was sloth itself compared to the move they got on themselves when they discovered another boat loaded with marines trying to head them off. The peninsula was joined to the mainland by a narrow neck of land with rather deep water on each side, so it was simply a question of beating the boat there or throwing up the sponge. However, in the language of Mark Twain's cowboy they "seen their duty and they done it." They beat the boat to the point by a neck and passed it gloriously, their pace being accelerated at the critical moment by the explosion of a big shell over their heads and a brisk fire from the marines in the boat, who now, realizing that they had lost, concluded to get an extra spurt or two from the land side of the race.

The mainland was reached, but there was that broad prairie, and for at least two miles the noble band would be within reach of the guns of the gunboat. Shells began falling in front, behind and all around them. There was no abatement of the pace. It was a mad headlong plunge forward, a mad desire to get anywhere, anywhere out of reach of the shells. Finally the shells ceased to fall, but the mad rush continued until an old deserted house on the prairie was reached. Here the gallant men fell in a heap and attempted to catch their breath and to still their throbbing hearts.

After awhile, one by one, they succeeded in crawling into the deserted house and lay there panting, bathed in perspiration, but silently congratulating themselves on their escape. The captain, a very large and fleshy man, was three-fourths dead, but after an hour or two regained sufficient energy to sit up and then announced that he would go upstairs and see if the gunboat had gone. The others sat or lay around too utterly played out to take the slightest interest in the matter or care whether it had gone or not so long as they were out of range.

A few moments after the captain had gone there was a tremendous crash as if the side of the house had been crushed in by a shell. There was but one thought—the gunboat had returned, had got the range of the house and had plugged it the first time. That thought cost the old house its front door for there was not room for the whole crowd to get out at once as they tried to do. Part of the old fence was swept away, too, as they, swerving neither to the right nor to the left, made a beeline for their camp in the live oak grove in the distance. It was another mad rush with the devil take the hindmost for several hundred yards, when, hearing no more shells, one of the boldest slackened his pace and then others, emboldened by his example, slowed down until they all came to a dog trot. Now, for the first time they thought of their captain and noticed his absence. A council of war was held, which resulted in a determination to return and bear away his mangled remains, for there was no doubt among them that the shell had found a shining mark in his manly form.

Slowly they wended their way back and when within long earshot they were startled by an unearthly rapping and kicking, mingled with smothered oaths and maledictions. There could be no mistake about that voice. It was that of their captain and he was very much alive and evidently very much enraged. They hurried round the house and found to their amazement that the sounds came from the inside of an immense wooden cistern. Yes, their captain was safe and not a mangled corpse as they feared. He was very much alive though a prisoner. They fished him out after a great deal of trouble and then learned the truth. He had gone to the second story to get a good view of the gulf and had incautiously crawled out on what he thought was a shed but which proved to be the top of a cistern. Old and decayed, it had given way with the great crash that had stampeded the company, and he had been precipitated to the bottom. Fortunately there was no water in the cistern so the consequences were by no means disastrous.

About ten days later a train of dilapidated cars, drawn by a squawking engine, drew into Houston from Brazoria. After all the passengers had gone, the captain of the great independent company of Texas Rangers and two or three comrades slipped off the step of the last coach and sneaked down a side street. The next evening other members of the company did the same thing and within a week they were all back and following their usual vocations just as though nothing out of the ordinary had ever happened.

How the judge ever explained Magruder not issuing that order, the fear of which had caused the gamblers to fall such easy victims, was never known. The fact that every member of the company was strictly on the defensive no doubt helped him out of the difficulty.

★ ★ ★

PLENTY OF ACTION—BUT NO GAME

A few days ago I was over at the Grand Central Depot when the Houston & Texas Central train came in and several hunters got off with well-filled game bags. The sight made me think of a hunt I once took out on that road. Hockley was a famous place at that time for duck shooting. Captain John Warren had the eating house at Hockley, and, being a great hunter himself, he always had parties from across the state visiting him. The captain had been a game-keeper in England before he came to this country and what he did not know about guns, dogs and anything pertaining to hunting was not worth knowing. He was rather stiff and offish at first acquaintance, but would thaw out soon and then he was a most delightful companion.

Dr. Alva Connell and I had an office on Texas Avenue right back of where the Binz building now stands, and as neither of us had a patient we concluded to go up to Hockley and have some fun shooting ducks. We sent a boy over to the depot with our guns and traps, and, sticking up a notice reading, "Called out of town on professional business. Will return tomorrow or next day," we followed the boy and were soon on our way to Hockley.

That was in the early 70s and it had been raining for weeks, so we knew there would be plenty of water and consequently plenty of ducks. We arrived at Hockley about 4 o'clock in the afternoon and called on Captain Warren as soon as we got there. He sized us up as two dudes and seemed to be rather afraid of us. He hesitated a long time about letting us have a rig, but finally consented to do so. I don't think he would have done so at all if Connell had not mentioned my grandfather, who was paymaster of the Central at that time. Having secured the rig, a two-wheeled gig, and Connell having negotiated successfully for a pony, the captain very reluctantly consented to lend us his dog. This dog was of royal descent and had better blood in his veins, in Captain Warren's opinion, than had any member of the royal family.

The captain gave us the most minute instructions about how to treat the dog and said he would not have anything happen to him for any money. The dog seemed to mistrust us as much as the captain did, for when we got ready to start he would not follow us at all. Then the captain got a rope and hitched the dog on behind my gig and we started off in great shape. The captain directed us where to go and we crossed the railroad track and set off across the prairie.

When we were about two miles out, several snipe showing the utmost contempt for us and our guns, settled down on the prairie not 20 feet from where we were. Connell jumped off his horse and, handing me the bridle, began to advance on the snipe. Just as he got by my horse's head the snipe flew up and Connell fired at them. Up to that point I had been using the whip on the horse to make him go at all. Now his whole character changed, as if by magic. He gave one mighty leap at the crack of that gun and spilled everything but me out of the gig. It was the funniest leap you ever saw. He went fully 20 feet and when he lit he came down on his hind legs and ran 20 feet further on his hind legs just like folks. Then he made a mighty plunge, lowering his head just as if he were going to turn a somersault. When he did that he snapped one of the reins off close to the bit. Evidently thinking that he was free, he began a series of the most disgraceful antics, and at times I really believe he thought of getting in the gig with me and riding home. His conduct was scandalous. Then he suddenly changed his mind, gave up his circus performance and bolted in dead earnest.

My horse completed one of the most graceful curves that was ever made on that prairie and was just beginning to make another near where we had started when some ducks flew over, and Connell took a shot at them. That settled everything. My horse became absolutely frantic. He whirled round first to the right and then, changing his mind when he found himself facing Connell and his gun, he gave a mighty leap, and it seemed to me, in two different directions at the same time. The result was that I was thrown out of the gig into a mass of mud and water, and the horse was free. There was a terrible splashing of water and mud as that horse passed me. He had the gall to take a good look at me before leaving for good and I fancied I could see him grinning. The next moment he was headed for Hockley at a gait that would have won him fame and renown had he been on a racetrack. As he departed I made a horrible discovery. There was that thousand-dollar dog of the captain's tied fast behind a gig being dragged at an incredible speed through mud and water, right into the captain's presence. Connell and I got together and held a consultation. We watched the horse and dog approach Hockley and to our consternation, just as they got to the railroad crossing a freight train blew its whistle and that fool horse took fresh fright. Instead of stopping at home, as he evidently intended doing at first, he took a fresh start, passed clear through the town and the last we saw of him he was trying to make his way into the next county north of Hockley. Connell and I started to walk to Cypress, stay there all night and catch the morning train into Houston, but the mud and water conquered even our fear of Captain Warren, so we trudged back to Hockley.

We found the captain so mad he could hardly talk, but fortunately the dog had sustained no serious injury. He was a sight, though, and if we had dared to do so we would have had a good laugh at him. He was such a mass of mud that you could not tell whether he was a dog, calf or what he was.

It was nearly dark now, so we had to give up all idea of hunting that evening; we sat by a good fire and dried our clothes while the captain told us about hunting in England. He promised to wake us at daylight, but he did not, and when we awoke it was nearly train time. I thought then and have thought ever since that he let us sleep on purpose to keep from turning us down when we asked for another hunting rig. We got up and after a good breakfast took our things over to the depot to catch the train, which we could see coming in the distance. Connell said he hated to go home without killing anything, so he took his gun and went back of a big barn where there were thousands of blackbirds. We waited to hear him shoot, but he did not do so. Then, just as the engine blew for the station, we heard his gun go off and he came from the barn terribly excited and running to catch the train, which stopped only for a moment. As he came up he cried out "Captain, I killed a big fox back of your barn. I did not have time to get him, but I wish you would and send him to me."

"Now," said the captain, almost speechless with indignation, "you have played. You have killed my pet fox."

We waited to hear no more, but dived onto the train and were thankful to feel it moving the next moment. That was about the most strenuous hunt I ever went on. It is true the only thing we killed was a pet fox, but we had action for our money during every moment we spent in Hockley.

★ ★ ★

A Hard Luck Story

I read a "hard luck" story the other day and it reminded me that Frank Le Mott had once told me one of the best stories of the kind I have ever heard. One day Frank said to me, "Did I ever tell you about Limpy Lewis' hard luck?" and when I answered in the negative he told me the following:

"This Limpy Lewis got his name from having a wooden leg that was always wearing off at the bottom, so that it was too short for his good leg. He walked lopsided when he pranced along the street and the boys got to calling him 'Limpy.' He was a no-count kind of a fellow, a tramp soldier of fortune and a gambler. When he won he rolled in good things to eat and when he lost he bummed for his grub. It was chicken one day and feathers the next with him. He was a good-natured sort of chap and the other gamblers helped him along occasionally, when they could. Those who owned the games gave him a commission on all the customers he brought them, so Limpy hung out around the hotels early in the evening, looking for suckers.

"One morning Limpy got hold of a greenhorn. When the bank got through with him Limpy had a real good stake coming. He thought he was in such good luck that he would go against the bank himself and did so. At first he won and had a big pile of chips in front of him for an hour or two. Then his luck changed and he lost everything he had. He got up dead broke and concluded to go out and find another sucker.

"While going to the nearest hotel to look over the situation, he met a tall stranger dressed like a cowman. The stranger asked him if he could direct him to a square game. Limpy told him he knew exactly where to go and invited the stranger to go with him. As they started the stranger told him he wanted nothing but a square game, and if he would lead him to one of that kind, he would give him a quarter of what he won, if he did win. He did that to protect himself, for with that prospect in sight Limpy would pull for him to win, even if he were playing against Limpy's best friend. There was no mixing of sentiment and business when Limpy had a case like that. Limpy was going to take him against a brace game, but when the stranger mentioned a quarter share for him, Limpy changed his mind and took him to the squarest game in town.

"When they got there the stranger bought $500 worth of chips and wanted to make two bets of the whole thing. That was too big for the bank. Considerable argument took place, with the stranger trying to get the bank to raise the limit and let him bet his money. At last the limit was raised to $200, except on 'case cards,' when it was fixed at $100.

"When the game got to going good, the proprietor took Limpy off on one side and told him he was glad to see him and his friend. He was going to be liberal with Limpy and give him 20 per cent of all the house won from the stranger and that he would do the same thing on all customers like this one Limpy could bring him.

"The stranger was a big cattleman who was famous for his big bets and gambling. In an hour or so it looked like he was going to break the bank. He had about $8,000 worth of chips in front of him and was scattering them in heaps of $200 all over the table. His luck came and went. It was daylight now and the game was just warming up. By 10 o'clock the stranger was in the hole for about $20,000, but still bought chips and showed no signs of quitting. Limpy sat there, half-dead for lack of sleep, but afraid to go to sleep or to leave for a moment. Luck shifted and the stranger began to win again. By 5 o'clock the stranger had all his money back and was ahead. At one point he was about $18,000 ahead. Limpy was crazy for him to cash in and quit but was afraid to say a word, so all he could do was to sit there and suffer while the game went on. The dealers and lookouts had been changed two or three times, of course, but Limpy and the stranger had to stay there.

"The value of the chips had been placed at $100 each, so it was not hard to keep track of the winnings and losses. About 4 o'clock the second morning the stranger took stock and found he was just $900 ahead of the game. He said to the proprietor: 'If you say so I will make one bet of this, for I'm getting tired. It's double or nothing. Shall she go?' The proprietor agreed, the bet was made and the stranger lost. He got up and quit, exactly even, and poor old Limpy fainted. He'd sat there for two nights and a day, drinking coffee to keep awake and with a sure winning for himself in sight all the time, until the last minute. That was the toughest luck I ever heard of."

★ ★ ★

HONEST BOB WILSON

"Honest Bob" Wilson has never received that justice from the writers of history to which his eminent services to the colonists, to the Republic and to the young state of Texas entitle him. He was one of the remarkable men of the early days and it is a shame that he is not better remembered.

Old Houstonians remember him, not so much for anything that they knew of his achievements, as from the fact that he was the father of the Hon. James T. D. Wilson, the first mayor chosen by the people after Reconstruction, when the Democrats gained control of the state. The younger generation know of him as being the grandfather of the Wilson boys, who have done so much for the growth and advancement of Houston and who, today, have their shoulders to the wheel, working for an even greater Houston.

It is scarcely credible that a man of such accomplishments should have his memory perpetuated only through the lesser accomplishments of his descendants, yet that is literally true of "Honest Bob" Wilson. His title of "Honest Bob" was not given him in derision, as is the case so often nowadays, but was the result of, and the expression of, genuine admiration for him by his fellow citizens.

I have heard my grandfather tell the story often. Bob was a member of the senate of the Republic of Texas. He believed in publicity and was silly enough, measured by later day standards, to think that the people had a right to know something of everything their servants did. Members of the congress knew more about fighting than they did about parliamentary matters.

Soon after Congress assembled it became necessary to hold an executive session and those who knew something about such matters warned the members that nothing must be divulged about any matter discussed. It was impressed on them that the meeting was to be a secret one. It was also impressed on them that any member who broke the rule of silence would be severely punished. Honest Bob listened to all that was said but did not say anything.

It was in 1838 during the Lamar administration and Burnet, being vice president, presided over the senate. Burnet had a scheme by which the bonds of the new Republic of Texas were to be exchanged for South Carolina state money, and he was urging the adoption of a resolution by the senate that would enable him to carry out his plan.

Honest Bob owned a line of sailing boats plying between Harrisburg and New Orleans, and through his captains he had heard that the South Carolina money was of little value. He never had agreed with Burnet on any question, so he made a most vicious attack on his plan.

It was during an executive session of the senate that the argument and outbreak occurred. The most unparliamentary language was used, and almost a free fight occurred. When the session closed Honest Bob went out on Main Street and told everybody he met what had taken place and what the vice president was trying to do. When the senate heard what he was doing the sergeant-at-arms was sent after him. He was arrested, brought before the senate and promptly expelled from that body.

A special election was ordered by the senate to fill the vacancy caused by his expulsion. Three days later the election was held and "Honest Bob" was re-elected to the senate by practically a unanimous vote.

The people did not stop at merely electing him, but when the result was known, they took him on their shoulders and bore him back to the senate chamber and deposited him before the members with instructions to leave him alone and not try to expel him again. That is, briefly, how he obtained the name of "Honest Bob."

He was a remarkable man and did much for the future great state. He was a progressive, alright. He came to Texas in 1828 and settled down about Harrisburg. He was a man of great energy and enterprise. His boats were the first to come up Buffalo Bayou and he made the first permanent improvements at Harrisburg, establishing quite an extensive manufacturing plant there. He had a sawmill, a blacksmith shop, a wagon and wheel shop and had several good houses for his workmen.

When the revolution broke out he contributed largely to the cause, and Santa Anna made him pay dearly for his patriotism, burning up everything he could lay his hands on. The war ruined him, but he would not stay ruined, and while the Republic and State of Texas, with the proverbial ingratitude of republics, failed to reimburse him for his losses, he succeeded in making what was considered at that time to be a modest fortune before his death.

I am not certain, but it is my impression that the body of Honest Bob Wilson lies in or near the old Catholic Cemetery down in the Second Ward. I have not been there for many years, but I am almost certain that there is a marble shaft erected over his grave.

★ ★ ★

JOE TYRAN AND HAMP COOK

One afternoon recently I was in a bookstore on Main Street when a gentleman who is a candidate for a county office came in. The bookman asked him how his campaign was coming on and the candidate assured him that he had everything going his way and that there could be no doubt of his triumphant election. He said he had a majority of the votes pledged to him already and that they were coming his way all the time. He was absolutely confident of his election.

After he went away the bookman told me that the chap would come out about fourth in the race. I don't know anything about local politics, nor about the candidates, either, but from what I know of elections in the past it will not surprise me if the bookman's prediction proves to be true. I could never understand why it is so, but it is true, nevertheless, that so soon as a man becomes a candidate for office he is seized with a species of insanity which may be called *cacoethes credendi*, or, in plain English, he becomes a sucker and believes everything that the voters tell him. He may be a hard-headed businessman and one who weighs everything and gives it its true value, but when he becomes a candidate he reverses his methods and becomes the most credulous being on earth. It is strange, but it is true. Perhaps the candidate loses no advantage by becoming that way, for each one of his opponents is equally guilty.

About the most amusing case of this kind of credulity that ever came under my personal observation occurred several years ago here in Houston. The Harris County Democratic convention was being held in the opera house; that was located in City Hall. I met Joe Tyran, who invited me to go up in the hall. He told me he was going to be nominated for one of the big county offices on the first ballot, that he had prepared a fine speech and wanted me to hear him. Of course, I went. On the way he told me that taking the ballot was a mere formality, as he had a sure thing, and would get the vote of nearly every delegate in the convention. When we got to the hall Joe and I went into one of the front boxes, so he could step right out on the stage when the time came for him to return thanks to the delegates. We had not been there long before the time came for balloting for Joe's office. One or two nominating speeches were made and then the voting began. The result knocked me and Joe out of the box, for out of the 86 votes in the convention Joe got only three. He looked at me and I looked at him and then he crawled out of the box onto the stage and raised his hand. There was a dead calm. Joe advanced to the front of the stage and said: "Mr. Chairman, I want to say that there are 83 of the biggest liars in this hall that God ever let live."

In a moment bedlam broke loose. Delegates were on their feet in all parts of the hall gesticulating and shouting, while everybody was yelling and hooting. One little fellow clear back in the rear of the hall, who had a voice like a foghorn, managed to make himself heard and finally the others stopped their racket long enough for him to speak.

"Mr. Chairman," he said, "I object to any such language being..." He got no further than that. Joe did not know who he was, but he shot in the dark. "Sit down, you infernal scoundrel. You offered to sell out to me this morning for twenty dollars."

Now everybody in the house knew this charge was absurd and groundless, and that Joe was saying what he did simply because he was mad, but the crowd enjoyed the situation and raised a yell that could have been heard for blocks away. The little fellow could do nothing and realizing his helplessness, he collapsed. It took a long time to restore order and get the convention down to business again. When things got quiet I left, feeling that I had been more than repaid for my trouble in going up to hear Joe's speech, even if the one he delivered had been a substitute.

Joe Tyran was a politician from way back—sometimes. He was a politician all the time, but a mighty poor one occasionally. He had an impolitic way of letting his personal friendships influence him and you know no successful politician can do that. From that failing Joe made a poor politician. He was a splendid fellow and everybody loved him. He would get to be so popular that it would actually hurt, and then, acting on impulse, he would do something that would throw all the fat in the fire. That was only when he was a candidate himself. When he was working for a friend he could do much that was valuable and he always could be counted on to do it. Joe sure was impulsive, and I can prove that by Col. Hamp Cook. There is a good story here and I am going to tell it, even if I have to dodge Col. Hamp Cook for the next month for doing so.

On one occasion there was a red-hot campaign on and Joe and Hamp were taking an active part in it. They boarded the old mule car to go down to the Union Depot on Congress Avenue. On the way down they jumped off the car and went into a grocery store to get some cigars. They were standing talking to the man when a big yellow negro came in. Joe looked at the negro for a moment and then, without a word, hauled off and smashed him in the face. The negro did not understand what it was about, but he promptly knocked Joe down and mounted him. That was more than Colonel Cook could stand, so he batted the negro, knocking him off Joe and engaging him himself. The negro had the Colonel on his back the next minute and proceeded to beat him up a whole lot. Hamp fought and fought, but he also yelled for Joe to help him out. Joe had gotten up and stood there with his hands in his pockets shouting, "Give him hell, Hamp. Give him hell!"

"Put him off, I tell you. Don't you see that he's giving *me* hell?" replied Hamp.

"No he's not," replied Joe. "Keep it up. You've got him."

Finally the store man pulled the negro off Hamp and restored order for a moment, but only for a moment, for Hamp forgot all about the negro in his anxiety to get at Joe. The man had hard work to prevent another fight, but finally restored order.

I had forgotten about that convention and the battle royal until that candidate came in the bookstore the other day and set the current of my thoughts backward to the days when there were more things happening in Houston that had life and vim in them, each day, than happen now in a month.

★ ★ ★

HOW HE LOST HIS EGGS

Someone asked me the other day how I managed to think of so many things of the past to write about. The truth is that I have more things, unwittingly, suggested to me every day than I could write up in a week. I rarely meet one of my old-time friends that some subject is not discussed which, directly or indirectly, suggests something of the past. Then, too, a line in the daily papers will cause me to think of some occurrence, which has no apparent relation or reference to the subject of the paragraph. To illustrate this I will say that the other day I read one editor's paragraph, in which he said that if he had a fresh yard egg he would put it in a bank and draw checks against it. That witty paragraph did not make me think of the high price of eggs so much as it did of an amusing fight I once witnessed in which a bag of yard eggs played a prominent part.

I have written of that grand old democratic war horse, Uncle Dick Westcott, and have told of how he "held the fort," sometimes almost single-handedly, against all comers. He was a Democrat first of all and then a Southern gentleman who would have willingly given up his life any time to prevent even the semblance of equality between the whites and negroes. He did not want them to have the same rights at the ballot box, but he could not prevent them doing so. Like all old-time Southerners, he had a warm place in his heart for the old-time negroes, and was always willing to help them along in the world, except in the direction of the ballot box. When the white Republicans and negroes marshaled their forces and beat him in an election, he let them take the fruits of their victory, for no other reason than that he could not prevent it. It was not because he was not willing enough to knock them out.

Uncle Dick always declared that the government had gone only halfway when they gave the negroes the right to vote, and that to make the thing complete the ballot should have been bestowed on the mules.

I dwell somewhat at length on Uncle Dick's political views, because they have bearing on what follows. One afternoon a very prominent member of the Houston bar got into a discussion with Uncle Dick, during which the prominent lawyer so far forgot himself in the heat of argument as to take the stand that the negro had as much right from a legal point of view to vote as a white man. Uncle Dick was forced to reluctantly admit that perhaps that was true, but he stuck to his point that the law was a fool, or as Mr. Bumble puts it, "the law is a ass." The discussion attracted quite a crowd, for it was hot and animated and Uncle Dick punctuated his points by waving a big paper bag of eggs he held in his right hand. The lawyer had the best of the argument, of course, and that did not add to Uncle Dick's equilibrium. Finally Uncle Dick lost his temper, and when the lawyer drew emphatic attention to "negro rights" Uncle Dick lost his head and his bag of eggs at the same moment. Before anyone knew what he was going to do, he smashed the lawyer full in the face with the bag of eggs. The bag and eggs broke and that dignified lawyer was turned into the worst scarecrow anyone ever saw. I had no idea until then that there was so much material in a bag of eggs. Of course the lawyer could not see nor hear, either, and before he could find his bearings, friends seized Uncle Dick and hurried him away. The lawyer swore vengeance and declared he would shoot the old man on sight, but before they met again their friends patched the matter up and while never the best of friends after that, they managed to endure the presence of each other on the earth at the same time.

Now, as I have said, when I read that newspaper paragraph, that egg fight came distinctly before me, and I could see that dignified lawyer clawing at his eyes and ears, with his fingers dripping egg all over everything. Uncle Dick was a warrior from away back yonder and everybody knew it. He used to publish editorials in the *Age* during a campaign that were so hot one wondered that they did not burn the paper. They were in pure United States language, too, and things were called by their names, or at least by names that Uncle Dick thought appropriate. One of those articles of his, if published in earnest today, would result in a million dollar libel suit if not in buckets of blood. I have said that he was a warrior, and such he was. I have seen him in one or two engagements, and in every one of them he forced the fighting. That was the strange part of it and I can't understand yet why a man who did so much as to arouse antagonism and invite attack should always have to make the attack. Perhaps one reason was that everybody knew Uncle Dick was fixed for trouble and they did not care to become the aggressors. They would venture to sass him, but that was as far as they cared to go.

Sometimes it makes me really hungry for the old times when I think of Uncle Dick and Uncle Dan McGary. There can never be two such characters as they in this community again. When it came to politics they had but one thought, one object in life, to save the country from the grasp of the "depraved Republican party." With them, any and everything was absolutely right that would result in downing the hated enemy.

★ ★ ★

FRANK LE MOTT'S POKER STORY

I met Frank Le Mott in the street the other day. He was either coming from the country or going there, I don't know which. He had the most mournful expression on his face when he greeted me, and he began at once to state his grievance. "That article you wrote about me being a reformed sport has injured me seriously. It has about destroyed my reputation as a citizen, and has done more than that, for it has caused me actual financial loss." Of course, I felt sorry and asked for particulars.

"It's this way," said he, "I have been in the habit of stopping over at a little town in East Texas and whenever I hit the town, the sheriff, the judge and a few of the leading citizens would get busy and organize a 'little game' for my entertainment. That game was always to be depended on to increase my funds from $12 to $20 and I looked for it regularly. The other day I hit that town, and while they all seemed glad enough to see me, not one of them said a word about the 'little game.' I did not understand it until the next day when someone told me about that article in the *Chronicle*. It seems the paper beat me to the place, and my friends were afraid to sit in with me after reading what you wrote."

"I have not seen the article yet," said he, "but it must have been awful, for I heard of it all over Texas. Everywhere I have been people have asked me about it."

Then his manner changed, and nudging me in the ribs he said, "Tell them about Farmer Bill, about Old Fish and about Weston, and if that don't catch them I will eat my head." He was referring to three distinguished citizens of Texas, New Mexico and Arizona who flourished in the early seventies and whose doings furnished Frank with some of his best stories.

One evening Frank and I were sitting on the gallery of the Surf Bathing House in Galveston when I asked him if gambling paid. He thought some time before he answered and then said:

"That's a hard question, for it has several sides to it and can be answered properly only after knowing which side of the table your man sits on if it's a bank game or how your man plays his hand if it's short cards. Offhand I would say that gambling does not pay, and yet I see no reason why a square man running a square game can't make good. He has all the advantage of making the other fellow do the guessing and to that must be added the legitimate percentage in favor of the bank. A sport like that who has a good game, has as sure a thing as a national bank, and if he sticks to business and does not go against some other sport's game, he is bound to get rich.

"The best poker player I ever knew was a fellow named Weston. He was a genius and could put the value on a set of threes, two pair or a bobtail quicker than any man I ever came across. It was an education to watch his play. He had real scientific poker sense and he won all the time. He wins at poker, but he can't keep away from faro bank and that game gets all his winnings. Of course, everybody has an explanation of how he wins all the time. They know his play is straight, for they watch him too closely for there to be any crooked work. They charge it up to luck and predict that it will change and run against him the same as it does with everybody else. But it doesn't and he continues to win. An old fellow named Wagner has a theory that becomes very popular. It is that Weston is a mind-reader and that when he is ruminating over his cards he is reviewing the minds of the gents who are sitting in with him to find out what cards they hold. If he has kings up and finds aces in some gent's hand he goes to the discard, but if he finds his hand is the best he raises them out of their boots. Wagner cinches his theory by pointing out that when Weston goes against faro bank the box ain't got any mind to read and that Weston stands to lose and loses the same as anybody else.

"Finally it gets so that nobody will sit in the game with Weston. But he must play poker and he gets to going against the public poker games, where one man does all the dealing and anybody can sit in who has the price of a stack of chips. His luck, or mind-reading, follows him there and he continues to win. He totes off a wad every night. Finally the fellows who were running the games got tired of it and concluded to put up a job on him. I had nothing to do with it, but they let me in to see the fun. The plan was to ring in a cold deck, give out four or five stiff hands and give Weston the next to the best one. When they mentioned it to me I suggested that Weston might not stand for a flimflam and as he always toted a gun there might be trouble. They told me they were on to that and had provided against trouble by giving Donovan, a big Irishman, who acted as bouncer, a sawed off billiard cue and telling him to stand behind Weston's chair and if he reached for a gun to pacify him with the club.

"That night Weston took his seat and placed a big roll of bills by the side of the chips he bought. The game opened and dragged along with no plays of any interest for some time. Then I saw Happy Jack shuffle the cards pretty fast, put them down like he was going to cut them and pick up a deck one of the house men had slipped near him, and I knew the play was on.

"Jack dealt out the hands and almost before he got through, a little shoemaker, who was playing a five-dollar stack, opened the pot. A butcher, who is next to the shoemaker, raises and the next man, who is a booster, tilts her again. The next man just comes in. The play then reaches Weston. He comes in and boosts her a fifty-dollar bill. The next man hesitates a long time and finally drops out. The next one, who is a booster, comes back at Weston with a hundred-dollar bill, only after looking up at Jack first. The shoemaker who had opened the pot shoved in what chips he had left and claimed a show for his money. The butcher quit. Then the first booster raised her $200 and the man between him and Weston quits reluctantly. This brings the play back to

Weston. He ruminates, as usual, for some time and then throws his whole bundle into the pot. Jack asks what is in her and Weston counts out four 100 and two 500-dollar bills. The last booster has only $300, but he shoves that in and claims a show for it.

"I saw one of the house men slip the first booster a big roll, and I know that Weston saw it too. There's a big fuss about how much money the booster who wants a showdown has in the pot, and Weston pretends to take a heap of interest in what is going on at his left, though I see he is watching the right, too, and his letting the house man in on the play that way does not look very good for the house to me. Still I know the hands are fixed and I construe it that Weston has a stiff hand he is willing to back on general principles, that he can't read the minds of the boosters because they are too excited, and that he is going on pure poker judgment; though I know, of course, that he is all wrong.

"When the dispute is settled the first booster nearly breaks his arm getting his wad in and Weston is called for the whole pot. Then cards are drawn. Everybody takes one card except the shoemaker, who takes two, and Weston, who stands pat. All the money is up, so its a showdown all 'round. Donovan draws up so as to be in easy reach of Weston with his club, and everybody leans over to look at the hands. Then the two house men nearly faint and Jack turns green, for Weston shows down four aces and rakes in the pot.

"Yes sir, justice had miscarried. Jack had made a fatal mistake and had given Weston the hand intended for the booster, who showed down four kings. The house is broke. The two house men look at me and I look at them. I want to laugh, but I don't do it till I get outside. Jack is scared nearly to death. Everybody looks foolish, but the worst looking man in the crowd is Donovan, who is trying to hide his club. Next day the story gets out and old Wagner's theory about mind-reading falls flat. The chaps who back the luck argument win out easy."

★ ★ ★

A FAMOUS DEER HUNT

In the good old days of the seventies, there was a much more intimate association between traveling salesmen and the citizens of the small cities and towns than exists now. At that time every drummer who traveled in this territory was as well known to everybody as the residents of the towns, and met with both a personal and professional welcome wherever he went. I suspect there is something of the kind prevalent today, but it is not so widespread as it was then. Salesmen have become more keenly alert to the business side of their calling and attach less importance to its social side, while the small towns have become more dignified and are striving to put on city airs.

The drummer who could tell the best and latest stories or work off a good practical joke was very popular everywhere, while the citizen who worked off anything good on a drummer became famous at once and was the talk of the whole country.

There was one well known drummer famous for his practical jokes and equally famous for his ability to dodge every trap set for him. From Houston to San Antonio there was not a practical joker who did not lie awake at night trying to devise some scheme to catch that fellow. He was finally landed, or rather he landed himself, by taking seriously a joke made by Colonel McCarthy of Eagle Lake. The colonel was a great sportsman and spent his time hunting and fishing. It was hard to say whether he was the king fisher or the king hunter, he was so good at both. He rarely went hunting that he did not come home with a fine deer or other big game, while his friends used to say that he could actually catch fish on dry land where there were no fish.

His constant and never-failing success as a hunter excited suspicion that he had some secret charm or something of that sort which gave him an advantage over the ordinary hunter. One day the colonel drove into town in his hunting wagon with two large bucks prominently displayed. Just as he passed the depot the train arrived and our drummer got off. He was delighted to see such fine game and asked a thousand questions about how and where the colonel had killed them. The colonel made no secret of where he had killed them, but he was less communicative about how he had done it. The drummer insisted on knowing, so, finally, the colonel, never dreaming that he would be taken so seriously, agreed to tell him, provided he would never reveal it to anyone.

"If it got out," said the colonel, "there would be no deer left, for it is so simple that even the boys can work it, and the deer would be exterminated." The drummer swore by everything holy, and unholy, too, that he would never tell, so the colonel gave him the great secret.

"You must know," said he, "that deer have more curiosity than any of the wild animals. They will run away from anything that scares them, but if there is anything mysterious about it they will come back to investigate. Now, I get my deer by taking advantage of that peculiarity they have. I drive a very gentle horse, as you know, one that will stand and keep quiet no matter where I leave him. I go out on the prairie and when I see deer I drive up as close as I can, then sit perfectly still until they go to feeding again if they have noticed me. Then I slip out, get behind the wagon and pull off every stitch of clothes I have on. I get down on my all-fours and back up to the deer. Never go head first. The deer will recognize you at once and light out. Be careful not to show your head at all. Take plenty of time, move slowly, and you will be surprised to find how close you can back up on a herd of deer."

Now all that sounded right to the drummer. He had often heard of the curiosity of deer and the colonel's plan was very much in line with other plans of which he had heard. He said nothing to the colonel about it but he made up his mind to try his hand at the new scheme the very next day. He hired a two-horse rig from the stable, got his gun and slipped off all alone before daylight the next morning. About six miles out he discovered a bunch of deer. He followed directions to the letter, and though the deer gave no indications of having seen him, he waited some time before getting out of the wagon to strip himself. Finally he got out, went behind the wagon and was soon in the condition that he was when he entered the world.

The next thing he did, after carefully placing his clothes in the wagon, was to get down and begin backing on the deer who were almost a mile away. He had a tough time of it with hard clods and tough pieces of grass, but he was so excited and elated at the idea of killing a deer that he did not mind the hardships. He crawled and crawled, or rather he backed and backed for a long time, keeping the general direction of the deer by guesswork. Finally he ventured to take a peep. The deer were gone. He took a good look and could see them nowhere. Then he looked back to the place he had left the wagon, but could see no wagon either. Then it dawned on him that the deer had seen him and had left for parts unknown and that the horses not seeing him had left for home and had taken every stitch of his clothes with them.

There he was, six miles from home, as naked as a picked bird and no way to get home without creating a riot, except by waiting until it got dark.

The horses trotted quietly back to Eagle Lake and went to their stable. When the drummer's clothes were found in the wagon the people, naturally, supposed that he had gone in bathing and been drowned. Searching parties organized and soon the whole town turned out searching for the dead man. They searched the prairie, dragged the ponds and searched the river. The drummer, who knew nothing about what they were after, saw them and took good care that they should not see him, for every time they started in his direction he hid himself. That continued all day and towards night the search was abandoned and the people returned home. They mourned for the drummer as for one dead. About midnight they heard shrieks coming from the back of the hotel and on rushing there found a half crazy negro stable boy who swore that he had seen a ghost. Investigation resulted in finding a very naked and half-dead drummer hiding in the horse lot. He had attempted to get into the back door of the hotel but unfortunately ran across the stable boy. In a few minutes the story was all over town and the drummer left town on the first freight train that passed without waiting to kill Colonel McCarthy as he had sworn to do more than a hundred times that day.

★ ★ ★

HOW THEY BEAT FARO

If Captain John Steel, Jim Martin, Jack Martin or any of the old-time sports could come back to life and see their former gambling "palaces" being used today as moving picture places, shoe shops and for other unworthy purposes, they sure would have the right to mourn over the degeneracy of modern Houston. In "the good old days" gambling was wide open, and while enough deference was paid to appearances to keep the halls on the second floors of the buildings, everybody knew what was going on and access was very easy and unobstructed.

It is true that every time the grand jury met, the keepers of the places were indicted, pleaded guilty and paid a fixed fine, which was looked upon as a kind of tax and therefore was considered perfectly proper, even by the proprietors themselves. Occasionally a grand jury would get too inquisitive and get after a bunch of the players and then there was sure enough trouble. I remember an occasion of that kind when a number of very prominent lawyers, doctors and businessmen were indicted for indulging in poker. Of course they did not want to appear in court and at the same time they did not want to pay a heavy fine. They clubbed together and employed Colonel Manley to defend them and, selecting the man in whose room they had played, they placed him on trial, all agreeing to abide by the decision in his case. I forget the details of the trial, but I remember that Colonel Manley won the case, on the ground that there was a bed in the room and that a bedroom was not a public place in the meaning of the law, which he read.

I just happened to think of that case and jotted it down here, for I did not intend to write about the moral or legal aspect of gambling. Perhaps the best known gambling saloon in Houston was the old Iron Clad, so named because its second story was covered with sheet iron, which was above Gregory's saloon on the corner of Congress and Main, where Krupp & Tuffly's nice store now is. That was a great resort and everybody who had sporting blood knew all about it. Some of the most prominent gamblers in Houston held forth there from time to time and thousands of dollars changed hands almost daily at that place.

There was a game of some kind going on all the time and the doors were never closed night or day. Some very amusing things took place there, too. One night there was a big crowd around the faro table and a big game was in progress when two men came up the stairsteps, one carrying a large sack. They were perfect strangers and no one knew who they were. They at once introduced themselves by commanding the gentlemen present to hold up their hands, backing their command with two nasty looking six-shooters. All held up their hands and while one of the intruders kept the gentlemen covered with his gun the other advanced with his sack and put the entire bankroll in it. Then he paid his attention to the guests of the house, taking all their money and jewelry. It was a clean sweep and when they got through there was not the price of a glass of beer in that crowd. Having gotten all the wealth in sight, the robber backed out of the room and went downstairs, leaving his partner to keep the crowd quiet. When he was safely out with his sack he whistled and robber No. 2 began to back out of the room. The crowd had been so taken by surprise that not a word had been spoken.

As the robber was just going down the steps a little fellow who was sitting at the end of the table said, "It's a good thing I didn't have my gun with me." The retiring robber took a step back into the room and, covering the little fellow with his pistol, asked him what he would have done if he had had his gun. "Why, I would have lost that, too, as well as my watch," was his reply.

The strange part about this performance was the fact that neither of the robbers made the least attempt to disguise himself. No one had ever seen either of them before nor has anyone ever seen either of them since. They simply came, conquered and disappeared. Probably they were the only men who ever beat that faro game.

Now of all of the superstitious people on earth, gamblers are the worst. Anything strange or unusual will get on their nerves and unfit them for any and everything. One night I saw a splendid illustration of this. Dick Fuller and I were going fishing and had gotten up about 3 o'clock to make an early start. We were near Gregory's corner and noticed that it was brilliantly lighted, so we judged that there was a good game going on. "I'll bet I can break that game up," said Dick, "and I will not go in the building either."

There had been a man killed near there a day or two before. Dick told me to hide behind the corner and watch him break it up. Then he took a seat on a big dry goods box near the corner and commenced pounding it with his heels, at the same time crying out, in a hoarse voice, "Whoa, you scoundrel! Whoa, you scoundrel!" Blang! Blang! He would hit the box and then utter that cry of distress. In a moment it sounded like a drove of mules coming down the steps and a whole gang of anxious players were on the sidewalk trying to see what the trouble was. They rushed up to Dick and asked what was the cause of all that racket. He pretended not to know what they were talking about and declared he had been sitting there for some time and had heard nothing. After looking around carefully they went upstairs again. In a little while Dick began the same performance and down they came with a rush. They found no horse kicking a buggy or wagon into kindling wood, nor could they see any horse at all. Dick expressed surprise at their action and declared that he had neither seen nor heard any horse or anything else cutting up as described. They hesitated for some time and one or two decided not to go upstairs again. Then in a few minutes all came down and went home, no doubt convinced that they had had an experience with a ghost.

Whenever I speak of gamblers and their ways I think of my friend "Frenchy." He was a gambler and was never guilty of speaking of anything in the past tense which, as everybody knows, is a habit with most gamblers. One night I was talking to Frank Le Mott about that robbery in the Iron Clad. Frenchy came up just in time to hear me say "hold-up" in connection with the story. He concluded that we were talking about that time the gambling saloon was dynamited and robbed here in Houston, so he butted in.

"Hell," said he, "that's no holdup. That's a bombshell. I am there. I am playin' bank. There's a big crowd so I can't get to the table. 'Limpy' George is in front of me and I have to reach over him to get my money down. Just as I get my bet placed hell breaks loose right behind me. I don't know what it is and I don't stay to find out. I breaks for the street and I thinks I'm the first one to get out, but when I hits the sidewalk I see Limpy George goin' up the street, 20 yards in front of me, and he ain't got no crutches, either. I tell you that bombshell shore works a miracle with Limpy's legs. He can't walk across the room without crutches before it goes off, but here he is downstairs and out in the street ahead of me with my two good legs."

If anyone will read that description over carefully they will know "Frenchy" as well as I do.

★ ★ ★

How the Rabbit Foot Worked

Professor Proctor, in one of his essays, draws attention to the fact that there is as much superstition involved in combating a superstition as there is in hanging on to it. He says that the man who holds that a ship that sails on a Friday will have a prosperous voyage is just as superstitious in one direction as the man who claims that the ship will have bad luck if it sails on a Friday. When one thinks of it Proctor is right, for both the good and the bad are problematical and each is likely to prevail. Therefore it is just as superstitious to believe in the good as in the bad, so far as the influence of Friday is concerned.

But I am not going to write about superstition from a scientific viewpoint, but am going to tell of some of the pet superstitions of some of my friends. I doubt if there are many telegraph operators except Colonel Phil Fall and Colonel D. P. Shepherd who remember little Jack Graham, the best operator and the gamest sport that ever handled a telegraph key or bet on a four-flush. Jack loved a "quiet little game" better than anything on earth and would have resigned the presidency of the Western Union had it come between him and a nice game. He was not a plunger, but loved a small game better than he loved to eat, and could always be counted on to take a hand when anything was doing.

In those days there were a number of us who had more money than sense, so we organized a small club and we had regular Saturday night games, which generally extended over until nearly daylight Monday morning. Jack was always there and among the first to get there, too. As I have said, it was a small game, and being table stakes, it was a safe game as well.

One Saturday night we had been playing for some time and Jack was having the most outrageous luck. Every hand he got he found that someone had a larger one. He had visited the "lamppost" (which in plain English means that he had gone out and floated a check or borrowed some money) two or three times and was fast losing his patience as well as his wealth. He got cranky and tried all the tricks of a poker game to change his luck. He swapped seats, turned his chair around, and did everything else he could think of. It was no use, and he continued to lose. Finally, after about the fourth visit to the "lamppost" he found he had misplaced his bag of tobacco and, searching for it through his pockets, he found a rabbit foot that he had put away and forgotten all about. You should have seen the smile that lit up his countenance when he found that foot. It restored his confidence and he was a new man at once. He came back and, taking his seat, he carefully dusted every one of his chips and then heaped them over the rabbit foot.

"Watch me do you wolves now," he said. "From this moment you are my meat."

Actually, I felt sorry to see an intelligent man give way so blindly to superstition as Jack was doing, for he showed absolute confidence in the potency of his talisman. He did not have a doubt.

Four or five hands were played with no features of interest about any of them. As a rule the opener took the pot without opposition. Finally I skinned my hand and found four eights pat. A man named Bright just ahead of me opened the pot and I simply trailed. When it reached Jack he came in and tilted the opener modestly. One other man came in, but merely stood Jack's raise. Bright stood the raise without tilting it and I "saw" Jack and doubled the pot as a raise. I was so certain of the pot that I did not want to scare anybody out. Jack saw my raise, but went no further; the man next to him dropped out, but Bright played, thus leaving three of us in the game. On the draw Bright took two cards, I took one; to our great surprise Jack took three, showing that he had only one pair.

Without looking at his draw, Bright threw a blue chip in the pot. I simply saw Bright's bet, but when it came to Jack he tilted the pot away up yonder.

I was certain that Bright had opened on a set of, threes and I was praying for him to catch a pair and make a full house, but he evidently did not, for he hesitated a long time about calling Jack's bet. The pot was now large enough for me to take an interest in it, and so I played my hand. I saw all that was in the pot and gave it a substantial boost. Jack instantly sized up my chips and then set in a stack more. I felt certain that Jack had come in on kings or aces and had caught his third man. Bright threw down his openers, three sixes, and quit. The play was now up to me. I knew the pot was mine and I hated to beat Jack further, but I saw a chance to beat him and at the same time teach him a lesson about the folly of depending on superstition in a poker game.

I looked at him and said, "Jack, you are in bad luck, and I hate to pound a loser, but I am going to teach you a lesson and impoverish you at the same time. I tap you," saying which I shoved all my chips into the pot. Jack liked to have broken his arm getting his chips in, but he said nothing.

"Now, Jack," I said, "I had you beaten all the way through, and I would not have bankrupted you except that I saw a chance to teach you a good lesson about the folly of playing poker with a rabbit foot. I had these four eights all the time." Saying this, I spread my hand out on the table and reached for the pot.

"Hold on there," said Jack. Then, without showing his hand he reached over and carefully inspected each of my eights. "Yes, you've got 'em," he said, "but why don't you stay out until you get something better?" He then laid down four jacks and raked in the pot. He had stayed on two jacks and had caught the other two on the draw.

Now I hate to confess it, but nevertheless it is true, that when the game broke up I tried to buy that rabbit foot from Jack. Instead of converting Jack he had converted me. It has been a long, long time since I played cards of any kind, but I admit that if I were going to get in a game tonight I would feel far more comfortable if I took a rabbit foot along than if I went without one, and I sure would let the fellow alone who had one in front of him.

★ ★ ★

POKER SUPERSTITIONS

People laugh at the negroes for being superstitious, and I suppose when all the returns are in they are justified in doing so. However, if the most superstitious and ignorant negro can beat the average well-educated white man who plays poker, then I am willing to quit.

I remember years ago, when I was young and giddy, sittin' in with a lot of professional men. There was one, a young doctor, one of the honor graduates, who had tough luck from the start. First he blamed his seat. Then he discovered that the man next to him had his foot on his chair. Then he located his hoodoo in the coat; then in his vest; then in the nice pink shirt he was wearing. One by one he discarded these garments, but his bad luck continued. Just as he was about to go further in his disrobing, his luck changed and he began to win.

"I knew it was that shirt," said he, and, that being the last garment he had taken off, he promptly ordered the negro boy who was waiting on us to put it in the stove and burn it up.

Some very funny things result from the active display of poker superstitions, as everyone with the least experience knows. I remember once in Galveston, before the electric cars were established and the old horse and mule motive power was used, I was in the car with a very distinguished newspaperman, who was a bit of a sport.

There was no conductor, and the driver rang up the fares as they were deposited in the box by the passenger. There were two cords extending the length of the car, one to notify the driver when a passenger wished to get off and the other to register the fares.

We were in the midst of an interesting conversation when the distinguished journalist leaped to his feet, grabbed the rope and began a series of most vigorous jerks, shouting at the same time for the driver to stop. In his excitement he got hold of the wrong rope and before the wild-eyed driver could get to him and release the rope from hand he had rung up about $14 worth of fares against the driver. I looked out ahead and saw a funeral passing down the intersecting street just of us.

"Why, that fellow liked to ruin me," he said to me. "He was going to pull us right through that funeral. I had that to happen to me once and I never held a thing for six months."

He was quiet now that the great disaster had been averted, but the driver was gone "off his nut" completely when he looked at the register and recognized that he was a financial wreck unless my friend paid for all those fares he had registered. I am convinced that he would have deserted the car right there in the street and never gone back to the barn again if my friend had not volunteered to go with him to Colonel Sinclair, the president of the company, and explain matters to him. The driver readily agreed to that arrangement and since the returns had been tampered with and the box stuffed, it gave him a splendid chance to fix the genuine figures at any point he pleased, which no doubt he did to his own personal advantage.

Another friend of mine, who is an educated man and who absolutely ridicules negro superstition, will immediately abandon any business enterprise he may be engaged in and will not resume it again that day if he meets a cross-eyed woman face to face. He claims that such a chance meeting is absolutely fatal and that every particle of luck abandons him right then and there.

The strangest part of the matter is that not one of the superstitious men has the slightest respect for the pet superstition of any of the others. Each fellow will ridicule every other superstition except his own. He feels that he has the only genuine article.

Anyone who has "fooled with cards" knows that there is such a thing as luck, in spite of the fact that it can be demonstrated mathematically that there is no such thing. With mathematicians chance does not exist. For instance, when a perfectly fair dice has been thrown and has shown "six," or anything else, for four times hand running, it will be mighty hard to keep a gambler from betting odds that the number will not show up again. I mean by odds more than the legitimate odds of 5 to 1.

There are six sides to a dice, therefore there is one chance in six of the same number showing again, and yet any gambler will be willing to give greater odds than that after the number has shown even twice consecutively. As a matter of fact, all the throws that have been made have not the least influence on those to follow, so the odds remain as they were at the be ginning, 5 to 1.

Now the mathematicians can prove all that, but what I would like for them to prove is that there is no good or bad luck when a fellow one night makes every hand he draws to and the next night can't hold a thing and loses every time he backs his hand. If it is not luck, what is it? Is it that great mystery the mathematicians have recently evolved called the fourth dimension, by which they can explain things that have no existence and have a man in jail and outside of it at the same time?

★ ★ ★

A LIVELY ELECTION

I hear that Houston is going to have an election next summer and that already the pot is beginning to boil. It may boil until it runs over, but it can never reach one-tenth the heat and animation that characterized our elections in Reconstruction days. Those were the hot times, sure enough, and no mistake about it. There was no Australian ballot, no registration, nor any of the modern devices to check an unlimited exercise of the franchise. A fellow could vote as many times as he had nerve to do so, and if he took care to vote "right" when the right crowd was around he could get away with it.

About the most strenuous election that was ever pulled off in those strenuous days was the one held in 1873 or 1874, I forget the exact date. Mr. William R. Baker was the Democratic nominee for the State Senate, and Colonel John T. Brady was supported by the Republicans, though avowedly running as an independent. Early in the action it became evident that the candidates who could get the most outside voters here would carry the day. The Republicans sent out their agents with dragnets and secured a large number of negroes from Fort Bend, Brazoria and adjoining counties. Some of these came in a week or two before election day and hung around attending torchlight processions and political meetings, but the bulk of the negroes were held in reserve to show up the day before and on election day.

The Democrats were apparently snowed under, for they gave no indication of doing anything to overcome the black overflow. It looked blue for "Billy" Baker and he apparently had no more chance than a snowball in that unmentionable place. The night before election the Democrats had a torchlight procession and public speaking, but that was done apparently more for appearance than anything else.

But Billy Baker, who was president of the Houston & Texas Central Railroad, had a card up his sleeve that was worth all those the Republicans were playing so openly. On the morning of the election trains began to arrive at the Central Depot from stations as far north as Denison, and every train had a full load of section men and other railroad employees who had come to

Houston to vote for "the boss." Every one claimed Houston as his home and every one voted for Baker, not once but as many times and under as many names as he could. Baker was elected, of course, but even with the enthusiastic support of the Irish brigade he was elected by the skin of his teeth. His majority was so small that it was scarcely worth the name. It would be a most difficult task for any mathematician to figure out just what Brady's majority would have been if Mr. Baker had not thought of his Irishmen.

He could not have secured a better following or one more determined to assert their "rights" than those Irishmen. They could not be browbeaten or intimidated, and took pleasure in bulldozing the negro voters, who showed good sense by keeping out of their way as much as possible. That was one day and one election on which Uncle Dick Westcott was in his element and perfectly happy. He had things going his way from start to finish. It took several days to get the imported Irish voters out of town. There were special trains that left on schedule time to take them back, but they stayed to enjoy the fruits of their victory, and they had a good time, too.

The next time Mr. Baker forgot to bring the Irish brigade, or thought he could win without them, and he got left. Colonel Brady beat him, but by only a small majority, as the negro vote also was rather lacking and lukewarm, owing to the vigilance of the white voters. The sheriff was after some of the leaders for various crimes, and they were afraid to show up in Houston.

I know all such statements as these sound queer to the present generation of voters, but they must remember that it was a case of fighting the devil with fire, and a death struggle for white supremacy. The most honorable men recognized that it was right to do any and everything short of actual murder to carry their point and they did not hesitate to do it.

Major Lowe used to tell of an election in Louisiana, when the Democratic manager telegraphed to an eminent lawyer and fine gentleman who lived in an out-of-the-way precinct, telling him he must send in returns showing 450 Democratic majority. A day or two after, he got a letter in which the gentleman informed the manager that he had done what he had been told to do, but that it was a rather difficult task, as there were only thirty-five votes in that precinct.

Now it must not be forgotten that the Republicans were doing exactly the same things and it was simply a question of who could do the most of it.

★ ★ ★

NEGRO
CRAPSHOOTERS

A fact that demands investigation and explanation at the hands of the scientists is the mortal terror inspired in the breast of the negro crapshooter by the appearance of a policeman. If there was a death penalty attached to crapshooting there might be a possible explanation, but there is only a light fine and a possible detention in the lockup for a few hours. Yet in spite of all this when a party of negroes are caught "rollin' the bones" by the police, there is nothing short of the indestructible being in their way that is going to keep them from trying to get away. They will take the most marvelous chances, involving loss of life and limb, and they think no more of leaping out of a third story window than they do of going out of a convenient door on the first floor.

It is just as impossible to keep a negro from playing craps as it is to keep a railroad sectionhand from getting drunk on payday. They will play in spite of everything or anything and no one can stop them. Some years ago the police of San Antonio, according to a story told me by an ex-policeman, made a rather neat thing out of the negro gamblers.

On Saturday evenings the negroes would seek secluded places along the river banks in order to indulge in their favorite pastime. The policeman would mark these places down and conceal himself nearby, waiting until the game became exciting. Then, at the critical moment, when the negroes had their money all spread out on the ground, he would suddenly show himself, fire his pistol in the air and, within but a moment, he would be left absolutely alone in possession of the field. He told me he had frequently picked up fourteen or fifteen dollars in dimes, quarters and larger coins abandoned by the negroes when they made their speedy exit. Of course he made no effort to stop any of them, for the sooner they got out of sight the better pleased he was.

It really seems that it needs the "rattle of the bones" to bring out the queer side of the negro's nature. They will do the most absurd and senseless things imaginable when under the exciting influence of gambling. Not long ago I was talking with Horace Baker, the big deputy sheriff who has had long experience with negroes, as everybody knows, and he told me an amusing story.

"I was coming up town and when I got to a point below Harrisburg, not far from the bayou, a black negro who knew me came out in the road and told me a tale of woe. You know we catch the negro crapshooters nine times out of ten through some negro squealing. This was one of the times, for the negro told me that a gang of negroes was down on the bank of the bayou playing craps and that they had got him in the game and robbed him of all his wife's money. I saw through the thing at once. He had lost his money and wanted me to pinch the crowd and get it back for him.

"That's the game. So long as they win the game is fair and the money belongs to them, but when they lose the game is crooked and the money, they say, was their wives. I got down off my horse and followed him. When we got near enough, I hid behind a clump of bushes and watched them for a while. There were six playing and one little, black, bullet-headed fellow was looking on. He was taking no part in the game, and the negro who had stopped me told me the little fellow had not played at all. After watching them for a little while I stood up and started toward them. Then the fun commenced.

"Two of them had their backs to me, but one of the others saw me and gave the alarm. The two on my side did not even look around but made a dive forward, knocking over everything and everybody in front of them and broke down the bayou bank like quarterhorses. The three that were knocked down got up and scattered, but the fourth one, a big negro with an old-fashioned wooden leg like a broomstick, jumped off the high bank and landed on a pile of clay the dredgeboat had scooped out of the bayou. When he came down, instead of landing on his good leg, he landed on his peg. That went into the clay and anchored him as firmly as a piledriver could have anchored a post. I knew I had him, so paid no further attention to him.

"Now, you would suppose that the little bullet-headed negro, who had been merely looking on and who had not been gambling at all, would have made no effort to escape, but he was the most frightened of all of them. When he caught sight of me, he let out a yell like a frightened woman and tore down the bank and plunged in the bayou. I saw I could not get him and as I did not want him particularly, I turned my attention to the others. I heard the anchored negro puffing and blowing and on looking down I found he was busy trying to unstrap his wooden leg, so he could leave it there and roll off into the bayou. He was determined to get away, so I thought I had best take him in charge. I crawled down to where he was anchored and when I got there I took a look for the negro who had jumped in the bayou. I knew he had not had time to swim halfway over the bayou, yet he was nowhere in sight. I could see along the bank on my side, but there was not a sign of him. Finally I concluded he had gone under and been drowned.

"I got my one-legged chap out and took him up the bank and was about to leave him, when I noticed a good-sized piece of plank floating along in the bayou and something peculiar about it attracted my attention. I watched it closely and then thought I could see a kind of bump at one end. I walked down the bank where I could get a better view and then I saw what it was. The negro had sunk his whole body, leaving only his mouth and nose sticking slightly out of the water and was floating along quietly with the board, waiting for me to leave. I told my one-legged man that I thought there was a turtle on the board and that I was going to kill it. I said that to scare the negro, but since his ears were under water he did not hear me. Then I took careful aim at the far end of the board and cut down with my six-shooter. No harpooned whale or sea monster ever cut up worse than that negro did. He fairly rose out of the water, yelling like a crazy man. It scared me badly, for I thought that I had hit him and I would not have done that for anything.

"He commenced yelling, 'I give up, Mr. Baker! I give up, Mr. Baker!' I ordered him to come to shore and was much relieved to find that he was unharmed. I took the two to Harrisburg and turned them over to the constable there, and came on to town. I was more amused than proud for all I had done was to capture a one-legged negro who actually caught himself by bogging down, and capture a negro who had done nothing to be captured for."

★ ★ ★
UNCLE DAN AND UNCLE DICK

When the Republicans and scalawags were manipulating the ballots and ballot boxes in the early 70s, they little dreamed that they were giving object lessons and introducing methods that were later to be used with telling effect against themselves. And that is just exactly what they were doing, and wherever the Democrats secured a foothold they took pains to insure against it falling into Republican hands again by doing a little manipulating themselves. Occasionally it was necessary to overcome a Republican majority by such crude and violent methods as carrying off a ballot box by stealth or force, thus destroying the vote of an entire precinct which was known to be largely Republican and which held the balance of power in the election.

Such things did occur, however, but the gentlemanly and clean way was to stuff the ballot box by removing the genuine ballots and substituting others. The present generation would hold up their hands in genuine horror if such a thing were proposed now and would cry out that tampering with the purity of the ballot box is striking at the very root of our government. That is eminently correct, too, for this day, but it must be borne in mind that at that day the ballot box had little or no purity about it and that the form of government the carpetbaggers and scalawags were trying to establish had such roots that it became the patriotic duty of every lover of his country to destroy them.

It may have been a technical and nominally legal offense to suppress or destroy the ballots, but the circumstances under which they were cast and the conditions they aimed to perpetuate made it a crime against good government not to destroy them. That is the way the white people felt then and I don't think there is one still living who passed through those trying days who doesn't feel something of pride in having taken part in the good work.

Occasionally funny things would occur when, for instance, an election was contested and it became necessary to open the boxes and recount the votes. Then it was often found that some loud-mouthed Democrat had voted for "the other fellow," which fact, no doubt, inspired "Uncle Dick" Westcott to compile his famous list known as his " ———— Book."

After the Democrats had succeeded in getting control of affairs in Harris County they had hard work in holding it, there being so many white Republicans and negroes here that every Democratic vote was needed, hence any backsliding or treason was looked upon with scorn and contempt. Uncle Dick Westcott was a Democrat at whose feet Thomas Jefferson and Andrew Jackson might have sat. He held Democracy far above religion or anything else. He was one of the most remarkable men I ever knew and was the first political boss Harris County ever had. His business was different from that of the modern "boss." He did not try to dictate to the voters who should be elected to office except in rare cases, when he was personally interested in a would-be candidate, but he made it his business to see that every Democratic voter did his duty and also to see that all delinquents were held up to scorn.

Now, early in the fight Uncle Dick had been elected county clerk and since all the ballot boxes were placed in his keeping after an election, he had a sure way of finding out just how every vote had been cast. If he had suspicion that Smith had not voted right, he would open the ballot from Smith's ward or precinct and set all doubt aside by looking at Smith's ballot. Of course, he never boasted of doing this and nobody was able to prove that he did it, but he knew too many things about the ballots and of how this man and that man had scratched the ticket to admit to any other explanation as to the source of his information. About the first intimation that he had real and genuine inside information about the ballots was given soon after an election in which Uncle Dick had been re-elected over quite a popular Republican opponent. A very prominent and well-known lawyer met Uncle Dick and congratulated him on his election.

"If you are so glad I am elected, why were you not glad enough before the election to vote for me and why did you vote against me?" he asked.

The lawyer was dumbfounded and did not know what to say. He mumbled something and left. He had a moment before been telling some gentleman what a fine official and man Uncle Dick was, but after his interview with Uncle Dick he was heard to say, "That old rascal has been opening the ballot boxes and should be in the penitentiary instead of in the county clerk's office."

Occasionally Uncle Dick allowed his zeal to get away with his judgment, and, as the gamblers say, he overplayed his hand. A striking and well remembered instance of that was when Judge John Kerlicks was a candidate for some county office against the late Captain A. K. Taylor. The returns, I believe, showed the election of Kerlicks, but the result was so close that Taylor contested the election and brought suit in the District Court. When the case came up for trial the first box opened was that from Westcott precinct, Uncle Dick's home box. There were more ballots found than there were votes out that way, and there was such evidence that the ballots had been manipulated that the whole vote from that precinct was thrown out, thus leaving a sure majority for Captain Taylor, who was given the office. While all the Democrats regretted the result, for they wanted to see John Kerlicks elected, yet they realized that the case was not so bad as it might have been, for though Captain Taylor was a Republican he was a clean man and had never affiliated with the scalawag Republicans and carpetbaggers. He made a good official and to the day of his death was one of the most honored and reputable citizens of Houston.

Uncle Dick Westcott and Uncle Dan McGary were two of the most remarkable characters who ever lived in Houston. Uncle Dan owned and edited the *Age*, and whenever an election was to be pulled off Uncle Dick helped him with his editorial work. Either one was a hot wire and made little use of parliamentary language when discussing a Republican candidate or his adherents, so when the two put their heads together and produced an article it was something long to be remembered. They said just what they thought and as it was generally understood that they willingly held themselves personally responsible for any and all of their utterances no one had cause to complain.

Uncle Dan was particularly bitter, for he had had experience. He had tried to edit a Democratic paper in Brenham but had made it so hot that the Republican voters burned down his office and the Republican officials placed him in jail where he remained for some time. When he got out of jail he came to Houston and started the *Age*. He and Uncle Dick joined hands and, though as a rule the *Age* was practically the same paper day after day with Uncle Dan using the same matter all the time, when an election was coming on all that was changed and the *Age* became one of the liveliest sheets imaginable. Both these old war horses have long since gone to their reward. Peace to their ashes!

★ ★ ★

TWO REMARKABLE HORSE RACES

It is quite evident, to me at least, that many of the other old Houstonians are beginning to look on me as a kind of historian since I have had the pleasure of writing a few articles for the *Chronicle*, recalling some of my memories of the past. My daily experience with these old Houstonians is amusing and at times very amusing. I seem to have struck a chord which has aroused their latent memories and I am every day asked about men and events that lived and occurred long before I was born. Then, too, there are the critics. These I always welcome, for, being conscious of the fact that I am not infallible, I am desirous of being corrected whenever in error. It is amusing, though, to hear some of the corrections. For instance, I met one of my old-time friends the other day. "I see, old man, your memory is bad," he said. "You get the general drift alright, but I see breaks here and there." I owned up to my fallibility and asked for particulars.

"Well," he said, "I noticed the other day you said something about a thing happening on Saturday, when I know it happened on a Thursday." I promptly admitted the probability of his being right, though I had reason to know that he was wrong. I asked for other "bad breaks" I had made.

"Well, you made one that made me nearly fall out of my chair when I saw it," said he. "You spoke of old man Jack Kennedy as William Kennedy when you wrote about those bombshells." I cleared myself easily on that point by telling him that I had written "Mr. Kennedy" and that probably my bad writing was responsible for the change of "Mr." to "Wm." by the printer.

Such encounters as these amuse me, but there are others that are not quite so pleasant. I don't mean to say that any of them is disagreeable, but some are rather boring. I have been approached, personally and by letter, by people who want information about early Houston on all conceivable subjects.

"When was so and so's headright located?"

"Who was the original owner of the lots where the Rice Hotel now stands?"

"Do you remember a man by the name of Jackson who came to Texas in 1836, located somewhere near Harrisburg and afterward went to Philadelphia in 1852 or '53 and died there?"

These are a few samples of the inquiries I receive nearly every day. The other day I received a call from a very pleasant old gentleman whom I had never seen before. I admit that when I heard him outside inquiring for "Old Man Young" I felt like going out and mounting him, but after he came in he was so pleasant and entertaining that I was sincerely glad he had come. He wanted information, of course, and it was about a racehorse. He wanted to know who brought a certain racehorse to Houston, cleaned up all the sports here, then went up the state and repeated the operation of skinnin' 'em up there. He knew all about the performances of the horse, but could not find out who brought him here. He explained that his question had a business rather than a sporting intent, for on the identity of the importer of the horse hinged the ownership of a valuable tract of land either in or near Houston.

I was sorry that I could not help him out, and told him so. After he had gone I got to thinking of old-time horsemen and racehorses I had known. I found that my acquaintance in that line had been very limited and that I could recall but two instances of where horse races had left any impression at all on my mind, and in both of these it was the results rather than the races themselves that I remembered. In both the results were disastrous to the too-zealous action of the admirers or owners of the horses.

In 1870, and for a few years after, the Texas State Fair was held in Houston. The first was over on the north side of the bayou in Macatee's warehouse. The next year the association purchased the old Hadley place out on Main Street, known for years after as the Fairgrounds. A racing association was organized and everything was done to encourage the raising of fine horses, stock, etc. There was a good race course laid out and some good races were pulled off every year. There was one fine horse named after Col. Scott Anderson of Eagle Lake. I am not certain, but I believe Col. Anderson actually owned this horse. On one point I am certain—Scott Anderson was one of the fleetest and best horses to ever appear on a Texas track.

As the boys say, he could hold one hand behind his back and whip any horse he ever came in competition with. Of course, when Scott Anderson showed up in a race his backers had to give big odds to get any bets at all against their favorite. One of the greatest admirers and strongest backers of Scott Anderson on any and all occasions was a man named Gregory, who owned a saloon on the southwest corner of Main Street and Congress Avenue. Gregory was a good old sport and gambler, but at times he was rather too emotional and allowed his enthusiasm to run away with him.

In one such instance, it was toward the close of the racing week, and a big crowd was out to witness the coming event, a race with half a dozen good and well-known horses entered, among them the famous Scott Anderson. The horses got away in a bunch, but Scott Anderson soon took the lead. As he pulled out from the bunch Gregory began waving a handful of bills over his head, shouting, "One hundred to twenty-five that Scott Anderson wins the race!"

There were no takers, for Scott Anderson was plainly increasing the distance between himself and his competitors, and no one cared to throw away money by betting against him.

"Two hundred to twenty-five!"

"Three hundred to twenty-five!"

"Four hundred to twenty-five!" shouted Gregory.

By this time Scott Anderson's lead was so great that even a blind man could see that he had the race grabbed. But Gregory was so anxious to get a bet that he raised his odds.

"Six hundred to twenty-five!" he shouted.

"That's a good bet if I lose it," said Rush Hutchins, who was more entertained by Gregory's capers than he was by the race. "Here Gregory, put up your money. I take your bet," he said.

Rush produced $25, which Gregory quickly covered with $600, and the whole lot was handed over to a stakeholder. The money had scarcely been placed when Scott Anderson stumbled and fell, injuring his leg so badly that he was out of the race at once. But Gregory was too good a sport to kick. He accepted his loss quite gracefully and if he ever kicked himself for allowing his enthusiasm to get away with him, he did it privately, when no one was looking.

Now, the other races I remember had similar results, but from a different cause. These were races being held out beyond Westheimer's place up on Buffalo Bayou. The city has extended away out there, but in those days it was clear out in the country. A man named Copping, who, with his brother, owned a saloon on Main Street, was considerable of a sport. His name was Tom, though I forget his brother's name. Tom was the proud owner of a bony-looking gray horse, which he swore could outpace anything that ever came from Pacerville.

There was good reason for his faith in his horse, for the old gray beat anything he went against. Tom was not only willing but anxious to pit him against anything that showed up. He would go against running horses, pacing horses, trotting horses and, I have no doubt had such things existed at that time, he would have pitted him against automobiles and motorcycles. His faith in his old gray was unbounded.

One day there were some races out at Westheimer's and Tom was there with his gray. He could not get a race against his horse, so he gave an exhibition spin around the track. The races were over and everybody was starting to town. There were wagons, carts, omnibuses, carriages and men on horseback.

Every mode of conveyance of that day was represented. Tom was feeling good, and he called to one of his friends, who was in a buggy drawn by a good horse, and offered to bet him $300 to $50 that he could give him a half a mile start and beat him to his (Tom's) barroom on Main Street between Prairie and Preston Avenues. The other fellow hesitated a moment and then took the bet. The whole crowd stopped to see the performance.

The money was produced and a tree some distance ahead was agreed on as representing a fair half mile start. Some carriages and buggies went with Tom's opponent to see that a fair start was made, but most of the crowd remained with Tom, who sat in his sulky awaiting the signal. When the tree was reached a yell was raised and the man in the buggy put whip to his horse and started for town. Tom put whip to the gray at the same time. But then the most wonderful thing occurred.

The old gray, who to that moment had never failed to respond to Tom's call in the most proper and orthodox manner, stood straight up on his hind legs and looked over his right shoulder at Tom. Tom was too amazed to do anything. He waited until the gray resumed his normal position and then touched him up with the whip again. The gray promptly rose on his hind legs again, and this time looked at Tom over his left shoulder. That was too much, and Tom lit into him with the whip in good fashion. For ten or fifteen minutes they had it up and down all over the prairie. Finally Tom conquered, but it was too late, and when he reached his saloon he found his opponent there "settin' 'em up" to everybody in the place. Now, these are the only race horses I remember anything about, and it is quite evident that neither of them could under any circumstances be of the slightest assistance in adjusting the ownership of a tract of land.

WHISKEY, WOMEN AND SONG

★ ★ ★

FRANK LE MOTT'S ROMANCE

I know exactly how a fellow feels after he has entered blindly into a dark conspiracy and agreed to do the will of a beautiful woman for no other reason than that she was a young and beautiful woman.

That was the way Frank Le Mott of Galveston began what proved to be one of the best stories I ever heard him tell. There was quite a crowd of us out at the Breakers bathhouse at Galveston, and everybody moved closer to hear the story we knew was coming. He began…

"Two weeks ago, I had an adventure, not four blocks from this very place, that fairly took my breath away. But it started downtown and was two or three days culminating.

"Monday afternoon I was standing on the corner of Tremont and Market when one of the most beautiful and prominent ladies in the city drove by. Just as she was opposite where I was standing she bowed and smiled. I thought, of course, that she was bowing to some acquaintance behind me and took no notice of it. She drove down the street and when she returned she repeated the bow and smiled so sweetly that there was no mistaking that it was all meant for me, and in a moment I was regularly sweeping the sidewalk with my hat. The next evening the same thing was repeated and when she came back she ordered her driver to come near the curb and beckoned for me to come to her."

At this point of the story a little fellow named Smith, which was really his name, butted in. He was so excited that he could scarcely talk. "I'll bet you a thousand dollars to one I know her name," he said. "Don't be afraid, Frank, I won't give you away, but if you will come here I'll whisper it to you and you'll see I'm right." Le Mott paid no attention to Smith, but continued.

"When I got near the carriage the lady leaned out, and calling me by my name, asked me if she could trust me. You bet I told her she could, and that I would willingly die to be of service to her. She told me not to make extravagant promises, because she was going to hold me to any promise I made. Then she drove away after asking me to be at the same place the next afternoon at 5 o'clock."

Here Smith butted in again, swearing that he knew the lady and he would bet anyone present a thousand dollars and leave it to Le Mott to say if he was wrong or not. He also repeated his assurance to Le Mott that he need not fear his divulging the name. Le Mott did not notice the interruption further than to remain silent until we could shut Smith off. He went on.

"The next afternoon I was on the spot an hour ahead of time. Promptly at 5 that carriage drove up and the lady, calling me to her, managed to slip me a dainty little note, which I slipped into my pocket."

Here Smith became terribly excited and insisted on whispering the lady's name in Le Mott's ear, but we interfered and got him quiet after some trouble.

"She then drove away, after giving me a sweet smile, and I hastened to a secluded place where I could read that note. It was very short and was simply this: 'Meet me tomorrow afternoon on the boulevard near the foot of Tremont Street at as near 4 o'clock as possible.' There was no address nor signature.

"That night I could scarcely close my eyes and time passed terribly slow. The next afternoon I was again way ahead of time and walked up and down the boulevard until I almost knew every brick in it. Finally I saw her carriage drive up at the foot of Tremont and she got out and came toward me. I walked forward to meet her, but when she drew near I was completely taken off my feet, for instead of looking at me she looked past me and sailed by, as coldly as an iceberg, without ever, apparently, knowing I was on the face of the earth. She cut me dead. I felt like a fool and, turning to see what could have caused her to act that way, I found the explanation, and it made my blood run cold, too, for not fifty feet behind me was her husband, who had been following me. "

Here Smith began to swear that now he knew he was right and could call the lady's name. Le Mott looked at him reproachfully and he went on with his story.

"The lady advanced to meet her husband, but instead of the scene I expected to see they met in the most friendly way, stood chatting for a few moments and then she turned and together they walked to where the carriage was standing. When they got there he got in and, smiling at her, drove away to town. She waited until he was a few blocks away and then she came toward me, smiling and holding out both hands in the most friendly way. I admit I was mystified and could make neither heads nor tails of the whole thing, but having gone that far, I made up my mind to see the whole thing through.

"She led me up the boulevard for two or three blocks and then turned down a side street. I am not going to say where we went, but she led me to an elegant residence and taking a key from her satchel she unlocked the door and invited me in."

Here we had almost to hold Smith to keep him from whispering to Le Mott the location of that house. He knew it exactly and could, with Le Mott's permission, lead the crowd there in a few minutes.

"The house seemed absolutely vacant. We passed through a hall and entered an elegantly furnished bedroom. Here for the first time her courage seemed to desert her and she realized what she was doing. She wanted me to leave the room and house at once. She seemed so scared and anxious that she began to get me rattled, but I had no idea of giving up after having gone that far. I begged her to calm herself and tell me what she wanted me to do for her. Instead of getting quieter she began to weep and cry out against herself for having acted so imprudently with an entire stranger. 'My husband would kill me and you too,' she said, 'if he caught us here alone, and I have an idea that he suspects me and is watching.'

"All that did not make me feel any too comfortable, but to tell the truth I would have rather had dealings with the husband just then than with the hysterical woman in a strange house. Finally I got her quieted enough to sit down and talk sensibly and she was just beginning to tell me her story..."

Here Smith butted in with the declaration that he was going to name both the husband and woman, whether Le Mott liked it or not. "Wait until I finish, Smith," said Le Mott, "and *then* if you know you may tell." That was the only time he had noticed Smith at all.

"She had just begun to tell me how she feared the vengeance of her husband, when there was a terrible crash right back of me and..." Here Le Mott paused a long time and looked steadily at Smith. "And then I woke up, for a window had fallen at the head of my bed and ruined my afternoon nap."

At this unexpected conclusion of the story, Smith subsided. We were all taken in, but Smith was obliterated completely.

★ ★ ★

EARLY SHOWS IN HOUSTON

Whether the war was responsible for it or not, the fact remains that for several years after its close society was in somewhat of a chaotic condition and "most any old thing went," just so long it was not outside the law. Men of fine social standing engaged in business that they would shun today, not because there is anything radically wrong with these things, but because they are now in the hands of professional people and are not considered just the things for businessmen of commercial and social standing to engage in. To illustrate what I mean I will state that the first organized vaudeville show ever in Houston was organized and managed, not by a professional show-man, but by Ed Bremond, the son of the great railroad builder and capitalist. Just why Ed ever thought of such a thing no one knew, but he did think of it and he made a great success of it, too. That show was the "Academy of Music" and was one of the most popular places in Houston. It was located on the corner of Main and Prairie, upstairs, and was crowded every night.

"Academy" proved so great a financial success that Ed began to get the big head and spoke of himself as an "impresario." He had looked the word up in a dictionary and, liking its sound, had adopted it. There was a very large lady, inclined to what the French call *embonpoint*, who could sing "Molly Darling," "Don't You Love Me Darling?" and songs of that description in the most entrancing way. She had a complete name, of course, but all the young fellows knew her as "Miss Joe" and spoke of her in that way so often that her last name finally became lost in the shuffle. Ed was never guilty of falling into the popular way of the boys, but always referred to Miss Joe as the "Charming Cantatrice." After his show got to making lots of money he grew more ambitious and spoke of Thuse Donneland, the fiddler, and Charley Finkelman, the piano player, as "virtuosos." His chorus girls, by the same reasoning, became "artistes."

Ed had one man in his company who afterward became famous as a negro delineator. That was Milt Barlow, the creator of "Old Black Joe." The song was introduced in Houston by Barlow and he afterward became famous through that one song alone.

But I did not start out to write anything about Ed and his "Academy of Music." Mention of him is only incidental. What I wanted to say was that right after the war there were a lot of fellows in Houston who had the initiative and who had the promoter talent well-developed. They would promote anything from a cockfight to grand opera. About that time the father of a young gentleman well known in Houston died and left him a pot of ready money. The young man at once began looking around for something to promote. He tried a cock fight, with only partially satisfactory results. Then he staged a crazy, stage-struck fellow who gave one of the most outrageously ridiculous performances ever witnessed. The absurdity of the whole thing advertised it extensively and an encore was demanded by the public. I nor anyone else who witnessed it will ever forget it.

The opera house (Perkins Hall) was crowded from gallery to pit with a male audience at $1 per. From a financial point it was a grand success and before the close of the performance everybody there felt that he had his full dollar's worth. It was a one-man show. The curtain rose to slow music and the great actor entered. He was going to give a Shakespearean reading. He came on the stage in a tight-fitting union suit which fitted him as though he had been melted and poured into it. He wore high-laced shoes and had an immense sword buckled around his waist. The sword was very long and kept constantly getting between his legs. The audience howled when he came on and he, taking it for applause, attempted to bow his thanks and came near falling down. The cheers continued, but had no effect on him, for he began his recitation at once. No one could hear a word he said, but that made no difference. He spoke for several minutes and then bowed himself off the stage. The audience was absolutely wild with delight by now. Then the great actor appeared again and began another piece. That continued for half an hour, when the promoter got on the stage and announced that "Senior De Pompeno" would next give an exhibition of living statuary. A barrel was placed in the center of the stage and the actor was led forth and mounted it.

He raised his hand for silence and when he could make himself heard announced that his first production would be "Ajax Defying the Lightning." With that he threw himself back, elevated his fists and shook them at the far gallery. The audience howled with delight. Then he gave "Faith, Hope and Charity." It was all ridiculously grand. After four or five renditions he announced that he would produce his masterpiece, "The Prayer." With that he threw back his head, raised his arms and began the most strenuous efforts to run while still on the barrel. The truth was that when he threw back his head he discovered seated on a beam just above him an old negro woman armed with a big tub of water which she was to empty on him at the close of the performance. His untimely discovery of her plot unnerved Fanny, for that was her name, and in her haste to empty the tub she lost her balance and she, tub and all came crashing down on the actor. It was heart breaking to have so many things to laugh at at once, and came near choking half the audience. Of course, when he tried to run he simply kicked the barrel backward without advancing himself the least bit, so that when Fanny landed she came down fairly on top of him and the barrel. Fortunately no one was injured. That was the greatest show that was ever pulled off in Houston and was talked about for weeks afterward.

★ ★ ★

AT THE MASQUERADE BALL

I suspect that the young folks have just as good times now as we used to have, but I doubt it. "Our times" were too near perfect. The balls, dances and social gatherings now are too formal, and then, too, the people do not know each other as well as they formerly did.

Houston was then not much more than a big town. Everybody knew everybody else, and it is a fact that society was something like a great family. There were several social clubs here. Two that devoted themselves to dancing the "German." These clubs were the O. C. and the E. C. The O. C. stood for Omnibus Club and the E. C. for Economical Club. Each club had a "German" every two weeks, so that there was a "German" every week. There were similar organizations in Galveston, Austin and Waco, and as mutual invitations were exchanged there were always some popular members of outside clubs at our dances or some of ours at theirs. The Omnibus Club got its name from a rule of the club prohibiting the use of carriages and requiring the gentlemen to take the ladies to the dances in one of Baldwin's omnibuses, which made the rounds collecting the couples for the party and distributing them after the dance was over.

In addition to these two clubs was the famous Z Z Club, which gave delightful dances and balls, and the grand Purim ball given by another association. That Purim ball was the grand social event of the year, and was looked forward to with pleasurable anticipation by the young people of Houston for weeks before it occurred. It was a mask ball and always an enjoyable event.

Now, what made me think of those gay and festive times was meeting my old friend, Mr. Henry House last week. I had not seen him in years and would never have known him had he not told me who he was. When I last saw him he was a frail, bright-eyed, rather delicate young man, while today, as everybody knows, he is a rather portly, handsome and dignified business-man. I remember his rosy cheeks and slight form of years ago, for on one occasion they led to my undoing.

In the spring of 1872 or 1873 there was given one of the grandest Purim balls in the history of the association. People talked about it for weeks before it came off. A great many people from neighboring cities were invited, and when the night for the ball arrived many were here from Galveston, Austin, Waco, Dallas and from points on the San Antonio Road.

Soon after I entered the ballroom, I met Captain Conradi, who told me that he wanted me to take charge of a young lady who was visiting his family and had arrived that evening from New Braunfels. She was not in costume or mask, but he did not think that would bar her from the dancing floor, and it did not. He introduced me to her and I danced with her. She was so graceful and danced so well that half the fellows in the hall wanted to be introduced at once. I saw her program filled for the entire evening in a few moments and soon she was easily the belle of the ball.

I had reserved one or two dances for myself and I enjoyed every one of them. I took her to supper and before the evening was half over, she had me head over heels in love with her. She was so pretty, so natural and altogether such a lovely girl that she captured the hearts of half the young men she met. I knew she had me, good and fast.

After supper the order came to unmask and then we began to find out who we had been dancing with. Of course, my young lady did not have to unmask, for she had none on, therefore we were all surprised when Captain Conradi gave her his arm and escorted her to the stage. Then he introduced her to the audience by her right name, which was—Henry House, Jr. All of us young fellows collapsed, but so many had been taken in, and the joke was so far-reaching that we took comfort in the fact that everybody else was fooled as badly as we were. The next day in its account of the ball, the *Age* said:

> But the very greatest imposition and cheat in the masquerade—the truth of which assertion some 20 or 30 young beaux can attest to their great mortification—was Mr. Henry House, Jr., whose lithe figure and undergrown proportions suited the impersonation of a young girl excellently. His flowing hair, flashing jewels, heavenly smiles and tell-ing glances led many an impressionable young man to his undoing.

During the continuance of these balls there were many fine characters taken and there were numerous splendid impersonations, but none that ever came within speaking distance of Henry House's "young lady from the country."

★ ★ ★

NO SECOND FORTUNE WANTED

The other night at the Press Club, a crowd was collected about the reading table discussing every imaginable subject under the sun. Finally one of the gentlemen asked me what I would do if I had a million dollars.

I told him the truth—that I would get a shotgun and shoot every real estate man or promoter who came within 50 yards of me with any scheme for me to invest in, and that after I got them all scared off I would proceed to gratify the greatest wish of my life, namely, to spend the money just as I pleased. Since my tastes are not expensive ones, a million would last me the remainder of my life, which remainder I placed at not more than 30 years.

The subject of gratifying one's wishes in the way of spending money brought to my mind a famous character who formerly lived here, but who has long ago been gathered to his fathers. His name was Fitzgerald and he was a full-blooded Irishman, and a typical one, too. He had a little oyster stand down on Travis Street and while his trade was not great nor very remunerative, he managed to make a fair living and was outwardly content and happy. He loved the flowing bowl, but was forced to play the game on a small limit because of his narrow finances.

He was content and happy, as I say, and doubtless would have passed through life in a very humdrum, prosy way had not an unforeseen incident bobbed up. His father, uncle or some one of his immediate relatives had preceded him and settled in Houston while the town was still in its infancy. Fitz, for such his intimates called him, knew nothing of this relative beyond the fact that there had been such a person, therefore he was greatly surprised one day when a lawyer came to his oyster place and told him that he was a wealthy man.

"If you are the heir of old Blank Fitzgerald," the lawyer told him, "you own the whole of the Third Ward of this city, and I can get it for you if you will sign these papers."

Fitz, having everything to gain and nothing to lose, promptly signed the papers and the next day or two saw the beginning of a real estate volcano.

There were suits and countersuits and, as the new Bible says, there was underworld to pay. The old Fitzgerald claim appeared to be all right and there was scarcely a lot holder in the Third Ward who felt safe.

In a week or two, offers to compromise began to pour in from these frightened people, and Fitz's lawyer literally did a land office business. In those days real estate was not selling for $4500 the front foot. That amount of money would have bought several blocks in most any part of the Third or any other ward of the city, hence compromises were not difficult to make.

Fifty dollars here, a hundred there and sums of that kind usually satisfied all claims and resulted in clear titles. The lawyer waited until he rounded up the whole lot and then he went to Fitz with his part of the money. It was only a few thousand dollars, but even that was more money than Fitz thought there was in the whole world. He promptly kicked his oyster counter over, threw his knives out in the street, tore the door of his shanty off its hinges, took his paint brush and went out in the town to paint it red. The chance that he had dreamed of all his life had come and he took advantage of it.

His field of operations was limited, so that while he spent his money freely and bought lots of whiskey for himself and friends, his roll actually lasted about three months. When he finally became a physical and financial wreck he had at least the doubtful satisfaction of knowing that no one who had preceded him had ever pulled off a similar stunt.

After laying up for repairs for a week or two Fitz went back to his old shack, repaired the counter, fixed the door, got new knives and settled down to his old business just as if nothing had occurred to interfere with the placid flow of his life.

About six months after he had settled down the same lawyer bustled in again. "Fitz," said he, "I have found that you own all of the Second Ward and I'm going to get that for you, too."

"You're not!" shouted Fitz. "I'll have nothing to do with it. I'm through with the whole thing. Why, man, I would not get on another drunk like that one I had for the whole city of Houston. Git out of me place."

The lawyer had actually discovered that Fitz had a good claim to lots of property in the Second Ward, but he could not get Fitz to assert his claim. "Send 'em to me," he said, "and I'll give every one of them a clean title and thank them for takin' it." He did it, too, and gave every man whose title was affected a quitclaim deed.

He knew of no way to enjoy a fortune except to spend the money for liquor and he had his fill of that. The lawyer was disgusted, of course, but could do nothing, so he accepted the inevitable. Fitz continued his oyster business to the end and got more enjoyment out of it than he did out of the few thousand dollars that he spent on his great spree.

★ ★ ★

SEEING THINGS

It is said that one-half of the world does not know how the other half lives, and it might be truthfully added that the first half does not know how the other half *has* lived. I was much struck with the truth of this one night when I heard two first-class stories and received at the same time two of the greatest surprises of my life through the confessions of the gentlemen who told them. Both are prominent men of position and standing, and each has a host of friends, so I shall have to be careful in telling the stories, and, for obvious reasons, refrain from mentioning names.

It was after a social meeting and we were getting ready to go home when someone suggested a round of drinks. Strangely, there was not a gentleman present who indulged except the one who suggested the round. The temperance character of the crowd led to a discussion of drinking and its results, when Billy, as I shall call the prominent merchant, led off by confessing that in his early days he had been a great drinker, and had gone the limit.

"Why, I have actually had the jimmies, and you know that was going some. I got drunk and I could not get sober. I kept it up day after day and week after week, and finally I gave up trying to get sober and went in for the limit. One afternoon I went in the grocery store of one of my friends and insisted that he should go out and take a drink with me. He refused and said he had better whiskey in his store than we could get elsewhere and asked me to try it. Of course I agreed. I took a big drink and it made me so drunk that the merchant had me taken to a room on the second floor of his store, where one of his clerks slept. I don't remember much about getting in bed, but I do remember about waking up. It was late in the evening when I awoke, and I was lying there wondering where I was when I heard a noise behind me, and turning over I saw the biggest skeleton anybody ever saw sitting on the bureau in front of the looking glass. He had a great big scythe in his hand and sat there grinning at me. You know all skeletons grin, but his grin was a different sort of thing; you could see he was enjoying the situation. In those days I was a bit profane, so I took a long look at him and asked him what in hell he wanted and what he was doing there.

"'Billy,' said he, very slowly and drawling. 'Billy,' said he, 'I am here after you and I am going to cut your head off.' Saying that he made one big jump, landed square across my chest, cut my head off with the scythe, and jumped back on the bureau again.

"That made me good mad. I don't know how I did it, but I could see just as well without my head as I could with it, but all the same I wanted my head back. 'Look here,' I said to him, 'you bring that head back here or I'll hurt you.'

"'You can't hurt me,' he said. 'You make me laugh.' With that he began to chuckle. It was the funniest chuckle you ever heard. It commenced in his teeth and then dropped down into him and went rattling along his ribs and sounded like a boy scraping along a picket fence with a stick. I had my .45 with me and I lugged it out.

"'Are you going to bring that head back?' I asked. The skeleton said nothing, but just sat there and grinned.

"I took good aim at his head and said, 'I am going to count three and when I finish, if my head's not back, I'm going to destroy you.' I commenced counting right slowly, 'one, two, three,' and I let him have it. I saw the looking glass fly to pieces and I saw that I had missed him, so I pulled down on him again. When the smoke cleared off the skeleton was gone, but he had taken my head with him and I was in a worse fix than ever.

"I heard a noise in back of me and there was the skeleton. He was trying to hide and I was trying to get a line on him when the crowd from downstairs broke into the room and grabbed me. They lugged me off to a hospital and the doctors finally pulled me through. That is the reason I don't drink. I have whiskey and that skeleton too intimately associated together to enjoy the whiskey part of it."

"That's a fine experience you had, major," said a retired ranch man, "and since you told it, I will give a bit of my own experience in the same line."

"I had been in Richmond for about two weeks enjoying myself with the boys. I had drunk lots of whiskey but had not eaten a thing. Finally I got so that I could not get any action at all out of whiskey. It would not make me drunk or do me any good at all except for a few minutes, when it would die out and I would have to fill up again. One of my friends was running a saloon, and upstairs over the saloon he had a faro layout and other fixtures, among them a billiard table. I was in his place one morning, feeling awful. I took four or five drinks and he persuaded me to go upstairs and lie down on the billiard table and try to get some sleep. It was a big room and was not sealed, with all the rafters bare.

"I lay down on the table and was thinking how much I would give to be sober so I could take a fresh start and enjoy myself with the boys, when I heard a scraping sound down at the end of the room on one of the rafters, and looking up I saw a big rattlesnake about fifteen feet long, trying to slip up on me without my knowing it. He'd creep along a little bit, slip, catch himself, and then begin it all over again. I got interested, and it aroused the sporting spirit in me, and I lay there betting, first that he would make it and then that he would not. He would stretch way out, get a good hold, and then try to draw himself forward, slip, nearly fall, and catch himself. I got so interested that I did not realize that he was gaining all the time, and the first thing I knew he was right over me. Then he turned himself loose and did not try to catch himself. But I was too quick for him. By the time he hit the table I was halfway downstairs, and the next moment I was across the sidewalk, heading for the other side of the street.

"Just as I left the sidewalk a man riding a big black horse came charging down on me with a long sword in his hand. I realized that he could not touch me so long as I was on the sidewalk and made a dash for it and just got there in time. I also realized that I had to cross that street, so I waited until the fellow's back was turned and started again, but he whirled his horse and nearly got me. Then I waited until he got way off and made another dash, but he saw me out of the back of his head and I just barely reached the sidewalk in time. Then I made like I was going down the sidewalk. As soon as his back was turned I made a quick dash, but he was there all right, and again I just barely saved myself. That made me mad and I started into the barroom to get a gun to do him up, when the saloon man and a number of my friends jumped on me and tied me. They sent for a doctor and for about three weeks I had a time of it. Like you, I associate whiskey with a snake and that fellow on a black horse. I have not taken a drink since nor do I intend to take another."

★ ★ ★

DYING FOR A DRINK

To follow is one of so many colorful tales recounted to me by Frank Le Mott. Although I might be able to capture the gist of it, I think it's best to let him tell it.

"I was sitting out in front of the old Gray Front Saloon in San Angelo, smoking a cigarette, when I saw a little old dried-up looking chap ride up on a dilapidated bronco, and recognized Old Fish. Now, 'Old Fish' did not get his name from having been named Fisher or anything like that, but he got it in a queer way.

"One night a crowd of cowboys found him all spraddled out in the middle of a trail over in Arizona. He was flat on his belly and was moving his arms slowly up and down and waving his feet about as if he were swimming. The boy hails him and ask for information. 'Don't muddy the water, boys. I'm a fish,' he said. He had the jimmies and thought he was a fish. The boys toted him to a doctor and he got rid of the jimmies, but he did not get rid of the name and from that time everybody calls him Fish.

"I hated to see him coming for I knew how trifling and no-count he was. He could drink more whiskey than any man I ever came in contact with, and it took more of it to get him drunk, but when he did get drunk he would be drunk all over. I knew he would prove to be a great nuisance, and I hated to see him, as I say. A man named Riley is keeping the big faro bank and owns the Gray Front, which I have told you before was the big thing in San Angelo. Riley being the big saloon man and big gambler has acquired big standing as a citizen and is eminently respectable, therefore it makes me laugh when Fish rushes up to him and shakes hands with him and gives it out right and left that he and Riley was partners out in Arizona. Fish was sober, but Riley and I knew that he would not stay that way long, and that when Fish got drunk it would lower anybody's standing to recognize him as an old friend and partner.

"Well, Riley shakes hands with him and pretends to be mighty glad to see him, but he's not. He asks all hands to the bar and introduced Old Fish and then slipped away. Fish acts pretty good for a few days, not that he don't drink lots of whiskey, for he does. But he is one of those accumulative drunkards who has to lay a big foundation for what's coming. A week passes and Fish ain't drunk yet. Riley sees him drinking all the time and can't understand it. Finally he concludes Fish has discovered some system by which he can drink all he wants without getting drunk and lets it go at that. It comes at last, just as Riley knew it was coming, and Fish strikes him for a stake.

"'Look here,' says Riley, 'I've been watching you and I think I can trust you to make your own stake. I won't give you money for whiskey, but I'll stake you for a monte game against these Mexican pikers.' Riley does it, and when he does so he makes Fergerson, who runs the regular monte game, mad, for Fergerson can't stand Mexicans around him.

"Riley gives him a place for his table and stakes him for about $40. Fish is happy and the Mexicans are happy, but Fergerson is mad plumb through. The first night Fish blows the whole bankroll in at the bar before Riley finds out what he is doing. When Riley comes in and finds what Fish is doing, he kicks him out in the street and chases the Mexicans out, too. Fish is in a bad fix. His money and loafing place are both gone, so he takes up at a low dive where Mexicans are treated the same as folks. In about a week they get tired of him there and chase him out and he is in for good. Fish finally takes up with a tinhorn gambler who lets him sleep in his room, but they ain't got no money for whiskey, so Fish gets sober. He comes whining to Riley and strikes him for enough money to buy a coat. Riley sees how ragged he is and feels sorry for him so gives him the money. Instead of getting the coat he buys a couple of gallons of whiskey and he and his tinhorn friend set in for a good drunk. Finally the whiskey gives out and Fish don't know what to do. He comes to Riley and fairly slobbers for help. Riley won't listen to him and tells him he better go off somewhere and die. Fish don't get mad. What Riley says to him about dying puts an idea in his head. "Look here," he says to Riley. 'That's a good point you makes. Suppose I just makes out I dies, won't that turn the trick?'

"Fish gets close to Riley and says, 'Supposing I make out I'm dead. Then you collect funeral expenses from the boys. You kin bury a box, give me the funeral expenses and I kin skip out of town.' Riley falls for it at once. He sees a chance to get rid of Fish and at the same time make the boys pay nearly all the expenses. He tells Fish to come up to his place and talk it over. They do talk it over and then Riley and Doc Matchet have a talk.

"The next evening Fish comes in Riley's place and he don't look good, either. He is feeling bad sure enough, for he is needing whiskey bad. Riley gives him a couple of scoops and some of the boys throw other drinks into him. After he gets to looking so much better that nobody notices him particular, and just when everybody forgets he's there, he throws up his hands, jerks up one leg, falls down on the floor and goes off in about twenty fits to the minute. You've seen chickens with their heads cut off. Well, they ain't deuce high to the capers Fish cut up. Finally he subsides a little and Doc Matchet and Riley makes a landing on him and lugs him into a room where Riley has a bed. Riley tells me to stay and help hold Fish and then sends everybody else out of the room. Soon as they are gone Fish sits up in bed and demands a drink. I'm astonished to see Fish get well so soon, but then Riley tells me what's doing and asks me to help him. So we got a lot of chalk and rubbed Fish's face with it. We pulls his clothes off and lays him out like sure enough dead folks. The Doc goes out to get a drink and tells the boys that Fish is playing nothing but white chips and ain't got more than a half stack of them left. In a little while he goes out again and announces that Fish has lost his stack and backed off from the table for good.

"It's pretty near dark now and we are having some trouble with Fish, who wants more whiskey. Finally we give him a big drink and laying him out again, we invites the boys in to view the remainders. Everybody comes except Fergerson, who stays away and sends in word that he's glad the deadbeat old bum is dead. After the review is over Riley goes out to the bar and starts a subscription to bury Fish. He heads it and in no time he has over a hundred dollars put down. Fergerson puts down for ten dollars and tells Riley he will pay next day. All the rest is cash.

"Riley brings the list in and shows it to Fish to let him see how anxious the boys are to bury him. Fish takes the list and reads it carefully. When he comes to Fergerson's name and sees it not marked paid, he raises a row. 'You can bet your sweet life that groundhog can't git no credit from me; I want the cash and I want it right now. He can't git no credit on my funeral!'

"Riley argues with him but it does no good. Finally Riley got mad and told him what Fergerson said about him and how glad he was when he heard he was dead. That makes Fish wild and he swears if he don't get that cash he will go out and whip Fergerson if it breaks up the funeral. Fish demands more whiskey. Riley gives it to him to keep him quiet, though he is afraid Fish will be too drunk to get away when the time comes.

"After awhile Fish gets quiet and Riley says he will go out and get a box to bury Fish in. He leaves me with Fish and cautions me to keep the door locked. As soon as he is gone Fish commences again. He is still thinking about Fergerson and can't get over the idea of his wanting credit on his funeral, and then abusing the deceased behind his back. He cusses Fergerson and then demands more whiskey. I argued with him and tried to show him that if he got drunk he would bust the funeral and then the boys would take back their money and run him out of town dead broke. That stopped him for a time, but not for long, for he came back demanding more whiskey. I saw there was no way out of it so after swearing him to keep quiet I slipped out to get a small bottle. He cusses Fergerson real good and hard as I go out, but stretches out in bed like he was dead.

"I walked out looking as solemn as I could and called for a drink. There is a big crowd there and everybody wants to hear how Fish cashes in. I am right in the middle of my tale, and I admit it has taken more time to tell it than I'd calculated, when the barkeep, who is setting out the bug juice for another round, gives one look over my shoulder, jumps over the counter and goes out of the front door like a prairie on fire. The crowd looks where the barkeep was looking and before I know what's doing I'm alone. I turns around and if I don't know that Fish is alive I'm here to tell you that I would have followed the crowd too. Fish was standing in the door with the sheet drawn all around him. His face was white like a dead man's and having so much whiskey in him made him wobbly in the legs just like a dead man who has just stood up from his grave. It sure was a scary sight. Before I could do anything Fish turned and made straight for the back room, where Fergerson was dealing monte. The room was pretty full and when Fish butts in nobody looks around, thinking its only some of the boys coming in to buck the game.

"Fish gets right in the middle of the room before anybody sees him. Then a Mexican sees him and instantly climbs over everybody in front of him and lands right on Fergerson's monte table. Fergerson rises to squash the Mexican and sees Fish. There's a window back of where Fergerson was sitting and he goes out of it backward. The other boys and the Mexicans see Fish and all hell breaks loose. They all try to get out the window at the same time and naturally tear the whole side of the house out.

"Riley hears the racket half a mile away and comes in his buckboard like a streak of lightning, for he guesses something has taken place. When he gets there he finds nobody but me and Fish. I am on the floor laughing, while Fish is behind the bar helping himself to a big drink out of a bottle. Riley don't ask for explanations. He grabs Fish, throws him on his buckboard and hurries away with him. He told me afterward that he gave a Mexican he could trust $20 to take him to the next town with orders to keep going if he wanted to keep from being hung by the boys.

"Riley explained to the boys that it must have been a case of 'revived mortality,' and that Fish must have wandered off and been eaten up by wolves. He gave Fish some money to live on and he gave the money back to the boys that they had put up to bury him with. Instead of getting rid of Fish cheaply, as he calculated, it cost him a good deal. Fish wandered around and died in San Antonio a few years ago. The funny thing was that when he died, and the boys were chipping in to bury him, Fergerson examined him carefully before he would subscribe a cent. When he found Fish was really dead he doubled his subscription, he was so glad."

★ ★ ★

CENSORS AND CAPT. BICKLEY

Nearly all the moving pictures bear this announcement: "Censored by the national board," etc. That, of course, is to guarantee that no improper shows slip by. I understand that Houston also has a board of censors, whose duties are to guard the good people from being shocked. In the olden days there was nothing of that kind attempted and the places of amusement had everything their own way and did whatever they pleased. Of course, some of the plays and exhibitions they put on were outrageous and scarcely fit for anyone, but there was no other remedy than to boycott them or literally run them out of town.

I remember a novel and most effective plan adopted by Chief Coyle and a number of the members of the Left Hand Fishing Club for suppressing one of those shows, which created immense amusement at the time. It was a sort of Adamless Eden Company and had about 15 or 20 girls who were traveling on their shapes. The first night the house was crowded, but nearly all the respectable people left before the show was half over. The next night the Left Hand Fishing Club took the matter in hand.

A number of them secured seats, all in a row, near the front. They sat quietly and with a wonderful amount of dignity, until the curtain rose on the great scene, which was the troupe of girls all dressed up, or more properly speaking, all undressed up. Then each member of the club, with a face as serious as if he were at a funeral, produced from under his coat a big tin cylinder, which he carefully extended into a telescope about four feet long and with it slowly reviewed the whole line of beauty. The effect was marvelous. The girls could not stand the thing and broke for cover behind the wings of the stage, while the audience went wild with delight and the show came to an abrupt end. The funniest part of the whole thing was the serious faces of the Left Handers. Not one of them smiled and all seemed puzzled to understand what had occurred.

In the early seventies there were several good amateur and semi-professional actors in Houston. There was Charley Wallace, a professional actor, who had great talent, and Charley Evans, a scene painter and actor, besides a number of amateurs. Above and far beyond all was Captain Charles Bickley, who wrote plays and often took prominent parts in them. He was a great favorite among the professionals, for he had written a play for a young actress which had made for her fame and fortune. He gave it to her and as it proved a success and had a long run in New York and made a fortune for her, all the actors watched the captain closely, hoping he would do something of the kind for them. They always gladly helped him to put on anything he would write.

On one occasion the captain produced one of his plays at Perkins Hall. He insisted on taking the leading part, but unfortunately he took so many drinks during the first act that it became necessary to kill the hero, which was Bickley, in that act, an event scheduled to come off at the end of the play. Then the plot was changed and the piece was played kind of backwards, presenting the most confusing and amazing complications imaginable. It was wonderful and to add to the fun of the situation, Captain Bickley could be heard behind the scenes, insisting that it was his time to go on. He and the other actors were having more work off the stage than were those on it. If anyone ever found out what the plot of that play was I never heard of it. It was said by some who had read it before its murder, to have been very good, but it never had a fair chance to display its merits. There is one thing sure, the audience would not have had such a good time as they did if the captain had remained sober.

Now I don't want anyone to form a false idea of Captain Bickley. He was just exactly as I have pictured him—a real Bohemian, and he would, if he could, write about himself just as I have written. He was really a remarkable man and a genius. He wrote the play I have mentioned in the foregoing, for a little actress named Elsie Weston. She belonged to a stock company here and had considerable talent both as a singer and actress. Captain Bickley wrote several songs for her and finally wrote a play for her. It was called the "Shadows of London" or something like that. Elsie went to New York, got the play put on by some manager and it met with instant success and had a long and brilliant run. Elsie then went to Europe and the play was successful over there. She made a fortune out of it, but I don't think Captain Bickley ever received but one or two short letters from her after she went North. I am sure he never got a cent of money from her.

The most amazing thing about Bickley was, when, where and how he found time to write anything at all. He was always on the street, night and day, and apparently did nothing but enjoy life. After midnight he was generally loaded and singing that favorite song of his which was a sort of barometer telling his condition.

I was talking to Dr. George McDonnell the other day and he told me about a green policeman arresting Bickley one night. The policeman, who was a new hand, saw Bickley staggering along and "pinched" him. Bickley was indignant and tried to explain. "I am Br-uic-ly," he mumbled, "Br-uic-ly, don't you know?"

"I don't care if you are a bricklayer," said the policeman, "you are going with me," and he took him to the station where he was at once released, of course, for he was as great a favorite with the members of the force as he was with everybody else.

★ ★ ★

Old Peg

I suspect that I have been rather more than half Bohemian all my life without ever being conscious of it. In no other way can I account for the fact that every tramp printer or telegraph operator that has been in Texas during the past 20 or 30 years has gravitated toward me as naturally as if I were the object point of his search. I have known them all, and I confess the wide acquaintance I have had in that line has given me more pleasure than annoyance. Jim Baker, "Shorty" Parish and one or two others among the printers, and "Peg" among the telegraph operators were characters whose acquaintance at times was rather embarrassing, but on the whole rather beneficial. All of the even moderately old printers remember the first two I have named, while I am sure all the telegraphers of the 1880s remember the last, for he was a character never to be forgotten. "Peg" was not his proper name, of course. He had a Christian and a surname, too, but he also had a wooden leg, and that took precedence over everything else, and he became Peg and nothing else.

He was one of the most expert operators that ever struck Texas. He was what was called an Associated Press Operator and could take and send more copy during a night than anybody. He was high-toned and swore he would never work for less than $35 per week, and as such jobs were scarce and, even when he got one, hard to hold because he would celebrate his success at the end of the first week when he was paid off, he was generally idle. He had lost one of his legs in a railroad accident, having gone to sleep and fallen off the brakebeam, or something of that kind. The railroad patched him up in one of the hospitals and gave him a fine wooden leg to say nothing more about the matter. The leg was really a fine one, and Peg could, and did, get from $10 to $15 on it at any pawnshop.

During his temporary pecuniary embarrassments he had another leg for everyday use. This was simply an old-fashioned broomstick-looking affair which, while not ornamental, was quite useful. It got so that one could tell the financial standing of Peg by the style of leg he wore. He had been all over the country, knew all the newspapermen from Chicago to San Francisco and in every city and big town in Texas. He was a great talker, and when only half-loaded was very amusing. He told some good stories, too. I remember one in particular that will bear retelling, though, of course, I can't tell it as he did. It was in the *News* office one night after "30" had been sent to the composing room and we were all indulging in a talk. Peg held the floor:

"Gent-teel-men, you can talk about your 'hot towns' as much as you want to, but Santone takes the cake. I was out there last winter and I had the time of my life. There was a big variety show going on down on one of the plazas and, of course, I went to see it. The place was crowded and I got a seat away back near the door, and I was glad afterward that I did. The show was nearly over when a drunken cowboy came in. He had two big guns strapped round his waist and a bowie knife that looked like a young sword. He refused to take his hat off and made a terrible row about it when a man asked him to remove his hat and sit down. He swaggered about and the show had to stop for a minute or two. He ordered a bottle of champagne and then, catching sight of the boxes on the edge of the stage, he made for one. Everybody seemed to be afraid of him and tried to quiet and pacify him. When he reached the box he tore down the curtains and ordered three girls to bring him three bottles of champagne, which they did in a hurry. The show had been forced to come to a standstill by now and everybody was watching the cowboy.

"While he was drinking his wine a fellow on the stage began to sing. The cowboy promptly ordered him to stop. The fellow paid no attention, but went on singing. The cowboy hammered on the box with a bottle and made a terrible racket. Finally the singer got mad and, advancing to the front of the stage, asked if there was not an officer in the house to take that drunken nuisance out and lock him up. There was no response, for the policeman, if there was one there, was hidden out. The singer repeated his request for an officer and finally the cowboy said to him that if he wanted him put out so bad he had better undertake the job himself.

"The singer was game and accepted the challenge and announced that he would do so. He advanced to the side of the stage and began climbing up to the box. It was about ten feet, being on the second tier. The cowboy sat right still until the fellow got nearly to the top, then he reached out and caught him caught him by the collar of his coat and dragged him into the box. They dropped to the floor in a clinch, but as they fell I saw the cowboy had his knife in his hand. The girls fled. The table was knocked over and there was a terrible racket for a few minutes. Then I saw them rise, the cowboy holding the singer by the back of the neck. He rammed him face foremost against the wall and rammed that big knife through him twice and then, slamming it plumb through him between the shoulders, he left it sticking in his body and, picking him up, hurled him out of the box to the stage below.

"It was all over in a minute and there was the biggest stampede you ever saw. The whole audience made for the door in one solid mass, and I was working well in the lead, in spite of having only one good leg to work with. When I struck the sidewalk I lit out in good style and ran two blocks before I stopped. I saw a policeman and I rushed to him. 'You better go down yonder,' I said. 'A cowboy just murdered a man in the theatre down there.'

"He looked at me and grinned. 'That's alright,' he said. 'They have been killing that same man for two nights now. It's all part of the show.' Then I realized that I had been sold and I took the policeman into the Buckhorn Saloon and threw a couple of scoops into him to keep quiet.

"The next night I went back to enjoy the fun of seeing the stampede, now that I knew it was all a part of the show. I got a seat near the end of a row near the middle of the house, and there is where I was a fool. The cowboy came in and went through the same performance. There was the same stampede, too, but it started sooner than I calculated. There was a big Dutchman near me and he stampeded at the first flash of the knife and took the whole tier of seats with him. In the rush they got my leg, the broomstick one, jammed in the seat and broke it square off. Then they walked all over me, and I never saw a thing. When the dust settled they found me all spraddled out on the floor. The proprietor acted pretty square. He set 'em up two or three times, sent me home in a hack and had a carpenter come round early the next morning to fix my stem, and that night I left for El Paso. Santone was too strenuous for me."

★ ★ ★

CAPTAIN CHAS. BICKLEY

One reads a great deal in newspaper circles about "Bohemians," but the fact remains that one seldom comes in contact with a genuine one. In all my experience I have never met but one, though I have met several of the spurious article, fellows who were simply more or less refined tramps and bums, and who were glad to be called Bohemians because it gave a bit of respectability and gloss to their otherwise dissolute behavior. There are tramp newspapermen just as there are tramp printers and telegraph operators, but there are few genuine Bohemians. The race, or whatever they may be called, died out years ago.

As I have already said, I have never met but one, but he was a good one alright, and all the old-timers will recall him with pleasure. I refer to Captain Charles Bickley. He was a comparatively young man when he first appeared on the scene in Houston. Of all of the devil-may-care, heedless and care-free fellows on earth he was the greatest. He lived, not for the day, but for the immediate present and gave no thought to the hour that was sixty minutes ahead. He was a brilliant writer, drunk or sober a fine talker, and, strangely enough, a highly honorable man.

He wrote poetry and drank whiskey, wrote plays, short stories and drank more whiskey. He could always get a job when sober and he could hold it as long as he could manage to hold his pencil, for he gave rather more than value received, for his writings were first class and editors were glad to have him with them. He would hold a job for a time in Houston, get drunk, get fired and move on to Galveston or San Antonio, go through the same performance there and then show up in Houston again. He got passes over the railroads whenever and wherever he wanted them and trusted to luck for drinks on the way.

His title of captain was genuine, for he had actually been a captain in the Confederate army. When the war ended he took a trip abroad, though he did it without money and simply on cheek. He came to Houston about 1867 and secured a position on the *Telegraph*. He at once became the best known man in town and was popular with everybody. He was stage-struck, of course, for one never finds a true Bohemian who is not, and he wrote several plays which were produced by amateurs and professionals. One of his plays made quite a hit, locally. It was somewhat on the order of the "Chanticleer" and was written at the time the old market house was being pulled down. The place was overrun by big rats who had possession of the building for generations of rats. The captain had these rats as his characters and made them review the history of the old building and of all the doings of the early Houstonians who had passed through it.

It was an historical review of Houston from a rat's point of view. The captain took a leading part and acquitted himself so well that he would have gone off with the first strolling company that passed through Houston and become a professional, if any of the managers would have taken him.

The captain revolved between the desks of the local papers and those of other Texas cities for several years and then disappeared and no one knew what had become of him until an announcement of his sudden death appeared in one of the New Orleans papers.

In those days there were no managing editors to blue-pencil things, but the local editor, as he was called, wrote what he chose to write and stood all the consequences. When an objectionable article appeared, the aggrieved one never thought of going after the editor of the paper but went directly after the local editor. Bickley rarely wrote anything that would get him in trouble, but occasionally he did.

On one such occasion, he wrote a local item that reflected rather severely on a well-known gambling saloon. The proprietor took his medicine and kept his mouth shut, but one of his dealers got drunk and the more he thought of it the madder he got. Finally about dark he was on the warpath good and strong and, taking his gun, he started out to destroy Bickley. Someone told him that Bickley was in Gregory's saloon and the fellow started down there after him. He had his pistol in his hand and went down Main Street knocking people over right and left in his haste to get at his victim. Sure enough, Bickley was there and he was ripe, too, for he was singing, and that was a good way to let people know his condition. Unfortunately for the gambler's plans, just as he made a rush through the latticed doors to get at Bickley he collided with Big Bill Williams, who was as large and almost as strong as John Sullivan. Instead of making an apology, the gambler swore at Bill and tried to pass him.

Bill was feeling pretty good himself and the next instant he swung onto the gambler's left jaw and curled him up on the sidewalk. Bill never said a word. He walked out to where the gambler was lying, kicked his pistol out in the street, and walked up the sidewalk, just as though nothing out of the ordinary had occurred. There was a dead silence and the captain's voice could be heard as he continued his song:

> I kissed her in the kitchen,
> I kissed her in the hall,
> Good morning, ladies,
> I've come to kiss you all.

One could always tell the exact condition of the captain when they heard him singing that favorite song of his. About the funniest scene I ever witnessed was seeing the captain, an eminent lawyer and a leading doctor all drunk in the back room of a barroom. Bach was singing his own song and paying not the least bit of attention to the other two. The doctor was singing, in a low, crooning tone:

> How in the hell did that gal know
> That I took sugar in my coffee-o?

The judge was singing at the top of his voice in a growling bass:

> The ship she lay four miles from shore,
> The ship she lay four miles from shore,
> And there came on board a gay buccaneer, etc.

The captain was singing the above mentioned classic and, as the negro porter put it, "They sho' was enjoyin' theirselves." Captain Bickley would last on a modern paper about half a minute, but in those days he was looked upon as quite the thing, so long as he could keep sober enough to write copy.

★ ★ ★

BURIED TREASURES

When I was a small boy I had an ambition, shared largely by other boys of my age, to grow up as rapidly as possible so that I would be big enough to go out and dig up buried treasures. That the treasures were there I never for a moment doubted, and my only fear was that someone would beat me to them. My faith had something tangible to rest on, too, for at that time it was generally believed that the great pirate, Lafitte, had buried his treasure, not on Galveston Island, but somewhere on the mainland. The discovery of the grave of the wife of one of his lieutenants on the north side of Clear Lake, not far from where Seabrook now stands, gave much basis for the belief that Lafitte made Clear Lake his headquarters and it was generally supposed that he buried his treasures there. Just why he should want to bury his treasures at all, no one undertook to explain, but as that was a long accepted habit, characteristic of all pirates, Lafitte was held to be no exception and the burial of his treasures was accepted as a fact.

Now, something that gave the buried treasure theory a decided boost was the periodical appearance in Houston of a most disreputable looking character, who came from time to time from no one knew where, to indulge in a ten days' or two weeks' drunk and then to disappear as mysteriously as he had appeared.

He was a villainously looking Greek or Italian, had but one eye and a scar from a sabre or knife cut across his cheek. His looks were sufficient to have proven him an ex-pirate, but in addition to that he always brought with him a lot of gold and silver coins of ancient date, Mexican and Spanish money. He was watched carefully, but no one ever discovered where he came from or went to. No one ever doubted his having been one of Lafitte's men and I am confident that every boy in Houston had implicit faith that this old fellow was the last survivor of Lafitte's gang and knew where all the treasure was buried. After awhile the old fellow's visits ceased and as time wore on interest in him and his treasure ceased also. There was too little information about Lafitte's movements and none at all to show that he ever buried any treasure at all, so when the old pirate ceased to visit Houston, the people soon forgot him and all he was supposed to represent.

While the existence of the Lafitte treasure was merely a matter of supposition, there was another treasure which was known to exist and which is known to exist today. That is the $600,000 in Mexican money known to have been buried somewhere on the Santa Fe trail between the San Jacinto River and the Brazos River. I don't know the exact date, but it was some time in the early 30s that a party of Mexicans started from East Texas for Mexico over the Santa Fe trail. They had with them $600,000 in Mexican government money. At some point between San Jacinto River and Brazos River this party was attacked by Indians. They took refuge in a sweet-gum island (a clump of trees on the prairie called an island) near a creek. They buried the money in a hole and then put up a fight against the Indians. The Indians were in strong force and the result was that all the Mexicans except one were killed. One escaped, though he was so badly wounded that he died soon after reaching a settlement and telling the story of the disaster, though he could not give the location of the fight nor any definite information beyond the fact that it was in an "island" on the banks of a creek.

Hundreds of people have searched for that "island," but its location has never been found. At one time it was thought that it was found, when some cowboys discovered a lot of arrowheads sticking in a sweet-gum tree on Cypress Creek, in the west part of Harris County. Those cowboys got spades and shovels, but though they literally tore the earth up for hundreds of yards all through and around that "island," they found nothing. On another occasion a German farmer out hunting for cattle found a Mexican dollar sticking in the bank of Cypress Creek not far from where the Houston & Texas Central Railroad crosses that creek. He showed the dollar, told where he had found it, and some of his auditors who had heard the story of the buried treasure spoke of it and at once there was another rush of diggers. The search was very thorough, but nothing was found and the treasure remains today where the ill-fated Mexicans buried it four score years ago.

Some rather pathetic and other rather amusing things have been connected with that buried treasure. One or two men became so fascinated by it that they devoted their lives to searching for it. I met one of them in 1873 and spent a night with him at his camp on Cypress Creek. I think his name was Shook or Schukes. Louis Hillendahl, who lives at Spring Branch, knew him well and told me the old man did nothing but search for that Mexican money. He was so certain that it was located in Harris County on Cypress Creek that he would search nowhere else for it.

Sometime about 1878 or 1879, Charley Fingerman, who was a great musician in Houston, and who is well remembered in Houston, heard of the treasure and determined to find it scientifically. Charley had married a lady who was a spirit medium and had the power of calling up the dead. He was about halfway a convert, though only halfway, but he was enough so to lay all the facts before his wife and consult her. "A sitting" was had and the spirits promptly told them where the treasure was and how to go about finding it. They were told to take a table with them and place it out on the prairie about a hundred yards from a certain island on Cypress Creek and then to await developments. They did as directed.

Charley told me the story himself. He said the day was very hot, for it was summer, and that he had slipped a few bottles of beer in a basket to prevent sunstroke. When they got to the creek he slipped off, took a good drink of whiskey and washed it down with a bottle of beer. He said it was so hot he needed something to strengthen his faith. There were five or six people in the party, all women except Charley.

After he had his drink they took the table out on the prairie as directed. They gathered about it and put their hands on it. Charley said his faith increased by leaps and bounds when the table at once began jumping up and down and started off hopping in the direction of the "island." The table led them into the little grove, and going to a large tree, halted and began jumping up and down. Charley was so excited that he nearly forgot to drink another bottle of beer when he went down to the creek to get his digging tools. The table was set aside and Charley went to work with his spade and for two hours labored faithfully. He found nothing. The ladies consulted over the situation while Charley slipped off to refresh himself.

Finally it was agreed to try it over, so the table was taken out on the prairie again where it cut up exactly as it had done before. When it led them back to the "island" it took them in at one of the sides and stopped at another tree. Charley went to the creek, took another big drink of whiskey and a bottle of beer and returned to his work again. This time he dug and dug, not only at the place indicated by the table, but for yards all around it in every direction. Finally his patience was exhausted and rising in his wrath he kicked the table over, cursing both it and the spirits. That settled it right there, for the indignant spirits washed their hands of the whole affair and quit in disgust.

The ladies were horrified. The table was carried out on the prairie again, but the insult was too deadly. They placed their hands on the table, sang soothing songs and began to plead with the spirits, but it was no use, the table refused to move. At last they took their hands off the table and tried to put them on Charley, but he was too quick for them and made his escape. Charley's wife and all the ladies blamed him for the disaster and said that if he had not gotten drunk they would have found all that money; that the spirits were testing their faith and would have led them to the proper place the third time if he had not spilled over and spoiled everything. Charley defended himself as well as he could and finally made peace with them, but they could never get him to go on another treasure hunt under the guidance of the spirits.

$$\star \; \star \; \star$$

IN SAN ANGELO

I am afraid I got myself into serious business by telling those Frank Le Mott stories, for at least a dozen of my friends have been doing the Oliver Twist act and asking for more. Even two of my lady friends asked me to please tell those two stories Mr. Le Mott spoke of, "Farmer Joe" and "Old Fish." Of course, I cannot tell the stories as Le Mott tells them. He is an artist in that line and one of the greatest charms about his storytelling is the fact that when he becomes interested he drops into the habits of all old sports and speaks of everything in the present tense. Le Mott has to he heard to be appreciated:

"Did I ever tell you about the Old Gray Front Saloon in San Angelo? San Angelo was the biggest thing in the biggest county in the biggest State in the Union, and the Gray Front was the biggest thing in San Angelo. It was a single-story adobe building, but what it lacked in height it made up in length, for it was fully 70 feet long.

"There were three fellows running it. 'Farmer Joe' deals monte for the Mexicans up in front. 'Frenchy' deals faro bank in the rear, while Billy, the bouncer, deals whiskey for everybody over a board counter that takes up nearly one whole side of the house. Billy got his name of 'Bouncer' from a habit he had of butting into every fight that got started, not playing any favorites, but choking off both parties engaged in battle. This habit of Billy's does not lead to peace; it leads the other way, for gents, even timid ones, felt safe to start war when they knew Billy was going to put a stop to it at the very jump.

"Now, Farmer Joe was no more of a farmer than you are. He gets his name from a habit he has of wearing his hair and beard long. He was the most peaceful man on earth. He hated a row worse than anyone and when war was declared by anybody he would not stay and witness it, he was so peace-loving. He was so gun-shy it was painful, and whenever two gentlemen started to argue with their artillery, Joe would leave the room even if he had to do the sash act in order to get out. You understand that the sash act was going out of the window in so great a hurry as to take sash and all with you.

"As I have said, Joe deals monte for the Mexicans in the front part of the building. He is not very strong financially, as his bankroll is typically only about $40. The Mexicans know Joe is peaceful and they give him a heap of their sass, for they know Joe would rather have abuse than a fight any time.

"I call to mind one of the funniest things I ever witnessed in which Joe played a leading part. There is a little consumptive Mexican playing against his game. A dispute comes up between them. The Mexican is very sassy. Joe sees Billy standing near and knowing he will stop the fight, he concludes to soak the Mexican one for luck. He bats the Mexican. The Mexican don't know anything about fighting and goes for Joe like a woman. He grabs him by the hair with one hand and by the beard with the other. Then he begins to pick Joe the same as if he is a chicken. He swipes a handful of hair out of Joe's face and another handful out of his head. In a minute he has Joe looking like a cross between a half-picked chicken and a dog with mange. At the first start Billy comes round from behind the bar to interfere, but changes his mind and stands there viewing the battle. It shore was a funny battle, too. They sways this way and they sways that way and finally they sways against Joe's table and upsets it, scattering his bankroll all over the floor. The other Mexicans, seeing everybody watching the fight, went for the money, and Joe told me afterward that he did not get but about $8 of it back after the war was over.

"'Don't that beat hell?' says Joe, looking at me when he and the Mexican drops loose from each other because they were out of wind and could go no longer, 'Don't that beat hell? Here I been for three years. There's been more'n five hundred fights started durin' that time and this is the first one Billy ever let go to a finish.' I wanted to laugh, but I held in because I saw tears in Joe's eyes. Being pulled to pieces that way by a consumptive Mexican goes hard with him. That Mexican did lots to him, for he don't leave but one little patch of beard on his face, and Joe's head looked like a whole tribe of Indians had been scalping him.

"But Frenchy is the big man of the works in the Gray Front. He deals faro bank. They call him Frenchy, though why they do so I never could understand. His place is way back near the stove, where it is warm and comfortable. He ain't got no box but deals out of his hand. He shuffles up the cards, shows the soda card, and then, turning them face down, proceeds to deal. It's a good way, too, and he has a game going nearly all the time.

"One night two fellows come in and buck against him. They have only passable luck. The next night they both come again, but only one of them plays. Soon one of them disappears. Nobody notices where he goes at the time, but it develops afterward that he goes under the table, where he can look up and see the cards Frenchy is holding in his hand, face down. He and his partner has signals, so the bank loses pretty constantly. After awhile the stranger who is playing makes a funny kind of bet on the nine and wins, of course. This excites Frenchy's suspicion and, placing the cards on the table and putting a stack of chips on them, he leans back so he can see under the table. There he sees the legs of the stranger's partner.

"Frenchy says nothing, but reaching over to the pile of cordwood that's there for the stove, he selects a good big stick. There's deep silence, for nobody knows what's up. The fellow under the table must have been a mind reader, or he has good instincts for danger; anyway, he knows something's wrong and he makes a break for freedom. He upsets everybody sitting in front of the table and starts for the front door. It's a long run but he wastes no time. The front door is a screen that swings back. He reaches it and just as he does Frenchy's stick of wood reaches him. It catches him in the small of the back, doubles him up and assists him through the door. As he emerges he collides with a man who is just entering and they both go down together. The stranger gets up first and starts for the door.

"'Come back! Don't go in there,' shouts the fellow on the ground.

"'Why not?' asks the man.

"'Because,' says the fellow, 'they are playing faro bank in there and paying off with cordwood. I don't win but one bet. If I had whipsawed them they would have killed me.'"

CRITTERS
(NATURAL AND SUPERNATURAL)

★ ★ ★

AN ENCOUNTER WITH A CAMEL

Monday when the circus was here, I saw an old horse hitched to a buggy making a fool of himself because there were two or three elephants marching up Main Street. Now if it had been camels instead of elephants there might have been some excuse for that old horse, for, as everybody knows, horses dread camels as the devil dreads holy water. An explanation of this fact is given in an old story to the effect that when God made animals He made a horse among the last. He told the horse that he should be man's servant and be a beast of burden. At that, the horse thought he would make some suggestions and said that if man were going to ride on his back he should have a natural saddle. God knew what he was doing and, just to show the horse the absurdity of his suggestion, He made a camel and placed it in front of the horse. The horse took one look at the horrible figure and then took to his heels. Since that day, the story concludes, the horse has never been able to come near a camel without having the most abject terror and fear.

Now, I don't know whether there is a word of truth in that whole story, except the concluding part, but I know that you can't get any horse to associate with a camel under any circumstances. I once had a very vivid demonstration of the truth of that. In 1871 Dr. Charley Owens and I went down to Galveston on a pleasure trip. There were no street cars then, as now, by which to reach the beach, so we went round to Gregory's stable and hired a horse and buggy. The buggy was a brand new one, but the horse was evidently second, or even third-hand.

We drove out Tremont Street to the beach and by the time we got there we were pretty well worn out beating on that horse. We could not get him to go faster than a slow trot. Charley was for turning back and making the man give us another horse, but I talked him out of it, telling him that on the beach the drive would be better and probably we would get more speed out of the horse. My prediction proved to be true, for after we got on the hard sand of the beach the old chap showed marked improvement.

After a short drive we returned and went to Schmidt's Garden for some refreshments. As soon as we got out of the buggy the old horse fell fast asleep, so Charley said there was no use to tie him, and there was not, for he slept profoundly during the whole time we were in the garden. We came out finally and, without awakening the horse. Charley and I got in the buggy, intending to play a joke on him and wake him up with the whip after we got well settled. But our joke was spoiled, for just as Charley gathered up the reins and I gathered up the whip a lot of boys came up behind us, making such a noise that they actually awoke that old plug and he turned his head to see what was the matter. We did the same thing, and saw waddling toward us one of the largest and ugliest camels on earth. He was right up on us before we knew it. The effect on that horse was magical. I have thought over what he did a thousand times, but I am no nearer being able to explain it than I was then. I don't know how he did it, but he raised his left hind leg slowly and carefully and poked his foot right in our faces without touching the dashboard. It was an uncanny thing to do, for he kept his other three feet on the ground. He kept that left foot right under our noses for the fraction of a second, and then he took it down. When he did so he took the dashboard and nearly all the front part of the buggy with it. There was nothing dignified or deliberate about the way he got himself together. There was a high board fence across the street that some billposter had erected to paste bills on. There was lots of room on both sides of that billboard, for it was all vacant land out there then. But that old horse must have gotten a whiff of the camel's odor, which drove all the little sense he had left clean out of him, for he actually made three attempts to climb over that fence.

After the third attempt, he looked over his shoulder and seeing the camel between him and town, he turned and headed for the Gulf of Mexico at a frightful speed. I heard an awful flapping, but could not see anything because the horse raised such a dense cloud of dust that we could scarcely breathe. When we struck the hard beach I discovered that he had gotten his foot through the remnants of the dashboard and that it fitted his leg like a bracelet. While the horse was trying to climb the billboard, I got a glimpse at the camel, and as scared as I was I could not help wondering at the little interest he took in the performance of our horse. He did not smile nor show the slightest interest in the performance of our plug, though he himself was causing all the trouble.

By the most strenuous effort Charley succeeded in turning the horse just as he reached the water's edge and headed him down the beach toward Tremont Street. It was Charley's intention to turn him into Tremont Street, where the sand was very deep, and thus stop his mad career. There was a big sand fort that had been erected at the foot of Tremont Street during the war and this shut off our view in that direction, so we did not see what was coming. Just as Charley began to work the old horse round so as to head him into Tremont Street, right there in front of us and not 50 yards away, two big elephants and three more camels came waddling out from behind the fort and headed right for us.

Charley and I abandoned hope at once, but our horse did better than that, for he abandoned everything. He squatted down on the ground, coming to a sudden halt, and actually groaned with terror. When he did that the buggy rolled up on him. That must have been just what he wanted, for the next moment he shot all four feet back at us and smashed everything free from himself. Then he turned and if the Old Boy and all his fiends had been behind him he could not have gotten away more quickly. He was there one moment and out of sight down the beach the next.

Charley and I had a long walk back to town. We threatened to sue the stableman for damages and he threatened to sue us, but finally concluded he had a better case against the circus people, who had just come to town. He finally fixed it up with them and aside from our long walk, Charley and I experienced no further inconvenience from our contact with a mixture of a Texas-raised horse and camels and elephants.

Being of an inquisitive mind and ever on the lookout for explanations of common things, I learned something that day. I had heard all my life about the fleetness and running qualities of the Arabian steed. I found the solution of the problem that day. They have camels in Arabia and the horses over there are so in the habit of running away from them and have been doing so for so many generations that it has grown to be part of their natures. If we had a few camels to stir our horses up for a generation or two, judging by the speed our old plug developed that day, our mustangs would have the Arabian steeds looking like 30 cents before long.

★ ★ ★

A DOUBLE-ACTION GHOST

The other night at the Press Club one of the members told about being nearly scared to death one night while passing a graveyard by an old white horse. The horse was simply grazing about among the tombstones, but he was white, was moving, and was in the graveyard. That combination could not be resisted and the storyteller left precipitately.

The story reminded me of an incident that happened a long time ago and of which I had not thought for years. A big crowd of us went fishing over on White Oak Bayou. The fish began biting late in the afternoon and it was nearly dark before we thought of leaving for home. May Stanley and I left before the others and hurried, too, because we did not care to pass the old city graveyard after dark.

When we got to the graveyard May suggested that we stop and play a trick on the other boys. I did not want to linger in that locality a single moment, but he persuaded me to stay and see the fun. There was an old brick, one-story house used as the city powder house, located near the far end of the graveyard, near the bank of the bayou.

The boys would have to come close past this place, so May set his trap there. He took off his white shirt and rigged it up on a stick so that when he stood up it looked like a man six or seven feet high. He took his stand or rather his squat behind the house and we waited for the boys to come. Soon we heard voices and thought the boys were coming.

I had become interested in the game by now and moved off down the fence so as to give the crowd a second shock as they passed me. Just as the voices drew near, I chanced to glance over in the graveyard and my blood grew cold, for there rapidly advancing right down on May was a great big white thing.

"Look behind you, May!" I yelled, and May looked. When he saw what was coming he let out a yell one could hear for a mile, and tore out from behind the house with his white scarecrow held aloft. He emerged at just what the scientists call the psychological moment, for his charge was made just in time to bring him face to face with, not the boys, but two negroes who were on their way to town.

The negroes were too scared to yell. They gave sharp grunts like two frightened hogs and the next moment dashed down the hill and fairly split the bayou wide open in their haste to get across. May was too badly scared to realize what he was doing or what was happening. He knew that something terrible was behind him and coming face to face with two negro men instead of the boys he expected added to his confusion.

He did not realize that he himself had scared the negroes, but thought that they, too, had seen the ghost and were leaving for anywhere to get away from there. He dropped his shirt and tore off through the woods in the direction of where Schneider's swimming hole was afterwards located.

I was too scared to run or to do anything but stand and gasp. However, I soon found out that the ghost was only a big white dog, presumably on his way home and taking the nearest way through the graveyard. I yelled to May and tried to stop him, but he was too frightened to hear me and kept going.

Not caring to stay near the graveyard alone and hating to pass it by myself as I would have to do, I took after May. I did not catch up with him until we reached a point near where the Grand Central depot is now located. He was completely out of breath and was panting like a dog.

I did not want to do so, but I offered to go back with him to get his shirt, but he swore that he would not go back there again for a thousand shirts. The other boys had heard the yells and when they came to the scene of the disaster they found May's shirt and brought it along to him.

May swore that he would not have become so demoralized if he had not have been thinking of a fellow who had committed suicide a week or two before right back of the powder house. May said that he was thinking what he would do if that suicide should appear suddenly when I called out to him to look behind him and he naturally concluded that the fellow had come sure enough.

What the negroes thought or said we never knew, for we never heard of them again. I'll bet that to their dying day they thought and swore that they had come face to face with that man who had killed himself near the old powder house.

All that part of town is thickly settled now and the old graveyard is almost obliterated and totally neglected. At the time I speak of, the graveyard was away out of town and there was a dense forest of pine and oak trees surrounding it. The bayou too was a large stream, and not the dried up dirty ditch it has since become. The setting for the play was perfect and the advent of the dog pulled it off to perfection.

★ ★ ★

DICK FULLER AND THE PROFESSOR

In the early seventies Dick Fuller returned home from college, having acquired at that seat of learning, in addition to a smattering of Latin, Greek and mathematics, something of an expert's knowledge of the games of billiards, pin pool and the use of a shotgun. He was and still is a famous shot and delights in hunting.

About the same time there visited Houston one of the most distinguished educators from an Eastern college. This was a gentleman who was every inch a "Southern gentleman," and a man who by his fine "mixing" qualities soon became widely known and respected by all who knew him. The professor was at heart one of the boys, and being far from his base of operation and out on a vacation, he relaxed and went in for all the good things in sight. He was no mean hand with a billiard cue and it was in that way that he and Dick became familiar. The truth is that Dick captured the professor by turning his own guns on him. The professor commented on Dick's bald head and was taken off his heels when Dick came back at him with a quotation from one of the Latin classics, proving that hairy animals are always the most stupid. The professor appreciated the novelty of hearing a Texas youth quote Latin so glibly and a friendship between the two began and lasted until the professor's unwilling departure. Had Dick been ambitious to secure letters of the alphabet to go behind his name, I am certain that all he had to do at that time was to follow the professor to his particular college and he could have become a "doctor" of anything he chose.

After the professor had been here a week or two he asked Dick to take him out shooting. It was August and prairie chickens were "ripe," so Dick gladly agreed to the proposition. The next morning by daylight the two were out on the prairie by Pierce Junction. But I suspect I had best let Dick tell the story of the actual hunt.

"When the professor came down out of the hotel to get in the buggy I scarcely recognized him. He wore a little skull cap and had on a canvas hunting jacket that was nothing but pockets. He had on knee breeches and high laced shoes and was the breathing picture of those photographs you see of kings and dukes in the magazines. He had a little shotgun swung over his shoulder and a big belt full of cartridges. His uniform must have weighed fifty pounds at least, and it was August, too, when I wanted to hunt in my shirt-tails. Well, the professor said nothing about taking a drink, but I could smell whiskey mighty plain, so I knew he had made his peace before coming down.

"The old fellow was very dignified and very silent all the way out. He seemed to be thinking of something and, like that famous racehorse, he did not seem to have his mind on his business. We started in with luck, for we started a drove of chickens just across Brays Bayou and I got two. After driving on a bit I smelt that whiskey again, though I saw no signs of it. When we got to Pierce Junction we soon got in among lots of prairie chickens. The sport was fine, for after flushing they would fly only a short way and come down again. I yelled to the professor to come on, but he stood like a post with his gun over his arm and did not pretend to take any part in the sport. I gathered up my birds, and going to him, I rammed them in his big pockets. It was the funniest thing I ever saw. He did not notice me but stood there gazing off in the distance. I concluded that some great problem had come to him and that it had so absorbed his mind that he was oblivious to everything else.

"Finally I killed two more chickens and when I got to the professor to put them in his pockets he looked at me in a far away manner and said, 'Dick, why are you discharging that fowling piece so often? I see nothing to cause such a fusillade.' When I told him I was killing chickens he would not believe me and I had to pull them out of his pockets and show them to him. As I did so I dislodged a quart bottle of whiskey, half empty, and discovered the truth. The professor was as drunk as a monkey. It was no common drunk, either, but it was a real professorial drunk with all the dignity of his high position thrown in. I have seen various kinds of drunks, but that was the first time I recognized the genuine article from which the name 'Stone, Stiff Drunk' came. The professor could do nothing but look. It scared me at first, but I got him in the buggy and drove back to town, took him to the hotel and had him put to bed.

"The strange part of the whole thing is that the professor didn't remember a thing about going hunting. The next day when I met him he said, "You rascal, you promised to take me hunting yesterday and never showed up." I tried to convince him that he had been out with me, but had to give it up. Finally I saw it worried him, so I dropped the subject. I left half the chickens at the hotel for him but I don't know whatever became of them."

★ ★ ★

EVERYBODY IS AFRAID OF GHOSTS

I don't care who he is, where he comes from or what he does, when I hear a man say he is not afraid of ghosts, I simply do not believe him. I will not go so far as to say that I think he is lying, but I will say that I think he is self-deceived and talks that way because he has never been tested and does not know whether he is afraid of them or not. There is a certain amount of latent superstition in every man, which is as much a part of his general makeup as is the color of his hair. This superstition may lie dormant throughout his entire life, but will spring into activity on the first favorable opportunity.

About the most material, hard-headed man I ever knew was Tobe Mitchell, who was managing editor of the *Houston Post* in 1883. He hooted at the very idea of haunted houses, ghosts and all those sort of things, and expressed a great desire to spend a night in a so-called haunted house I had told him about. I sat down and gave him a detailed and truthful account of what had happened to me, and when he found that he was to neither see nor hear anything, and was simply going to feel that the room was full of ghosts, all anxious to catch him off his guard so they could nab him, he backed out ignominiously. He still swore the whole thing was a lot of rot, but he absolutely refused to enter the room after I had made all the arrangements for him to occupy it. My story got on his nerves and brought out all the latent superstition he had in him. It was all there, though he knew nothing of its existence. If he was not afraid of ghosts, why did he back out?

Now, what made me think of ghosts at all was the fact that Sunday I took a walk out through Sam Houston Park, and while there I thought of an old single-story, two-room brick building that stood for years in front of the old Nobles residence on San Felipe Street—or rather road. Just when that old building was put up I never heard. It must have been at a very early period in Houston's history, or else it must have been constructed of very inferior material, for when I first became acquainted with it, in the late fifties, it was almost a ruin, with one side almost completely demolished and the other not much better.

The truth of the adage about giving a dog a bad name was never better exemplified than in that old building. For no cause on earth, someone started a report that the house was haunted. All specific information and all details were wanting, and yet in an incredibly short time you could not get a negro or a boy in Houston to go near that house after dark. I link the negroes and boys together in the preceding paragraph, for when it came to believing in ghosts or any other superstition they were in a class peculiarly their own.

Now, there was an exception to this fear of ghosts in the person of John Steel, son of the man who afterward killed Colonel Kirby of Hempstead. John was a great big healthy boy, and was as game as a gamecock. He was not afraid of anything, living or dead, and talked so contemptuously about our haunted house that it made us angry. Finally Charley Gentry bet him five dollars that he would not go into that house and remain there until daylight alone. There were some other conditions, among them being that John should read a certain book. How I remember that book! It was called *The Night Side of Nature*, and was a compilation of the most horrible ghost stories, all sworn to and authenticated. I borrowed it afterward, but took care to read it only in the daytime.

John agreed to everything, and when the fatal night came we escorted him to the house, avoiding the Episcopal graveyard in doing so. We had an old chair for him to sit on and left him three candles. He was really the only cool and indifferent boy in the crowd.

We went off and hid among some coffee bean weeds near the side of the road and watched for developments. We could see the light shining through the cracks in the door and also in the wall of the old house. We waited and waited, but nothing happened. One of the boys crept up and peeped in and came back and reported that John was sitting there reading and smoking a pipe, "just like old folks."

Charley Gentry began to get anxious about his five-dollar bet, and realized that something had to be done. Finally he announced that if anybody would go with him he would get something that would move John out of that house in a hurry. One of the boys volunteered and they left. They were gone a long time, and when they returned we all realized that something was going to happen sure enough. Charley had gone to Dr. Robinson's office and stolen a skull. It was a horrible looking skull, too. It had no lower jaw, but was well-supplied with upper teeth, with only one or two missing ones, which added to its outrageous appearance. Charley had gotten a big newspaper, to do duty as a sheet. He decorated a pole with the paper and then stuck the skull on the end of the pole. It was about the scariest thing I ever saw. One of the boys slipped up and took a look at John. He found him as quiet and well satisfied as ever, and so reported to us. Charley was a bit anxious about being alone in the dark with that skull, so I knew what the thing was, of course, but I swear I came near running when I saw that skull come through the window. It was simply awful. John took one look and then Charley realized that he had won his bet, for things began to happen. John leaped to his feet with a cry like a wild bull. He turned over his chair and knocked the candle over, leaving the place in darkness. The next moment he was out of the door, carrying it and part of the frame with him. When he got outside, he headed for town and the boys hidden in the weeds said that it sounded like a drove of army mules when he passed them. They yelled at him, but that simply added to his speed, if that were possible.

We did not see anything of him for several days, and the queer thing was that, although Charley Gentry had won the five dollars, he was afraid to ask John for the money. John swore that if ever he found out who did it he would kill the fellow who poked "that dead man in on him."

Now, if anyone doubts the potency of a skull stuck on the end of a pole, let him stick one in the door or window of a nonbeliever in ghosts about midnight, and if he does not get good action I stand prepared to eat the skull. I believe even a dead man would get up and leave the room.

★ ★ ★

A TRUE CAT STORY

I see the *Chronicle* is publishing a regular series of animal stories, so I conclude that one that is absolutely truthful in every detail will be acceptable. My story is about my personal experience with two cats that for several nights and running destroyed not only my sleep but the ease and comfort of my neighbors for two blocks around me. Those were, in appearance, only ordinary cats, but when it came to loud talking and the use of profane language, they had all other cats I have ever known backed clear off the boards. They seemed absolutely oblivious to outside interference when they started a row, and old shoes, bootjacks, empty bottles and such things hurled at them seemed only to add to their sense of importance and they received them very much as a chorus girl receives a bouquet thrown on the stage to her—with only a moment's silence, a side-step and a smile. I know, because I bombarded those cats until I gave up in absolute despair.

The absolute depravity and meanness of those two cats may be seen from the fact that neither belonged in my yard, though both made free use of it for their meetings and subsequent battles. Often I have heard the big black fellow crying out, "Maria, Maria, come over in my yard!" thus showing that he laid claim to ownership of the place. But everybody has had the same experience with cats that I have outlined in the foregoing, but what everybody has not had is the extreme delight that I had in turning the tables on the cats and giving them an experience of their own and furnishing them a new sensation.

One bright, moonlit night I was awakened by the two cats who had gotten under my bedroom window and were using the most outrageous language to each other, in tones that would almost wake the dead. I searched the room for something to drop on them, for they were directly under the window and I could not have missed them. While I was making a fruitless search and wishing for a stick of dynamite, it occurred to me that my boy had purchased some large firecrackers the day before and had some left over. I went to his room and was fortunate enough to find one. It was not the great cannon cracker, but was the next size and the very thing I wanted. I lit a cigarette so as not to disturb the cats by lighting a match when I got ready to fire my cracker, pinched off the fuse, stuck it to the light and dropped it. I will say here that if any gunner in the army or navy could cut a fuse as accurately as I cut that one, his fortune would be made. The cats were in the midst of the most animated discussion and were just on the verge of blows. As I turned loose the firecracker I heard one say to the other, "You liar, you!"

Then the firecracker reached a point about four inches from the ground, directly between them, and exploded. I can't describe what took place. Each cat thought the other had shot at him. There was no scramble nor anything like that. There was plenty of action, but it resembled lightning more than anything else. There was a high board fence about ten feet behind one of the cats. He simply turned a back handspring, barely touched the top of the fence and was half a block up the street before the flash from the firecracker had died out. The other fellow went in the opposite direction and disappeared behind the stable. I have seen in scientific journals pictures of flying bullets moving 2,000 feet a second taken by instantaneous photography. They looked like they were standing still. I am willing to make a small wager that if one of those scientists had had his photographic machine trained on those two cats that night all he would have gotten would have been two long streaks.

While I was nearly choked with laughter and also lost in admiration over the record speed of the two cats, one of them came sneaking out from behind the stable. He had evidently thought the matter over and, finding he had not been hit by the pistol fired directly in his face by the other cat, he had gotten his "dander up" and, securing his razor, had come out looking for blood. That is the way I sized the situation up. He advanced very cautiously, without saying a word. I longed for another firecracker. I waited until he got nearly to the fence and, having nothing else to throw, I dropped my cigarette down just behind him. Again the effect was magical. He did not wait for the explosion of the bomb he thought the other cat had thrown at him from an ambuscade. He saw the sparks from the scattered burning tobacco and moved off like a rocket. There was one leap of ten feet to the top of the fence and he was gone.

Now, the remarkable thing about the whole circumstance was that neither of those cats opened its mouth or said a word after the first shock. All their energy was concentrated in their efforts to get away from there in the quickest time possible. I don't know how they ever settled the matter or what explanations they made to each other, but I do know that from that time on nothing on earth could induce either of those cats to come in my yard either during the day or night. The mystery of the affair was too much for them. Had I thrown a firecracker down on only one of them he would have known it was I who did it and acted accordingly. But the introduction of doubt and suspicion into the problem, which made each one doubt and mistrust the other and suspect him of having attempted to assassinate him, made the case of mystery complete. They dodged me and they evidently dodged each other, for we heard no more of their outrages.

★ ★ ★

ABOUT ALLIGATORS

Once when I was living in New Orleans, a young fellow asked me if I had ever been on a big cattle ranch and when I told him I had. He offered to bet me that I could not tell how a cow, that was lying down, got up. I had seen thousands of them get up, but when I got to thinking about it, I could not tell him to save my life. Then he asked me how a horse got up, and I could not tell that, either. Since that day I have always known that a cow gets on her hind feet first and a horse gets on his front feet first. That shows how little we observe things that occur constantly under our very noses.

Now, while most *Chronicle* readers may be better informed on cows and horses than I was, I am willing to take a small amount that not half a dozen of them can tell how an alligator opens his mouth. All the rest of the thousands will say that he opens it by raising his upper jaw; that the lower jaw lies flat on the ground and that the upper one rises. Last week, I admit, I would have said the same thing, but I know better now, for I have been reading up on alligators, and the natural history sharp whose book I read says that the alligator's jaws open far back, even behind the ears, where they are hinged or articulated into each other. The effect is that when the alligator opens his mouth his neck becomes somewhat bent upward, giving him the appearance of having moved the upper instead of the lower jaw. That was a new one on me, and I made up my mind to spring it on the public the first chance I got.

Speaking of alligators reminds me that there used to be quantities of them in Buffalo Bayou. I don't know how many Mr. Erichson, the father of Otto, killed in his day, but I know of several, and one of the largest I ever saw was killed by him about where the Louisiana bridge now stands. It was so large that it attracted public attention, just as that whale did a year or two ago. He cut the head off, had it prepared and shipped it to a museum in Germany. I remember seeing the head. It was in a large washtub and stuck up two or three feet above the top of the tub. The old man was a dead-shot with a rifle, and it took a dead-shot to kill an alligator with the guns of that day, for the only way to kill them was by shooting them in the eye. He could do that and he rarely failed to get them on the first shot.

As a boy, I heard stories of men being eaten by alligators, and I believe there are one or two well-authenticated cases reported. We boys paid no attention to the stories, however, and went in swimming just as though there were no such thing in the world as an alligator. The very evening Mr. Erichson killed that big one the bayou was full of boys not a hundred feet from where he killed it. But boys are hardly responsible for their fool capers.

On one occasion I witnessed a funny scene in which a 10-foot alligator was one of the principal actors. I was living out in the country with Louis Hillendahl. There was, and is yet, I believe, a large German settlement out there. One of the great summer sports was getting up a big fish fry. We had a great big seine and caught our fish that way. A week or two ahead a lot of the boys would select a nice stretch in Buffalo Bayou, and would strip off, get in and remove every snag. That was to give the seine fair play. Usually a space of a hundred yards or more would be cleared of snags, so as to catch as many fish as possible. The work was done some time before the seining so as to allow the frightened fish to return to their accustomed haunts. When everything was ready, on some bright Sunday morning, the whole neighborhood would turn out and meet at the bayou. There were men, women and children and everybody. The ladies would make fires and prepare for a big dinner while half a dozen young fellows would retire to the woods and don old clothes. These were the seiners. When everything was ready a whoop would announce that the seining was about to begin, and a rush would be made for the bank of the bayou, to watch the fun.

One Sunday morning the seining was going on finely. Two or three hauls had been made and quite a number of fish had been caught. Finally, just at a bend in the bayou, the seine became entangled in a deep hole. There was a big discussion, and the boys who had done the cleaning were roundly abused for having left such a snag there. Effort was made to clear the seine by pulling it sideways, backwards and every other way, but it was no use, it was evidently badly entangled. One or two of the boys volunteered to dive down and untangle it. It was rather deep, so none of them stayed down very long. Finally one fellow, whose sweetheart was watching him from the bank, took a long breath and went down with the evident intention of getting the seine free, even if he had to haul the log out that was holding it. He was down less time than any of the others, for he came up like a rocket, rose away up out of the water and made for the shore, shouting at the top of his voice the German equivalent for alligator. He hit the bank, scrambled out, and when he got breath enough to talk we learned that he had gone down and actually seized the alligator round the neck before he realized what it was. When he did find out what he was hugging he turned loose in a hurry and came out like a tornado.

Then you never heard so much excited talk. Every man there knew so well what should be done to capture that alligator that no one would listen to what anybody else said. Talk about the French being excitable, why a crowd of Germans with an alligator tangled up in their only seine 10 or 15 feet under the water can give the Frenchmen cards and spades and then beat them out. Finally it was determined that the only way to get the alligator out was to pull him out, and the whole crowd set to work doing so. It was hard work, for at first the alligator refused to budge. At last they got him started and you could hear those fellows shout for a mile or two. When finally they got him safely on the bank, he was fighting mad. He had not torn the seine while he was in the water, but he proceeded to rip it up right and left now that he was on land. Everybody who had an axe or hatchet took a dig at him, and that part of the seine which he had not destroyed was finished by the axemen. It was a wild, howling crowd that surrounded that alligator, and if he had been the least sensitive he would have died of fright long before they succeeded in killing him. No pack of coon dogs ever made such a racket about a fighting coon as those fellows made around that alligator. After it was all over they realized what foolish capers they had cut and laughed heartily at each other's antics. It was the best and most surprising seining party I ever attended.

There are no alligators in Buffalo Bayou today, at least not in the city limits, but I suspect that if a careful search were made one or two might be found up near the head of the bayou. The little lakes and ponds over in San Jacinto bottom were full of them a few years ago, and on one occasion I killed four or five without hardly getting out of my tracks. After doing such excellent shooting, I shot at a water moccasin five times at a distance of ten feet and missed him every time. The only way I can account for it is that the snake got on my nerves, for I dread even the sight of one.

★ ★ ★

BUD RANDOLPH A SCIENTIST

If anyone thinks that the Houston Press Club is not an interesting place and full of surprises, that one is badly mistaken. One can always meet there someone who knows something about everything on earth. There is where the surprises come in.

I came in contact with one of these surprises the other night when I discovered that "Bud" Randolph is one of the most profound entomologists in the state and that he has devoted many years to the study of bugs. He can tell you, offhand, without the least hesitation, the official names of bed bugs, cockroaches, boll weevils, tumblebugs and of more kinds of beetles, better than any fellow I ever met. He is a wonder.

Having tackled and mastered bugology, Bud evidently looked about for new fields to conquer and took up the study of natural history. His knowledge of rats, owls, skunks, cats, cur dogs, *et hoc genus omne*, is equal to his knowledge of bugs. The best part of the thing is that he does not have to be "drawn out." The other night someone mentioned a night made wretched by bed bugs and in a moment Bud had the floor.

"Oh, there is a most interesting member of the bug family. In my opinion the bedbug, or more properly speaking the *coccyclus indica myonsims*, is the most intelligent and thoughtful member of the dryonian family. He has sense like folks; he takes no chances and makes careful calculation before making an attack. He hides out when a light is on but comes to the front the moment it is turned out. He knows what he is doing all right and so do you when he gets to work.

"I have studied him and his habits and find that his bump of local attachment is wonderfully developed. He never leaves a place when once he establishes himself and he invites about a million of his friends to come and share the good thing he has found. When he has established himself, the only thing to do is set fire to your house, lock the doors and windows, and back off and watch the fun. It is expensive, but it is the only sure remedy.

"The bedbug has a terrible enemy in the tiger beetle, which we scientists know under the name *drastus lionions fabrista*. He could and would eat a bedful of bedbugs in two minutes if he could only get at them. The trouble is that the bedbugs get inside the mattresses and into the cracks of the bed while the tiger has to content himself with a mere surface examination of the bedspread.

"Speaking of rats," though no one had mentioned rats or even thought of them, "they are interesting members also. When I first began to study them, I was prejudiced, but I soon learned to admire them, for they so often do the unexpected and constantly spring cute little surprises.

"I remember one morning my lady stenographer pulled open her desk drawer to begin her day's work. Without a word of warning seven rats, one big one and six smaller ones, leaped out on her—we had to haul her out in the yard and pour water on her to bring her back around. Don't you know those rats planned the whole thing and laughed over the success of the joke afterward? I feel certain that they did.

"When I built my residence I built it rat-proof, of course, but the contractors did not. I had not been there long before I could hear the rats dancing and frolicking above my bedroom. Occasionally one would leave his place and fall down between the walls. In trying to catch himself on the rough plastering on the inside he would make a terrible racket. If you did not know the space was too small you'd think it was a dog or a calf falling.

"I stood it as long as I could and then I got a spring trap and set it out in the hall. The first night, about 2 o'clock there was a terrible racket out there, and I realized that I had got some game. I turned on the light and went out.

"By the time I got there the rat was halfway up the stair steps, lugging the trap with him. He was caught by one of his hind legs. When he saw me he abandoned the idea of going up, turned a summersault and came down, trap and all, in the middle of the hall. He was fighting mad, too, and made for me with blood in his eyes. As I had on only a nightgown and was both barefooted and barelegged I retired promptly, slamming the door as I did so. I got a chunk of stovewood and then finished his ratship.

"I sunned the trap next day and set it again. Nothing doing. Same result the next night and for several nights succeeding. I was congratulating myself on having scared off the rats and was sleeping peacefully one night when the most horrible racket you ever heard broke out in the hall.

"I realized that it was the trap again, but could not imagine what it had caught. I could hear the trap hit the floor, then hit the ceiling, bound off to the wall and come back to the floor with noise enough to wake the dead. It woke the whole neighborhood up and I could see lights being turned on in half a dozen nearby houses. They must have thought that I had caught a burglar or that a burglar had caught me and that I was trying to get away from him.

"Finally I switched on the light and peeped out in the hall. The mystery was solved. I had caught my wife's pet tomcat and he did not like it either. I had an 'underworld' of a time getting him free from the trap, too. I found a corn sack, wet it so it would stick, then threw it over him. I got him by the head and held him firmly until I could safely open the trap. When I released the cat, he did not stay to have his leg dressed, but went out of the open window like a streak of lightning. He did not show up again for ten days or two weeks and when he did come he examined the hall thoroughly to see if it was safe for him to come in. It seems that he entered through an open window that night and, in a stroke of bad luck, jumped down right into the trap. Of course, he thought it was a put up job and I don't think he ever forgave me for it.

"Yes, I have had experience with skunks, too. We know them under the scientific name *Magnus Odoriferous Felenus Americanus*, and they are all that the name implies.

"I and four or five cur dogs had an experience with seven of them in one bunch. The dogs corralled them on the prairie in a bunch of weeds and I was fool enough to get close up and take a shot at them. When I and the dogs got through vomiting, I realized that I had killed all seven of them and that they had nearly killed me and the dogs.

"I was with some boys in a wagon but they made me walk all the way to town, about six miles. When I got home they made me burn my clothes out in the yard and get under the hydrant and scour myself with lye soap. It was awful. It was a very cold day but I had to do it anyway."

★ ★ ★

HANTS AND HOODOOS

I was amused when I read in the papers the other day about the negroes being so frightened by the report that the "Axe Man" had reached Houston and was looking over the field before beginning his destructive work here. The description of how the negroes were using charms to ward off the disaster, which they feared was pending, was peculiarly amusing to me because I recognized that the negro of today is the same as the negro of my boyhood days. They are better educated, of course, but you can't educate superstition and the belief in charms out of a negro, and it is useless to try. "Hants," "hoodoos" and "spirits" are just as potent today as they have ever been with the negroes.

When I was a boy I had as implicit faith in the reality of ghosts as I had in anything, notwithstanding the fact that I was born a Doubting Thomas. The negroes taught me all kinds of nonsense and I became as superstitious as they. I was not alone in this for my state was common to all boys raised in the South among the negroes. I would no more dream of going in swimming without a string tied round my ankle to ward off cramps or to allow another boy to stunt my growth by stepping over me while I was lying down than I would have thought of jumping off the highest building in town. All three would prove fatal and I knew it.

Ghosts, however, were our strong points. Graveyards were shunned, even after early twilight, and after dark no boy would venture near one alone for anything. One of the greatest panics I ever was mixed up in was caused by this universal fear of ghosts. Four or five of us had been out hunting up Buffalo Bayou beyond the old San Felipe graveyard. We had stayed longer than we intended and it was quite dark when we came down the road by the side of the cemetery. Each boy recognized the dangerous position we were in, but not the slightest reference was made to the graveyard. We walked along boldly, each trying to get as far away from the cemetery fence as he could without attracting especial attention to what he was doing. There were several negro boys with us, for in that day no hunting party was complete unless there were as many negro boys as white ones. These negroes were frankly afraid and did not try to disguise the fact that they were shunning that fence. We talked loudly about everything we could think of except ghosts, though each boy knew that these latter were on each boy's mind and most prominently so, too. The real trouble was that none of the boys wanted a stampede, through fear of being left alone behind or of getting too far ahead and thus finding himself alone there.

All went well until about half of our perilous journey had been made. Then inside the graveyard a great white object was seen to rise up and the only boys left on the scene were those who had not seen it. Be it said to their credit, however, that they asked no questions and started after their more fortunate companions at a breakneck speed. It was only a newspaper which someone who had carried flowers out there had thrown aside, but had it been a devil with ten horns it could not have been more potent in starting that crowd. We did not stop until we reached town and then we halted only because we were out of breath. That was quickest time ever made over that old San Felipe road and that piece of newspaper was responsible for our getting home much sooner than we otherwise would have gotten there.

The other day I read a story of a negro who had been left in a haunted house with a bottle of whiskey and the promise that he would be given $5 the next morning if he remained there all night. About midnight something happened and the negro promptly tore out the front side of the house and left. Four days after he was seen coming up the road. "Where have you been?" asked one of the fellows who had hired him to stay in the house. "Why, boss," the negro replied, "I been comin' back." That was our fix exactly. We reached our goal so quickly that getting there did not count at all.

But the negroes' strongest belief was, and is yet, centered in the hoodoo and they fear a hoodoo negro worse than they fear the devil himself. It is somewhat remarkable that they are prepared to believe in hoodoo white men as well as hoodoo negro men.

I remember a laughable instance of this kind of faith on their part. A friend of mine had a negro cook who was absolutely no cook at all, but his wife liked something about her and would not consent to the cook being discharged. My friend was in despair, but finally thought of a plan for getting rid of her. He acted mysteriously and when she was in hearing he would mumble nonsense and repeat a kind of jargon in a low tone. This bore fruit and she began to watch his every movement with evident suspicion. One day he saw her go in her room, which was in the backyard, and he could see that she was watching him through a crack in the door. He slipped up and made a mark on the steps with a piece of red chalk. When she came out she avoided that mark as though it were a snake and she poured hot ashes and lye all over it.

My friend, a few days later, saw her go into her room again and take a position from which she could watch him. He had prepared himself for just such a situation. He slipped up and placed a small package, done up in red flannel, under the steps and crept cautiously away. He waited to see what the cook would do, but he waited in vain. He saw nothing of her. Finally his wife wanted her for some purpose and, receiving no reply to her calls, went out to investigate. She found the room empty. The cook had crawled out of a back window, had climbed over a high board fence and had made her escape into the street. That evening a dray man came for her things, but she herself never did show up again, not even to get a small amount of wages due her.

Right after the war there was a little old negro here who was known to everybody simply as "Crazy Harry." He was very eccentric and would abuse and curse whites and blacks with equal impunity, though no one paid any attention to what he said or did. The negroes, however, got it in their heads that he was a great hoodoo doctor and that he could summon the devil to help him whenever he chose. They feared and hated him, but they treated him with marked consideration and courtesy whenever he was around. Harry recognized his advantageous position and did everything to add to his evil repute.

Some of his capers were amusing in the extreme and at some future time I intend to devote an entire article to him and his doings, for Harry was a character whose memory deserves preservation. I will say here that his leading characteristic was hatred of the Yankee soldiers who were in possession of Houston right after the war. He hated every one of them, from the commanding general down to the lowest private, and played no favorites when he distributed his abuse of them. But enough of Old Harry for this time.

★ ★ ★

YELLOW FEVER, GHOST TALES AND FELINES

The present agitation over meningitis reminds me of some of the really exciting times they used to have in Houston when that great enemy, yellow fever, made an invasion. For the first few days pandemonium broke loose, and then people settled down and waited, in grim desperation, for the inevitable, knowing full well that only a complete exhaustion of material or a frost could stop the ravages of the fever.

Of course no one knew anything about the mosquito causing the disease, and some of the methods used to kill the "miasma" that was regarded as its cause, were novel. For instance, every exposed place was inundated with lime and, at night, huge bonfires, composed largely of tar barrels and tar, were burned at the street crossings. I remember, when I was a child, seeing those bonfires, which were ordered by the city authorities. Now, no doubt, both the lime and the fires did good, the first preventing the breeding of mosquitoes and the second by driving them away with the smoke.

The present generation cannot appreciate the horrors of a yellow fever epidemic. One case would appear, then a few, and then people would be taken down by the hundreds. In a week the death roll would begin to swell and business, except at the drug stores, would be suspended. Those who had had the fever became nurses and looked after the sick. One good thing was that yellow fever requires nursing rather than medicine, and as there were numerous nurses and few doctors, the patients generally got along pretty well. The doctors were so overrun that when they found a patient in the hands of a competent nurse, that they knew to be such, they turned the case over to the nurse and went elsewhere, where conditions were not so favorable.

I will never forget the time I had the fever, and as my case will give a fair idea of how the disease was treated, I give a short description of my experience. It was in 1858, on a Sunday morning, that I was stricken. I got up that morning feeling as well as ever, dressed, ate a good breakfast and started to Sunday school. On the way to Sunday school I was stricken suddenly with a terrible pain in the back of my head and then my head began to ache so terribly that I could scarcely see. It was with great difficulty that I managed to walk the two or three blocks home, and when I got there I was in such pain that I could scarcely talk. My mother knew at once what was the matter, for she had had much experience with the fever. I was hurried to bed and given a hot mustard footbath, and then blankets were piled over me. They gave me a dose of castor oil. That is one feature of the treatment I shall never forget, for after I had taken it they found I had eaten a large breakfast and they gave me a mustard emetic, made me throw it all up and then repeated the dose of oil.

The weather was warm, but they kept the bedclothes piled on me and the only thing they allowed me to drink was orange leaf tea. There I lay and sweated and famished for water for three days, or until the fever left me. There was no ice in those days, and if there had been any, the man who tried to give a yellow fever patient any would have been looked upon as a would-be assassin. It was tough treatment, but it did the work, and wherever people got the same treatment and nursing that I got they got well.

Where patients could not get proper nursing, they died like sheep, and they died in a hurry, too. I remember the great epidemic of 1867. I had come home from college during the summer vacation and just about the time I was getting ready to go back, the yellow fever broke out and I could not go because Houston was quarantined again at once and travel ceased.

Since I had already had the fever, I was safe in going everywhere and saw a great deal of the devastation. I remember four young men who had just come to Houston from the North. They were not the least afraid of the disease and laughed at their friends who warned them against exposing themselves to the night air. I remember ex-Mayor I. C. Lord telling them of the danger and warning them to be careful. They had rooms in the Kennedy building on market square and were over at the market at the time the conversation took place. That night the oldest one was stricken, the next morning the others were down and four days after Old Man Pannell buried all four of them.

There used to be all kinds of queer stories floating about, saying this and that one died, came to and then died again. One story was to the effect that a horse drawing a drayload of coffins to the graveyard became frightened, ran away and spilt part of the load. It was said that one of the coffins burst open and that its occupant, a negro woman, got up and made a beeline for home, got in bed again, got well and "lived happily for years after." Now, I don't vouch for the truth of any of these stories, but some funny things did happen. Dr. Massie died and was laid out. All preparations were completed for burying him, when he came to life. He was placed in bed again and heroic efforts were made to save him, but all in vain. He lived 24 hours and died, the last time for good. It was during that epidemic that one of the funniest panics on record took place. As all grown folk who were able to nurse were engaged in that way, it became necessary for the boys to sit up with the dead, if a death occurred too late in the afternoon to permit of burial at once.

The editor of one of the leading newspapers in Houston died late in the afternoon and Dick Fuller and Fish Allen volunteered to sit up with the body. The editor was living in the Ennis residence on Courthouse Square at the time of his death and the body, after being placed in a coffin, was placed in the back parlor on the ground floor. Dick and Fish began their lonely watch. All went well so long as they could hear people moving either in the house or in the street. Finally about midnight everything became quiet and they began to feel depressed. Like boys, they endeavored to cheer things up by talking about ghosts and such cheerful subjects. Dick asked Fish what he would do if the dead man should rise up in his coffin. Before Fish could reply there was a terrible shriek near the open window and with a great bound an immense black cat leaped on the window sill and with arched back and bristling tail, let out another blood-curdling cry. Then, without warning the single lamp in the room went out, leaving them in darkness. Neither Dick nor Fish could ever tell how they got out of the place, but when the neighbors arrived and went in to find out what had happened, they found the dead man on the floor, the coffin overturned and most of the furniture that stood between the window and door totally wrecked. Nothing could persuade those two boys to go back in the house, so substitute watchers had to be found. The boys worked themselves up to the highest point of nervousness and excitement, talking about ghosts and dead men, and that cat managed to put in an appearance just at the psychological moment. I don't blame the boys for not going back, neither do I blame them for coming out.

I don't care whether people believe in ghosts or not, I know everybody is afraid of them just as I am.

★ ★ ★

BEST FIGHTER IN THE ARMY

The other day I told about James Longstreet, the famous mule that was the mascot of Hood's Texas Brigade. Soon after the article appeared I met Captain Mat Ross, who was a member of Company H, Fifth Texas Regiment, of that brigade and he jumped on me for not having mentioned another equally famous member of the brigade, another James Longstreet, too. That was a little red rooster, the pride and glory of Company H, but the immediate property of Mat Ross and Major E. G. Goree, now a resident of Huntsville. Mat related the following to me about the latter James Longstreet:

"That rooster was the greatest little fighter in the Army of Northern Virginia. That is how he got his name. He would fight anything that had feathers on it and when he got stirred up would tackle a man or anything that got in his way. Why, it is a matter of regimental history that our rooster kept Ed Goree and me in ready money for a year or two. There was no rooster anywhere that could stand up in front of him. He whipped everything and never put on the least bit of airs over the fact. He got one eye knocked out in one of his battles, but that did not seem to interfere with his fighting qualities the least bit. I really believe it helped him, for it had a kind of demoralizing effect on the old roosters to have James Longstreet come at them with his head turned sideways so he could get a focus on them. They were not accustomed to that kind of an advance and he generally 'got their goat' before the fight lasted one round. We kept him in perfect condition and while we had no gaffs, we took charcoal and rubbed down his spurs so that they were always bright and sharp as needles.

"Ed Goree and I thought as much of that rooster as though he had been our son. We took turns in carrying him when we were on the march and if we had only one handful of corn for our ration, Jim got half of it. He was always getting in some trouble by being too familiar with the men. Usually he roosted on me or Ed Goree, but one night he took a notion to roost on Jim Langston, who was perfectly bald. About daylight Jim Longstreet woke up, and, stepping over on Jim's bald head, he threw back his head and sounded reveille. Now if Langston had remained quiet nothing would have occurred, but instead of doing so he made a grab for Jim Longstreet, who, in his haste to get away, closed his claws and cut three or four long gashes on Langston's head. He jumped up and, grabbing his gun, tried to shoot James Longstreet.

It was all we could do to keep him from shooting our rooster, but finally we got him quieted down.

"When we went down to the peninsula, Jim Longstreet went with us and won a small fortune for us, for we met some North Carolina troops down there and they had some fighting chickens with them. One great secret of our success was that Jim was mighty deceiving in his looks. He was mild-mannered and to look at him you would not think butter would melt in his mouth. He would walk about looking as if he would rather eat than do anything else and would actually pretend not to know what we were talking about when we were trying to arrange a fight. He was awfully cute that way. But after he found we had covered all the money the other fellows could rake and scrape, his whole manner would change and he became a warrior at once. It would have done your heart good to see Jim going into battle with his head cocked to one side so he could get a focus on the other fellow with his one good eye, and picking out the exact spot he was going to puncture. Ed Goree and I had as much faith in that rooster winning as we had in General Lee, and neither one of them ever deceived us. We would follow Lee anywhere, and we would bet our last dollar on Jim Longstreet.

"It is rather remarkable that both our favorites, Lee and Jim, should have met their first reverses at Gettysburg. General Lee had taken us into Pennsylvania and we had taken Jim Longstreet with us, of course. When I realized what a big fight it was going to be at Gettysburg, I took Jim back to the commissary wagons and gave him to Jim Stanger of Company A, who was acting commissary clerk. I told Stanger that from the looks of things there was going to be hell to pay and that some of us were going to get hurt. I told him if anything happened to me, to give Jim Longstreet to Ed Goree, and that if anything happened to both Ed and me, that he could have the rooster, but he must promise to take good care of him.

"We had been in the fight all the morning when the fire grew so fierce that we could hardly hold our position. So many men had been killed and wounded that our line had become dreadfully thin and weak. Colonel Powers ordered me to go back and bring every available man to the front, even those who had been wounded but were not entirely disabled. I went back and got about twenty men. I went as far as the wagons and there I saw Jim Stanger. He was almost crying and was pointing to a wrecked wagon and several dead horses beside it. 'Poor Jim Longstreet is gone,' he said. 'A little while ago a stray shell landed square on that wagon and you see what it did.'

Jim had been roosting in the wagon and the shell did not leave even a grease spot of him.

"You see, Jim died the death of a soldier and warrior. I know that if he had been given the choice of deaths he would have taken what he got. After I had gone back to the firing line and broken the sad news to Ed Goree we lay behind some rocks and discussed the matter. We finally concluded that the shell had come up on Jim's blind side and thus caught him, for we knew him so well that we felt certain he would have gotten well out the way before it lit, had he seen it coming.

"Jim Longstreet, the mule, was alright in his way, but at best he was a camp follower and loafer, while Jim Longstreet the rooster was an ornament to the regiment and a producer. After we had been camped near any other troops for a few days there was not a dollar left among them, for Jim would whip any chicken they could produce and we would rake in the money. The loss of Gettysburg was a sad blow to General Lee, but the loss of Jim Longstreet just naturally knocked the stuffin' out of Ed Goree and me. It was a great financial disaster."

★ ★ ★

Proof that Flies Think

Being somewhat bald I have had rather more difficulty and trouble with flies than the average man. They have acted meanly with me, too, and at times, have actually gone out of their way to annoy me. I have read all about their spreading disease and of how filthy they are and furthermore I know that everything that has been said to their disparagement is true, yet in the face of all this I have learned to admire and to almost honor the fly. I have discovered that they have sense just like folks and that they have a fine appreciation of the humorous side of things.

Not long ago they formed the habit of coming in my room and sitting on my bed waiting for me to try to take my afternoon nap. I got a towel and went for them. They simply dodged, laughed and made such a lot of fly racket that others from the outside came to see the fun and having come, stayed to join in the play.

Those flies thought I was playing tag with them and they entered into the spirit of the game in a whole-hearted way that discouraged me. Actually my efforts to kill them with a towel increased their number and I gave up in despair. One day I spoke of my trouble to a friend and he suggested that I go to the drugstore and get a "swat-the-fly," a piece of iron screen hitched to a handle. As he explained, the wind from my towel blew the fly aside before the towel reached him and that is why the fly enjoyed the game so much. He knew he was in no danger and that he was exhausting me by hanging around and encouraging me to hit him with the towel.

Well, I got the swat thing and laid for my flies. So soon as I made out I was going to take a nap, they put in an appearance, abandoning everything else they were doing to devote themselves to me. But I fooled them. Two settled down on the bed and pretended not to be noticing me, sat there as if it were they who were going to take a nap instead of I. I brought down my swat thing on them and as there was no wind to warn them I got both of them. Others came and others fell, too, and for half an hour I had everything going my way. I killed every fly in sight and, having become bloodthirsty by now, I hunted for more. Some who had seen the slaughter and retreated must have spread the news, for I longed for more flies to swat, but none came. They would come as far as the window and look in but you could not hire a fly to enter the room and strut around as they had all been doing.

Having thus been brought in such close communication with flies I learned to respect them greatly. I also learned that they are keen observers and, that having seen a thing once, they recognize it thereafter. Now sometimes when I am absent the flies will take things easy just as they used to do. They even go so far as to ignore my presence completely and pay no attention to me at all. But they watch me closely and stand prepared to act promptly. When I get ready to clear the room of their presence, I do not exert myself at all. I merely pick up my swat-the-fly machine and they leave in a body.

Learned professors may argue that flies can't reason and that they can't talk, but I want those professors to explain to me how those flies know the difference between a towel which gives warning of its approach and the wire contraption that gives none. Furthermore, how do the flies inform each other that I have picked up the swatter? They can't all be watching me at the same time and yet every one of them departs at the sight of the swatter. As a matter of fact, I have not been able to get near a fly with my swatter in a week and if I want a quiet nap all I have to do is to place the swatter on the bed where the flies can look in the window and see it and not one will venture in the room.

I don't know anything about flyology, if there is such a thing, but I do know that a fly has as much sense as a man about some things and that the fellow who takes Mr. Fly for a fool is almost one himself.

Now, the concerted action on the part of flies when I pick up my swatter precludes any other idea than that flies can talk. If I could hear and understand their language I am confident I would hear some old fellow call out, "Git! He's got his swatter. This is no place for us!" When you see dozens of them take wing as one fly and rush out of the window, you can safely bet that something like that has been said by one of their pickets and that they have acted promptly on the warning.

This is not written to fill space but is a record of actual occurrences and of the evidence of high intelligence of the fly. He has simply got more sense than anybody credits him with having.

★ ★ ★

HUNTER MYER

I have told of the boy hunters of Houston and of what fun we used to have chasing rabbits, shooting birds and roaming over the prairies and woods which are now thickly settled portions of the City of Houston, and now I am going to tell of a sure enough hunter, one whose exploits in that line equalled those of any of the great hunters of this country.

In the late 40s there came to Houston a gentleman who was apparently in the advanced stages of consumption. He was tall, being over six feet, and as straight as an arrow. He was a man of family and had but little of this world's goods. The doctors told him that he must not seek employment that would keep him indoors or be in any way confining; that he must go somewhere where he could be in the open air and get all the sunshine possible. The advice was the proper thing and it was easy enough for the doctors to give, but it was not so easy for Mr. T. B. Myer, the gentleman himself, to follow, since its adoption meant the starvation of his family while he was attempting to get well. He thought it all over and then concluded that there was but one way in which he could follow the doctor's advice and at the same time support his family, and that was by becoming a professional hunter.

Having formulated this plan, he set about putting it in practical operation. Among his friends was a San Jacinto veteran, a Mr. Arnold, who gave him a long rifle which he had used in the battle of San Jacinto. Every schoolboy raised in Houston remembers the long rifle, which was as well known as

"Hunter" Myer. It was very long and very heavy and we boys used to wonder how anybody could ever handle it at all. Having probably done some execution among the Mexicans at San Jacinto, it was destined to do much greater among the deer, turkeys and other game near Houston. Hunter Myer used this rifle for over a quarter of a century and when too old and infirm to hunt longer he gave it to Tom Padgitt, then a Houston boy, but now one of the leading merchants of Waco, who still has it.

Hunter Myer was a remarkable man in many respects. He was over six feet high, did not have an ounce of fat on his body and was nothing but bone, sinew and muscles. He was a powerful man and had a grip like a vise. One of the most vivid remembrances I have of him was seeing him one day scare a little Jew almost to death. The Jew kept a store on or near the corner of Preston Avenue and Milam Street and had done something that angered Hunter Myer and he had gone to the Jew's store evidently with the intention of chastising him. When he got there and the Jew realized that Hunter Myer was after him, his terror was so evident and his attitude so groveling that Mr. Myer changed his mind about giving him a whipping and concluded to give him a good scare instead. He suddenly reached over the counter and catching the Jew by the back of his coat lifted him bodily over the counter as easily as if it had been an infant he was handling. Then catching him by the collar of his coat he bore him, shrieking, to the sidewalk. There holding him out at arms' length he quietly pulled out his long hunting knife and pretended to be searching among the Jew's ribs for a soft place to shove the point of the knife in. Sheriff Hogan, who lived across the street on Milam, heard the shrieks of the little fellow and concluding that someone was being murdered, came on a run. Mr. Myer winked at the sheriff and he saw it was only fun, so he did not interfere.

The Jew did not see anything but the big knife and all he heard was the grit and grind of Mr. Myer's teeth, who pretended to be fairly crazy with anger. He would lower the little fellow to the ground as though he was going to let him go and then, changing his mind, he would elevate him again and begin searching with the point of his knife for fresh places in the Jew's side. The Jew's shrieks and prayers for mercy were pitiful. Finally Mr. Myer released his grip sufficiently to allow the Jew to escape, which he did very promptly, going toward Main Street and leaving all his earthly possessions behind him. He was thankful to escape with his life.

All that took place, of course, after Myer had regained his health and after he had made his name as a mighty hunter. His hunting outfit was simple—a little two-wheel wagon with a canvas cover, drawn by a single horse. This horse was trained and was of great assistance to him while out on his hunts.

As there were no such things as cold storage and ice in those days, Mr. Myer had to get his game to town as soon after killing it as possible. Hence he could not go very far off to hunt. His favorite hunting grounds were up Buffalo Bayou, the head of Clear Creek, Chocolate Bayou, Austin Bayou, San Jacinto bottom and other nearby points, none of them more than 12 or 15 miles from Houston. An idea of the abundance of game near Houston at that time may be found from the statement that when Hunter Myer died in 1880 he was credited with having killed, within 20 miles of Houston, over 11,000 deer, and turkeys and other game too numerous to mention, all of which he sold in Houston.

He was a quiet and peaceful man, slow to anger, but when once aroused it was well to keep out of his way, for he became terrible. He was absolutely honest and fair in all his dealings and he demanded and saw, too, that all with whom he came in contact accorded him the same treatment. He played no favorites in disposing of his game and, unless some one of his customers had spoken in advance for a part or the whole of a deer or for other game, he sold everything in the open market on a first come, first served kind of way. He would come down Main Street, if he had been hunting out that way, and often before he had reached Preston Avenue he would be sold out, for a sight of his little wagon jogging down the street was notice enough for the people living on Main Street that they could get venison or other game. He never had the least trouble in selling all the game he could kill.

★ ★ ★

TROUBLESOME GHOSTS

Houston has had its full quota of haunted houses. There have been a number of them in different parts of the town and, no doubt, if one took the trouble to look for them others could be found today just as real and just as scary as were the old ones. The old ones, of which I speak, were conducted by quite a variety of "hants." There were serious-minded ghosts, lively ghosts, noisy ghosts and others who said or did nothing, but who merely made their presence felt in the most awe-inspiring way.

I have had personal experience with all the varieties, for I was ever curious about such matters and never let an opportunity pass to make an investigation. I can say from my own experience that the worst ghost of all is the one you can neither see nor hear, but which you can "feel" is in a room or some part of the house with you, and which you fear is going to lay hands on you at any moment.

Occasionally one meets an amusing, though mischievous, ghost or set of ghosts and it is of that sort I am going to speak now. I am not afraid of the story not being believed, for not only is it absolutely true, but there must be hundreds of citizens yet living who will remember all about it when they read this. It was too remarkable an occurrence to have escaped their minds completely. The only point on which I am doubtful is the exact year it occurred, but I am rather certain it was in 1869. That, however, is a minor matter.

One evening during the summer of, let us say 1869, a saloon keeper who lived out on McKinney Avenue, two or three blocks beyond Austin Street, took his seat with his wife at the supper table. They had scarcely commenced the meal when half a brick, coming from nowhere, apparently, landed on the table, smashing a dish, and rolled off on the floor. The man rushed out of the house, thinking some one had thrown the brick through the window or door, but he saw no one. He returned to the supper room and as he entered it another half brick smashed a picture frame that was hanging on the wall. Then other bricks and things began to fall on top of the house and on its sides.

This bombardment continued for several days and the house soon presented the appearance of a general wreck. There was not a pane of glass left and everything breakable in the home was in fragments. A remarkable thing was that while all the window panes were broken none of the woodwork of the window was touched. The place became famous and hundreds of people, watched and guarded the vacant blocks all around there every night, but still the missiles came. I was there one night when the bone of a cow's leg, a tin can, a large piece of wood and a brickbat were hurled all together against the front of the house with great force. It would seem that numerous accidents would have happened and that many people would have been injured by such promiscuous bombarding, yet I believe that only one person, the occupant of the house, was ever struck and his injury was trifling.

Many theories were advanced to account for such things, the most popular one being that it was the work of some enemy of the man, but the fatal error in that theory, aside from the man's statement that he had no enemy, was to account for the way in which such enemy accomplished the feat of hurling the projectiles without being caught in the act of doing so. One or two hundred people guarded the house on all sides and in every direction and yet no one ever saw anything that could account for the phenomenon. It would seem impossible for a half brickbat to be hurled from a great distance through a window pane without touching any of the woodwork and then smash a picture or looking glass hanging on the wall with unfailing accuracy, and yet that was exactly what occurred night after night.

Finally everybody gave it up and left the poor fellow alone at the mercy of the ghosts. The bombardment continued for some time and finally the man concluded to go to headquarters for a solution of the problem. He went to a spirit medium. One or two "sittings" were held and he was informed that there was great wealth buried in the earth under the house and that he must bore for it. I forget whether it was oil or gold they told him was there. His house stood immediately over the place where he must bore, but under no circumstances must he move the house. He was absolutely desperate by now for his house was a wreck surrounded by cartloads of bricks, bones, tin cans and every other kind of trash one could think of. He was willing to do anything to get rid of the ghosts, so he sought out a well-borer, made a contract with him and in a few days work was begun. A derrick was erected on top of the house a hole was cut through the roof and through the floors and the well-boring commenced. So soon as active operations were commenced the ghosts quit. Not another stone was thrown from that time.

The boring continued for several weeks and almost as many people went out to see the well bored as had gone to try to see the ghosts, for it was a strange sight to see a well being bored right through the roof of a house. I don't know whatever resulted from sinking the well beyond the fact that the ghosts were apparently pleased to have living beings complete the destruction of the man's house which they had begun, and so withdrew from the job. If gold or oil were ever found the man kept it a profound secret, for no one ever heard of it.

Those ghosts were amusing fellows, that is for everybody except the owner of the property, and as the spectators were generally out in the yard with plenty of company it was not the least scary to be there. I afterward had experience with one of the silent fellows, one of those kind you can neither see nor hear but whom you can "feel" is there all right. I stayed in a room with one of these one night until after midnight. Then the lamp went out suddenly, something blew in my ear and I left. I can give the street and number of this place, but I will not do so, for I passed it the other day and saw on its front: "Furnished Rooms to Rent." I don't want to empty the place, and while it is a good story and absolutely true, I will not tell it.

★ ★ ★

SINCLAIR'S GOAT RACES

One hot day during the summer of 1892, Wm. R. Sinclair and Nat Floyd were standing on Congress Avenue near the corner of Main Street when two boys came along driving two dilapidated-looking goats, hitched to wagons made out of soap boxes and mounted on baby buggy wheels. Sinclair's attention was drawn to the activities of the two boys who were trying to get some action out of their respective goats. Turning to Floyd, Sinclair said, "Floyd, I'll bet you that the far goat beats the other to the courthouse."

"What'll you bet?" asked Floyd.

"Drinks for you and me and a quarter as a prize for the winner of the race," said Sinclair.

"You're on," said Floyd. "Line up your goats."

Sinclair halted the two boys and explained the situation to them and they readily agreed to make the race. Sinclair and Floyd got out in the street and began the preliminaries.

At that time Congress Avenue had a so-called pavement, but it was good on one side only. There were no traffic laws then, as now, so anybody used the side of the street that seemed best or more convenient. The result was that only one side of the street being used when the two newspapermen took charge of the goats, they blocked traffic in both ways. A big crowd began gathering and everybody wanted to know who had been killed, what accident had happened or what was the matter. Floyd and Sinclair made no answer, but went ahead with their work. Just as they got their goats in line a rough voice was heard and then Captain Jack White showed up behind the voice. The moment he saw Sinclair he knew something wrong was going on.

"Oh, it's you, you rascal," he said, addressing Sinclair. "I could have closed my eyes and known that some devil's work was on foot had I known you were here. What are you going to do now? It's nothing for the peace and law and order I know."

"Why Captain White," said a lady who was in the crowd. "The gentleman has done nothing wrong that you should speak to him that way. He and the other gentleman are assisting those two boys to do something, that's all."

"Madam," said Captain Jack, "Ye do not know this chap as I know him. He has given me more trouble than all the other rascals in town. Wherever he goes and wherever he stops I look for trouble. It may look innocent to you, but I know better, and think I'd best take him in just to avoid trouble."

It may be said right here, that Captain Jack White thought Sinclair one of the finest fellows in the world, and while he abused him to his face, it would not have been a healthy thing for anyone else to do in Captain Jack's hearing.

"Now, Captain," said Sinclair, "keep your shirt on. Floyd and I are doing nothing except trying to pull off a goat race and we can't get the street clear of carts, wagons and horses." Sinclair then told the captain of the bet with Floyd and the prize for the boy who won.

"Is that all you're doing?" said the captain. "Clear the way there," he shouts, waving his club, and in a few moments he had the right side of Congress Avenue clear from Travis Street down to the courthouse. There were five hundred people lined up on the sidewalks to see that initial race and the winner was cheered to the echo.

That, briefly, is a history of the beginning of Sinclair's famous goat races which for a time attracted national interest and attention. While Sinclair never had much in common with a goat he always had a great deal in common with a boy and was a bigger crank about boys than Jud Lewis is about babies. He was every newsboy's friend and confidential adviser and knew all their trials and tribulations much better than their parents did. Whatever he said to do they did. His influence was not confined to the newsboys, but extended to every boy in Houston. That being true, it was an easy thing for him to organize the boys into a great racing association, goats being the "ponies" used.

Sinclair took only the boys in his confidence and no one knew of the first goat race until Sinclair announced, in the morning paper, that it would occur one afternoon on San Jacinto Street and would be run from Preston Avenue to Congress Avenue.

That afternoon San Jacinto Street was lined on both sides for the entire length of the course. Everybody was talking goat and the whole town thought of nothing else. A committee of leading citizens called on Sinclair and asked him to organize a grand race for the next year, to be held where everybody could see it. Magnolia Park, then in its glory, was selected as the place. Sinclair got busy and after talking to his boys they went to work with a will and soon every boy in Houston who could beg, buy or borrow a goat had a private training establishment of his own. The morning newspaper gave Sinclair all the space he wanted and when he began his "publicity" work he had the publicity department of the No-Tsu-Oh of today looking like thirty cents. The state papers entered into the spirit of the thing and Houston's Goat Races were soon the best advertised things in the state.

The next year, 1893, Sinclair grew ambitious and invited Governor Hogg to come to Houston and act as official goat starter. The governor was equal to the occasion and promptly accepted the great honor. That cinched things. The idea of a great governor of a great state like Texas, leaving his arduous duties to come to Houston to start goat races, caught the people. The railroads at once established excursion rates to Houston from all parts of the state.

When the great day came, every bank, the railroad shops, every wholesale and retail house in Houston was closed and the day was made a real holiday. By noon there was hardly a man or woman to be seen in the city, and not a single boy. Everybody had gone to Harrisburg, where the races were held.

It is out of the question to attempt to describe the scenes on the grounds. Hundreds of prizes had been offered by the merchants and everybody had contributed something for the pleasure of the boys. There were tons of watermelons and hundreds of cases of soda water. There were regular hills of cakes and pies and nothing could have been more attractive to the average boy than the display of good things to eat and drink.

Captain Jack White was about right when he told the lady that Sinclair could not keep from doing something outrageous. Sinclair had invited the governor to come to Houston and had given him the coolest place to rest in during the heat of the day, namely, the tent where the watermelons were stored, amid chunks of ice. When Sinclair saw the big governor sitting back, fanning himself, the devil tempted him and he fell. He got about two hundred boys, drew them up in line behind the tent and told them that the first boy to get in the tent from the rear could have the biggest melon. Then he gave the signal to charge and the next moment Governor Hogg, chunks of watermelon and two hundred boys were struggling amid the torn-down tent. It was merely a side play, but the governor enjoyed it as much as anyone.

After that race Houston became famous as a sporting center, and before long a challenge was received from Pittsburgh, Pa., saying that Pittsburgh had the fastest goat in the world and that if the Houston champion would come up there, Pittsburgh's pet would wipe up the earth with him. The challenge was promptly accepted. Sinclair sent his champion goat and boy owner, a young chap named Bailey, and when the race came off "Black Bill" won and was officially declared to be the Champion Fast Goat of the World.

The people of Houston used to turn out to welcome the Houston Light Guard when they came back home victorious from an interstate drill, but those Light Guard receptions sank into in significance compared to that given Black Bill when he returned from Pittsburgh. Everybody, who did not have a broken leg, was down at the depot, and when Black Bill and his proud owner appeared, the heavens were rent with cheers. A procession was formed and, headed by a brass band, marched down Main Street. It was a day of triumphant rejoicing. I think that if proper influence were used, Sinclair could be induced to revive those famous races. He is just as great a favorite with the Houston boys now as he was with those of years ago and he can get them to do things quicker and more heartily than any other man alive.

FIGHTING HOUSTON MEN, IN WAR AND IN PEACE

★ ★ ★

HOOD'S BRIGADE MASCOT

During the winter of 1869, I was sitting in the reading room of the old St. Charles Hotel in New Orleans, when I saw in a stray copy of the *Houston Telegraph* the following startling headline:

"DEATH OF JAMES LONGSTREET"

Naturally I supposed that General James Longstreet, the great Confederate general and the loved and admired leader of the Texas brigade in Virginia, which brigade was so immediately under his command, was the Longstreet referred to. I read the article eagerly and was relieved to find that it was the death of a famous mule rather than that of the famous general that was chronicled. That mule was famous indeed, for it had the distinction of being the "mascot" of Hood's Texas Brigade in the army of Northern Virginia.

Just where Jim Longstreet came from I never knew. All I know is that Major W. D. Denney, who was commissary of the brigade, owned him as early as 1862 and that Jim was a conspicuous object around the commissary wagons during the four years of the war. Major Denney was killed at Elthams Landing the first time the brigade was under fire, on May 7, 1862, and was succeeded by Major Robert Burns, who fell heir to the mule and also to a big gray horse owned by Major Denney. I mention these facts so as to get Jim Longstreet's war record straight. He shared in the glory of the first battle, though from a safe distance, and laid down his ears at Appomattox.

Jim was a beautiful animal. He was about the size of a small Shetland pony, perfectly formed, graceful, quick in his movements and, though by no means lazy, he never did a lick of work in his life. He was a camp follower in the strictest sense of the word, and before the war had continued very long he was considered the very best authority on the nearness of a fight. At the sound of the first gun Jim would break for the rear and remain there until the trouble was over. He was a great forager and would go off alone on private expeditions, but at the sound of a cannon he would duck his head and make a beeline for the wagons. His track was about the size of a silver dollar and was easily recognized, so that it frequently served as a guide for the two-legged foragers to find camp. Jim shared in all the hardships through which the army passed, but they seemed to do him good instead of harm, for he was always fat and sassy. He was with the brigade when it went to help Bragg out at Chickamauga and in Tennessee. He followed Lee to Gettysburg and finally, as already remarked, laid down his ears at Appomattox. When the end came Major Burns brought his gray war horse and Jim to Texas. How he managed to do it is a mystery, but he did it and late in 1865 he arrived in Houston with both animals. He presented James Longstreet to Dick Fuller, whose brother, B. P. Fuller, had been captain of Company A in the Fifth Texas Regiment.

From the moment that Jim became Dick's property, his comfort and ease were assured and he led a life that suited him down to his toes. He was the personal pet of every boy in town and from the dignified air he assumed I am confident he felt his importance and knew how great a mule he was. He had sense just like folk and had the most cunning ways about him. There was absolutely nothing vicious about him.

James Longstreet, like many men who did no actual fighting during the war, never was convinced that the war was over. For him the war went on for many years after Appomattox. This was shown in a decided way. James continued his foraging expeditions to the day of his death. He would wander away and go clear out on the prairie, though he never crossed the bayou and went into the woods. No matter how far away he was or what he was doing, if a thunderstorm came up he would duck his head and break for home at the first thunder clap. He was certain that a fight was about to begin and he hunted for safety at the discharge of what he thought was the opening gun of the engagement. When at home a thunderstorm had no effect on him and he paid no attention to the most terrible crashes, but away from home he was keenly on the alert.

James Longstreet died in 1869, full of years and honors. He was given a decent burial, as was befitting his station in life, and the *Houston Telegraph* published a column obituary of him, reciting his many virtues. His record was remarkable and his life he made an easy one. He was the pet of the soldiers of Hood's Brigade four years and the pet of the boys of Houston during the remaining years of his life after the war was over. He lived at peace with himself and the whole world and died lamented by all who knew him.

★ ★ ★

EARLY FIREMEN GALLANT SOLDIERS

Judge James K. P. Gillaspie, who was at one time chief of the old volunteer fire department, has in his possession the books of Hook and Ladder No. 1, which he allowed me to look over a day or two ago. I found much of interest in these books, but, as was the case with Judge Anders' old court records, it was the memories evoked rather than anything else that appealed to me. One portion in particular was the record which began in 1859 and broke off suddenly in 1861, to be resumed again in 1865, with nearly all new names. The great war had intervened between those two dates. The last meeting of the company, before the war, was held in May, 1861. As a matter of general interest I give the roster of the company at that time:

Officers—E. R. Bremond, foreman; Ed Riordan, assistant foreman; J. B. Cato, secretary; G. L. Griscom, assistant secretary; D. K. Rice, treasurer; J. C. Baldwin, president; F. H. Bailey, vice president.

Members—R. A. Allen, W. H. Allen, T. P. Brain, J. S. Benton, E. A. Burke, C. Buckley, W. H. Clark, C. A. Darling, R. W. DeLesdernier, T. P. Evert, Charles Eika, C. G. Fisher, H. Fleishman, A. J. Hay, F. L. Hoffman, A. J. Hurley, J. W. Mangum, J. R. Morris, C. H. Merriman, A. S. Mair, George Merriweather, J. D. McClary, Thomas O'Donnell, Louis Pless, G. W. Perkins, F. A. Rice, I. C. Shaffer, J. H. Sawyer, W. C. Timmins, Ed White, W. F. Wright, W. Williams, C. Westlake.

Some person has marked in the book certain notes giving, here and there, information concerning these old members. These notes are very brief and do not do justice to the memory of the men. For instance, opposite the name of F. L. Hoffman, is this entry: "Killed by the Yankees." The others are equally as brief and unsatisfying. Since I know some of them and the records they made in the Confederate army, I propose to give a brief history of them and ask Judge Gillaspie to paste it in the old book. Nearly every member of the company went into the Confederate army. I. C. Stafford organized the first company that left Houston and rose to the rank of major. Ed Riordan also left as captain of a company. Captain F. A. Rice served on Magruder's staff, I believe. There were many others, who I know were in the army, though I am not certain where they served. I do know all about five of them, because they were members of Hood's Texas Brigade. All but one, Captain Dave Rice, belonged to the Bayou City Guards, Company A, Fifth Texas Regiment.

T. P. Bryan was killed at the battle of the Wilderness, on May 6, 1864. J. W. DeLesdernier was killed at Gains' Farm, June 27, 1862. W. H. Clark belonged to Company A, and after Onderdonk, the color bearer, was disabled at Gains' Farm, he became color bearer for the Fifth Regiment. Clark was badly wounded in Chickamauga, September 19, 1863, and was again dangerously wounded while bearing the colors at the Wilderness, May 6, 1864. This last time he was incapacitated for further service and was sent home. He lived several years after the war and died in Austin.

C. A. Merriman belonged to Company A, Fifth Regiment. He was wounded in one of the first skirmishes his company got in, and was then attacked by what the doctors said was galloping consumption. He was honorably discharged from the army and returned to Texas to die. During the winter of 1862 the Federal war vessel, the *Harriet Lane*, had anchored in the Potomac and kept up an almost constant bombardment of the winter quarters of the Texas brigade. Charley Merriman got back to Texas late in the fall of 1862 and when he learned that Magruder was organizing his forces to take Galveston and that the *Harriet Lane* was one of the vessels there, he volunteered to go down on the *Bayou City*, one of the Confederate boats, that was to attack the Federal vessels. He was more than half dead anyway. He was in the fight that took place January 1, 1863, and had the pleasure of getting even with the *Lane*, by helping to capture her. Now here a miracle was worked. Merriman had his arm badly shattered by a piece of shell and he was shot right through the lung. His arm got well and what was more remarkable, the bullet through his lung cured his consumption. He was never troubled with his lung after that and got so fat and healthy that he returned to Virginia and remained with his comrades till the close of the war.

The other member whose record I know was Captain Dave Rice, the youngest brother of Wm. M. and F. A. Rice. He was one of the handsomest men to be found anywhere. He was perhaps too effeminate looking, as he had the complexion of a girl. His complexion was the only effeminate thing about him, for he was a man, every inch of him, and one of the most gallant soldiers in Lee's army. He was captain of Company C, First Texas Regiment, but did more duty as a field officer than as a company commander. He was in command of the First Regiment at the battle of Chickamauga, September 19 and 20, 1863, and had quite a strange experience there on the first day's fight. He was captured and taken before General Rosecrans. Of course he refused to give any information, but the general kept him with him and for two hours he was literally under the fire of both armies. I say "under," for that's what he was. His own brigade was on one hill and the Federals were on an opposite hill, while Rosecrans and his staff were in the narrow and deep valley, so that all the fighting went on over their heads. Late that night an opportunity presented itself and Captain Rice made his escape, but was unable to get back to his command for several weeks.

I wish I knew something about the war records of the other members, for it would give me great pleasure to write them down here.

$$\star \; \star \; \star$$

DESPERADOES AS SOLDIERS

Houston has introduced some remarkable characters in the past, and some of her sons have established enviable reputations in the world. There are others of her sons who have made names for themselves as great warriors in private life; in a word, as desperadoes, and others as near-desperadoes. In the early days each community had its "bad man," who was pointed at with something like pride, for he was sure to shed a kind of luster on the community. Houston had several of these "bad men," gunfighters or whatever is the proper name for them. There was Kane Norton, who was killed in the battle of Mansfield, over in Louisiana; Tom Clarke, who was knifed to death by a dozen Mexicans in the market house in San Antonio, after he had killed several of them and exhausted all the shots of his six-shooter, and last, but not least, Buck Stacey, of whom I am going to speak at more length now. Buck did not have the glory of dying on the field of battle or of dying amid the bodies of those who had fallen before his deadly pistol, but he did have the honor of being the first man condemned to death by a court-martial and executed on this side of the river during our great war. But we will come to that later.

Buck was a "throw-back" if ever there was one. His father died when he was quite young and he was raised by his mother, a God-fearing, praying, Christian woman. His home life and surroundings were such as should have produced a preacher or at least a Sunday school superintendent, but they produced, if they had anything at all to do with it, something exactly the opposite. He was a magnificent looking young man. Nearly six feet high, with hair and mustache as black as the raven's wing, while his eyes were those of the typical desperado, steel blue and as clear as crystal. He was a handsome fellow, and yet, strange to say, he was no lady killer and avoided female company.

Buck's first appearance on the stage as a shooting man was a surprise to everybody, for he made his debut suddenly and unannounced. Mr. T. T. Thompson, the great jeweller who afterward moved to Galveston, had a large jewelry store on the northeast corner of Main and Congress Avenue. He had a young fellow from New York to clerk for him. This young man was one of the "flip" kind and had more impudence than sense. One day Buck's mother went to the store to make a purchase and could not find exactly what she wanted. The young clerk grew impatient and finally got so impertinent that she left the store, intending to complain to Mr. Thompson when she met him. At dinner she mentioned the incident, not dreaming that Buck would act in the matter. Buck ate his dinner, took his hat and strolled down to Thompson's. He walked in and, catching sight of the young fellow, opened fire on him. Buck had only two derringers. His first shot missed and the young fellow, screaming like a scared Indian, attempted to get upstairs behind a large jewel case. Buck saw his victim was about to escape, so he shot at him through the case, wrecking watches, brooches and everything else in the line of fire. He missed again, but he had scared the young man so badly that he rushed upstairs, escaped through a window, slid down a post and made good his escape. It was said that he ran all the way to Harrisburg.

Whatever he did, he never showed up in the store again. Buck's mother paid all the damage that had been done and the matter was dropped. I doubt very much if the courts would have noticed the case if she had not paid anything, for in the early days it was hard to convict a man for resenting impertinence to his mother or to any other lady. That affair died out, but Buck had had a taste of "high life" and he liked it, so he went from bad to worse, became a professional gambler and was a "bad man." His greatest failing was his quick and ungovernable temper. That was a bad asset for a desperado and would have led to his undoing in the end had he been permitted to run his course. Coolness and quiet decision were the mainstays of all the desperadoes I have ever known, and I have known several of the most prominent of them. Buck's passion always got the best of him and he was always at a disadvantage in consequence.

When the war broke out there were several companies organized in Houston and at nearby points. These troops were for service along the Rio Grande and in New Mexico and in Arizona. Buck was among the first to volunteer. I am not certain, but I think he and Frank Le Mott were in Captain I. C. Stafford's company, the first company to leave Houston. There were a lot of mighty good men in that company and there were some pretty tough ones, too. Among them were gamblers and desperate men who had always been accustomed to have their way about everything, and to act as they pleased.

These could not understand the necessary restraints that were placed on a soldier, and before a week had expired they were for kicking over the traces. The company, with other companies, was placed under command of General John R. Baylor, a born soldier and fighter. He started in at once to establish discipline, but he had hard work. The men gambled constantly and there were several shooting scrapes among them. Nearly every day somebody got shot. Finally General Baylor prepared an order which he had posted and also read at dress parade, announcing that the next man who was aggressor in a shooting scrape would be tried by drumhead court-martial and shot. That very evening Buck Stacey shot the sergeant of the company. He was arrested and put in the guardhouse. That night the sergeant died. The next morning Baylor called a drumhead court-martial, Buck was tried, convicted and shot. When he first realized that Baylor was in earnest and was going to shoot him, sure enough his nerve gave way and he broke down. Then when he saw his end was inevitable he braced up, and when the fatal moment came he faced the firing squad as coolly and bravely as if he were not the least interested in what they were about to do. He was ten times more self-possessed than anyone on the ground, and died with his eyes open, facing his executioners. He refused to let them blind his eyes, but stood calmly facing the firing squad.

That execution brought order out of chaos and established discipline in a way that nothing else could have done. The men realized that when Baylor said anything he meant it and that if he said he would punish certain offenses with death he would keep his word if he had to shoot every man in the regiment. The command became one of the best in the Trans-Mississippi department, and did fine work for the four years of the war.

Tom Clarke, who was killed in San Antonio, enlisted in the Bayou City Guards, the crack infantry company from Houston that formed part of the Fifth Texas regiment of Hood's Brigade in Virginia. How Clarke ever got out of the company and back to Texas I never knew. He did get back and afterwards joined Captain W. M. Stafford's company of artillery. He had not been with that company long before he slipped into San Antonio, resented a Mexican slapping a woman, and killed the fellow, who made at him with a knife. Then a whole crowd of Mexicans attacked him. He killed them as long as his pistol held out and when he had fired his last shot he hurled the empty gun at them and was then cut to pieces by the survivors. It was reported that he killed six of them before they got him.

Kane Norton, the other distinguished Houstonian, was not so fortunate in the mode of his death. He was killed by a Yankee drug clerk, just at the close of the battle of Mansfield. He rushed into the drugstore, and the badly rattled clerk thought Kane was going to kill him, so he shot him dead. The next moment Kane's comrades entered and slew the clerk. If Kane had known that he was going to be wiped out, not by a desperado or soldier, but by a little, panic-stricken drug clerk, he would have been terribly humiliated.

★ ★ ★

SAN JACINTO VETERANS

Recently I have been reading Texas history. The Alamo and Goliad made my blood boil with indignation, but San Jacinto more than paid the debt that was due the Mexicans. The account of San Jacinto battle is charming reading for all native Texans, and I take particular pleasure in reading about it, because I knew so many of the men who took part in that glorious victory. When I was a boy, the San Jacinto veterans were as thick about Houston as Confederate Veterans are today and you know that is a strong statement, for the latter appear to be numberless. The most conspicuous of the San Jacinto veterans was old man Tierwester, who had a powderhorn with a Mexican bullet in it. I have told before how he would commence drinking early in the day on April 21, and keep it up all day. The more he drank, the louder he talked and the more viciously he would shake the horn and tell the history of the bullet it contained. He was a Frenchman and lived down in Frostown, not far from where the gas works are now located. There was old man Jarmond, too, and a score or two of others. I speak of them as being old, but they were not really aged. They seemed old to me, but they could not have been more than 40 or 50 on an average.

One thing I have never seen mentioned in print and which seems forgotten by everybody, was the old Liberty Pole that was erected near the

Houston House by the San Jacinto veterans and the people of Houston to commemorate Texas independence. A few days ago I met Captain William Christian and he asked if I remembered the old pole. I remembered seeing only a part of it that was preserved by the veterans for many years. This liberty pole was a pine tree that had been trimmed and converted into a fine flagpole from which flew the Lone Star flag on festive occasions and always on San Jacinto day. It did duty as long as Texas remained a republic, but by the time it was admitted as a state the old pole had grown so decayed and weak that it broke off and fell to the ground. The veterans of San Jacinto, who had used the pole as a rallying point for years, secured a piece of it, about 20 feet long, and on April 21, after an appropriate salute had been fired from the Twin Sisters, the two brass cannon used by the Texans at the battle, the Veterans shouldered the piece of liberty pole and headed for the nearest barroom. Placing the old pole on the counter was all that was necessary to "put the drinks on the house" and the veterans had whatever they called for without money and without price. Then would begin a procession that would include every barroom in town. The veterans were welcomed everywhere, for it would have been considered as an unfriendly act by the proprietor had any saloon been overlooked.

After about the fourth or fifth drink, the war talk would commence and the battle of San Jacinto would be fought over and over in the way that men of only one battle can do. It is a pity that some live reporter of today could not have been around, for Texas history would have been much enriched. I have made up my mind that if there is any truth in the theory of reincarnation, or whatever it is called where a fellow lives again in a different form but with the same surroundings, that I will be certain to arm myself with a notebook and a sharp pencil, for I see so many elegant bets the early Houston newspapermen overlooked.

I don't know whatever became of the piece of Liberty Pole the veterans used in place of drink checks, but it would be a priceless relic if it could be found, if still in existence.

Now it must not be supposed from what I have written, that the veterans were drinkers and roisterers. They were anything but that. They were the most honored and honorable citizens of the land, and having given the world a glorious republic, they had a right to celebrate the anniversary of the event in any way they saw fit. It is singular how time changes a person's ideas of things. When I was a boy I looked on the veterans as just plain, ordinary men, who had had an opportunity to do a great thing and had done it. That was all. Old Tierwester with his horn, in my eyes was simply a funny old Frenchman who cut up clownish capers, while some of the others I looked upon with anything but veneration. Now when I look back on those men and appreciate the grand and lofty principle that inspired them and their willingness to die for the freedom of Texas, I feel like "Texas Thompson," one of Lewis' characters in the "Woolfville Tales," said he felt when he met an old gray-haired lady. I feel like getting down on my knees and asking the pardon of every one of those heroes for having walked the earth at the same time that they did.

Speaking of the Twin Sisters, reminds me of a good story Otto Erichson told me the other day. He and I were talking about the two old cannon, and of how often they were fired when Texas was contemplating secession. His father's gun shop and residence was on market square and the firing of the cannon disturbed him greatly. He was disturbed in two directions. Being an ardent Union man he did not like the reason for the salutes and the cannon being so near his house made it disagreeable for him. Erichson was a high-tempered, irascible man and perfectly fearless in expressing his opinion on any and every subject. He denounced the secessionists and their noise and made a row in every way. Otto and Alex Erichson concluded that they would relieve the old man of some of his trouble, so one night they got a couple of rat-tail files and spiked both of the cannon. The next day when it was discovered what had been done, there was great indignation, but the culprits could not be found, for Otto and Alex took good care not to blow about what they had done when they found what a row was being made. The cannon were taken to Mr. Erichson's shop and he, not knowing that his own boys had spiked them, charged $20 to get them in shape again. The boys sneaked out and spiked them again, but the citizens either grew suspicious or for some other cause, took the guns elsewhere to get them unspiked.

"Now," said Otto, "as bitter as the old man was before the state seceded, the minute Texas left the Union, he turned around and became the bitterest man in Texas on the other side. He called me in the shop and literally rammed me in the army. He said every man able to shoulder a gun ought to be in the army fighting for the South. It was funny what a change took place in him. He cursed the Yanks as bad as he had cursed the secessionists, and if he had not been so old, I am certain he would have enlisted in the Confederate army himself."

★ ★ ★

A WAR STORY

I have no patience with the latter day heroes. A telegraph operator is on a sinking boat that he can't leave, much as he would like to do so. He sends a wireless message, secures aid and is proclaimed a hero and given a reception on his arrival in New York. An engineer discovers a burning bridge in front of his train. He reverses his engine, puts on the air brakes and rides to his death and is proclaimed a hero. Now the case of the telegraph operator is too ridiculous and absurd to discuss at all, while the engineer is scarcely better. When he had reversed his engine and applied his air brakes he had done all that possibly could be done, and when he did not jump or try to save himself he showed that he was more of a fool and idiot than a hero. Perhaps one reason why I am so prejudiced against the latter day "heroes" is that I have known one or two genuine ones.

For a number of years Houston entertained an angel unaware in the person of a man who was regarded as a crank and miser, but who was in fact one of the grandest men and heroes that ever lived. This was Judge John Duncan. As I write that name I can see some of the old-timers who thought they knew him, sit up and take notice. I admit that I would be with them in doing so too, if I did not know the judge's history. As a matter of fact, only two persons in Houston knew anything about the judge, for he was not given to talking about his private affairs and resented all attempts to pry into them. He told me part of his story and Judge George Goldthwaite told me the latter part of it. The judge had but one leg, having lost the other while in command of a Mississippi regiment during the war. He had an old-fashioned wooden leg and one could hear him coming down the sidewalk a block away. He was very sensitive about his missing leg and no one ever made allusion to it in his presence. One evening he and I were sitting in front of the Capitol Hotel and I asked him where he lost his leg.

"Sir, it is a story that sounds so absurd and improbable," he said, "that I hate to speak of it for fear that my friends will doubt either my veracity or saneness. I lost it in battle, which, of course, was not strange, but the circumstances were most wonderful and almost incredible.

"I was lieutenant colonel of my regiment and we had been sent up in Missouri to take part in the campaign there. Our colonel had been wounded the day before and I was in command. Early one morning I received an order to advance my regiment, drive off a small detachment of the enemy from a woods on the opposite side of a big field and hold the position until more troops could be sent to me. It was supposed that the enemy had only a small force there, so you can imagine my surprise when, as we reached a point about halfway across the field, the enemy opened on us at easy range with a withering rifle fire. Instead of a small force we found ourselves confronted by a full brigade that had been moved up during the night. There was an old rock fence, about two feet high and I ordered the men to lie down behind it, knowing that more troops would be sent us so soon as our desperate situation was discovered by our people. Fortunately, the enemy had no artillery or else they would have exterminated us right there. The rifle fire was fierce and one need only raise a finger above the stone fence to have it shot off. I was lying there expecting relief every moment, when I heard a voice behind me and, looking around, I saw a boy about 16 years old, seated on a big white horse. The bullets were flying all about him, but he seemed to have a charmed life, for none of them struck him. 'Why don't you charge?' he called out. 'Get up and go at them.'

"The question and command were so absurd that nobody thought of paying any attention to him. Then the climax came. 'If your officers are a lot of cowards I will lead you,' he said and spurring his horse he leaped the low wall.

"The regiment rose and made a dash forward. The next moment the ground was strewn with dead and wounded. I was among the latter with a shattered thigh. Human blood and bone could not stand against that wall of lead. The regiment broke. What few were able to do so got back to the shelter of the fence. The boy was unhurt and rode up and down the line trying to get the men to make another charge. I shall never forget the conflicting emotions that wrenched my soul and body at that time. One moment I prayed that the young fool would get his head shot off and the next moment I was so afraid that he would get hurt that my heart almost stood still. There were thousands of bullets fired at him, yet not one touched him or his horse. Seeing his efforts to move the men were hopeless, he waved his hat, put spurs to his horse and rode away. I was left on the field and fell in the hands of the enemy. When I came out of prison I could never learn who the boy was or anything about him."

That was the story Judge Duncan told me, and since the only hero mentioned was an unknown and foolish boy, you may be wondering where Judge

Duncan's heroism comes in. That was the part of the story told me by Judge George Goldthwaite after Judge Duncan's death. Goldthwaite had been Duncan's confidential friend and attorney.

Judge Duncan was practicing law here in Houston and was apparently starving to death when his friends interested themselves and got him elected city recorder. The salary was not a princely one, but it was about $1800 a year, and the judge's friends expected him to live a little more comfortably than he had been doing. It was at this time that he earned the name of "miser." He had a little office and an old lounge. He made this lounge his bed and took his meals at some cheap restaurant near the market. He made no explanations to anyone and all the people knew was that he was too close-fisted to spend a cent. Finally, he died and after his death Judge Goldthwaite told me this part of his story:

After the judge was shot down, the Confederate army fell back, and he, having had his leg amputated, was left at a house near the roadside with a lady whose husband was away in the Confederate army. She nursed and cared for the judge, despite the fact that the commanding general in Missouri had issued a proclamation announcing that anyone who harbored a "rebel" would be put to death.

While Judge Duncan was yet unable to get out of bed, the lady's husband came home on a furlough one afternoon. The same night the house was surrounded by Federal troops and the husband was captured. He would have been simply made a prisoner of war had they not found Judge Duncan there. When they discovered that the people had been harboring a "rebel," a drumhead court martial was held and the husband ordered to be shot at daylight. Judge Duncan begged them to shoot him instead, but they refused and the next morning they took the husband out and shot him. The poor woman was left a widow with two little children. Judge Goldthwaite told me that Judge Duncan had deprived himself of everything except the actual necessities of life, to send money to that woman. Being a cripple, past middle life and extremely poor, it was uphill work, but he faced it manfully and at the time of his death, he had succeeded in giving the two children a fair education and had kept the lady from actual want, at least.

When I heard that story I felt like tearing my hair and kicking myself for ever having even thought that the judge was simply a miser. He was a noble man, and I and all others who had laughed at him were unworthy to fasten his shoes. One might ask why he didn't widely tell of his circumstances. Had the judge ever told his story it would have been different, for then it might have seemed that he was asking for sympathy or trying to get praise for his magnanimous act.

He did nothing of the kind. He went through life quietly and silently, performing the great duty he felt rested on him. Now by the side of this man, place your wireless operator calling for help or your fool engineer staying on his engine because he had lost his head and was too scared to jump—these so-called heroes—and note the difference. Once or twice I have thought of writing this story for the *Confederate Veteran*, but I am glad now that I did not do so, for it is much better to tell it through the columns of the *Chronicle*, where it will be seen and read by hundreds who thought they knew Judge Duncan, but who will find that they did not, and like me they will want to breathe a prayer for the rest of his soul, since it is too late to do anything else.

★ ★ ★

SOME OF THE NOTED BAD MEN

I had a most interesting talk a few evenings ago with my old friend, Dr. William Daniels. I know of no one who has had a more intimate acquaintance with the thrilling days of Texas and the men who furnished the thrills. The doctor, having served as one of the surgeons of Sibley's Brigade on the Rio Grande and in New Mexico and Arizona during the Civil War, had exceptional opportunities for knowing all the real "bad men" of that day. It is pretty safe to say that from the beginning to the end one or more of them was connected with his command at some time. The doctor is one of the quietest and most peaceable gentlemen. Had he not practiced medicine for many years, one might safely say had never killed a man. In spite of all this, he took great interest in "bad men" and made a study of them.

"One hears often of the gameness of bad men. They are game, of course, but so are you, so am I and so are 90 per cent of the gentlemen one knows. It takes more than gameness to make a desperado or bad man, and that fact was recognized by the people who first gave them the name of desperadoes. Cold-blooded murderers who killed merely for the pleasure of killing and who gave their victims no show at all, should be classed as human fiends and not be dignified by calling them bad men. Billy the Kid belonged to that class. He killed just as a wild animal kills—merely for the pleasure it gave him to see his victims die. He was a fiend in human shape and should have no place in the honorable (?) list of killers.

"The true bad man differed from the ordinary man in many ways, the main one being his absolute indifference to taking human life. The only care he took about the matter was to have the semblance of being in the right before he acted. Ben Thompson, for instance, was noted for never firing the first shot. He always allowed the other fellow to shoot at him before he shot. It never required but one of his shots to get his man, and both he and the man knew that. No doubt it had influence in getting the other fellow's goat, for I don't think any of Ben's many antagonists ever succeeded in hitting him, while if he ever missed one of them the fact is not on record.

"I knew Cain Norton, Tom Clark, King Fisher, Ben Thompson, Billy Thompson, Matt Woodlief and others of lesser prominence. There was one who, had he lived, would have made his mark. That was Buck Stacy, whose career was cut short by General John R. Baylor, who had him court-martialed and shot for killing a fellow soldier after Baylor had issued an order against any further private killings. Buck was really a very game man and had all the elements about him that go to make the real bad man.

"The gamest man among all the game ones was Cain Norton. In all his private wars I don't believe he ever gave himself a single thought. His own safety was a matter of utter indifference to him. He made no calculations about the future or the present, except to get his man, which he always did. On one occasion I saw him when another bad man had the drop on him. Cain had only a knife, while the other fellow had a pistol. Cain first laughed at him, and then cursed and taunted him, daring him to shoot. He was willing to risk being killed so that he would get a chance to close in with his knife and take the fellow with him. The man he was facing had a reputation as a killer, but Cain's coolness got his goat and he ended by backing out of the door and leaving town.

"Tom Clark was another cool one. I have often thought about Tom's case and have concluded that among some of his ancestors was one of those old knights errant, who spent their time hunting up wrongs or imaginary wrongs of other people, or doing something for the advancement of their lady love. Tom was a great lady's man and would fight for the protection of any woman, the wrinkled old hag as quickly as for the fairest girl. One or two notches on his pistol's handle represented the exit of men who had so far forgotten themselves as to strike women in Tom's presence. It was that knightly feature in his character that led to his taking off. One Sunday morning Tom was in the old market house in San Antonio when a Mexican struck a woman in the face with his hand. Tom knew none of the people, but he promptly bent his six shooter over the fellow's head. The chap drew a knife and made for Tom, who shot him dead. There was a big crowd of Mexicans there and they made a rush for Tom. He fired three shots and got three of them. Then the cylinder of his pistol got jammed and he snapped on an empty chamber and then, hurling the useless pistol in their faces, folded his arms and quietly waited the inevitable. About 20 Mexicans mounted him with knives and when they got through they had him cut into shoestrings.

"Cain Norton was killed in one of the battles over in Louisiana, and, so far as I can recall, he was the only one who met a soldier's death among the whole number. Every one of them died with his boots on, however.

"If I could find time I would write a book telling of those stirring days and of the men who kept things at fever heat all the time. That would be one book where style and literary excellence would be at a discount, for the contents of the book would carry it along."

★ ★ ★

HOUSTON'S LAST AFFAIR OF HONOR

I saw the other day where a Frenchman had offered to give anyone 10,000 francs who would furnish him with a new sensation. I don't know what that Frenchman's record in the sensation line is, but if I could fix up the stage, as it was once fixed up for me, I could get his money easily.

I know of only one sensation I have not experienced—that of having killed a man. Now as I practiced medicine for about five years, I can see some of my friends raise their eyebrows over that statement, but if I have ever killed any, I did so scientifically and did not know it, hence my conscience does not hurt me. I have experienced the sensation of being nearly killed myself two or three times, and on one memorable occasion, I came face to face with the ghost of a dead man I had cut up half an hour before, and I had the time of my life in the sensation line when I did so. That was what I referred to when I spoke of fixing up the stage for that Frenchman a moment ago. I am not going to tell any ghost story now, and I refer to it merely to let the reader understand that I am a bit of an expert when it comes to sensations.

To be guilty of taking human life must be the most terrible thing on earth. No matter what the circumstances are, there must be keen regret, if not agonizing remorse at all times. I once knew a man who had killed three men. He was actually afraid to go in the dark, not afraid of the living revenging themselves on him, but afraid of the dead. It was said that he killed the second man to get rid of the first, and the third to get rid of the second. He got tired of the ghosts and wanted a change of companions. Now all this is simply a prelude of the story of a young man who resides in Houston, who is prepared to go in court and swear to the agony a sensitive person feels after he has "got his man."

Some years ago there were two young gentlemen here who were great friends but who were constantly falling out with each other—kind of lovers' quarrels, as it were. One (perhaps both) is here now, so I shall not call names, though the truth of the story will be vouched for by hundreds when this recalls it to their memories. One day these two youths had a most bitter and serious quarrel, and their companions saw a good chance to have some fun. Instead of trying to bring the two together, they widened the breach and magnified its importance until finally they induced one of the boys to challenge the other.

They took the challenged party into their confidence and told him that no balls would be put in the pistols and only blank cartridges would be used. Under these safe circumstances, he readily accepted the challenge and chose pistols at 16 paces. He was told that he must fall dead at the first fire, and stay dead until they could get his slayer out of the way. The plan worked beautifully, for the other fellow was game, even eager, to fight, so they had no trouble with him. Early the next day the principals and their seconds appeared promptly on the field of honor way out somewhere beyond the city limits in the Third Ward. The men were placed, the word given and at "three" both fired. The challenged man threw his hands over his heart, wavered a little and then dropped dead, all in proper form. When he saw his friend fall, the survivor was panic-stricken, and, for the first time realized that his whole life was to be one of remorse and regret. He wanted to rush forward and throw himself on the body of his dead friend and plead for forgiveness, but was restrained by his seconds, who pointed out to him the necessity for immediate flight. He took one wistful look at the place where his friend's body was lying on the grass and then, panic-stricken, he started for Mexico on foot, like a racehorse.

After his "killer" was well out of sight, the dead man got up and the whole party returned to town to enjoy the joke. There was only one thing they overlooked in their calculation, that was the agony and remorse of their victim. He wandered aimlessly all the morning and finally concluded that there was only one thing to do to drown his sorrow—return to the city, give himself up, and be hung for the murder. He felt easier after making up his mind to return and be hanged, so he started for town, and when he got there he went to the courthouse to look for the sheriff. As he turned the corner of Preston Avenue, he saw what he supposed was the ghost of his murdered friend standing in the courthouse door. The ghost saw him at the same time and attempted to hide behind the door. The young man rushed eagerly toward the ghost, but the ghost, concluding that he had been found out and that his friend was coming to take revenge on him for the part he had played in it, concluded not to wait for him and fled.

Then commenced one of the most wonderful flights and pursuits that has ever been witnessed on courthouse square, or anywhere else, so far as that goes. The ghost rushed through the courthouse with the victim close behind him. The ghost gained some slight advantage by diving into a cigar store, knocking down two or three people who were in there, wrecking the stand and thus blocking the way long enough to allow him to reach the backyard, mount some dry goods boxes and crawl over a fence into the next yard. The advantage was only slight, however, for the victim was a good second and reached the next yard by the same route, almost as quickly as the ghost. Then, in a perfect agony of fear, the ghost made for the sidewalk again, choosing for his route the first open door he saw, which chanced to belong to a little tailor shop. In they went, like a couple of wild horses, knocking down shelves, overturning tables and wrecking the place completely.

By this time the ghost was convinced that the victim had secured a bowie knife and was only waiting to get near enough to him to rip him into bits. The thought put new life and energy into his legs, and reaching the sidewalk he lit out in true marathon style. He had seen the folly of trying to dodge into stores, so kept to the open street. The victim was as anxious to capture him as he was to escape, and took after him, also with renewed energy. Not one word had been spoken up to this time. The chase, barring the crashes in the cigar store and tailor shop, had been conducted amidst profound silence. After going four blocks in something like a fraction of a second, the victim managed to get near enough to the ghost, and to find breath enough to say, "Hold on, you fool. I don't want to fight you; I want to kiss you for being alive."

That was all. He was so glad that he was not a murderer that he wanted to kiss his supposed victim. It was a terrible load that was lifted from his mind and heart and he was crazy with joy. He felt such relief that he forgave everybody who had anything to do with the duel and the subject was allowed to die out by the principals. The joke was so evenly divided between these two that neither had any advantage. That, I believe, is the last "affair of honor" that has occurred in Houston.

★ ★ ★

FOUGHT TO THE DEATH

After the war, a number of young men came to Houston, seeking employment. There were some professional men but the majority were young fellows just out of the army, with nothing to do and whose entire capital consisted of nothing more tangible than youth and good appetites. Some of them later rose to prominence in the commercial and financial world, while many drifted away and were lost sight of. Among these young men were two who were destined to establish a tragic mystery here. One was the son of a gentleman of Galveston, a man of means, who established his son in business on Congress Avenue, between Travis and Main Street. The young merchant who was so fortunately established was named Ed Brown. The other young man was Ed Prewit, who had come to Houston from somewhere up the state and had secured a clerkship in the freight department of the Houston & Texas Central Railway with Mr. J. Waldo, local freight agent.

Brown and Prewit became great friends. They roomed at the same place and after business hours were almost invariably together. They were both slender, weighed about 135 pounds and were between 19 and 20 years old. Aside from physical resemblance, no two men could have been more unlike one another. Brown was full of life and animation. He loved a joke, whether at his own expense or not, and was always ready for fun or frolic. Being on "easy street," he could afford to take life easy and did so. Prewit, on the other hand, while not morose, was very quiet and sedate. With him, life was a serious affair. He was polite and gentlemanly and made many warm friends, who admired him for his sterling qualities. Both young men were favorites and each numbered among his friends the friends of the other.

Late in the summer of 1867, I was standing on Main Street, a few doors north of where Kiam's place now is, in company with Charley Gentry, Andrew Hutchinson and Prewit. Someone asked Prewit where Brown was.

He replied that he did not know. Just at that moment Brown turned the corner of Preston Avenue and came toward us. When he saw Prewit he hesitated for just a moment and then advanced, walking very slowly. Prewit moved a little nearer the middle of the sidewalk and stood facing Brown as if awaiting his coming. Both were very pale and we saw at a glance that something was wrong. Brown came slowly forward and Prewit stood there as if awaiting him. For a minute it looked as if Brown intended to walk right over Prewit, but just before reaching him Brown turned slightly and passed Prewit so closely that he nearly grazed his coat. As he did so he raised his hat with mock politeness, and saying, "Good afternoon, gentlemen," passed on. Someone in the crowd called to him to come back, but he paid no attention and passed on down the street.

Prewit stood for a moment, then rejoined us with a smile and a casual remark as if nothing out of the ordinary had taken place. Of course we pressed him, trying to find out what was wrong between he and Brown, but he expressed surprise that we should think there was anything wrong and declared there was no cause for our assumption to the contrary. In a few minutes we separated, Prewit, Andrew Hutchinson and I going toward the Capitol Hotel, now the Rice. As we walked Andrew remarked that Brown had come near running into Prewit. "It's a good thing he didn't," said Prewit.

"Why, what would you have done?" asked Andrew.

We were near the corner of Main and Prairie Avenue now and Prewit did not answer at once. Just as we reached the corner Prewit turned to Andrew and said, "If he had run into me I would have cut his damn heart out, that's all." He turned the corner abruptly and walked down Prairie Avenue.

That night I met Brown on Main Street and had a long talk with him. He seemed much depressed and was low-spirited at first, but this gradually wore off and before we parted he seemed to be as bright and happy as ever. He explained his low spirits by saying that he had seen a ghost the night before and that he was either haunted or going crazy, he did not know which. He said this half in fun and half seriously. He denied emphatically that there was any trouble between Prewit and himself and laughed at the idea of my thinking there was. Of course I said nothing to him of Prewit's remark, merely giving as the reason for my asking the question his and Prewit's conduct on the street that afternoon.

The next day I did not come downtown until late in the afternoon and the first thing I heard was that Brown and Prewit had killed each other on the corner of Fannin Street and Congress Avenue on the northwest corner of Courthouse Square.

The particulars as I learn them were as follows: Prewit, in company with Mr. Waldo and another gentleman, was coming toward Main Street along Congress Avenue, while Brown, with a companion whose name I forget, was going in the opposite direction. Neither would give way and they collided. Each jumped back, Prewit drawing his knife, a big butcher knife, and Brown his pistol. To my mind, Brown did not want to kill Prewit, for he could have done so easily, as he was an expert with a six-shooter.

Instead of shooting Prewit down he tried to shoot the knife out of his hand. His first ball went through Prewit's right wrist, completely disabling his right hand. However, Prewit quickly changed the knife to his left hand and began advancing on Brown, moving in a zigzag course, so as to disconcert Brown's aim as much as possible. Brown fired at Prewit's left hand, but missed, and instantly fired at his arm. The ball passed through the arm, but did not break the bone.

Prewit kept advancing like a cat, preparing to jump. The gleaming knife and the cool, cat-like movement of Prewit evidently got on Brown's nerves and disconcerted him. He fired point blank at Prewit and missed him. Prewit, with his knife, was uncomfortably close by now, so Brown stepped back to gain a better position. As he did so his heel caught on a wooden bridge that spanned the gutter and he fell full-length on his back. The next second, like a wild tiger, Prewit made the long delayed leap and, landing astride of Brown's body, he drove the butcher knife through his heart. Prewit was about to strike again when Brown's companion rushed up and struck Prewit on the side of the head with a six-shooter, knocking him off several feet to the side, where he lay insensible. In spite of his frightful wound, Brown staggered to his feet and fired again at Prewit as he lay on the ground. Brown then turned and walked half a block before he fell dead.

Prewit was taken to the old Fannin House nearby, where he died the next day from loss of blood, Brown's bullets having severed several arteries causing Prewit to lose a great quantity of blood.

★ ★ ★

KIRBY-STEEL FEUD

I like Waller County. I like Hempstead and I like the people who live up that way. There are many reasons for this. Personally I have none but the most pleasant of memories of the old town of Hempstead, for it occupies first place in my own "first experiences."

My first stage ride was made from Houston to Hempstead, though I must admit that my memory of it is only in spots, one of the spots being a large drove of wild horses which we saw on the prairie about fifteen miles from Houston, and another spot being our arrival at Hempstead. The first railroad ride I ever took was from Houston to Hempstead when the Houston & Texas Central Railway was completed to that place. There was a big barbecue and everybody in Houston went on that excursion. Later I spent some very happy school vacations at the hospitable home of Mr. Jarad Groce, near Hempstead.

All these things combined render my memory of Hempstead and Waller County very pleasant. The people up that way are noted for their hospitality and kindly reception of strangers. That, of course, is commendable, but it is not the reason I like them. I know I may shock some of the *Chronicle's* readers when I say it, but my real admiration for the Waller County people is due to the fact that they are not "pikers." Whatever they do, they throw their whole heart and souls into it and do it completely. They remind me of a sleeping volcano that lies dormant for years and then suddenly blows up and leaves only the fragments behind.

When they are peacefully inclined, jack rabbits are as raging hyenas compared to them, but when they start on the other tack they do not raise any Sunday school "Hades" or "Gehenna," or anything so euphonious sounding as that, but start right in with the genuine article and raise unadulterated hell. It has been said that any sport who, ambitious of becoming a bad man, was on the warpath seeking trouble, could find more of the genuine article, done up in a greater variety of styles, in Hempstead than in any other place in Texas. Just why this is so no one seems to understand, for as a rule the people of Waller County are among the best in the state and year after year the most profound peace, law and order prevail.

Still there are always toes to be trodden on, and a Waller County man was never known to thwart the intentions of a would-be treader by withdrawing his toes. The trouble hunter is always sure of being met fully half way. There must be some cause for the existence of so much latent pugnacity, such dogged persistency.

I have thought over the matter and concluded that it is all a question of heredity. It was born in them and they can't help it. My reason for saying this is that I know something of their fathers and grandfathers. In early days that section was settled by some of the best, most prominent and influential families who came to Texas.

Conflicting interests, political differences and other causes led to individual quarrels and difficulties; personal friends and relatives took sides and soon there were feuds that resulted in bloody conflict. The fights were always clan fights—the stand up, give and take kind. Such a thing as an assassination was almost unknown and when one occasionally occurred ten to one both the assassin and his victim belonged to the lowest order of criminals. The genuine feuds frowned on the work of an assassin and when a Brown or two were killed by a Smith or two there was no effort made to conceal the fact. It was done in the open and everybody knew how, why and when it was done.

In those days, there was a powerful and influential planter living near Hempstead—Colonel Kirby. There was also another man there who was less prominent in social and financial circles, but one possessed of strong character, personal bravery and other admirable qualities that enable a man to establish himself anywhere as a man. This latter was Captain John Steel, a hero of San Jacinto. He had a farm which he and his son cultivated. For some unknown cause, Steel and Kirby quarrelled. Kirby had a hundred friends where Steel had one, but that made no difference to Steel, who would not yield an inch. Kirby ordered Steel to leave the county, while Steel flatly refused to go.

Some of Kirby's friends caught young Steel one night and just for fun made out they were going to hang him. They did not hurt him, but turned him loose after scaring him badly. This enraged Captain Steel and he sent word to Colonel Kirby that he was going to kill him on sight. Colonel Kirby treated the message with contempt and sent back word to Steel that he was going to treat him as a common criminal and that if he (Steel) were found in Waller County by midnight the next night he was going to have him hanged to the first tree he could find. That settled it. It was no longer a matter between two men, but was one of a single man against a dozen or more. Steel knew Kirby would do exactly what he said he would do. So he acted with discretion and left for Houston at once. He had to sacrifice his home and everything to save his life, but he did so, bearing in mind all the time that someday he would be able to square his account with Kirby.

Steel remained in Houston until the close of the war. The army of occupation came in and everything was under semi-martial law. One day Colonel Kirby came to Houston to consult with the commander of the post, whose office was on the second floor of the old Wilson building, corner of Main Street and Congress Avenue. On the same day and at the same hour Captain Steel went to consult Judge Hamblen, his lawyer, who had an office in the same building just opposite the commander's office. Their business completed, both Kirby and Steel stepped out in the hall from the respective offices and for the first time since their trouble, came face to face. Not a word was spoken by either. Like a flash Steel drew his pistol and fired and Kirby sank to the floor and died. Steel was arrested and placed in jail. He was soon admitted to bail and then his case came to trial and he was acquitted.

At the time when Colonel Kirby was killed he had a young son only four or five years old. This boy was too young to appreciate the great loss he had sustained, but as he grew up he learned all the details, and though he never gave a hint of that fact, he evidently brooded over it and determined to be avenged. He was sent away to one of the older states to receive his education and graduated from a leading college with honors. He then entered a law school, developed fine oratorical power and graduated at the head of his class. He returned home, and as his fame had preceded him, he was given a royal welcome by his own friends and by those of his father.

In the meantime Captain Steel had moved back to Waller County and was living in or near Hempstead. Young Kirby never mentioned Steel's name and gave no indication that he knew of his existence. Kirby did know it, though, and had made all his plans. The following Sunday morning Steel, now an old man, was coming out of the church door with his old wife holding to his arm. As he got completely out he was confronted by young Kirby, who had stepped from behind a tree, with a gun in his hand. Again the old tragedy was restarted. Steel and Kirby again faced each other, though in this last meeting the ground of vantage was shifted and Kirby held the winning hand. Again not a word was spoken. There was a sharp report and Steel was sent to his final account in identically the same way that he had sent Colonel Kirby to his. Young Kirby disappeared at once. If any effort was ever made to catch him it was only perfunctory and half-hearted, for everybody felt that he had done only right in killing the man who had killed his father and doing it in precisely the same way.

Now, this is only one of many similar cases that took place in Waller and neighboring counties, and while there are no feuds up that way now, there is lots of the same blood that caused the old ones. And while conditions now do not favor family bickerings and contentions, there is the same old martial spirit up that way that occasionally slips its bridle and, as remarked already, proceeds to raise genuine hell.

★ ★ ★

THUGS AND YELLOW FEVER

Last Sunday I spoke of the first Federal troops that ever came to Houston, "the army of occupation," and told of the good conduct of the men and of the conservative administration of the officers. Of course, in an army such as that, there were "toughs" and a few of those broke out from time to time and caused trouble. However, they did not always get away with the play, for when a six-shooter was at that time as much a part of a man's toilet as his boots or shoes, there were always two sides to an attempted knockdown and robbery or the creation of a "hot house," when circumstances did not justify such creation. Of course while the town was under military rule—as a fact, if not really so in name—it was not a healthy thing for a citizen to kill a soldier, no matter what the provocation might be, so that while two or three such killings did occur, those who did such excellent killings took good pains to avoid taking credit for them.

The slungshots used by the thugs were made of lead and were about the size of a large egg. They were fastened to a leather thong and this was slipped over the wrist and securely knotted there. It was a fearful weapon and with it skulls and bones could be easily crushed. An old German was once found on Washington Street one morning with a crushed skull, while a negro had his shoulder smashed somewhere out on Main Street. No doubt there were other cases, but if so, I have forgotten them.

I do remember three casualties on the other side. One was a soldier found on Main Street just above where the Rice Hotel stands. He had been shot through the head and the slungshot attached to his wrist told the story of why he had been shot. Another was a soldier found one morning at daylight just in front of the gate of the old Episcopal Cemetery. He, too, was shot through the head, but as the ball entered at the back the supposition was that he had missed his victim when he struck at him with the slungshot and had then tried to get away. The slungshot attached to his right wrist told what part he had played in the tragedy.

Another case that occurred out on Main Street had more of the ludicrous than the tragic about it. A negro was going home late one night. He was met by a soldier, who walked directly up to him and without a word made a lick at him with his slungshot. Instinctively the negro threw up both hands to protect his head and the lead ball struck him on the palm of his right hand. His hand closed and he hung on for dear life. He was afraid to turn loose and the soldier who, having the leather thong knotted around his wrist, could not get loose. They fought and struggled there, the negro shouting "Murder! Help!" at the top of his voice. They made such a row that people in the neighborhood were aroused and help came. The soldier was captured and taken to the provost officer in the old courthouse. He was locked up and presumably punished, though I never heard how.

Soon after the troops had been located at desirable points in the state, the reason for their presence became more apparent. All state, county and city officials, who had been chosen by the people, were turned out of office and their successors appointed by the President of the United States and by the state officials so appointed, and the work of "reconstruction" was begun. Houston was reconstructed, of course, and though it had escaped all the horrors of war, it was made to realize that there are some things worse than war. A lot of scalawags were put in office and as they were backed by Federal bayonets, they proceeded to loot the county and city in the most up-to-date manner. I will not say anything on that subject now, but shall simply jot down some memories that come to me as my mind goes back to the long ago.

The army was not much in evidence, for its mere presence was all that was necessary to give the looters free hand. The citizens accepted the inevitable and did the best they could. For about eighteen months a sort of armed peace existed between the soldiers and citizens and then, in 1867, the great yellow fever epidemic broke out. With hundreds of soldiers, camp followers and carpetbaggers from the North, who had never been exposed to yellow fever, the camps and town were soon hotbeds of pestilence and the death rate was appalling.

At that time there was only one undertaker in Houston, though he called himself and was called by others the city sexton. He was known to every man, woman and child in Houston as Old Man Pannell, the "old man" being a term of affection, for in spite of his gloomy calling, everyone loved Old Man Pannell. He was a great character and one of the most uncompromising rebels that the South ever produced. He never was reconstructed and died as he had lived, hating the Yankees to the end. At first he was constantly in hot water and was once or twice taken to headquarters by the guard of soldiers because of intemperate language, but finally the commander concluded that he would have to do one of two things—shoot Pannell or ignore him altogether, and wisely concluded to follow the latter course.

When the yellow fever broke out Pannell found himself the busiest man in Houston, for in addition to his regular customers in the city, he had to provide for the dead soldiers. He hired negroes with drays, negro grave diggers and extra carpenters to make coffins, but was still swamped. The soldiers died faster than he could bury them. There was an accumulation of dead soldiers at the camp and the officers became suspicious of Pannell and had him arrested for not performing his duty. He was taken before the commander, who said to him, "Mr. Pannell, they tell me you dislike to bury my soldiers."

"General," declared Pannell, "whoever told you that told a damned lie. It's the pleasantest thing I've had to do in years and I can't get enough of it. I would like to bury every damned one of you."

The interview ended abruptly, for the general ordered Pannell to jail. He did not stay long, for his services were in too great demand and he was released and went back to work. According to his story, he had his revenge. "You see," he would say, "these Yankees think a nigger is as good as they are and better than we are, so I'm giving them their own medicine. In mixing up the cards, so to speak, I plant a nigger and then I plant a white soldier. Sometimes I put a white one with three or four niggers and then I reverse it and put a nigger with three or four white ones. Those relatives up North are going to have a hell of a time getting things straight and the chances are that some nigger is going to rest under a big tombstone meant for a white man." Pannell died years ago and with him passed away one of the most remarkable characters that ever lived in Houston.

★ ★ ★

EARLY TRAGEDIES

An evening or two ago I dropped in to see some moving pictures on the southeast corner of Prairie Avenue and Main Street. While I watched a mimic tragedy pictured on the screen, it occurred to me that identical locality had been the scene of more real tragedies than any other place in Houston, or perhaps any other single point in Texas. The reason is obvious when it is said that on that corner was located one of the most fashionable saloons in town and the spacious second story was devoted to gambling and billiards.

Before the war the saloon was owned and run by a man named Charles Harris. He was a man of good manners and considerable polish, was known to be a "square man" and had numerous friends. In those days the modern club was unknown, and lawyers, doctors, bankers, merchants, and in fact everybody went in saloons and billiard halls and thought no more of doing so than they do today of going to a restaurant or a soda fountain. Harris, as I have said, was popular and his place was generally well filled, while the billiard hall and faro bank upstairs did a thriving business.

When gambling and whiskey get together there is more than apt to be trouble, and Harris' place was a shining example of this fact. There were a number of very large sycamore and cottonwood trees growing both on the Main Street and the Prairie Street side of the place, so Harris chose to call his saloon The Shades. On one occasion, a young lawyer congratulated Harris on the appropriateness of the name, but suggested that it would be still more appropriate if he could have the "S" painted out and leave it "Hades." "Then," said he, "the only objection that could be raised is that yours is the home of imported spirits while the other is the home of exported spirits."

When I was a little fellow I remember seeing a big blacksmith, who had a shop on Travis Street between Preston and Prairie Avenues, come running out of the saloon with something that looked like an axe handle in his hand. He was closely followed by another man, without a hat, whose head and face were covered with blood. This man had a big bowie knife in his hand and just before the blacksmith reached the corner where Dr. Robert's residence stood, but where now stands the Lumbermans National Bank, he caught up with the blacksmith and sank the knife in his shoulder. The blacksmith turned and dealt him a terrific blow with his stick, and both fell in the street. I don't think either was killed. I know the blacksmith was not, for on the following San Jacinto Day, I saw another fellow chase him from the north side of market square clear to his shop, which he reached in time to shut the door and keep the other fellow out. This other fellow had an ugly looking bowie knife, too, but his friends came up and took him away. I don't remember the name of the blacksmith, but I judge from what I saw of him when I was a boy that he must have been rather contentious and fond of bickering and argument.

I remember, when I was a child, hearing of shootings and cuttings at The Shades, but I was too young to grasp the details. The first tragedy that came under my personal observation occurred about 1858 or 1859. I was coming up Prairie Avenue from the direction of the bayou, when about Travis Street I saw a small man struggling out in Main Street with a big fat man. The big man had the small man grasped from behind and was evidently trying to prevent him using a six-shooter he held in his hand. At a window on the second floor of the building another man appeared and poked what looked like a walking cane out of the window. The movement of the two struggling in the street became more animated and then the little man turned his pistol under his arm and shot the big man through the chest. The big fellow dropped and without turning to look at him, the little fellow began shooting at the man upstairs.

It was all over in a moment. The little man in the street was one of the leading businessmen of Houston, while the man upstairs with the cane was a fashionable physician. There had been serious trouble between the two which had resulted in the merchant ordering the doctor to leave town within 24 hours. The 24 hours had expired that afternoon and since the doctor was still in town, the merchant had gone gunning for him. He armed himself with a shotgun and six-shooter and, finding the doctor taking a drink in The Shades, he pulled down on him. The doctor, whose back was to the door, saw his enemy in the looking glass and just as the gun was fired he dropped to the floor and the bartender, who was in front of him, received the full load in his chest. The doctor jumped to his feet and rushed for an enclosed stairway leading upstairs. Just as he was disappearing up the steps the merchant discharged the other barrel of his shotgun at him. Only one buckshot took effect and that passed through the doctor's heel. The merchant then went out in the street, where he was grabbed by his too-zealous friend, whom he had to shoot in order to have a chance to protect himself from the doctor, who was armed with a rifled shooting cane.

Two men were seriously wounded and the doctor was only slightly injured, yet strange to say the two men got well, while the doctor took lockjaw and died a few days later.

The next sensational shooting that took place there was just before the war. It was between one of the leading physicians of Houston on one side and a distinguished citizen of Texas, a veteran of the Mexican war, and his son on the other. Fortunately, while both father and son were terribly wounded, no one was killed and all three rose to prominence during the war that soon followed.

There had been a feud of long standing between the doctor and the captain. Mutual friends had patched this up and no one was looking for trouble between the two. The captain and his son came to town that morning and they had not been here long before the captain began abusing his old enemy and making threats against him. The doctor, hearing of this, went home, for his bravery and courage were of such high order that no one could question his motive, and he could afford to do so in order to avoid trouble.

About four o'clock some injudicious friend went to the doctor's house and told him the captain was in The Shades abusing him and declaring that he (the doctor) had run to the hole. The doctor said nothing but after his friend left, got his six-shooter and went down to The Shades to investigate. The captain and his son had gone upstairs and were playing billiards. The doctor entered the room smoking a long-stemmed meerschaum pipe. Drawing his pistol he said, "Defend yourself, captain. I have come to kill you."

The captain was as eager for a fight as the doctor, but he was by no means as cool as the latter. They both fired together, the captain's shot going wild, but the doctor's ball piercing the chest of the captain, who went down in a heap. Old Man Pannell, whom I've written about on other occasions, grabbed the doctor from behind and attempted to pinion his arms. The captain's son reversed his billiard cue and was advancing on the doctor for the purpose of braining him with it. The doctor, finding it useless to argue with Pannell and being unable to free himself, turned his pistol on Pannell and shot him through the arm. Now free, he then shot the captain's son and that ended the affair. The captain lingered between life and death for three or four months but got well. The son soon recovered, while Pannell was taken in charge by the doctor and soon restored to health.

Of course, there were a number of killings took place on this corner, where the killers and victims were sports and hard characters. I remember one or two of these, but I pass them by and use only the two I have given above, for they were between persons of high social prominence and serve to illustrate the cosmopolitan character of The Shades, if I can use the term in that connection.

★ ★ ★

FAMOUS STREET DUEL

Everybody remembers Matt Woodlief. Some because during his lifetime he inspired them with dread and fear for he was a typical desperado and killer, and others with feelings of gratitude, for he was charitable and generous and his purse was always open to an appeal from the needy. Matt must have been a "throwback," and one of his warlike ancestors must have come back in him, for there was nothing in the history of his immediate family to account for him. His father was a leading physician of the state and the whole Woodlief family was one of the best and most prominent in Texas. All its members, with the exception of Matt, were peaceable, law abiding citizens, and there is no way of accounting for such a volcano as Matt breaking out among them except to assume that he was a "throwback."

Matt had a reputation for cool courage and desperate bravery second to none of his dangerous associates, and when it is said that those associates were such men as Ben Thompson and King Fisher, the full meaning of this assertion can be understood. He was a very handsome fellow; tall, with hair and mustache inclined to be blonde and with, common of desperadoes, steel gray eyes. His manners were those of a gentleman; he dressed well and with good taste, and no one, merely meeting and conversing with him, would ever have taken him for a desperate character.

For years he lived at various points in the interior—at Austin, San Antonio, Columbus and other places—but in 1873 he came to Houston to make this his home. He was a professional gambler and before he moved to Houston had nearly always owned and operated a gambling house. When he came here, however, he made no effort to open a game himself, though he had money and could have gotten all he wanted had he needed it, but contented himself with playing against the games of others. Luck was against him and he lost heavily. Then he got to drinking from time to time, and as whiskey always made him a fiend, everybody kept out of his way when he went on a spree.

There was one exception to this. At that time there was a little fellow here who was chief of police and if he ever kept out of anybody's way or ever wanted to keep out of anybody's way no one ever heard of it. He was Alex Erichson, the coolest, bravest man I ever knew. I saw him right after he had killed a man one day and if he was any more excited or agitated than the six-shooter with which he had done the killing, it was not visible.

One day Matt got to drinking, and soon got to raising a rough house in a saloon. Alex Erichson heard of it and went there to arrest Matt. He walked in on him and told him he was under arrest. Matt was not so drunk that he did not recognize the danger and folly of resisting an officer in the discharge of his duty, so he submitted and handed over his pistol. Erichson took him down to the police station allowing him to stay in the front room to await the arrival of some friend Matt sent for to go on his bond.

During the delay Matt had time to think over the situation and he began to feel the humiliation of his position. This made him angry and he began to abuse Erichson for having arrested him and to express regret that he had submitted to it and had given up his pistol. His language was very personal and finally Erichson, forgetting that he was an officer and Woodlief a prisoner, lost his temper and told Woodlief exactly what he thought of him. He did not use Sunday school language in doing so, either. Just then Woodlief's friends arrived, the bond was given and he was released.

So soon as he was free he walked up to Erichson, and, pointing his finger in his face, said, "You —— —— little Dutch —— — — —— ,I am going to kill you before night for what you have to me." Erichson sneered in his face and told him to pop his whip whenever he got ready.

Matt left and headed to a gunsmith, purchased a Colt six-shooter, since his own gun was locked up in Erichson's safe at police headquarters. Police headquarters at that time was down on a side street, one block below Milam Street. Erichson was detained there for some time by his duties and then walked toward Main Street. As he got to the corner of Main Street and Preston he saw Matt Woodlief on the northeast corner and Matt saw him at the same time. Each drew his pistol and began advancing, firing as they advanced. When each was about twenty feet from their respective corners, they fell.

By a strange coincidence each had been shot through the thigh and the bone had been shattered. Their wounds were identical. They fell, but that did not stop the fight, for they began dragging themselves toward each other, shooting as they advanced. Neither of them spoke a word as they slowly writhed along the street, getting closer and closer and shooting all the time. Both were noted shots, but somehow, after the two shots that had brought them to the ground, all the bullets went astray. Finally their ammunition was exhausted and the crowd rushed in and they were borne away and placed in the hands of surgeons. After weeks of suffering both recovered, though each was left a cripple for life.

Woodlief was tried in the criminal court on a charge of assault with intent to murder. The evidence was very clear and full against him, but the jury saw fit to bring in a verdict of aggravated assault and battery and assess the punishment at a fine of $250. When Erichson heard the verdict he lost his head again and allowed his temper to get away with him. I heard him tell one of Woodlief's witnesses, quite a prominent young man, that he was a perjured S.O.B. and that he (Erichson) would not believe him on oath, and then, turning to Sheriff Con Noble, he expressed the wish that Woodlief would beat him out of the fine. He was as game as a fighting cock and as vindictive and unforgiving as an Indian.

Woodlief remained in Houston for some time after his trial and then went to St. Charles, Louisiana, where he committed suicide. I say he committed suicide, for that is just what he did, though, perhaps, not exactly in the orthodox way.

Here's how it happened. He and one of his friends had been drinking and cutting up. His friend was arrested and put in jail for an offense which Woodlief claimed that he himself had committed. He sent word to the officers that if his friend was not released by a certain hour, let's say 2 o'clock, he was coming down to the jail to take him out himself. Woodlief's reputation was such that the officers knew he would at least try to carry out his threat, so they swore in some deputies and placed a strongly armed guard in front of the jail. Promptly Woodlief showed up, smoking a long stem pipe. He advanced to within 20 feet of where the guard was standing. Then waving his hand and ordering them to stand aside he reached for his pistol. The next moment he fell dead, pierced by a number of balls, for the guard literally riddled his body. If that was not committing, suicide, what was it?

Like most of the gunfighters who were picked off in their prime, Woodlief deteriorated toward the end, but the deterioration was physical and moral only, for his gameness stayed with him to the last and he died as he had lived, without fear of God or man.

★ ★ ★

A FAMOUS ROBBER

I took a car ride out to Woodland Heights the other day. As I passed Beauchamp Springs I thought of old man Kirkendall, one of the famous characters of early days, whose home was on the hill on the north side of the bayou, not far from the big spring that used to be just south of the bridge that crosses White Oak Bayou. Kirkendall was an intelligent, cool, calculating scoundrel and was the most hated and best feared man in or near Houston. He was so bold in the manner in which he stole cattle and horses and committed other depredations that it was a wonder he was never caught and convicted for some of his many crimes. He was generally credited with committing every crime except murder and, though he was arrested and tried seven times he always managed to get free.

Kirkendall was a powerful man. His frame was massive. He stood about five feet seven or eight inches high, broad of shoulder and as strong as an ox. His right-hand man was one of his slaves who went by the name of Pompey. Had Pompey been free and therefore able to do as he pleased, he could have made a fortune exhibiting himself as a giant. He was so tall that one feels inclined to become indifferent in speaking of his height and to say that he was either six feet seven inches or seven feet six inches tall. After seeing him one would be inclined to accept either statement as true. As a matter of fact he was six feet seven inches and he was superbly formed in every way. He was loyalty and devotion itself and absolutely devoid of fear. He knew nothing except to obey Kirkendall, who had absolute confidence in him, knowing that he was too courageous to be frightened into giving any of his dark secrets away.

For years Kirkendall stole cattle, branding those that were not branded, and changing the brands of those that were, until he owned one of the largest herds of cattle on Montgomery prairie, which was north of his home. He did not confine his operations to stealing cattle and horses, however. When opportunity presented itself he was a burglar and frequently he made the opportunity when one did not present itself! He was a wholesale burglar, too. When he had made his way into a grocery store, he was not content with a few cigars, a plug or two of tobacco, a box of sardines or a bottle of pickles; none of that kind of burglarizing for him. He took the whole works.

One night he broke into Dan Huebner's grocery store, corner of Preston Avenue and Travis Street, and he and Pompey loaded everything in the store in a two-horse wagon and drove off with it. It must be remembered that the stores in those days were small affairs and none of them carried big stocks as they do now. Of course, Kirkendall was suspected and officers searched his place, but they found nothing, for he had carefully concealed everything in the woods far away from home. Both he and Pompey were arrested but as there was no absolute proof against them, they were released again. Sheriff Tom Hogan and City Marshal Bob Boyce tried to frighten Pompey into making a confession, but soon had to give it up, for he did not scare easily and only laughed at them and held his tongue.

But this success in robbing Huebner's store led to their undoing. One night Kirkendall and Pompey came to town with their wagon and broke into the store of Mr. Cornelius Ennis, which stood where the office of the Western Union Telegraph Company is now located. They took what groceries they wanted and then picked up the iron safe, which was not a very large one, and loaded that on their wagon. They took their plunder out near their home, dug a big hole on the bank of the bayou, buried the safe, and left it there to be opened at their leisure.

The next morning when Mr. Ennis discovered his loss, he called in the sheriff and city marshal and they did not waste any time by looking elsewhere, but went right out and brought Kirkendall and Pompey in and placed them in jail. Then they gave Pompey a taste of what might be called the third degree. They took a rope, took him out in the jail yard and swore they would hang him if he did not tell them all about the robbery. Pompey really believed they were going to hang him, but he did not weaken. He did something worse, he made a blunder.

He told them he was not going to say a word and if they wanted to know where that safe was they would have to go to Mr. Kirkendall for the information. Now, as neither Kirkendall nor Pompey had been told what they were arrested for, when Pompey made his break the officers knew they had the right men. They went out to Beauchamp Springs and made a thorough search of the house, the woods and the bayou, and they found the safe where it had been buried by Kirkendall and Pompey. Kirkendall was subsequently indicted, tried and convicted, but I don't know what was done with Pompey. Kirkendall was sentenced to a long term in the penitentiary. When the time came to take him to Huntsville, he was placed in the middle of a big wagon with two guards in front and two behind and one riding on each side of the wagon. They knew that Kirkendall was a desperate man and was the head of a band of outlaws of unknown strength, and it was feared an attempted rescue would be made.

It was a week or two before Christmas when they started with him and as they drove off he rattled his chains and called out to Captain Boyce, telling him goodbye, and also informing him that he intended eating his Christmas dinner in Houston. The captain laughed at him, but Kirkendall was telling the truth, for a day or two after Christmas officers from the penitentiary came to Houston looking for him and told how he had mysteriously escaped a few days before Christmas.

After that Kirkendall left the country and was seen afterward in California, where he had evidently gone direct from Texas. As everybody was glad to get rid of him and to have him brought back would have consumed both time and lots of money, no effort was made to catch him and he died there several years ago.

★ ★ ★

FRANK LE MOTT'S STORY

Frank Le Mott frequently makes appearances in the stories that I tell and, as readers of the *Chronicle* will attest, he is one of my favorite characters. The other day I had the good fortune of hearing Frank talk about one of his favorite characters.

"I have known some queer characters in my day, but the queerest I ever ran across was an old, one-eyed chap that taught school for several years out west of San Antonio. If I did not know that Conan Doyle had never heard of the man, I would be tempted to believe that he had him in mind when he created Sir Nigel. This old fellow was on the warpath all the time and spent his leisure moments reading about chivalry, knights errant and all that sort of foolishness.

"The old chap had only one eye, and the way he lost the missing one was in keeping with everything he did. He belonged to a cavalry regiment that served on the other side of the river during the war, and they say he made one of the best soldiers in his command. I can't swear that the story is true in every detail, but I have heard it so often that I am inclined to believe every word of it. Once his regiment was camped on one side of a big bend in a river and a Yankee regiment was camped on the other. As a matter of fact, the two regiments were on the same side of the river, but there was a big bend in the river, coming down to a narrow neck that made them appear to be on opposite sides.

"One day, a crazy Yank came down to the bank of the river and rode his horse up and down, waving his hat and making signs and signals. No one could make out what he was up to until finally our old chap solved the mystery.

"'That chap is making a defy,' he said. 'He wants to run a tilt for the advancement of his lady love. Don't you see he holds up one hand and then points up the river? He wants a private war, and I'm going to give it to him. I ain't got no lady, but I will stop his advancing his.' So saying he saddled up his horse, buckled on his six-shooter and motioning to the Yank to come ahead, he rode off to the big bend in the river.

"The Yank must have been out for what the old man said, for as soon as he saw him start he put spurs to his horse and aimed for the bend, too. They commenced shooting as soon as they got in range and about the second shot the Yank's bullet knocked the old chap's eye out. That made him so mad that he charged down on the Yank, yelling like an Indian and shooting like a fiend. That charge was too much for the Yank. He forgot all about the advancement of his lady love and thought only of the retirement of himself. He turned tail and broke for his camp with the old chap right behind him, coming like a prairie fire. In spite of the danger, the boys could not keep from yelling, and the Yanks were doing the same. The old fellow chased that 'knight' right into his camp and tried to hit him with his empty six-shooter after he caught him.

"The Yanks were dead-game sports. They had seen that it was a fair fight, and they refused to take advantage of the situation. They had their doctor fix the old chap's eye and then they turned him loose and let him go back to his own regiment. Some of the boys used to say they sent him back with a guard of honor, but I always omit that part when I tell the story.

"Now if you knew the old fellow you would be prepared to believe this story, or any other that would bring out his gameness. He was like one of those blue-legged crabs in a tub that throws up both arms, ready for battle every time anybody looks at him. The old man was always looking for trouble, with the result that, after his reputation was established, he was always treated with the most distinguished consideration and courtesy.

"Now, from what I have told you about the old man you would think that nothing on earth could rattle him, and that he had nerves made out of galvanized iron. He had nothing of the kind, but was one of the most nervous men you ever saw. He would stand up and fight the devil himself with knife or pistol, and never a whimper, but if anyone sprang a surprise on him he would go all to pieces. I suspect he was ticklish. I remember I gave him a great surprise and he gave me one in return that I remembered for a long time. He was walking down Houston Street, in San Antonio, and I walked up behind him and slapped him on the shoulder. He squatted down on the ground and squealed like a wildcat and then rose with a bowie knife in his hand and chased me for two blocks. He was simply crazy from nervousness and did not know what he was doing. I heard afterward that he did the same thing in the legislative hall at Austin and came near killing one of his friends who came up behind him and nudged him. You can bet I never tried to flank nor come up behind him after that. I would dodge him until he could see me advancing from in front, and even then I watched out for signs of war from him. The old fellow always carried two derringers and a bowie knife and it is a wonder he did not kill off half his friends.

"He was a great believer in duelling, but I don't think he ever fought a duel unless that tournament with the Yankee might be called one. He was always in too great a hurry to wait for the seconds to arrange the affair. Poor old fellow. He has been dead now many years, but the next time you are in San Antonio and come across any old-timers you ask them about Professor Pete White, and listen to the tales they will tell you. You can get enough to make a book if you want to."

★ ★ ★

FRANK BATES

I had the pleasure of meeting my old friend, Frank Bates, on Main Street recently. Of all the young men I knew when I left Houston, Frank has changed least and looks today exactly as he looked thirty years ago. It is marvelous what little change has taken place in his personal appearance though, of course, Frank is by no means an old man. He was scarcely more than a well-grown lad when I last saw him. There are wonderful changes that have taken place in him otherwise, for he is now a sedate, dignified country gentleman, married and settled. Back then he was the wildest, hair-brained, fun-loving fellow that ever lived. If he ever had a serious thought no one found it out.

Frank lived about twenty years too late. Had he been older and more mature at the time when real bad men flourished, he would have been one of them. There was never anything vicious about him. He was always the soul of honor and was loyal to his friends, but his tastes ran towards fights and skirmishes, and having a Southern gentleman's distaste for a fistfight or anything so low as that, his inclinations were towards six-shooters and knives.

Frank loved to talk of private battles and told marvelous stories of his fights with Indians and frontier desperadoes. He was and is still a great favorite with everybody, for I defy anybody to be with Frank for half a day without falling in love with him.

Frank was a member of the famous world-beating Light Guard, and when we went to Philadelphia he went along as one of the substitutes. As a substitute, he did not have to drill, so had abundant leisure to go where he pleased. The second day after our arrival, Dr. Carrycross, a large wholesale druggist of Philadelphia, came out to Fairmont Park, where we were camped, and asked for the Texas company. He introduced himself and invited every member of the company to call on him when they went into town and asked them to make his place their headquarters. Some of the boys called on him the next morning and that evening he came out to see us again. After that he came every afternoon. He adopted the company and the company adopted him.

He and Frank Bates became inseparable. He got Frank to talking—not a hard thing to do, by the way—and was never so happy as when listening to Frank's stories of Indian warfare and life of the frontier. Had a dime novel writer been present and taken down those stories his fortune would have been made. Frank saw the deep interest that Dr. Carrycross took in his stories, so he spread himself. I remember only the main points of one he told, but it serves well to show what and how Frank was doing in his efforts to entertain a genuine "tenderfoot." He was describing a wild ride he claimed to have taken once. "Yes, sir," he said, "I rode from near my plantation to Navasota, fifty miles, in little less than three hours. Let me see. What was I in such a hurry about? Oh, yes, I remember, I had shot a man that morning, and, then, feeling sorry, I went after a doctor for him."

Frank stuffed Carrycross full of such stories and made him believe that his life had been one great tragedy from the time he left his cradle up to that moment. Carrycross swallowed it all and asked for more. Day after day he entertained the boys who went to town in the morning, but was entertained by them every afternoon at our camp.

On the Sunday before we left for New York, we invited him out to dinner. After dinner we laid out on the grass, smoking and talking. Frank was making the best of his last opportunity and was telling some thrilling stories when Carrycross interrupted him: "Now boys," he said, "I want to tell you how much I have enjoyed your visit. There are 5000 or 6000 troops here, but you may have noticed that I have never gone near any of them. I have enjoyed being with you Texans too much. That enjoyment arises from two causes—first, because you are from Texas, and, next, because you have my dear friend, Frank Bates, with you. I have enjoyed hearing him talk more than I can make you understand. His descriptions of wild and woolly Texas have been perfect. I am a competent judge, too, for now I am going to tell you all something which will further explain the great interest I have had in you. I was for nine years a Texas Ranger in West Texas and served under Captain Baylor along the Rio Grande for three years. I said nothing about this because I was afraid Frank might stop talking. Now, that you are going away, it makes no difference, so I tell you."

When the crowd realized that Frank had been stuffing a Texas Ranger with blood and thunder stories for three weeks under the impression that he was an ignorant tenderfoot, a great shout went up and Frank took to his hole. We teased him all the way to New York and home again, but it was hard to tease a fellow who enjoyed a joke on himself as much as anyone else did, and Frank did that.

Good old Frank. May his days be long and happy ones. He is dignified and sedate now, but somehow I rather prefer the happy-go-lucky Frank of a quarter of a century ago to the staid country gentleman he is today.

★ ★ ★

FIGHTING HOUSTON BOYS

Last winter I was out walking with a gentleman near San Antonio when he suddenly turned to me and asked: "What has become of all the tumble bugs?" The question was so uncalled for, so foreign to all we had been talking about, that for a moment I suspected him of being the victim of sudden insanity.

"What do you mean?" I asked.

"I mean just what I say; what has become of all the tumble bugs?" said he. "When you and I were boys there were millions of them everywhere, bright shiny fellows with yellow and gold on their wings and back, and black and brown ones. You could see them everywhere, but now you stop and think and see if you don't find that you have seen only a stray one, now and then, for years past. What has become of them?"

I did stop and think, and the more I thought the more I realized that what he said was true, and now I am like he and would like to have some scientific bug-sharp answer his question. I have heard that quail and some other birds go with civilization and accompany the footsteps of the pioneer. If that be true, I see no reason why the tumble bug should not have his own individual peculiarity, which causes him to get out of the way completely when civilization shows up. Perhaps that is the proper answer to my friend's question.

But I am not going to write anything about the disappearance of the tumble bug, for I don't know anything to write, beyond the fact that he has disappeared. The question I had in mind is one of equal importance and is related also to a disappearance—that of the fighting boy of long ago, who loved nothing better than a good scrap and who felt lonesome and somewhat humiliated unless he had a black eye or bore the evidence of past combat. In the early days fightin', fishin', swimmin' and huntin' were the greatest joys of a boy's life, and, looking back on those happy days, I really believe the fightin' portion of the program held first place in the hearts of all of them.

There was no regular organization, each tub stood on its own bottom, and yet there were divisions of territory and the boys who lived in such divisions, while they fought freely among themselves, always banded together against an outside, common enemy. In the Fourth Ward, west of Main Street, there were a number of big boys, such as Phil Fall, Os and Matt Conklin, the two Lilly boys, George and John Harman, Ed and Billy Brown and others whom I have forgotten. They were the recognized bosses of that part of town and any big boy who, like the knights errant of old, sought adventure "for the advancement of his lady love" or for any old thing, could go out that way any day and any time of day and find enough of it to last him for a week or two, or until he could get his eyes sufficiently open to see to get back for more. The fights were all fair and square, too; no doubling up or having a big boy jump on a smaller one. A boy had to tackle a fellow of his size. The rules of the game were simple, too, and no deadly insult or loudly proclaimed challenge was necessary. The simple fact that a big boy from another part of town had dared to show himself at their favorite swimmin' hole or town ball games was taken as all sufficient *casus belli* and active hostilities were at once under way.

The Fourth Ward was the best equipped of all for warfare, for a larger number of big boys and good fighters lived there, but what is now the Third Ward but which then was in two or three divisions, was not far behind. There were three gangs in this territory, but none of them had brilliant leaders. There were too many of them nearly evenly matched to admit of anything like leadership. I remember many battles royal that took place down at the arsenal swimming hole, which was a favorite battleground, between the Howard boys, Mag and Vic Rogers, Bud and Prat Mathews, Henry and Jim Thompson, John and Milt McGowan, Joe Wills, Hiram and Billy Church and a number of others whose names I have forgotten. I was a little fellow and therefore immune from attack, protected by my size, but occasionally, quite often as a matter of fact, they would produce a boy of my size and I would have to fight for the privilege of remaining there.

Those who remember the quiet, good-natured gentleman that Dr. James Blake grew up to be will no doubt be surprised to hear that he was one of the greatest scrappers of his day when a boy. He was terribly handicapped by his size, for he was a great big boy for his age and always had to fight uphill, that is, go against boys of his size who were much older than he. If no such material was at hand he would take on two boys smaller than himself, and I remember on one occasion he became overzealous and took on three with the result that he got beaten nearly to death. As I remarked, those were fair fights. No knives, sticks, bricks or other weapons were used and the strange part was that very little anger or temper was ever shown. Five minutes after a fight the boys were as good friends as ever and never bore ill will or resentment toward each other.

It was really a painful and trying thing for a Houston boy to have to go to Galveston or for a Galveston boy to have to come to Houston, for in either case the visit was simply a continual round of fights. Then as now the Galveston boys were "sandcrabs," while the Houston boys were "mudcats," though the use of such names was considered a deadly insult then and always resulted in a fight.

I understand that it is not considered the proper thing for school boys to fight now and that there are any number of them who have never had a single fight in their lives. It makes me feel awful sorry for them, for in that fact I discover another great misfortune they have in being born in a place where there are no old-fashioned swimmin' holes, no place to go huntin' and fishin' except way off.

★ ★ ★

Fun at the Fairgrounds

I think it was at the State Fair that was held in Houston in 1871 or 1872, I forget which, that one of the funniest sights I ever witnessed occurred.

At that time there was a very prominent physician here, who had been a lawyer before studying medicine and who was one of the finest speakers I ever heard. He could make a speech at any time on any subject, and when he got about half-loaded he was very eloquent. He delighted to hear his own voice and never missed an opportunity to give himself a treat in that way. I mention this because it has bearing on what occurred.

That year Colonel James, who had charge of the military school at Austin, brought the cadets down to the fair. There were several hundred of them and they made a fine appearance. Major Brokenbourough, who was the military instructor at the school, had command of the battalion. He and I had been college mates in Virginia and I was delighted to meet him again. His father was Judge Brokenbourough, one of the most distinguished lawyers in Virginia. While the major and I were talking, my friend, the doctor, came up and I introduced him to the major. The doctor was loaded just right, and was very effusive. "Is it possible," he said, shaking the major's hand, "that I grasp the hand of a son of my old and esteemed friend, Judge Brokenbourough of Virginia?" Now, as a matter of fact, I don't believe the doctor had ever heard of the judge until I mentioned the fact that he was the major's father, but he made the play alright and created the impression on the major's mind that he and his father had been raised together. "This occasion," he said, "deserves to be commemorated. Come and take a glass of wine with me."

He led us over to a stand and ordered a quart bottle of champagne. The major protested against such extravagance and declared he would rather have a glass of beer, but the doctor would not listen to him and the champagne was opened. Just then a band nearby began playing and the wine and music combined to make the doctor feel awfully good and talkative.

There was to be a grand parade of the cadets at 4 o'clock and as it was near that hour the major tried to excuse himself so as to go and get ready. Then a happy thought occurred to the doctor. He told the major he would like to give the boys a talk. The major thought it was merely a passing whim and made some casual remark about being most happy to hear it and things of that kind. The doctor insisted and then the major told him he would go and get Colonel James' permission.

Now, had the major known the doctor as well as I did, he would have gone to the colonel and secured his permission, for the talk would have been a good one. As it was, thinking that the doctor would forget all about it after taking the next drink, instead of going to Colonel James, he went directly to where the cadets were and commenced preparing them for the parade. The parade and drill were to take place on the race track in front of the grandstand, so, taking my arm, the doctor led me out there and took up his position where the colonel generally stands during a dress, parade. Major Brokenbourough was busily engaged in forming his battalion across the track. The grandstand was crowded with ladies, the band was playing and the doctor was absolutely in the seventh heaven of delight. He was feeling mighty good. He took off his hat and the wind blew his long hair about and he evidently felt like a war horse about to charge. The charge was there all right, but it was to come from the other side. After a little while Colonel James showed up on a fine, prancing horse.

If he noticed the doctor and me standing there he said nothing, but, drawing his sword, Colonel James took command of the battalion, which the major had formed. For the benefit of the ladies he put the boys through the manual of arms and then gave the order: "Fix bayonets." His next order was "Charge bayonets," and then "Forward, quick time, march." I saw what was coming and deserted the doctor at once, getting away on one side. The doctor thought that the colonel was bringing his battalion up closer, so the boys could hear his speech, and he stood his ground with his head thrown back and his nostrils distended. He was in his glory. Some soldiers to talk to, a fine brass band playing and thousands of pretty women to hear him talk. He held his hat in his hand and the wind was scattering his long hair about in the most charming manner.

In the meantime that solid wall of bayonets was sweeping down on him. I was off on one side in a safe position where I could watch him and see the expression on his face. When the battalion reached a point about thirty feet away and continued to advance, a troubled and surprised look came over his face. The next moment he realized that there had been a blunder committed and that he was in a tight place. People began to shout to him to get away while he could. At last he realized the truth, but it was too late to reach the end of the line and escape that way. He realized that and did not try it. He slapped his hat on his head and turning his back to the advancing troops bent over and awaited them. There was a sudden break in the line, the ranks parted on each side and the doctor emerged, tail foremost, from the confused mass. The grandstand gave vent to a mighty shout and the doctor straightened up and came over to where I was rolling all over the ground, half dead with laughter. He was so angry he could scarcely talk.

"Where is that ———— ?" he asked, referring to the son of his supposed old and highly esteemed friend. "Get up. I want you to take my card to him. He must answer to me for this outrage. He must have been drunker than I thought, for evidently James knew nothing of why I was out there." I had hard work to keep him from attacking the battalion right there so as to get at the major, who was hopping along before the girls and entirely oblivious to the proximity of the great volcano he had stirred up. Finally I got the doctor to wait until he got to town, where he could draw up the challenge in regular form, which I promised I would take to the major.

After another drink, the doctor's mood changed. "I find myself in a nasty position," he said, "I can't make up my mind to kill the son of my old friend and comrade-in-arms, for his father and I served together in the Army of Northern Virginia. The boy deserves killing, of course, for he has made a monkey of his father's most intimate friend, but then he is only a thought-less boy. I might execute James, but that would be unjust, for he knew noth-ing of what he was doing. What do you advise?"

Of course I told him that I'd drop the subject and never think of it again. That night, the cadets left for home and the major left with them. He left in absolute ignorance of the terrible fate that came so near overtaking him.

★ ★ ★

RELICS OF THE WAR

Walking down Main Street the other day I saw in one of the show windows an assortment of shot and shell which, according to an attached card, were taken out of the bayou near the Milam Street bridge. These had all been nicely cleaned and painted black, so that they looked as good as new, despite the fact that they had remained so many years in the mud of Buffalo Bayou.

One would naturally suppose that they had been thrown in the bayou to keep them from falling into the hands of the Federals who at that time were expected to invade Texas. Such, however, was not the case. Lee had surrendered; Johnson had surrendered and the Trans-Mississippi department of the Confederate States was alone in its glory to represent the Confederacy. However, the soldiers of the Trans-Mississippi department did not care for such an honor and those stationed at Galveston, Houston and other points on the coast, having no enemy in sight to whom to surrender, concluded to take matters in their own hands and just quit.

Having quit they concluded to take with them everything movable that belonged to the Confederacy. Horses, wagons, guns and ammunition were seized wherever found, and of these powder and lead were more sought after than all else. At that time there was a large two-story brick house on the corner of Travis and Congress Avenue, north side of market square, owned by Jack Kennedy, the father of the late John Kennedy and father-in-law of Wm. Foley. The building extended back on Travis Street where Foley's store now is. This building was occupied by the Confederates and was used as a factory for making percussion caps and cartridges. Where Foley's store now stands was used as a warehouse and in it were stored boxes of cartridges, caissons filled with ammunition for field guns, rifles and any kind of ammunition except that for heavy guns.

There was a large quantity of cannon powder, hand grenades and large bombs stored over in the old powderhouse near the city cemetery, northwest of the Central Railway depot. The powderhouse was broken open by the soldiers and its contents, proving undesirable, were scattered over the ground or rolled down the hill into White Oak Bayou. The next move was on the Kennedy building and here they reaped a rich harvest. Boxes of cartridges were broken open and their contents appropriated. Sacks of powder were ripped open and when found to be cannon powder, they were thrown on the floor. Soon the floor was covered with powder, loose percussion caps and an indescribable assortment and litter of dangerous things. There were hundreds of roughshod men trampling and stamping over this and the wonder is that the whole place and everybody for blocks around were not blown to bits.

The remarkable thing is that no one seemed to realize that there was the least danger and it was a good-natured, jolly crowd that went on with the work of looting. One shining example of an opposite opinion was the owner of the building, Mr. Kennedy. He realized the danger to the fullest extent and did all in his power to check such recklessness. He begged and implored the crowd to get out and let him lock the doors and pointed out the almost certain explosion and consequent destruction if a halt were not made. All his talk fell on deaf ears and finally in desperation he took matters in his own hands. He hired a lot of men and giving them buckets full of water he flooded the place. There were no hydrants or water works at that time so the water was drawn from a cistern and the buckets passed from hand to hand until the place was flooded. Late in the evening everything worth saving had been carried off by the soldiers, but the shells and hand grenades with a lot of fuses remained. These were all dangerous, of course, so Mr. Kennedy concluded to get rid of them. He hired some drays and teams, loaded the shells on them and, carting them down to the Milam Street bridge, known then as "the iron bridge," he had them cast in the bayou.

There must be hundreds of them there yet. From time to time during the prevalence of a norther, the water in the bayou falls so as to reveal those which were dumped off near the banks. These were fished out and saved as relics, but no doubt hundreds of others lie deeply buried in the mud or in such deep water that they are never exposed.

In 1866 a severe norther blew the water out of the bayou, revealing a number of these shells near the bank. Two young men, who were machinists in McGowan's foundry, fished one of the shells out of the mud and placed it on the bank to dry. When dinner time came they took their hammers and tools and tried to get the fuse out of the shell. They had worked but a few moments when there was a terrible explosion and both young men were instantly killed and horribly mangled.

A negro living out near the Hardcastle place in the Fourth Ward got two or three of these old shells out of the bayou. He left them lying around his yard for a long time, not knowing they were dangerous. One day while cleaning up his yard, he raked the trash up over one of the bombs and set fire to it. The explosion that followed alarmed the whole neighborhood, but fortunately did no damage to anyone. It is safe to say that the other shells belonging to the negro's collection now rest at the bottom of the bayou which runs near his place.

★ ★ ★

Fought with Fireworks

I have never seen it mentioned in any history of Texas, though I remember that a long account of it was published in the *Houston Telegraph* of December 25, 1871; nor is it generally known today that one of the most remarkable battles of modern times was fought on Preston Avenue and on Main Street for several blocks on Christmas Eve, 1871.

This great combat was the result of a joke. It started in a small way, but soon grew to great proportions, involving prominent railroad men, staid bankers professional men, merchants and a good sprinkling of everyday kind of people. An account of that great battle is worth giving, and as I witnessed the firing of the first shot and actually dodged the first ball, I feel that I am competent to give it.

Dr. Louis A. Bryan and I came out of Conlief's drug store, on Preston Avenue, about 9 o'clock that night. As we stepped on the sidewalk, Captain J. Waldo, who was on the opposite side of the street, shooting off a big roman candle, lowered it and sent a great, green ball directly at us, following it with others in rapid succession. We dodged into a nearby store, which happened to have a good supply of fireworks on hand and each of us got the largest roman candle we could find. Out we went and opened fire on Waldo. Andrew Hutcheson came to Waldo's assistance, then Sandy Ewing joined Dr. Bryan and me. Mr. Fred Stanley joined Waldo and Andrew. It kept up that way until within 15 minutes there were fully 100 men shooting at each other with roman candles. At first they kept apart and fired from across the street, but getting excited they closed up, made charges and almost reduced it to a hand-to-hand conflict.

By common consent Dr. Bryan was chosen as leader of one party and Captain Waldo was chosen as leader of the other. They kept boys busy bringing up ammunition and it was not long before they had bought every roman candle to be found within blocks of the battlefield. Dr. Bryan and I were wearing stovepipe hats, and, of course, we received marked attention.

Our hats were something wonderful to look at within a few minutes after the fight got under headway.

When you consider that nearly every man engaged in that battle was a leading and prominent citizen, that nearly all of them were prominent merchants, bankers, railroad officials or professional men, it will be seen what a remarkable fight it was. Had it been a lot of boys it would have been quite natural, but it was nothing of the kind. It was a spontaneous determination on the part of a lot of grown men to be boys again, and the battle was the result. I can remember only a few, but the mention of their names will show the character of the crowd, for they were all of the same class. There was Dr. Louis A. Bryan, Captain J. Waldo, Captain A. Faulkner, Mr. Fred Stanley (right-hand and confidential adviser of T. W. House, Sr.), Sandy Ewing, Andrew Hutcheson, Judge George Goldthwaite, Dr. Alva Connell, Dr. James Blake, Charley Gentry and a score of others whose names escape me.

Just imagine the general officers of the railroads, the leading merchants, bankers, doctors and lawyers of today getting up such a racket as that. Why, the mere idea is preposterous! I was talking to Dr. George McDonald, the only one of the old crowd left, the other day and he remarked that the people of Houston do not know what fun is, and I believe he is right. I don't remember whether Dr. McDonald was in the roman candle battle or not, but if he was, he and I are the only survivors, for all those I have named have crossed over the river. That is the one sad feature about recalling the happy days of the past. There are so many sad thoughts connected with the subjects I write about.

★ ★ ★

MIXED TEXAS HISTORY

The other day I was in a Main Street store making a small purchase. The young man who waited on me was an intelligent looking chap and was as talkative as the proverbial barber. I did not know him but he knew me, and after discussing the paving question and kindred matters he made pleasing reference to some of my articles in the *Chronicle*, saying he had enjoyed reading them very much.

"I read your article on the battle of San Jacinto," he said. "It was fine and I enjoyed reading it very much. I was greatly surprised to find that Col. Hamp

Cook was as old as that makes him out to be. Let's see, the battle of San Jacinto was fought in 1861, was it not?"

I thought he was joking, of course, but a glance at him convinced me that he was in dead earnest, so I said, "Oh, no, the battle was fought in 1873."

"Why, of course. What was I thinking about? It was the battle of the Alamo that was fought in 1861. Somehow I always get the two mixed up." That remarkable interview actually took place just as I have described it. One marvels at such ignorance of Texas history, yet that ignorance is more general than anyone imagines. To the credit of the Texas boys I am glad to be able to record the fact that the young clerk was not a Texan but had come to Houston a year or two ago from Chicago. I have never met a Texas boy who could not tell all about the Alamo and San Jacinto.

Last winter I met with a more remarkable example of ignorance than my clerk exhibited. It was in San Antonio at the Gunter Hotel. There was a large party of excursionists going to California. They stopped over in San Antonio for a day. In the party was a young man who had just been graduated from one of the theological schools in Massachusetts. He was on his way to some place between Los Angeles and San Francisco to take charge of a church. He was an Episcopalian and was well-educated in everything except Texas history. We took a walk and when we reached the plaza I pointed out the Alamo to him.

"Really, I am ashamed to ask the question, but what is the Alamo and what does it stand for?" he queried.

I thought he was trying to make fun of me at first, but a glance at his face showed me that he was seriously seeking information. With such context, with the Alamo itself in front of me, I was able to make rather a good talk and when I finished up with San Jacinto, my young preacher was about as enthusiastic over Texas history as I was. We returned to the hotel and after lunch he asked me to go with him to the smoking room. When we got there, I found that he had gathered about a dozen of his traveling companions and after making a short talk himself, he begged me to repeat what I had told him about the Alamo and San Jacinto for the benefit of his friends.

For the first time in my life I found myself lecturing on history. I began with Bradburn's misdeeds at Anahuac in 1831, which really started the Texas Revolution and ended with San Jacinto. They were all greatly interested in what I told them and I was intensely proud of being a native of a state which has such a history. The preacher became enthusiastic again and before he left the city he purchased every book he could find that had any Texas history in it.

It seems strange to us that there should be anybody ignorant about our state's history, and yet the average Texan is about as ignorant of the history of most of the other states of the Union. It is true that no other state has a history so striking and so worthy of being known, yet some of them do have worthy histories and the average Texan knows no more about them than those northern gentlemen knew about Texas.

I suppose the self-confessed ignorance of the Massachusetts gentlemen is more general and widespread than is supposed, for those who do not know what the Alamo is are wise enough not to admit the fact, but keep their mouths closed until they inform themselves. That is what I know I would do if I visited Massachusetts and any point or incident in the state's history came up for discussion about which I knew nothing.

The Alamo has always been an incentive to Texans urging them to the performance of deeds of patriotism and valor, and at times it has been something of a heavy handicap. Everybody remembers the speech made by President Davis at the breaking out of our great war to the Texas troops in the Army of Northern Virginia. "The troops from other states," he said, "have reputations to make; you Texans have one to sustain."

★ ★ ★

HOUSTON TURNVEREIN

The other night I was passing along the Carolina Street side of the Turnverein grounds when it occurred to me that just in the middle of that block was where I had seen the first dead Confederate soldier. I saw thousands of dead ones after that but none that left such an impression on my mind as did that first one. He was a member of the Turnverein company organized and commanded by Captain E. B. H. Schneider at the outbreak of the war. The company was one of the best that left Houston for the front and made quite a name for itself. It was composed entirely of members of the Turnverein, which organization had been perfected some years before. To be exact, the Verein was organized on January 14, 1854, and on the first page of its old minute book its story is told in the following simple and touching language:

We, the undersigned, assembled this forenoon in Gable's house, to confer in regard to the institution of a Turnverein. It was the wish of all to belong to a society where each feels as a brother to the other and lives for him and with him as a brother. We have, therefore, associated ourselves under a brotherly pressure of hands and promised each other to organize a Turnverein with energy and love in the cause and assure its existence by continued activity.

(Signed) T. Heitmann, F. Reitmann, Marschall, Louis Pless, John F. Thordale, Robert Voight, E. B. H. Schneider, August Sabath, B. Scheurer and L. Scheihagen.

Captain Schneider was a great athlete and to him was assigned the task of organizing a gymnastic class. He organized two—one for the men and one for the ladies. He was most thorough in his teaching and it was not long before the Houston Turners gained name and fame for themselves in athletic circles.

At the beginning there were very few members, but it was not long before the association grew to such proportions that they were enabled to add other features to their gymnasium. A fire company was organized, a good German-English school was established and then, when war was talked of, the famous military company was organized, composed entirely of members of the Verein. It was of this company I started to tell you.

Captain Schneider was born a soldier and had thorough military training, of course, before coming to this country. He at once started in to apply the most rigid discipline and exhaustive methods in training his men to be soldiers. He would load them down with all their camp equipment, heavy guns and cartridge boxes and march them for hours, way out in the country and back again, and would put them through quick and double-quick time for the amusement of people who had gathered to see them drill.

It was while putting the men through one of these gruelling marches that the soldier I speak of lost his life. The captain marched the company down San Jacinto Street to the bayou. The wharf was about eight feet high and the water was twelve or fifteen feet deep, right up to the wharf. The captain marched the company right over the wharf into the bayou. He wanted them to cross to the other side and march on as if nothing had happened. After some floundering all the company except one man got across. Strange to say the one who failed was considered the best swimmer and all-round athlete in the company, but he lost his life. The body was recovered almost immediately and was borne sorrowfully to the armory of the company, which was a modest little building near the middle of the block about where the hall is.

The dead soldier was given a military funeral which was probably the first that occurred in Texas at the beginning of the war.

The people of Houston really do not appreciate what the Turners have done for the city and the state. The first semi-public school in Houston was established by the Turners two years after the close of the war. Those who could pay for the education of their children did, but there was always a deficit and the Turners made this good from their treasury. By misrepresenting the South, the emigration agents were turning the tide of emigration to the West and North. To counteract this the Turners prepared and had printed, at their own expense, thousands of pamphlets which they sent broadcast over Germany and other points from which desirable emigrants were coming to this country. In this way they secured for Texas numbers of the best citizens the state has today.

I say nothing of their record as musicians for everybody knows that but for the Turners, Houston would never have attained its prominence as a music-loving community as soon as it did, nor have attained the high position it now holds in the musical world. That is the one thing that everybody knows about the Turners, but the things I have mentioned are not so generally known nor appreciated as they should be.

★ ★ ★

OLD MAN LAKEN

Of all the remarkable characters who lived in Houston in the early days "Old Man" Laken occupied a place very near the head of the class. He was the most serious man I ever knew. I don't think anybody ever saw him even smile, let alone laugh, and I am sure I never did. He had been a policeman, a jailer or private watchman all his life, and having occupied only subordinate positions, he did not know anything except to obey orders. Being old and somewhat feeble, Marshal I. C. Lord always gave the old fellow an easy berth at police headquarters and his principal duty was to keep order in the recorder's court. During his long career as a policeman and jailer it had fallen to his lot to kill several men and no enthusiastic hunter ever displayed greater pride in telling of the game he had bagged than did Old Man Laken when telling of what he had done in the killing line. He did not speak of them often, but when he did his face showed the only animation that was ever seen on it:

"You see, it was this way. I'm all alone in the jail, when one of them fellows puts up a holler and says he wants a doctor, for he is sick. I goes to the cell and peeps in. He's stretched out on the floor and is all doubled up, and when he sees me he begs for water. Thinkin' he's sick shore enough, I opens the door and steps in. Just as I gits in the other fellow, who is on one side, slugs me good and hard right behind the ear and knocks me down. Before I can git up both of 'em is on top of me and begins chokin' me to keep me from hollerin'.

"Then they throw me in the bunk and piles all the bed clothes over my head and sits on top of the pile to smother me. Before they throw me in the bunk they takes my gun and my keys. They nearly smother me, but I manages to git my nose where I can breathe a little. I see what their game is, so after a little kickin' I laid right still and they got up and went out in the corridor. They went to the big door and unlocked it and went out in the yard. There was a big fence and, as the sheriff always carried the key to the door of that, they knew I did not have it and got ready to climb the fence. The fence was about eighteen feet high, but they got a pole and one of 'em climb up and dropped down on the outside.

"I had got up and had got one of them old hoss pistols, the only thing I could find, and was watchin' 'em. When the first fellow got over, the other one commenced climbin' the pole. He was the fellow who had knocked me down and I wanted to git him bad. I slipped out and got right behind him, but he was too busy to see me, and just kept on climbin'. I waited until he got to the top of the wall and then I raised my pistol. It was so heavy I had to hold it in both hands. I took good aim and made the best shot I ever made in my life. I got him right in the middle of the back of his head and that fellow don't know till yet what happened to him. We caught the other fellow that evening but I could never get a chance to shoot him, for he would never give me an excuse to do it."

"But, captain," said I, for I always called him captain, and he liked it. "But, captain, why did you not catch him instead of killing him? You could have done so easily." He did not like my suggestion and answered a bit hotly.

"Because I didn't want to catch him. Wasn't I hired to work for the best interests of this community, and that's what I done. If I'd made him come back there would have been his board and then his trial would've cost a lot more. I plugs him in the back of the head. It costs about $15 to plant him and there you are. Look at the money I save the community."

Being a policeman was second nature with the old man. Although he had married a widow who owned a snug little farm near town and could have lived in comparative ease the rest of his life without working, he hung on to his job to the last. He did not have a tooth in his head and as he disdained to wear "stone teeth," as he called them, his nose and chin nearly met every time he closed down on his quid of tobacco, which was all the time, for he was an incessant chewer.

One afternoon Alex Erichson was showing Marshal Lord and a few other gentlemen, who were in his office, a Manhattan six-shooter, so called because the New York police had just been armed with them. After admiring the pistol, Marshal Lord went to his safe and brought out an old Allen pistol, also known as a "pepper box." A good many jokes were made at the expense of the old pistol, but old man Laken took up for it.

"You can laugh at it as much as you want, but all the same I got three dagoes with one of them pistols over in New Orleans one night. That is, I got two right there and the other one croaked next day in the Charity Hospital." Of course, he was pressed for particulars and told the story.

"It's thirty years ago and I was a watchman at one of the big warehouses on the levee. I noticed three dagoes moseying 'round and acting queer, so I watched 'em. One night I saw 'em go in an old shanty, so I snuck up and tried to get a peep at 'em. I could see 'em but couldn't hear what they were saying, so I snuck around back of the house where there was a window. There I could hear 'em, but it didn't do no good, for they were talking dago, and I didn't understand what they were saying.

"While I was trying to get close to the window I stepped on a bottle and liked to fell down. I made lots of fuss trying to catch myself and the dagoes look around and saw me. They jumped up. One pulled a long knife and another made a dive at the candle to blow it out. I dropped him before he got to it and the other two ran to the front door and commenced trying to open it. I ran around the house and got there just as they came out of the door. I pulled down on the one in front and got him and then I lammed it to the other one."

"Why, you old murderer," said someone, jokingly. "It's a wonder they did not hang you for wholesale murder. How came you to shoot people like that?"

"Well, I done it on suspicion and I'm dead right, too, for the one that died in the hospital comes across and makes a clean breast that they were counterfeiters the government is trying to catch. I didn't have anything but one of them pepper box pistols, but you see it done good work for me."

A young man named Gillespie was local editor on the *Houston Telegraph* at that time and made quite a feature of the police court. A great many negroes and loafers filled the courtroom every morning, so Marshal Lord issued an order to Old Man Laken to keep everybody out except lawyers and witnesses. The next morning the old man took a stand at the foot of the stairs and when Gillespie showed up he refused to let him in. Gillespie tried to argue with him, but it was no use.

"You ain't a lawyer and you ain't a witness and you can't get in. So don't try," he said. Finally Gillespie got word up to the marshal who came down and let him in. The next morning Gillespie had a humorous story about the occurrence. He thought nothing of it and was therefore greatly amazed when he arrived at court to have Old Man Laken come up and whack him over the head with the hickory stick he used instead of a club. Of course, he was indignant and demanded an explanation.

"You've done plenty," said the old man. "I won't let any man call me a brute in the paper or anywhere else."

"I never called you a brute," said Gillespie.

"The hell you didn't," said Laken. "Here it is as plain as printing, and it *is* printing, too," and he pointed to the heading of the article which was:

"ET TU BRUTE"

Gillespie explained that it was Latin and that he had used it for the purpose of expressing his sorrow that so good a friend as he considered Laken, had gone back on him even for a few minutes as he had done the day before. That settled the matter and they were as good friends as ever, though Gillespie was careful to use only English when he referred, even remotely, to Old Man Laken in his articles after that.

Marshal Lord, who is now ex-Mayor Lord, told me the other day that Old Man Laken died several years ago. He said the only change that ever took place in the old man was that his chin and nose came a little closer together when he chewed and that he used a little more tobacco, if that were possible, toward the end. There was only one Old Man Laken and there can never be another like him.

★ ★ ★

A DEADLY FIGHT

A few evenings ago I was talking with Captain T. H. Hunter, formerly of Huntsville, but at present a citizen of Houston, about the Cortina trouble on the Rio Grande in 1859. Captain Hunter was a Texas Ranger at that time and took an active part in the campaign against the Mexican outlaw and his followers. During the conversation Captain Hunter mentioned the fact that he and some members of his command had on one occasion escorted Judge E. J. Davis into Brownsville. The mention of the name of Judge Davis awakened in me many bitter memories, as it always will do with any old Texan, for this Judge Davis was later to become Governor E. J. Davis, who earned such an undesirable reputation during Reconstruction.

Judge Davis was a Union man, so when Texas withdrew from the Union he went North. Having gone North, he did more than some others who left with him—he went into the army and fought against us. Since in refusing to stand by Texas in its fight against the North was a matter of principle with him, I do not blame him at all for what he did. His entering the Federal army showed that he was willing to fight for his principle and I admire him for that. Had he stopped then, no Texan would have ever had the right to complain, but after the war his acts as a governor, backed by bayonets, were so outrageous that no true Texan can or ever will forgive him.

I am not familiar with his record as a soldier during the war. All I know of it is the last and closing chapter. Soon after the Federal troops took possession of Houston Colonel E. J. Davis arrived with his regiment. It sounded very funny then and sounds a bit funny yet, but this regiment was called the First Texas Regiment, and was known to the remainder of the army as a genuine Texas regiment, loyal to the Union. I know it is not prejudice that makes me say it, for anyone who ever saw that regiment will say the same thing. They were the greatest aggregation of scoundrels and cutthroats that ever disgraced a uniform. So far as being Texans is concerned, I don't think there was a genuine Texan in the whole lot, though doubtless there were some who had a right to claim that they had lived in Texas. They were mostly low-down Mexicans with a good sprinkling of negroes, and they all looked as if they had been recruited from the jails and penitentiaries. Where Colonel Davis ever found so many outlaws and how he ever kept even the semblance of authority over them has always been a mystery to me.

They had not been here long before highway robberies, sluggings and other outrages, of which I have already spoken, became of almost nightly occurrence. Finding that their would-be victims were prepared for them too often for their own safety, and after one or two of them had been found dead on the streets with the telltale slungshot knotted to their wrists, they turned their attention to other and safer modes of plunder. They took to raiding nearby farm houses, ill-treating the occupants and carrying off everything of value they could lay their hands on. They did not go in twos or threes, but went in force and, as no notice of their intended raids was ever given, they had things their own way.

One bright moonlit night in the fall of 1865, Mrs. W. E. Rogers, widow of the gallant Colonel Rogers, who died so bravely at the head of the Second Texas regiment at Fort Robinett, near Corinth, Miss. during the war, was aroused from her sleep by blows on her front door. She and her two daughters were alone at their home near Eureka, on the Houston & Texas Central Railway, five miles northwest of the city. The ladies were badly frightened, of course, and were terrified when, on peeping out, they saw a crowd of men on the front gallery and others in the yard. They paid no attention to the raps on the door and those outside, growing impatient, burst the door open with the butts of their guns and entered the house. The nearest neighbor was two miles away, but the outlaws took no chances of outcries being heard or of an escape being made or of help being summoned. They bound and gagged the ladies and, tying them securely to bed posts, they proceeded to ransack the house at their leisure. They broke open trunks, bureaus, wardrobes; in fact, everything they thought might contain money or jewelry, and made a clean sweep of everything they could lay their hands on. After they had gotten everything in sight they left, leaving a scene of ruin and desolation behind them.

Had they been satisfied with the plunder they had, all might have been well with them, temporarily at least. That was not to be, however. Their thirst for plunder was insatiate and they turned from the Rogers home to that of an old German named Bache, who lived with his wife and two sons on a small farm about two miles nearer town, about opposite where Houston Heights now is. Old Man Bache was about as tough a customer as they could possibly have tackled. He would rather fight than eat any time and everybody except those outlaws of Davis' regiment knew it. His sons, though quite young, were "chips off the old block," so the trio made a strong combination.

About two hours after the Rogers robbery, Old Man Bache was aroused from his sleep by a noise in his yard. He got up and saw a couple of men coming toward the house. He seized his gun and called to them to halt. They paid no attention to him, but continued to advance. He fired and one of the foremost fell. The fire was returned and the doors and windows were riddled. The sons came to the rescue of their father and for a time a pitched battle was fought. The casualties were heavy, but they were all on the side of the outlaws. Finally the ammunition of the Baches gave out, a fact which was recognized by the outlaws when the brisk fire from the house ceased, and they prepared to take the place by storm. Finally they charged and broke the door down, thus gaining admittance to the house. That move on their part was fatal, for Old Man Bache had a cavalry sabre, which he used with such skill and deadly effect that he killed three of them before they could escape. The others fled, leaving their dead on the ground, but taking away their wounded.

It was nearly daylight now, so Old Man Bache sent one of his sons to town to notify the authorities to come out and take the dead men away. When it was learned that the dead men were soldiers, a detail of soldiers was sent after them, but by the time the detail got there Old Man Bache had changed his mind and had become so well-pleased with his performance that he concluded to keep the bodies himself. The argument he used was that he had killed them and that they were his personal property, just as a deer or bear would have been. Finally his friends persuaded him to give them up and the bodies were turned over to the soldiers.

When the bodies were searched, some of Mrs. Rogers' jewelry was found on them, showing that they were the same scoundrels who had robbed her house.

When I heard Captain Hunter mention Davis' name, memory of this outlaw regiment came back to me, and I thought of the last fight some of its members ever made and of what a proper and fitting ending it would have been for the whole regiment.

A Thumbnail

History

of

The City of
Houston, Texas

From Its Founding in 1836 to the Year 1912

By Dr. S. O. Young

TABLE OF CONTENTS

AN INTRODUCTION
BY MARK PUSATERI

When S. O. Young wrote this book, he was sixty-four. His subject, Houston, was but seventy-six years old. In three quarters of a century, it had grown from a population of 12 to over 80,000. There had been earlier books published on the history of the Bayou City, but most were "mug books" which featured glowing biographies of prominent men, published be sold to those same prominent men. Dr. Young set out to fill a need for a serious history, a sober recording of the facts regarding Houston's development. He poured over original documents in the city and county archives. He further made extensive use of old newspapers housed in Houston's Carnegie Library.

1912 was a landmark year. It can be seen as the cusp of Houston's transformation from a city of regional importance to a national commercial center. Dredging had been finished on the ship channel, prompting city boosters to adopt the slogan: "Where seventeen railroads meet the sea." The Rice Institute (now Rice University) was set to open. The current Harris County Courthouse had just been completed and Jesse Jones was building the Rice Hotel. There was a new city auditorium on the site where Jones Hall now stands. Lumber was booming and, while cotton was still king, oil had all but taken the crown.

Samuel Oliver Young, Jr. (1848-1926) was a native Houstonian. He was born just two months after the death of his father in the midst of a Yellow Fever epidemic. He grew up among veterans of San Jacinto and the most prominent citizens of early Houston. His mother reared him in the home of her father, Nathan Fuller, one of Houston's early mayors. Young served in the Civil War, enlisting as teenager in the Bayou City Guards (Company A, Fifth Texas Infantry), a unit of Hood's Texas Brigade. Like his father before him, S. O. Young became a physician, practicing from 1870 until 1882, when he abandoned medicine to become a newspaperman.

Some readers will already know S. O. Young from his account of the 1900 Galveston Storm which is detailed in Erik Larson's book, *Isaac's Storm*. He was Secretary of the Galveston Cotton Exchange at the time and was determined to ride out the storm in his house. The storm destroyed the house leaving Dr. Young to surf across the island on his front door.

Dr. Young had grown up with Houston. It's history was his history and he presents it within these pages in detail and with pride.

A Word in Advance

In presenting this little volume to the people of Houston for their consideration, I feel that a word of explanation is due. I wrote the book to supply a badly needed "need," of course, but I wrote it more for my own pleasure than for anything else. I have made no attempt at fine writing and have given no thought to literary excellence. My sole object has been to attain accuracy, and every precaution has been taken to guard against error. Wherever possible I have consulted original documents and newspapers. Yet, in spite of this, I fear that some errors have crept in and that the readers will find many statements which they may think erroneous. I say this because there are some stories and traditions that have been repeated so often that many suppose them to be true.

If the readers derive as much pleasure from perusing these pages as I have from writing them, I shall feel content. I have enjoyed writing every line, and add "The End" with regret.

S. O. YOUNG

Houston, June 5, 1912

TO THE MEMORY OF MY MOTHER
MRS. MAUD JEANNIE YOUNG,

whose life was largely devoted to the cause of education and to the creation of a taste for literature and the sciences in the minds of the earlier citizens of Houston, this little volume is lovingly dedicated.

—THE AUTHOR

CHAPTER I:
FOUNDING & GOVERNING A GREAT CITY

A fact not generally known nor appreciated is that Houston is the result of a disagreement between the Allens and the Harrises. There was no serious quarrel or anything of that sort. They simply differed about land matters, with the result that the Allens, instead of joining the Harrises in their efforts to build up the already established town of Harrisburg, came five miles by land and about sixteen miles by water further up the bayou, and laid the foundation for the rival town, which was destined to become the greatest city in Texas and one of the greatest in the Southwest.

Now, as a matter of fact, there was no good reason for the new town. The location at Harrisburg was ideal and had many advantages, naturally, that Houston had to create artificially. There was, to begin with, sixteen miles of very crooked and hardly navigable bayou to be overcome in order to reach Houston, while the new site had absolutely nothing to compensate for this disadvantage.

However, there was an element injected into the controversy that helped the Allens wonderfully in carrying out their scheme. Santa Anna's soldiers showed up just at the critical moment and burned Harrisburg. Before the Harrises could recover from the blow, and while their town still lay in ashes, the Allens acted and not only had their town laid out, but were actively engaged in selling town lots to settlers. Not much progress was made during the first year, however, and there was not much of a city in evidence and scarcely more to indicate where that city was to be.

Governor Frank Lubbock, in his memoirs, gives an amusing description of his search for the town, even after he had reached and passed the foot of Main Street. He came to Houston on the first steamboat that ever arrived here and it took four days to make the trip from Harrisburg to Houston. That being the pioneer trip, an immense amount of work had to be done to clear the stream of sunken logs and overhanging trees. There was plenty of water, but there were numerous obstructions in and over the channel. After that first boat there was little or no delay, and before long there were other boats that came to Houston. In a year or two there was a regular service established between Houston and Galveston.

The question of transportation was one of the most serious with which the early settlers had to contend. Transportation by land was not only difficult, but actually dangerous, for there were hostile Indians and predatory bands of Mexicans ever on the watch for unwary settlers. There were no roads, ordinary trails being the only guides for the traveller, and therefore when communication was established with the outside world by water from Houston, it was looked on as a blessing, since it saved many miles of difficult and dangerous travel. The bayou soon became popular and Houston sprang at once into the greatest prominence as a receiving and distributing point. It is remarkable that Houston should have had all those advantages, and that in the early days and then after the lapse of many years she should still retain them through the commercial activity and business foresight of her citizens.

During the first eighteen months of the new city's existence there was little accomplished aside from perfecting the plans and arranging the divisions of Houston, for there was not much more of a city than a name and some surveyed streets and lots until late in 1837. By then the town began to show some life and activity. It is true that the city was more like a military camp than anything else, for it was composed largely of tents, with here and there a small log cabin. During 1837 there was a large storehouse built at the corner of Commerce Street and Main and at the same time work was begun on the Mansion House, Houston's first hotel. This was located on the corner now occupied by the Southern Pacific offices.

But it was not until 1838 that Houston took on genuine city airs. That year an election was held to decide whether the city should be incorporated or not. The result was an affirmative vote and the same year the Texas Congress granted the City of Houston a charter. Having become a chartered city, it was necessary for Houston to elect a mayor and board of aldermen. Unfortunately all the records of the city have been twice destroyed by fire, but tradition and the oldest inhabitants declare that Dr. Francis Moore, Jr., was the first mayor of Houston.

Now there is really no good nor substantial reason for doubting that Dr. Moore was the first mayor, and the question is brought up in this way so as to give place to a doubt introduced by Maj. Ingham Roberts, who has made a close study of all that relates to the early history of Houston. Major Roberts, in the *History of Southeast Texas*, of which he was one of the editors, publishes a list of Houston's mayors and gives the honor of being the first to James S. Holman. The Major gives as his authority for doing this, a notice published in the *Telegraph* of Sept. 29, 1837, calling an election to fill

A. C. ALLEN
Co-FOUNDER of
HOUSTON

CHARLOTTE M.
ALLEN
WIFE of
A. C. ALLEN

JOHN K. ALLEN
FOUNDER
of
HOUSTON.

S. L. ALLEN
BROTHER OF J. K. & A. C. ALLEN AND
A PIONEER & PATRIOT OF HOUSTON

MRS. S. L. ALLEN
WIFE OF S. L. ALLEN.

vacancies caused by the deaths of two aldermen, which notice was signed Jas. S. Holman, "Mayor."

Major Roberts is a most careful student and accurate writer, and yet one is constrained to believe that a serious error has been committed by himself or by the paper publishing that notice. In the first place, Houston was not incorporated until a year after the date of that notice and, therefore, could not have had a mayor or board of aldermen. In the next place, James S. Holman was clerk of the Eleventh District Court from February 1837 until 1842, and it is not likely that he could have been mayor of Houston at the same time. As a matter of fact he was clerk of the court at the very time that notice was published, as the court records show. The matter is given space here so as to bring out all the facts for the guidance of future historians.

When the Moore administration took office, its first act was to extend the city limits, which to that time had been the bayou on the north, Walker Street on the south, Bagby Street on the west and Caroline on the east. The limits were extended so as to embrace nine square miles. This was done in order to increase the taxable area and to include within the city limits many citizens who had built residences just beyond the old city lines. The nine mile area was maintained many years, or until the city fell in the hands of the carpetbag Republicans appointed by E. J. Davis during Reconstruction. They found it necessary, in order to create more plunder, to increase the taxable area so as to embrace twenty-five square miles. When the carpetbaggers were turned out of office by the home people who had regained control of affairs, the city limits were reduced again to nine square miles. That was in 1874, and until 1903 no change was made. But by that time the city had so extended beyond its limits that an increase was demanded in justice and fairness to all, so the area was fixed at sixteen square miles. A remarkable feature is that since those limits were fixed, the city has again far outgrown its bounds, so that a very large number, perhaps 15,000 or 20,000 nominal citizens of Houston are living outside the city limits.

Aside from fixing the city limits and placing some pine trees across the streets, so that people could get across from one corner to another without bogging down in the mud, there appears to have been nothing accomplished by the Moore administration, or by that of G. W. Lively, the second mayor.

It was reserved for the Charles Biglow administration, in 1840, to take the first step towards permanent public improvement. That year, a contract was let for the erection of a market house and city hall on Market Square. That old market was pointed to with pride for many years by all Houstonians. It was really a pretentious building for it had length, if not height, being only a single story high. It extended from Preston to Congress and on the Congress side it was two stories high. The upper floor was used as a city hall, while the lower one was devoted to a city jail or "calaboose."

The market part was given over to the butchers and vegetable people, who had stalls arranged on each side, while a broad alley extended down the entire length of the market. There was no floor, only the bare earth serving for that purpose. The building soon became famous for the number of rats that took possession of it. Perhaps, in no part of the world were there ever so many rats gathered together in a limited space as were found in that old place. However, it was a great improvement on conditions that had prevailed to that time, for the market vendors had been forced to do business in the open air, or under a dilapidated shed that someone had erected. There was a tent, not on the square, however, that was used for market purposes, but that was a private affair with which the city had nothing to do.

The old market house stood for many years and was finally torn down to make place for the famous market house erected by the Scanlan administration. The story of that famous building is worth telling.

Mr. Alexander McGowan had been elected mayor of the city in 1867, but was turned out of office by E. J. Davis, the Reconstruction Governor of Texas, in August, 1868. Some other changes were made, but it was not until 1870, that Davis showed his hand by turning everybody out of office and appointing his own henchmen.

T. H. Scanlan was appointed mayor and four ignorant negroes were made aldermen by Davis. Then the plundering began in real earnest, and by the time they got through Houston had a debt of almost two million dollars and had but little or nothing to show for it. It was no public spirit or local pride that gave Houston the finest market house in the South. Houston got the building finally, but Houston paid a fancy price for it. It was merely the opportunity to extend the loot field that lay behind the market that resulted in its final construction.

Having decided to erect a market house, plans were drawn, specifications made and bids were invited. Col. William Brady was the successful bidder at $250,000. He was backed by some New Yorkers. He agreed to take the city's bonds in payment, the bonds to bear 8 per cent interest and to run twenty-five years. That part of the contract was alright, perhaps, but after actual construction of the building began, things began to show up that were never expected. Col. Brady built according to the plans and specifications, but when those were examined it was found that they contained no provision for blinds, some doors, and in one or two instances, for floors for the building. The whole thing was found to be merely an outline of plans and specifications, but Col. Brady claimed it was what he had bid on and he held the city strictly to its contract with him.

There was only one thing to do—issue more bonds—and that was when the city limits were extended, so as to take in more taxpayers. The tax area was increased, more bonds were issued, and before the market house was completed its total cost was $470,000 instead of $250,000 as originally contemplated. The building was insured for $100,000, but when it was burned down in 1876, the insurance companies refused to pay even that, and, after much haggling, finally agreed to restore the building, which they did at an outlay of only $80,000. The restored building was also destroyed by fire some years later, after which the present magnificent building was erected.

A so-called election was held in 1872, and by importing negroes from the surrounding counties and obstructing the white voters, the Republicans were able to elect the entire city ticket and keep the same gang in office. Retribution was near at hand, however, for the next year the Democrats swept the State and elected Coke Governor. In January, 1874, Houston was granted a new charter by provision of which the Governor was authorized to appoint the city officials of Houston. Governor Coke lost no time, but turned the Scanlan crowd out of office. He then appointed Mr. Jas. T. D. Wilson, mayor, and also appointed a board of aldermen composed of respectable and prominent citizens. A few months later an election was held and all the gentlemen appointed by the Governor were regularly elected.

There was little accomplished by the new administration during their tenure of office. The affairs of the city were so badly tangled and the bonded and floating debts were so large that the city was absolutely without money or credit. Under conditions such as these it was not expected that anything could be done beyond staving off clamoring creditors and answering court summonses, for the city was being constantly sued.

After holding office for one year the Wilson administration retired and Mr. I. C. Lord was chosen as mayor in 1875. He had all that his predecessor had to contend with, and in addition there came up the question of disposing of the interest the city had acquired, in some way, in the Houston East & West Texas Railroad. The interest owned by the city was in that part of the road surveyed as far west as the Brazos near Bellville, but which had been abandoned and has never been built. There were suits and countersuits and the whole question became very much involved. Finally the city sold its interest for $35,000 and went out of the railroad business for good. But it was a case of jumping out of the frying pan into the fire, for so soon as it was known that the Lord administration had a little cash on hand the courthouse feature became aggravated and everybody was clamoring to get hold of it. Old notes, old and new claims, popped up from unexpected quarters and the situation became desperate. Mr. Lord held office for two years and then quit in disgust.

Mr. Wilson, having had a two years rest, was persuaded by the citizens to try his hand again. This was literally true for at that time a man had to be talked into taking such an onerous office as that of the debt-burdened city. It required patience, honesty of purpose and fine executive and financial ability to keep the affairs of the city going, even for a day, and those who were qualified to act were not anxious to do so.

The second administration of Mr. Wilson resulted in the establishment, or rather in the inauguration of the movement that resulted in establishing the water works here. Before that time Houston depended entirely on underground cisterns for its water supply, both for drinking and for fire protection purposes. Soon after the beginning of his second term, Mr. Wilson sent a special message to the council drawing attention to the great need of water works. The city had no money to build such works, but was prepared and willing to deal most liberally with any private company or corporation that would undertake the work.

Nearly a year later such a company was formed, and some months later, in August, 1879, the company actually constructed the first water works on the north side of the bayou near what was called "Stanley's brick yard," where they have remained ever since. The service, however, was abominable and pleased no one. The company built a dam across the bayou so as to shut off tide water and secure as pure water as possible from the upper bayou. It was totally unfit to drink and no one ever thought of using it for that purpose.

In the early nineties it was discovered that an abundant supply of the purest artesian water could be obtained anywhere in Houston, and the water works company sank several artesian wells. That gave Houston an abundant supply of pure drinking water. However, the standpipe was too small, or for some other reason the company claimed they could not supply the city with both drinking water and water for protection against fire, and every time a fire occurred they would pump bayou water into the reservoir, with the result that the water became unfit to drink for some time after every fire.

The people complained, but that did no good. Finally, in 1906, under the administration of Mayor Baldwin Rice, the city purchased the plant outright, for $901,000, and since that time there has been no complaint nor any reason for complaint. This is the only public utility owned by the city, but its record has been a good one, so much so as to create something of a general desire that the city take over some others and run them in the interest of the people as the water works are now run. As one evidence of how the people have gained by the change, it may be said that the old company was charging 50¢ per thousand gallons for water, but the city at once reduced this charge to 15¢, employed more men to add to the efficiency, and has done all this without the loss of a cent of the taxpayers' money.

After serving two terms, Mr. Wilson retired and was succeeded by Mr. A. J. Burke. There was nothing accomplished during this administration for the very good and simple reason that nothing could be accomplished. Efforts were made to compromise the huge city debt, but the bondholders stood firm and nothing could be done.

When Mr. Burke's term expired, some of the leading men of Houston conceived a great idea. They determined to apply expert business methods and nothing else in settling the city's affairs. A committee, composed of the best businessmen of the city, called on Mr. Wm. R. Baker and asked him to devote his superb financial ability towards solving the great financial problem which confronted the city. He, after some hesitation, consented to do so, but made it one of the conditions that he should name the men who were to serve as aldermen with him. This was granted and he named a number of the leading bankers, merchants and businessmen as his staff. There was no serious opposition to the ticket and it was elected by practically a unanimous vote.

When the city was turned over to those gentlemen, the bondholders became very confident. Before that they were growing uneasy, to say the least, for the people were becoming desperate and everybody was talking about throwing up the city charter and repudiating the unjust debt that had been forced on the city. However, when Houston was placed in the hands of such prominent businessmen and great financiers, doubt and fear disappeared, for the bondholders knew that these gentlemen could not afford to be mixed up in anything such as repudiating a debt. Already something like repudiation had taken place, for the citizens had held an election and decided that not more than 50¢ on the dollar should be paid for the bonds. This action tied the hands of the Baker administration, of course, and they could do nothing, for the bondholders would not accept 50¢ on the dollar.

Towards the middle of the Baker administration a final effort was made. Mr. Wm. D. Cleveland and Mr. J. Waldo, two of the aldermen, went to New York for a conference with the bondholders, who were showing an inclination to "listen to reason." After some discussion the bondholders agreed to compromise for 60¢ on the dollar and to take forty-year bonds, a new issue. The aldermen explained that the action of the citizens precluded their paying more than 50¢.

Then the bondholders made a proposition. The compromise would be made ostensibly for 60¢ on the dollar, but really for 40¢. A prominent Houston banker, Mr. Baker, and Mr. Cleveland were to guarantee that the new bonds would be issued by the city and for doing this the bondholders would divide the difference between 40¢ and 60¢ with these three men and keep quiet about it. The aldermen returned to Houston, and Mr. Cleveland, Mayor Baker and the banker went over the proposition.

Mr. Cleveland pointed out that the plan proposed offered the only solution of the problem and suggested that the three gentlemen draw up an agreement, together with a statement of facts, by which the city would get all the bonds that were, ostensibly, set aside for themselves; that this agreement be witnessed by reputable witnesses and locked up securely in a safe. The bondholders had said they would treat the matter confidentially. Mr. Cleveland and Mr. Baker saw the advantage to the city and were anxious to close the deal, but the banker was afraid and dreaded adverse criticism and discussion by the people who would know nothing of the truth of the deal until it was all over. He refused to have anything to do with it and as the bondholders insisted on his taking part, the thing fell through. Houston lost the opportunity of compromising her debt on the most advantageous conditions that were ever offered.

With so many bonds out, some of them were in weak hands. These small holders, either willingly or unwillingly, parted with their holdings for about

35 cents on the dollar. The Baker administration was enabled to pick up a great many bonds in that way, but the large holders stood firm. Buying the bonds, as Mayor Baker did, reduced the bonded debt, of course, but it was borrowing from Peter to pay Paul, for at the close of the Baker administration the floating debt of the city was about $200,000 greater than when it went in.

Having tried expert business methods and failed, the people arose in their might and went to the opposite extreme. They turned out the financiers and put Mr. D. C. Smith and what was called a "short hair" board of aldermen in office. The labor ticket was elected triumphantly, and in electing these gentlemen, the citizens did a wise thing. When the news reached New York that the city had been turned over to the labor element, there was consternation in the bondholders' camp. They could see nothing but repudiation and ruin ahead of them, and their greatest fear was that the debt might be repudiated before their agents could get here with offers of compromise. After some bickering, which served to delay action by the council if in no other way, the bondholders came to an agreement with the city by the terms of which the debt was compromised on a basis that permitted the city to make needed improvements and pay interest regularly on the reduced debt. Since that day the city has been free from great financial embarrassment.

It seems strange to say in one breath that Houston has the best and the most dangerous form of government that could possibly be conceived. And yet that is literally true. The form, as all know, gives almost absolute power to a few men chosen, not by wards as was done formerly, but by all the people of the city regardless of ward and sub-ward divisions. The advantages of this method are apparent, for the Mayor, or Chairman, and each Commissioner represents the whole city and not any particular part of it. Each is responsible to the whole people and not, as formerly, to that one part of it where he might chance to have lived and from which he was chosen by the votes of his friends and neighbors only. He owes no political debt to any single ward and it becomes his duty to legislate for the good of the city as a whole and not for any subdivision of it.

The dangerous feature is the power the commission form gives a few men. Should a dishonest or incompetent Board of Commissioners chance to secure election, the result might be disastrous before the people awoke to their peril and took steps to check it. Of course, such a condition as that is very unlikely to occur. Still there is a possibility of its occurring and in that one thing alone lies the danger. The mere fact that there is danger in the form assures its safety, for it puts the voters on their guard and they are more careful than ever they were under the old method, in selecting their servants, so that it is almost impossible for unworthy or incompetent men to be elected. If the commission had nothing else to recommend it, this placing the voters on their guard would be a sufficient endorsement of its merits.

The evolution of the Commission idea has been slow and tedious, and it is remarkable that it has taken great disasters to impress its merits upon the minds of interested communities. Following the two great yellow fever epidemics of 1878 and 1879 in Memphis, Tennessee, the people of that city found themselves bankrupt and forced to adopt the untried and desperate remedy of ceasing to be an incorporated city and instead becoming a taxing district under a commission. That was, as a matter of fact, the first time the commission idea was applied practically to the management and direction of municipal affairs. It was not until the great disaster at Galveston in September, 1900, that anything like a practical commission for the government of a city was devised. Galveston, by act of the Legislature, was granted a new charter which did away with the old mayor and board of aldermen and placed municipal affairs in the hands of five commissioners—a mayor, or chairman, a commissioner of finance, a commissioner of streets and alleys, a commissioner of water works, lights, etc., and a commissioner of police and fire departments.

These are all elected by the whole vote of the city and each commissioner is given full charge of his department and held responsible for its working. The other commissioners have the authority to overrule and veto any undesirable act of any one of their members, but this has never been necessary, for the ability and honesty of the men thus far elected by the people have been such as to render unnecessary the exercise of the veto power by the other commissioners. If argument were necessary to show the merits of the Commission form of municipal government, the success of that in Galveston would be sufficient.

The success of the Galveston Commission attracted wide attention and in 1904 the plan was submitted to the voters of Houston and, they having adopted it, the next year a new charter was granted the city, under which Houston became a Commission city. Houston's charter differs in

many respects from those of Galveston, Dallas and other cities that have
gone under commission rule. Its practical working is so well shown in an
address delivered by Mayor Rice before the Chicago Commercial Club in
December, 1910, that it may be well to take the following points from that
address so as to best illustrate the commission:

> The essential differences between the old form of municipal gov-
> ernment and the commission form are three. The substitution of
> a smaller number of aldermen elected from the city at large, in
> place of a large number of aldermen elected from different wards
> or subdivisions of the city; vesting of a coordinate power in the
> mayor as in the city council to dismiss any officer of the city gov-
> ernment, except the controller, at any time without cause, and
> the essential provisions safeguarding the granting of municipal
> franchises. Instead of a body of twelve aldermen elected from
> different wards of the city, under the Houston system four alder-
> men are elected from the body of the city by the votes of all the
> citizens, in the same way in which the mayor is elected.
>
> These four aldermen, together with the mayor, constitute the
> city council or legislative department of the city government.
> The executive power is vested in the mayor, but by an ordinance,
> for the administration of the city's affairs, a large part of execu-
> tive or administrative power is subdivided into different depart-
> ments, and a committee is placed over each department, and one
> of the four aldermen, nominated by the mayor, is what is known
> as the active chairman.
>
> The mayor and all four aldermen are members of each com-
> mittee. The active chairman of the committee practically has
> control of the administration of the department, unless his views
> are overruled by the whole committee, but by the organization
> of the committees the active chairman does the work, to a cer-
> tain extent, under the supervision and direction of the mayor,
> who is, in the last analysis, the head of each committee and the
> person in whom the executive power of the municipal govern-
> ment ultimately rests.
>
> Under the old system of government, by which twelve alder-
> men were elected from as many different precincts of the city,

it frequently happened that unfit men came to represent certain wards of the city council. Now, unless a man has sufficient standing and reputation throughout the body of the city as a fit man for the office of alderman he will not be elected. Again, each alderman under the present system represents the whole city. Under the old system the conduct of public business was continually obstructed by a system of petty log-rolling going on among and between the representatives of the numerous subdivisions of the city. Then, too, the smallness of the number of aldermen now affords opportunity for the transaction of business.

An executive session is held previous to each meeting of the city council, at which matters to come before the council are discussed and action determined on. The small number of aldermen enables the city administration to act on all matters of importance as a unit. In other words, the system makes it possible to administer the affairs of the city in a prompt and businesslike way.

This is one of the strongest arguments in favor of the present commission form of government, for with a majority of the aldermen always in session, public business can be, and is, promptly attended to. It is no longer necessary to go before the city council with petitions to have something done. Any citizen who desires to have a street paved, taxes adjusted, a nuisance abated, or anything else, has only to call at the mayor's office and have the matter promptly adjusted. After a hearing, the matter is decided by the council in the presence of the applicant. To illustrate the great difference between this method and the old one, the following comparison is made:

By the old method a petition was addressed to the council. This was then referred to a committee, which acted when convenient. Then a report to the council was made by the committee. After the action of the council, it went to the mayor and from the mayor to someone else for execution. The people do not pay their taxes for such treatment. They want their business attended to promptly and that is what is being done under the commission.

This July, the commission will have been in existence seven years, and during that time it has accomplished wonders. In 1905 the floating debt of the city was about $400,000. Every cent of that has been wiped out and the taxpayers have been given, out of the treasury, without the issuance of a single bond for any one of the items, the following permanent improvements:

City Attorney, Law Library......$974.10
Assessor & Collector,
Block Book System................10,000.00
City Hall,
Furniture & Fixtures...............1,123.67
Police Department...................4,096.03
Fire Department,
Buildings & Equipment........66,239.67
Electrical Department...........37,461.47
Health Department.................7,340.94
Parks.....................................116,451.09
Streets & Bridges...................71,004.96
Asphalt Plant.........................,3,000.00
Auditorium..........................390,340.92
Ship Channel......................102,536.05
Sewers.................................132,047.56
Paving Streets.....................221,006.00
Water Department,
Extension of Mains &
Improvements......................325,757.33
Wharves and Slips.................33,109.89
School Buildings.................356,477.20
Total Improvements........$1,878,966.88

Extraordinary Expenses
Storrie Certificates...............$73,300.00
Refund Paving Certificates...141,418.68
Sinking Fund......................120,220.00
$334,938.68

This makes a grand total of $2,213,905.56, all of which was paid out of current revenues, and the elimination of a floating debt amounting to a little more than $400,000. One need go no further than those figures to be convinced of the benefits and advantages of Commission form of government.

Unquestionably the magnificent form of government that Houston has, and the thoroughly businesslike manner in which the affairs of the city are administered, have had helped in establishing confidence in the stability of the city both at home and abroad. Though the commission may not have caused it, the fact remains that coincident with the establishment of the commission Houston began to grow and expand in the most marvelous way. Strangers who come here and find a large and beautiful city are amazed to learn that modern Houston is only about seven years old. All the great strides forward, all the large corporations, all the great business enterprises, are less than ten years old, while the city has more than doubled her population in seven years.

Houston is today a city of skyscrapers and large buildings, and their number is being added to monthly. There are today a number of new ones going up and nearly every principal street in the city is the scene of building activity. There are hotels completed and being constructed, office buildings, business buildings, bank buildings, to say nothing of the hundreds of residences being constructed. Houston stands in a class of its own when it comes to apartment houses, for there are more and finer ones here than in any other Texas city. They are nearly all strictly up-to-date and several of them are luxurious and costly affairs.

Just what Houston is doing today and how it is being done is well shown in the reports made by the mayor and the commissioners and heads of departments at the close of the fiscal year, February 29, 1912. Mayor Rice says:

> *Gentlemen-* According to the law, I submit the annual report of the various departments and the budget for the ensuing year.
>
> You will notice that the appropriations recommended and the budget called for is some $200,000 in excess of last year, one half alone being increase of the interest and sinking funds on bonds and additional school appropriations.
>
> The rapid growth of the city and its numerous requirements means that the growth if yearly maintained, as it has for the past

several years, the city of Houston must expend annually more revenue to maintain in efficiency the various departments and satisfy local conditions.

I shall briefly discuss the important demands of the city and make recommendations for their improvements and needs.

The water department is in splendid condition and with the extension of mains this year will probably place every one within the limits of the city of Houston in easy access of pure water and charging the lowest rate for consumption.

Houston has an efficient and up-to-date fire department, and but for the unfortunate fire which occurred in the manufacturing district on the north side of the city during a tremendous gale, would have probably maintained the smallest loss in any one year since Houston's growth. I call attention to this great conflagration from a commercial standpoint, as the great losses from the immense quantities of cotton and manufactories destroyed ran into large sums of money. While numerous small homes were destroyed, yet, I am glad to state, the majority of those thus afflicted asked for no assistance and are making plans to reconstruct their homes upon a better and safer basis.

For those who were left destitute, too much praise cannot be given to the United Charities and the kind citizens who came forward and cheerfully made subscriptions for relief. Knowing the character of people who make up this community, and feeling confident of their generosity and grit, I, as mayor, declined all outside help and subsequent events justified my position. While deeply grateful for all offers of aid from all parts of the country, Houston demonstrated that her people can and will take care of almost any calamity that may overtake them. I recommend that an appropriation of $25,000 be made for a new fire station and equipment at Westmoreland station, as suggested by Fire Commissioner Kohlhauff.

I call your attention to the annual report of streets and bridges. It demonstrates what an immense amount of work and expense it requires to drain and make passable the streets in a level country like ours. A great viaduct connecting the north and south sides of the city is now under good headway and promises when completed to be one of the most substantial structures in the State, as well as giving rapid transportation for the people. Nearly all the bridges over Buffalo Bayou are out of date and fail to properly accommodate the traffic. I recommend that the bridges at San Jacinto and Preston Streets be removed and that more substantial bridges be constructed out of reinforced concrete. I also recommend that a reinforced concrete bridge be built over Buffalo Bayou at the foot of Texas Avenue, which will relieve congestion of traffic on both Washington and Preston avenues. Houston Avenue viaduct, now being constructed, will give immense relief to that section of the city.

During the past year $500,000 of bonds were voted for school purposes, and several schoolhouses will be constructed during the fiscal year, which will give the additional facilities that are so badly needed in our growing city.

Both the school board and city commissioners have for some time been acquiring additional property for school sites and playgrounds for the children. I believe in the near future, Houston's schools and playgrounds will be a model for any city to copy.

As we have no swimming pools for boys or girls in this community, upon the recommendation of Mrs. James A. Baker, president of the Settlement Association, who is taking a deep interest in their welfare, I suggest that a natatorium be constructed on the new Rusk school site, and that the feature be gradually extended to every other school in this city. I think Superintendent Horn's recommendation, that all public schools should be used as social centers, be adopted. These school grounds and buildings cost the taxpayer a great deal of money and should be utilized in various ways. School children are dismissed daily at 3 p. m. and there is no reason after that time why the immediate neighborhood should not use the building for any social custom they desire without going to the expense of renting halls. By such gatherings in a public building, that they have helped to construct, the people will not only become better acquainted, but better satisfied with taxation.

Houston should no longer wait for a park system. Land is becoming dearer every year. While the city has purchased additional park ground during the year, yet we are very deficient in this respect. We have a splendid board of park commissioners and I recommend that the city of Houston issue at least $250,000 in park bonds or more this year in order to secure a good start.

Now that the auditorium is completed I recommend that it be used for the best interest of the community. I am very anxious to see the social conditions of our people improved, especially on Sundays. On the first of May next Houston will have one of the finest bands in the United States. It will be maintained by the city. Not only will there be instrumental music, but some of the best vocal music in the country.

In addition to the musical part of the afternoons' and nights' entertainments on Sunday there can be secured good, whole-some picture shows, lectures and other entertainments that will tend to educate the people and make them happy and contented. All these entertainments will be free for the people and espe-cially to the working classes will this program be satisfactory, as they can enjoy the best music and best lectures at absolutely no cost. Once inaugurated and well established, I believe this work of our city government will go a long way toward exterminating some of the vicious tendencies that trouble our cities.

This government, in fulfilling its promises, created a public service department last year, and appointed a commissioner for that purpose. I recommend that every citizen read Mr. Gaston's report and know what has been accomplished.

I am glad to state that the efficiency of the police department is gradually being raised, and I trust in the near future that it will be up to the standard.

During the present year the Somers system of taxation has been established in Houston, at the suggestion of Commissioner Pastoriza. It seems to be a very efficient system, just and equita-ble to all. The tax board has adopted the system of assessing land values at 90 per cent and improvements at 25 per cent of their value. Under this system the valuations have been increased from $77,000,000 to $123,000,000, which is very great. All tax prob-lems are difficult, and very few, if any, are satisfactory. I would suggest that the citizens thoroughly investigate this system and understand it. If it is satisfactory, so much the better; if not, then some better plan should be proposed. The city council will not be arbitrary, but will be glad to listen to any one or all citizens upon this subject. Last year the tax rate was $1.70 per $100. This year it has been reduced to $1.30 per hundred for all purposes, being the lowest rate of any large city in the State.

With the exception of a few cases of meningitis...the health of this community has been splendid. Too much praise cannot be given our health officer, Dr. G. W. Larendon, and specialist, Dr. F. J. Slataper, and their associates for the way the health department has been managed. On account of the amount of work and the risks that these gentlemen are required to run I am decidedly in favor of increasing their respective salaries.

Now that the national government will soon commence work upon our waterway, I suggest that the city acquire more territory at the turning basin. I suggest steps be taken to condemn all land that is needed for practical purposes, and also that the city of Houston build and maintain a modern dredge boat on the channel.

The city has recently adopted a front-foot plan of pavement. It is a great step forward in progress and means that Houston will now go forward with rapid strides. Already petitions have been placed with the council for over ten miles of pavement. I caution the people that no permanent pavement should be made until all water, gas and sewer mains are first laid. I earnestly recommend that a million dollars be issued in bonds for sanitary and storm sewers alone. A short-time paving bond can be issued, redeemable at the rate of, say, $200,000 per year, which will give immediate relief in regard to the pavements and not increase the bonded indebtedness.

The city needs a city jail and additional fireproof rooms to the city hall to preserve city records. I recommend that an annex to the city hall be constructed to care for all these various features.

Thanking you for your hearty cooperation, I am,

Respectfully,

H. B. Rice

An idea of what it costs to run a big city like Houston may be formed from the following recommendations, made by the mayor, for the coming year:

Mayor and Commissioners	$13,600
Controller and Secretary	7,500
Law Department	12,000
Treasurer	620
Assessor & Collector	18,000
City Hall	4,000
Elections	1,000
Damages	1,000
Interest on bonds	265,000
Sinking fund	140,000
Miscellaneous expenses	15,000
Electric lights	50,000
Police	110,000
Corporation court	2,500
Fire department	125,000
Health department	25,000
Scavenger department	13,000
Electrical department	8,000
City engineer	20,000
Streets and bridges	100,000
Repair of shell & gravel streets	25,000
Sewer department	25,000
Garbage department	25,000
Market	7,000
Schools	210,000
Parks	10,000
Carnegie library	10,000
Refunding certificates	21,000
Buffalo Bayou	5,000
Mayor's emergency fund	1,000
Westmoreland fire station & equipment	25,000
Water department (general)	80,000
Interest	55,000
Sinking fund	28,000
Total	$1,458,220

Perhaps more interest attaches to the report of City Tax Commissioner Pastoriza this year than to any of the others, because of some radical changes that have been made in methods of taxation during the year just closed.

He states in his report that in the beginning of 1911 city officials were confronted with the necessity of raising the assessment over $12,000,000 to produce the additional revenue needed. He says that while the work for 1911 was fairly well done, the experience gained has convinced him of the necessity of a scientific plan of assessment. The Somers system largely solved the problem with its system of equalizing the value by a mathematical rule for calculation. A contract was entered into with the Manufacturers' Appraisal Company of Cleveland to install the system and for the past four months that work has been in progress. In his report Commissioner Pastoriza says:

> The application of the Somers system has revealed the fact that portions of many streets of Houston, some of them of exceeding value, are being used by individual citizens and corporations without bringing the city any rental or compensation whatever, and I recommend therefore that I be given authority to immediately institute suits to recover this valuable property for the city and to have removed such buildings or other obstructions as now occupy them.
>
> I also discovered that the area of many pieces of land were not accurately stated upon the block maps. There was not sufficient time to enable me to have these lands surveyed for the 1912 assessment, and I ask to be given authority to have these lands surveyed and that the engineering department be instructed to place at my disposal such help as is necessary to do this work without interruption and with the least delay possible.

The report shows that the tax rate was reduced from $1.70 in 1910 to $1.30 on the $100 in 1911. Commissioner Pastoriza explains in his report:

> To the average mind this might indicate a reduction in the rate of taxation, but Houston is a growing city, growing at a rate which few people realize, and the ever increasing need for street paving, drainage, sewers, extension of water mains, schools and playgrounds, for police and fire protection and a hundred and

one improvements not enumerated, calls for an ever increasing revenue.

In conclusion permit me to say that we do not claim our values are absolutely correct, but we do claim that they have been equalized as nearly as is possible, and that if our valuation of any particular piece of property in a block is considered too high, at least everybody else in that block and in the block across the street will be equally high; if we are low, everybody in that block and across the street will be equally low and there will be no discrimination. We have learned that it is not so much a question in the mind of a taxpayer whether our values are too high or too low, so long as we assess everybody the same, and only make the rate high enough to give the administration sufficient money to economically administer its affairs.

The report compiled by Building Inspector W. X. Norris shows that during the last fiscal year of the city permits were issued out of his office for the construction of 110 buildings of all kinds at an aggregate cost of $3,997,000. The permits issued during the previous fiscal year reached an aggregate of $3,152,820. Besides the permanent improvements permits were also issued last year for temporary work, aggregating $281,375, as against temporary work amounting to $189,270 during the previous year.

In his report the building inspector recommends that the electric sign ordinance be revised so as to provide for all electric signs to be hung vertical with the building. The permits issued by the building inspector have been classified by him in the following manner:

Permits	Kind of Building	# of Bldgs	Valuation
1	18-story fireproof hotel	1	$500,000
1	10-story fireproof hotel	1	$195,000
1	7-story fireproof office bldg	1	$150,000
1	6-story fireproof hotel	1	$70,000
1	6-story fireproof office bldg	1	$135,000
1	4-story fireproof bldg	1	$150,000
2	3-story fireproof bldgs	2	$117,000
1	3-story brick hotel & theatre bldg	1	$65,000
2	3-story brick flats	2	$31,300
4	3-story brick bldgs	4	$126,500

Permits	Kind of Building	# of Bldgs	Valuation
1	3-story brick warehouse	1	$4,500
1	3-story brick office bldg	1	$14,000
1	3-story concrete bldg & remodeling	1	$60,000
5	2-story brick warehouses	5	$61,000
2	2-story brick flats	2	$32,000
2	2-story brick stores	2	$9,000
1	2-story brick office bldg	1	$33,000
5	2-story brick bldgs	51	$36,300
3	2-story brick residences	3	$87,500
1	2-story concrete bldg	1	$40,000
1	2-story concrete warehouse	1	$14,000
3	2-story frame apartments	2	$22,000
1	4-story fireproof bldg	1	$150,000
5	2-story wood warehouses	5	$59,350
1	2-story stucco residence	1	$16,000
247	2-story frame residences	262	$811,985
1	Brick church	1	$56,000
6	1-story brick bldgs	6	$37,100
1	1-story brick office & car shed	1	$20,000
2	1-story brick warehouses	2	$12,000
2	1-story brick bldgs (not built)	1	$8,000
1	1-story cement block bldg	1	$3,000
3	Frame churches	3	$4,650
1	Frame clubhouse	1	$2,500
589	Cottages	748	$576,235
18	Iron & frame farehouses	19	$34,040
1	Open air theatre	1	$4,000
1	Automobile garage	1	$500
1	Fireproof addition	1	$14,900
1	Storage oil tank	1	$5,000
1	Oil plant	1	$10,650
1	Bread plant	1	$16,500
1	Viaduct	1	$350,000
2	Remodeling	2	$47,500
926		1101	$3,997,010

Valuation of 926 permits, year ending Feb. 29, 1912.........$3,997,010

Valuation of 868 permits, year ending Feb. 28, 1911.........$3,152,810

Increase in value, year ending Feb. 29, 1912.........................$844,190

Valuation temporary permits, year ending Feb. 1912...........$281,375

Valuation temporary permits, year ending Feb. 1911...........$189,270

Increase for year ending Feb. 29, 1912 over 1911...................$92,105

Total value temporary & permanent for year 1912.............$4,278,385

Total value temporary & permanent for year 1912.............$3,342,090

Increase in last 12 months over previous 12 months............$936,295

The following is a list of Houston's Mayors. The list is the one prepared by Major Roberts, though, for reasons given in the foregoing, Mr. Holman is not placed at the head:

1838	Dr. Francis Moore, Jr.
1839	G. W. Lively
1840	Charles Biglow
1841-42	J. D. Andrews
1843	Dr. Francis Moore, Jr.
1844	Horace Baldwin
1845	W. W. Swain
1846	Jas. Bailey
1847-48	P. B. Buckner
1849-52	Dr. Francis Moore, Jr.
1853-54	Col. Nathan Fuller
1855-56	Jas. H. Stevens
1857	Cornelius Ennis
1858	A. McGowan
1859	W. H. King
1860	T. W. Whitmarsh
1861	W. J. Hutchins
1862	T. W. House
1863-65	William Andrews

1866	H. D. Taylor
1867	A. McGowan
1868	J. R. Morris
1870-73	T. J. Scanlan
1874	J. T. D. Wilson
1875-76	I. C. Lord
1877-78	J. T. D. Wilson
1879	A. J. Burke
1880-84	W. R. Baker
1886-88	D. C. Smith
1890	Henry Scherrfius
1892-94	John T. Browne
1896	H. Baldwin Rice
1898-1900	Sam H. Brashear
1902	O. T. Holt
1904	Andrew L. Jackson
1905-12	H. Baldwin Rice

When one reads the names of the early Houstonians, it is almost like reading an early joint directory of Houston and Galveston for, in the forties, many of the men who aided in establishing Houston were also instrumental in building up Galveston and their names became inseparable from the history of the two places. General E. B. Nichols was, after the fifties, one of the most progressive citizens of Galveston, but to that time he was one of the pioneer workers in Houston. In the case of Mr. B. A. Shepherd, conditions were reversed. He was first a citizen of Galveston and then of Houston. Gail Borden, who surveyed the city of Houston and made the first map of the new city, was for years a resident of Houston and then removed to Galveston, where he became one of the most enthusiastic citizens there and prophesied most of the great things that have been accomplished by that city.

The first frame house in Houston was a small affair erected by the Torrey brothers who used it as a trading post for Indians. It was located on the north side of Preston near what is now the east end of Preston street bridge. It was afterwards purchased by Mr. H. D. Taylor and used by him as a residence for many years. It was one of the most beautiful and attractive places in Houston, in the midst of a grove of magnificent magnolia trees.

On the south side of Preston and on the east side of Smith there was a single room board house, erected about the same time as the Indian trading post. This was purchased by Col. N. Fuller, in 1837, and he added other rooms to it and built the residence which he occupied until the day of his death. That and the residence erected by Mr. A. C. Briscoe on Main and Prairie were unquestionably the first two-story houses erected in Houston, and both were built in 1837, the year after the founding of Houston. An item of interest is that when the Fuller residence was torn down a year or two ago to make place for the great brick building that now occupies its site. The old and original beams and rafters were found to be in perfect preservation and resembled steel beams more than wooden ones. It was with difficulty that they were torn apart, showing how thorough and honest were the early Houston builders.

The year 1837 also witnessed the erection of the first large warehouse in Houston. This was located on the northeast corner of Main and Commerce

Streets and was built by Mr. Thomas Elsberry. It was in this building that Messrs. Allen and Pool did business for many years, and it was there also that some of the great financiers of Houston had their early training. Mr. Doswell and Mr. Wm. R. Baker had their first experience as businessmen there, and others of less prominence worked for Allen and Pool from time to time.

All the early cotton crops of Texas passed through that old building, for it was the only cotton warehouse here and its location was ideal for conditions as they prevailed then. The building fronted on Commerce Street and extended back to the crude wharf of that day. The bales were simply tumbled out of the back door and landed near the steamboat, on which they were rolled by negro deck hands. Transportation by water was the only way to reach the markets of the world, and the bayou was of far more practical importance then than it has since become.

While the carpenters were erecting the Allen and Pool warehouse, workmen were busily engaged in hewing logs for the building of Houston's first hotel, which was erected on the corner of Franklin and Travis, where the Southern Pacific offices now stand.

It was built by Major Ben Fort Smith, one of the Texas pioneers, and its first proprietor was Mr. George Wilson, father of Mr. Ed Wilson, who is still an honored citizen of Houston. This old house stood for nearly twenty years and then, in 1855, it fell down through old age and decay. In the *Houston Telegraph* of May 16, 1855, is an interesting account of its fall, and still more interesting reminiscences connected with the old building.

> It had been in its day the hotel par excellence of the Capitol and commercial metropolis of the glorious old Republic of Texas. The President and his cabinet and the senators and representatives and officials of the first and second Congresses had dined there and so, too, had foreign ministers.
>
> Rusk, who was a great man before the Republic, was once glorified at its tables with a sacrifice of good things—fowls at $6 a pair, butter at $1 per pound, eggs at $3 per dozen and champagne at a fabulous price per bottle. It has been said that the dinner was planned to encourage a reconciliation between Rusk and Houston, and that it was so far successful that Rusk, in toasting Houston, his old opponent, said: "Houston, with all thy faults I love thee still."

Texas had great men in those days and their name was legion. It was an insult to take a man for anything but great, brave, chivalrous and even rich. Everybody was rich, or in the army or navy or public service, which was the same thing. The City Hotel had a barroom, one of perhaps twenty that flourished in the town, where steam was kept up at the explosion point, and the collapse of a decanter, pitcher or tumbler, as it came in contact with the brains of some unlucky devotee of the shrine of chivalry or bravado, or the kindred virtues usually worshipped "when the wine was red in the cup," was no uncommon occurrence.

Those were the days of duels, bowie knives and pistols, poker, keno and faro, when ten, twenty or fifty thousand dollars would be lost and won in a night. Texas was the prophecy of California and Houston a very San Francisco. No mines were dug, but gold was plenty and men managed to live without sweating their brows. If a man worked at all he earned from $8 to $10 a day, but precious few worked at all.

Buck Peters and Jeff Wright were the practical jokers then. Judge Shelby was on the bench and was indicted by his own grand jury for playing backgammon with his wife. Gus Tompkins, fertile in expedient but fractious, with his big brain and little body, was a terror to evildoers. Felix Huston commanded the turbulent army. Commodore Moore had not come to Texas then, and the navy was divided with several competent but less ambitious commanders, not less distinguished among them was our old friend Boots Taylor, a very Chesterfield in manners. Carnes and Teel and Morehouse and Deaf Smith lived in those times with a host of other noble spirits whose lights have long since gone out.

We notice a few survivors of those glorious days still among us. Col. Frank Johnson, one of the heroes of the storming of San Antonio, and the surrender of the Mexican garrison under Cos, sat with us on a log under the very eaves of the old building the day before it fell, and with him another survivor, Honest Bob Wilson, who was expelled from the Senate of the old Republic, but was re-elected and borne back in triumph upon the shoulders of an indignant people to the Capitol.

During 1837-39 there were a great number of houses erected in Houston, but all were wooden structures or primitive log cabins. Not until nine years after the town was established was a brick building put up. In 1845 Mr. Cornelius Ennis and General E. B. Nichols erected two brick buildings on the east side of Main Street, between Congress and Commerce Avenues. One was where the Western Union Telegraph Office now is and the other was where the Converse building is located.

Seven years later, in 1852, Mr. Paul Bremond erected a brick building and the following year Mr. B. A. Shepherd erected his bank building on the corner of Main and Congress, across the street from the present magnificent Union Bank building. All these first brick buildings were small two-story affairs, and as small as they were they seem to have been ahead of the time for in most of them the second stories were used only as lumber rooms.

On March 10, 1859, the first note of Houston's real progress was sounded by the fire bell. At the time it was regarded as a great disaster, and from a money point of view it was something of the kind, since the loss was placed at about $300,000, with little or no insurance. A great fire broke out at midnight on the corner of Main and Congress, and raged for eight hours. All the block on the west side of Main between Preston and Congress was destroyed and half of the block on the opposite side of Main was also consumed. These houses were wooden shanties and their destruction was the best thing that could have happened.

Almost before the ground grew cold again workmen were busy digging trenches for foundations, and in a short time several really fine brick buildings were erected. Mr. Wm. Van Alstyne, father of Mr. A. A. Van Alstyne, now of Galveston, had the honor of erecting the first three-story building in Houston. It was a very attractive building and stood on the corner of Main and Congress, directly opposite the present Krupp and Tuffly building. But Mr. J. R. Morris outdid Mr. Van Alstyne, for he put up a four-story iron-front building, not only the first of its kind in Houston, but the first ever erected in Texas. The building was in the middle of the block on the east side of Main, between Preston and Congress Avenues.

It was not a fire, or disaster of any kind, that gave Houston its first great hotel. During the same year that the Van Alstyne and Morris buildings were erected, Col. Wm. J. Hutchins began the erection of a large four-story hotel built of brick on the historic site of Houston's first hotel. This was the famous Hutchins House, made famous by the fact that most of the State associations, societies and many of the large commercial enterprises had their inception in its parlors.

To that time and ever since 1837, when the State Capitol building was erected, which was later the Old Capitol Hotel, it had been Houston's chief hotel. This was a rather commodious frame building, two-stories in height, and stood on the site where the new 18-story Rice Hotel is now being erected, corner of Main and Texas avenue. The Hutchins House was not completed until after the war; that is, not completely so, and there was a long delay before it could be used for the purpose for which it was designed. This historic house was burned down several years ago and the ground was allowed to remain vacant until 1911 when it was purchased by the Southern Pacific Railroad and the present magnificent office building of that road was erected on it.

In 1859 and 1860 Houston had something of a building boom and a great many really pretentious (for that day) buildings were erected in various parts of the city. One or two rather extensive fires occurred about that time, which cleared the ground of wooden shacks and enabled the owners to build more substantial houses, which they did.

For some years after the war there was very little in the way of improvements. During the war it was impossible to do much and after peace had been declared the people were too poor to do anything that was not absolutely imperative. The skyline of Houston underwent no changes until 1894, when Jacob Binz erected the first skyscraper in Houston. This building is still standing and though there are many others that tower high above it, it is justly considered one of the most useful and substantial buildings of its class in Houston. This building occupies one of the historic sites of the city, for it stands where the first Land Office of the Republic was situated, when Houston was the capital of Texas. Its erection marked the beginning of a new era for Houston architecturally. It was the introduction of the modern skyscraper, buildings for which Houston has since grown famous. Today Houston has more skyscrapers than any city in Texas and many more are planned.

The first public buildings in Houston were the County courthouse and the County jail, erected in 1838 by Harrisburg County, as Harris County was then called. They were both primitive in every sense of the word. The courthouse was a double log cabin, with a broad passage between the two rooms, such a building as is still occasionally seen on old plantations. The rooms were each sixteen feet square, the court being in one room and the clerk's office in the other. The jail was something of a curiosity, being simply a square log box with neither doors nor windows. There was but one opening, that being a trapdoor at the top. Access to the jail was through this trapdoor. A prisoner was taken to the roof by means of a ladder. The ladder was then drawn up and lowered into the jail. The prisoner descended and then the ladder was drawn up and the trap shut. It was all very simple, but very cumbersome as well.

Both the jail and courthouse were located on the Congress Avenue side of Courthouse Square, near Fannin. They answered very well for the court needs of that day, but the city and county soon outgrew them and it became necessary to provide better and more commodious quarters. Since the city had constructed the old market house and provided quite a serviceable city lock-up, or calaboose, the county solved the jail problem by making a contract with the city whereby the county was allowed to make use of the city prison as a county jail. The old log courthouse was still used, however, until 1850, when it was torn down and the first brick courthouse was erected. The building was placed almost in the center of the block, but a little to the Congress side. It was a two-story brick building, cost $15,000, and was regarded as the finest building in the country by the early Houstonians.

Owing to poor material, faulty construction or some other cause, this first courthouse did not stand long. Its walls cracked so badly and it showed such evidence of decay that nine years after its erection it was condemned and torn down to make way for a second brick building.

The second brick courthouse was erected in 1859. This was a much larger and more expensive building than its predecessor. It was placed on the north side of the square, fronting Congress Avenue. It was really a three-story building for it had a large basement, which was used for offices by some of the county officials. The other county officials were located on the second floor, while the third floor was used entirely for court purposes, there being two large courtrooms. During the war the basement was fixed up for a guardhouse, iron bars were placed in the windows and doors and, at various times, prisoners of war, captured at Galveston and Sabine Pass were confined there. It was not used permanently for that purpose, however.

Ten years after it was built, this building also began to crumble and in 1869 it was torn down and another larger building was erected almost on

the same site, only a little further back from Congress Avenue. This courthouse was an improvement over those that had preceded it and was also
more substantially constructed, for it stood thirteen years. In 1882 it was
somewhat damaged by a windstorm, and, since it was rather dilapidated in
every way, the County Commissioners decided to tear it down and erect a
new and finer building.

There was a great deal of friction between the members of the court over
plans and financial matters, but finally everything was amicably settled and
the courthouse was built in 1883. The new building was much more pretentious than any of the others that had preceded it and it was evidently better
constructed for it served the purpose for which it had been constructed
for nearly a quarter of a century, from 1883 until 1907. In 1907, a special
election was held and an issue of $500,000 of bonds was authorized for the
purpose of building a courthouse in every way worthy of the great County
of Harris and the great City of Houston. The bonds were issued and the
present magnificent courthouse was erected. It is one of the finest buildings of its kind in the South and would be a credit to a city fives times the
population of Houston.

Mr. O. L. Cochran, who has the distinction of being the oldest citizen
of Houston, and who for many years was the postmaster here, furnishes
the following information about the early locations of the Houston Post
Office:

> During the days of the Texas Republic it was located on the west
> side of Main Street, about the middle of the block between Pres-
> ton and Congress Avenues. After Texas became a State of the
> Union, in 1845, the office was removed to the old hotel, corner
> of Franklin Avenue and Travis Street. It was then removed to Dr.
> Hull's drug store, corner of Preston and Main, the site of the pres-
> ent Fox building. Then it was removed to Courthouse Square and
> located on the northeast corner of Congress Avenue and Fannin
> Street. It remained here for many years and then was removed just
> across the street to the northwest corner of Congress and Fannin.
> The next move was to the rear of the Fox building on the north
> side of Preston. Then it was taken to the Miller building on the
> northwest corner of Fannin and Preston. Its stay here was not long
> and its next move was to the Taylor building on the southwest cor-

ner of Preston and San Jacinto. It remained in the Taylor building until 1890, when the government purchased the southeast corner of Franklin and Fannin and erected its own building there. That building was behind the times and Houston grew so rapidly that by the time it was completed, substations had to be established to handle the business.

In 1903 the Government purchased the block in front of the High School and erected on it the present fine building, completed only a few months ago. Although the building is very large and thoroughly equipped, Houston has again outgrown it, and it has been found necessary to retain the old building, which is to be remodeled, improved and used as a substation.

As told elsewhere, Houston's first market house was erected in 1840 and stood until 1871, when it was torn down to make place for the great brick market erected at such immense cost to the taxpayers by the scalawag Reconstruction city administration. This famous building was destroyed by fire in 1876 and a similar structure was built on the same site, though for significantly less cost. In fact, the new building cost only about $80,000 to build, while the old one cost $470,000. This new building was also destroyed by fire in 1901, and then the present magnificent market house and city hall combined was erected. Today there is to be found no equal so far as usefulness, beauty of architecture and honest construction in the entire South.

It is a singular fact that Houston formerly had a volunteer fire company that was older than the city itself; that is, older than the chartered city. This was Protection No. 1, which was organized in 1836. It was not only Houston's first fire company, but it was unquestionably the first fire company organized in Texas. Houston at that time was only an aggregation of tents and log shanties, so there was no great danger of big conflagrations, and fighting fire was not the serious thing it became after more pretentious buildings were erected. Still there was danger and the company was organized to meet that danger.

For the first fourteen or fifteen years of the company's existence the method and appliances for fighting fire were extremely crude, consisting only of the formation of a line of men and the passing of buckets filled with water. The company was merely a bucket brigade, but it did good work. About 1850 the company purchased its first engine, which was a hand engine, worked by beams on each side. This old engine was used for many years and figured prominently at all the early fires, including the two or three great ones that occurred in the late fifties. It is regrettable that the names of these early Houston firemen have not been preserved.

Protection No. 1 was Houston's only fire company from 1836 until 1858. Since the city had grown and since a great fire had occurred in 1858, it became evident that better protection against fire was an imperative necessity. Hook and Ladder Company No. 1 was organized in 1858 and two years later, in 1860, Liberty No. 2 was organized. Then the great war came on and it was not until between 1866 and 1870 that further additions to the department were made. During the latter part of the war the engines were handled by negroes under control of white officers.

Mr. T. W. House, Sr., who was Mayor of the city in 1862, organized the first Houston Fire Department. The Department was composed of Protection No. 1, Hook and Ladder No. 2, and Liberty No. 2. Mr. E. L. Bremond was made Chief of the Department, and H. F. Hurd and Robert Burns were appointed First and Second Chiefs. The Department was not a great success and did not last long. There was friction between the companies and so each one pulled out and acted independently and the Department died a natural death.

It was not until 1874 that another attempt was made to organize a Department. That year Mr. J. H. B. House, son of the organizer of the first Department, succeeded in getting all the companies in the city to consent to the organization and he formed a really strong and efficient Department. Mr. J. H. B. House was unanimously elected Chief, and Messrs. Z. T. Hogan and C. C. Beavens were elected 1st and 2nd Assistants, as named. Mr. House and Mr. Hogan resigned before the end of their first term, and Mr. W. Williams was elected Chief, C. C. Beavens, First Assistant Chief, and Fred Harvey, Second Assistant.

The following is a synopsis of the report of the celebration of San Jacinto Day, as well as information about the participation of the companies in the day's festivities, as taken from the files of the *Houston Telegraph* of April 22, 1875.

There was a great street parade in which were large delegations from several interior cities, mostly from points on the Houston & Texas Central railroad. Col. J. P. Likens delivered an address during the afternoon. The following local companies were in line:

Protection No. 1—Charles Wichman, foreman; L. Ollre, first assistant; S. M. McAshan, president; Robert Brewster, secretary; R. Cohen, treasurer.

Hook and Ladder, No. 1—H. P. Roberts, president; L. Blanton, vice-president; William Cameron, secretary; O. L. Cochran, treasurer; Dr. Thorn. Robinson, foreman; J. C. Hart, first assistant; G. W. Gazley, second assistant.

Stonewall, No. 3—Joseph F. Meyer, foreman; L. M. Jones, first assistant; F. J. Frank, second assistant; W. Long, president; F. Ludke, vice-president; W. E. Smith, secretary.

Brooks, No. 5—I. C. Ford, foreman; William Alexander, first assistant; J. C. Thomas, Jr., second assistant; J. C. Thomas, Sr., president; I. Snowball, vice-president; S. L. Mateer, secretary; Thos. Milner, treasurer.

Eagle, No. 7—John Shearn, Jr., foreman; Willie Van Alstyne, first assistant; Ed. Mather, second assistant.

The *Telegraph* added the following bit of information about the companies taking part in the parade:

> Protection No. 1, organized in 1836.
> Houston Hook and Ladder No. 1, organized April 17, 1858
> Liberty No. 2, organized 1860.
> Stonewall No. 3, organized in the late sixties.
> Brooks No. 5, organized in the late sixties.
> Mechanic No. 6, organized October 28, 1873.
> Eagle No. 7, organized in 1875.

At that time the Department had two steamers, one extinguisher engine, two hand wagons and one hook and ladder company. It cost about $9,000 annually to run the department.

The old volunteer department existed as a whole for nineteen years, then, in 1893, it became a part pay and a part volunteer department. That proved unsatisfactory and the city took over the whole department in 1895, with the result that Houston has, today, one of the most useful and efficient fire departments in the South. There are thirty pieces of fire-fighting apparatus, of which nine are powerful modern steamers. In 1875 it cost $9,000 annually to run the department. Today it costs very nearly $125,000.

For some years after Houston was founded there was little or no necessity for crossing to the north side of the bayou. Very few people lived on that side and these came and went on small foot bridges which answered very well for the requirements of the limited travel. It is true that there was a growing wagon trade with other parts of the State and Houston but this was easily accommodated. All the trade from the west and northwest came in over the San Felipe road. That from the north came into the city by Stockbridge's ford, which was situated at the foot of Texas Avenue, while trade from the San Jacinto and Trinity came by the way of the Harrisburg ferry. The old San Felipe road remained unchanged to the end, but the trade from other parts of the State soon grew to such large proportions that the primitive methods of ford and ferry had to be abandoned and, in 1843, the first bridge over Buffalo Bayou was built at the foot of Preston Avenue.

That bridge stood for ten years, but was swept away by a great flood which occurred in 1853. The bridge that was constructed in its place had remarkable height and length. Its builders determined that it should not share the fate of its predecessor, so they built its center very high and extended its ends high up on each bank of the bayou. It was appropriately named "Long Bridge," and though seriously threatened by high water on several occasions it always escaped destruction. Finally, in the great flood of 1878, it was so badly damaged that it became necessary to remodel it and the present Preston Street bridge is the result. At about the same time that the Preston bridge was built a bridge was built across the bayou at the foot of Milam Street and another across White Oak bayou at the same point the present White Oak bridge occupies.

These bridges were originally cheap wooden structures, but were remodeled and ironwork substituted for wood, except in the White Oak bridge. It is utterly impossible to estimate the value of goods and produce that have passed over these bridges. For years everything grown in Texas for the outside markets was brought to Houston over them, while all goods and groceries shipped to the interior went out by the same routes. In time the Preston bridge became of chief importance, because the section north of Houston became more rapidly developed and the trade was consequently immense in that direction.

Of course when the railroads were built, the bridges were no longer needed for the purpose for which they were originally built. By that time, however, the city had grown and extended so that the bridges became equally as necessary for intercommunication between the various sections of the city as they had been for communication with the interior of the State. More bridges became necessary and more were constructed until now there are half a dozen passenger bridges and numerous railroad bridges spanning Buffalo Bayou, while an immense bridge is being constructed at the foot of Main street so as to connect with the Fifth Ward.

Ask ten men and the chances are that nine of them will say that the first railroad ever built in Texas had its start in Houston. This is no doubt due to the fact that the first road that ever amounted to anything, in the early days, the Houston & Texas Central, actually did have its beginning here. As a matter of fact, railroad building began (though nothing was accomplished) thirteen years before work on the Houston & Texas Central commenced. The mistake is quite natural for Houston has been the starting point for so many of the things that have made Texas great that it seems safe to credit her with being the mother of them all.

The first railroad construction ever done in Texas, if grading a few miles of track may be called construction, was at Harrisburg in 1840. Mr. A. Brisco was the moving spirit in that enterprise and he formed a company, putting up as a bonus a number of lots in the City of Harrisburg. The company he formed had no charter nor did they try to get one. Their idea was to build the road from Harrisburg to the Brazos and, after they had earned enough money by the traffic from that rich section to justify it, extend it further west towards Gonzales.

A large force of negroes was put to work grading the roadbed and nearly two miles were completed and ties purchased for that length of road when it was found that the cost of the iron rails would be too great, so the undertaking was abandoned. The next year, however, they took out a charter under the name of the Harrisburg Railroad & Trading Company. Though they had a charter now, they made no further attempt to actually construct the road. Everything was allowed to lie dormant until 1847 when General Sidney Sherman associated himself with a number of prominent Houston and Galveston men, secured the lots offered by Mr. Brisco, and after being assured of financial support by New York capitalists, he reorganized the road and secured another charter for it under the name Buffalo Bayou, Brazos & Colorado Railroad. That road afterwards became the Galveston, Harrisburg & San Antonio railroad of today.

Though General Sherman and his associates organized in 1847, it was not until 1851 that actual work was commenced. The preparation of the roadbed was commenced and pushed as rapidly as possible, but it was a year before rails were laid. That part of the work was done rapidly, however, and before the close of the year the road was actually completed as far as the Brazos, 32 miles from Harrisburg. No stop was made, but the road was pushed forward and in 1860, Alleyton, 79 miles from Harrisburg, was reached. Here a halt was made and before work could be resumed the war came on and nothing further in the way of construction was possible.

The Houston men who had taken a leading part in the construction of this first railroad were W. M. Rice, W. A. Van Alstyne, James H. Stevens, B. A. Shepherd and W. J. Hutchins. These same men and others had organized a purely local company at Houston, one year before construction had begun on the Harrisburg road, and had obtained a charter under the name of the Brazos Plank Road. Their object was to grade a road from Houston to some point on the Brazos and then plank it over so as to enable the ox wagons, which were the only means of transportation in those days, to reach Houston easily at all seasons. That was in 1850, and the work of grading had extended the load twenty-three miles, though no planks had been laid, when some of the citizens of Chappell Hill, Washington County, issued a call for a great meeting to be held at Chappell Hill in the interest of building a railroad. Houston was invited to send delegates to that railroad convention, and a meeting was held in June, 1852, at the old Capitol Hotel for the purpose of discussing the question.

The meeting was largely attended and the stockholders in the Plank Road project were rather conspicuous among the other attendees. They had something of a double interest in the meeting for, while they knew the value of a railroad, they also knew that a railroad would completely destroy the value of their plank road. However, that fact seems not to have influenced their action, for they voted for sending a strong delegation to the Chappell Hill convention. This action was taken not without opposition, however, for while making no direct attack on the proposed railroad, Dr. Francis Moore, the editor of the *Telegraph*, made a vigorous fight for the plank road, which he argued was a present necessity and one which could be supplied at once, while it would take years to secure a charter for a railroad and again years to build the road after the charter was secured.

A fact worthy of special mention is that at that meeting Mr. Paul Bremond took a most prominent part in advocating the building of the railroad. This was his first appearance as a railroad advocate, and it deserves notice for it was he who was destined to become the real pioneer in railroad building in Texas. He had been one of the incorporators of the railroad chartered in 1848 under the name of the Galveston & Red River Railroad, which road, after many changes and amendments of its charter, finally became the Houston & Texas Central.

Mr. Bremond opposed adhering to the plank road if it was going to delay the building of the railroad and advocated speedy action on the latter proposition. The whole situation was gone over at that meeting with evident good results, for while neither the plank road nor the Washington County railroad was ever built, there was started a movement towards railroad building that resulted in work actually beginning on the Houston & Texas Central railroad on January 1, 1853. Mr. Paul Bremond had the honor of throwing the first shovel of dirt.

It may seem strange that anyone should have raised the least objection to railroad building at a time when the urgent need of a railroad was so obvious. That, however, may be explained by the fact that the Houston merchants had become used to the means of transit then in vogue, namely the ox-wagon, and had seen such good results following it that they were beginning to feel that they could do very well without other means of transportation. It must be borne in mind that the wagon service was not desultory nor intermittent. It was slow but it was certain and regular. For fourteen years it had been in force and was thoroughly organized. Its very magnitude and the numbers engaged in the business rendered the service almost continuous, and while individual teams might be subject to unreasonable detention and delay, there were so many others to take their place that such gaps were not noticeable.

As remarked, at the date of that Capitol Hotel meeting in 1852, the wagon service had been in force for fourteen years; had answered very well and met all conditions except that of speed. It is no wonder that the ox-team should have had its advocates at the meeting among those whose fortunes it had contributed so largely to build.

The service was indeed of great magnitude for it extended as far west as the Colorado River and up to Austin; as far as Waco to the northwest and to all points in East and Southern Central Texas. There were three or four thousand wagons engaged in the traffic and as each wagon required from sixteen to twenty-four oxen. When these numbers are considered, an idea of the amount of money involved may be formed. In those days every bale of cotton, every bushel of corn, every hide and everything else raised in Texas for the market came to Houston while all merchandise and groceries used in the interior, were hauled away from Houston by ox wagons. The business was a gigantic one.

But the success of starting the Buffalo Bayou & Colorado Railroad and of actually constructing 82 miles of it in 1852, was too great a demonstration of what could be done and it spurred the Houston people on, so that, as already remarked, Mr. Bremond actually threw the first shovel full of dirt for what was destined to become one of the greatest roads in the country, on January 1, 1853.

The story of Mr. Bremond's trials and tribulations has been told so often that it is needless to repeat it here. He accomplished something that was never accomplished before and has never been attempted since. He built fifty miles of good railroad on very little cash and a great deal of faith. He had absolute confidence in himself and in his own honesty and, somehow, he managed to inspire others with his own faith and confidence. He was the first railroad builder to water the stock of his road, but his method was different from that of his successors for he used faith, faith and then more faith, and that was all.

Mr. Bremond had hundreds of Irishmen working for him as section hands, and it is no exaggeration to say that before the expiration of the first six months he knew every one of them by sight, if not by name. This was not because of any great democracy on his part nor was it because of the prominence of good social qualities in him. It was based on something more reasonable and useful, for it was a measure of self-protection on his part. He used his knowledge of his men to enable him to keep from coming in contact with them. They were so unreasonable as to want pay for their work, and tiring of promises, they began to take matters in their own hands, with most unpleasant effects for Mr. Bremond.

No one ever knew how he accomplished it, but he actually built the road as far as Hempstead, fifty miles from Houston, with scarcely enough money to build ten miles, but with promises enough to have built the road to the North Pole. When the road reached Hempstead it struck a rich territory and began doing a large and lucrative business. Mr. Bremond's first care was to fulfill the promises he had made to his men, and their claims were the first that were settled. No man who ever trusted Paul Bremond, whether willingly or unwillingly, as those Irishmen did, ever lost a cent by doing so.

Twenty-three years later, in 1876, Mr. Bremond undertook the construction of another great road. He tried to get sufficient outside backing to enable him to build it without any of the friction and worry he had encountered with the Houston & Texas Central. His success in getting the financial aid he sought was only partial, but he had made up his mind to build the road and he did. Again he threw the first spadeful of dirt, and before he got through with his work, he had added the Houston East & West Texas Railroad to the iron ways centering at Houston.

When the war began Houston had made considerable progress in railroad building. The Texas & New Orleans had been constructed for about 111 miles, the Buffalo Bayou & Colorado had been extended to Alleyton, about 80 miles, and had been connected with Houston by the Columbia Tap road which extended from Houston to Columbia on the Brazos, 50 miles. The Houston & Texas Central had been extended to Millican, 81 miles from Houston, while the Galveston, Houston & Henderson road connected Houston and Galveston. The latter road was of the greatest military importance and was therefore kept up, in some way, during the four years of the war, but it was the only one. The other roads were, necessarily, allowed to go to ruin and when the war ended it was flattery to speak of them as "streaks of rust." The roadbed and right-of-way were about all that was left of them. The owners of the roads were in about as bad shape financially as were the roads physically, the result being that through reorganization and other methods, by 1870 virtually every railroad in Texas had changed hands.

With the completion of the Houston & Texas Central to Denison and its connection there with the Missouri, Kansas & Texas, thus forming a through line to St. Louis, the completion of the Texas & New Orleans line to New Orleans, and the extension of the Galveston, Houston and San Antonio to San Antonio, Houston became a railroad center at once. Then the International & Great Northern was built and, since the late seventies ,nearly each year has seen additions to Houston's railroads until now there are seventeen roads centering here and Houston is now one of the greatest railroad centers in the country.

It is interesting to note the difference in the railroad situation in Texas, and in Harris County, in particular, since the close of the war. As noted in the foregoing there were, at the close of the war, less than 370 miles of railroads in the whole State. Today Harris County alone has 450 miles within its limits, valued at $20,000,000, and, of this there is invested in terminal facilities at Houston about $12,000,000.

According to the most recent census report, there are 2,843 trainmen and clerks and 3,000 shopmen, or a total of 5,843 employees of the railroads paid off here. The total amount of their salaries and wages foot up $7,000,000 in round numbers. Really Mr. Bremond should be allowed to come back to life just to see what has grown from that first shovel of dirt he threw on that January morning in 1853.

The real importance and magnitude of the railroad situation is shown much better by the terminal facilities and trackage of the roads within the city limits. Placed end to end these sidetracks and switches would make a line of railroad 275 miles long, or just about the total length of the Houston & Texas Central Railroad.

The Houston yards of the Southern Pacific are the largest in the Southwest, with a trackage of 131 miles and a capacity of 10,000 cars. The Harriman tracks in Houston accommodate 123 different industrial plants, handle over 50,000 cars monthly and employ in that work 547 men. The roundhouses contain 72 stalls and 1,600 men are employed in the roundhouse and shops of this company. Twenty-two switch engines are kept constantly in use in these yards, taking cars to and from the industrial plants and in making up trains.

The Southern Pacific has 738 switches in the yards here. Among the other properties of the Southern Pacific are water tanks for the locomotives with a capacity of 100,000 gallons, and fuel oil tanks with a capacity of 225,000 barrels. The payroll of the Harriman interests in Houston is $4,000,000 annually.

The Houston Belt & Terminal Company's terminals aggregate trackage of about fifty-five miles. Among other properties of this company, in addition to the handsome passenger terminal and the convenient freight depots, are a roundhouse and machine shops, oil tanks and water tanks. Over 200 men are employed in these yards and shops. The company uses five switch engines, all of which burn oil. Practically every industrial plant in the city is reached by these tracks. The Houston Belt & Terminal company facilities are used by a number of the roads entering Houston. The Missouri, Kansas & Texas, the Santa Fe, the Trinity & Brazos Valley, the Frisco lines east and the Brownsville line all use the passenger station. The same lines, with the exception of the Katy, use the freight facilities.

The International & Great Northern has fifty-six miles of track in its local terminals. Its yards are mostly located on this side of the ship channel, though several miles are in the north side, where they touch a number of Houston industries. The principal shops of the company are located in Palestine, but fifty-seven men are employed in the repair shops here. About 120 other men are employed in the yards. The tracks of this company touch eighty-three different industrial plants. There are twelve switch engines operating in these yards, which accommodate 2,500 cars. The oil tanks of this company in Houston have a capacity of 190 barrels and the water tanks 75,000 gallons. There are six stalls in the roundhouse and 194 switches in the yards.

The Missouri, Kansas & Texas has about fifteen miles of track in its yards here. These yards have a capacity of 1,500 cars. Forty-three men are employed in the car department of the shops here and nine men are employed in the roundhouse, which has six stalls. In the yards there are forty-five men employed. Five switch engines are used in the yards constantly. The water tanks of this company here have a capacity of 100,000 gallons and the coal chutes forty tons.

The San Antonio & Aransas Pass has a yard track mileage of thirteen miles. Over 1,100 cars can be accommodated in them and three switch engines are necessary to handle the business. Nineteen men are employed in the yards. This company maintains a freight depot here, but its passenger trains enter the Southern Pacific depot. This company is also closely allied to the Southern Pacific and can touch most of the local industrial plants on the Harriman tracks.

All the other lines entering this city operate very little yard trackage, but have agreements with some one of these roads. The Galveston, Houston & Henderson and the Santa Fe both have small stretches of track here, but the mileage is small.

It must not be supposed that land transportation occupied the attention of the early Houstonians to the exclusion of everything else. Water transportation was given a great deal of attention, though in that direction not so much was required. There was plenty of water in the bayou to float the largest steamboats of that day, but there were one or two very troublesome features. There were obstacles to navigation near Morgan's Point, where there were two bars known as Red Fish and Clopper's bars. The water was shallow at these two points and whenever a severe norther blew the water out of Galveston Bay, these bars became impassable. At that time there was no remedy for the evil, so it was endured. At this end of the bayou there was a less formidable though serious obstacle. Between Houston and Harrisburg, for a distance by water of about sixteen miles, the bayou was very tortuous and overhung by large trees. The limbs of these trees played havoc with the woodwork of the steamboats and sometimes did serious damage to the boats themselves.

The work of improving navigation of the bayou was done exclusively by the people of Houston, without outside assistance. This is strange, for among the first measures passed by the Texas Congress was one setting aside $300,000 for the improvement of Texas rivers and harbors. For some unknown reason no request was ever made for this money and certainly not for the improvement of Buffalo Bayou. The work was rather crude and simple and consisted chiefly of cutting off overhanging limbs, removing sunken logs and cutting down trees that could be gotten rid of in no other way.

The importance of the bayou has always been recognized by Houstonians first, and then by the people of Texas and of the Southwest. In the early days it afforded the only safe communication between the people of Texas and the outside world, and in later days it has been made the basis for adjusting fair and equitable freight rates over the railroads. Aside from its importance as a freight carrier for Houston, it is important in regulating freights for the entire Southwest, and that fact creates interests in the bayou in territory remote from Houston. Buffalo Bayou should have pages devoted to it instead of this, necessarily, brief mention.

A year after Houston was laid out as a "city," the first steamboat, the *Laura*, came up here from Harrisburg, though she had a terrible time in accomplishing the passage from Harrisburg to Houston. The *Laura* seems to have cleared the bayou of so many obstructions that after that, several steamboats and sailing vessels came here and soon there was a regular service established between Houston and Galveston, which continued for some years after the war. The railroads finally destroyed the passenger business, and since then the immense traffic, amounting to millions each year, has been done by means of barges.

During the latter years there were some magnificent steamboats engaged in the Houston-Galveston trade, the two most magnificent ones being the *Diana* and *T. M. Bagby*, sister boats which compared favorably with any of the famous Mississippi river boats. They were each 170 feet long, 32 feet beam and five feet hold and were furnished in the most luxurious manner. Each was a veritable floating palace.

There are only stray pieces of records and statistics in existence relating to cotton shipments during early years. In 1839 only eight bales of cotton were shipped down the bayou. By 1844 those eight bales had grown to 7,000. The next year, 1845, a large cotton crop was made in Texas and the receipts and shipments here amounted to 12,000 bales. Nine years later they had grown to be 38,000 bales and the growth has been steady ever since. Today Houston handles more actual spot cotton than any other market in America. The local sales of spot cotton in Houston average about 750,000 each season, while its receipts and shipments are between 2,500,000 and 3,000,000 bales yearly.

CHAPTER IV:
OF DOCTORS AND LAWYERS

Although there were such men as Ewing, Ashbel Smith, McAnally, and others of lesser prominence practicing medicine in the very early days of Houston there seems to have been no effort made by them to form a medical association. By the 1840s there were several additions to the profession. Among the newcomers were Dr. S. O. Young, Sr., Dr. William McCraven, Dr. W. D. Robinson, Dr. W H. Howard and Dr. L. A. Bryan.

Another decade passed before a successful attempt was made to form an association. In 1857 the first Houston medical association was organized. Dr. J. S. Duval was elected president; Dr. H. W. Waters, vice president and Dr. R. H. Boxley, secretary. The full membership consisted of J. S. Duval, W. H. Howard, Greenville Dowell, R. H. Boxley, and H. W. Waters. The objects of the organization were "to cultivate the science of medicine and all its collateral branches; to cherish and sustain medical character; to encourage medical etiquette and to promote mutual improvement, social intercourse and good feeling among members of the medical profession."

The first resolution adopted by the association was one aimed at the Homeopaths, and was as follows:

Whereas, the scientific medical world has proven Homeopathy to be a species of empirism, too flagrant to merit the confidence of rational men, and too fabulous to deserve even the passing notice of an educated physician, and as we are convinced that it is a delusion, far surpassing any other ism known to the world, witchcraft not excepted, therefore we will not recognize, professionally or privately, any man who professes to cure diseases through the agency of Hahnemanic teachings.

Be it Resolved, That as a diploma from a regularly organized medical school is the only evidence of qualification which our community can obtain in regard to the doctors in their midst, we respectfully recommend to the citizens of this flourishing city that they demand of every man who assumes the responsibility of a physician to their families, their diplomas as certificates of their worthiness of patronage, and that they see to it that they are not imposed on by a diploma from a medical society or a certificate of qualifications as a dresser in a hospital.

Two years later, in 1859, the Houston association issued a call addressed to the physicians of the State asking them to meet in Houston for the purpose of organizing a State Medical Association. There is reason to believe that such meeting was held but there is no record of it. The best evidence that there was such an association formed is the fact that Dr. W. H. Howard, who was a member of the City association in 1859, always spoke of the formation of the present State Medical Association as the re-organization of the old association.

The following named physicians met in the parlors of the Hutchins House on December 8, 1868, for the purpose of forming the Harris County Medical Association: L. A. Bryan, W. H. Howard, J. Larendon, D. F. Stuart, T. J. Poulson, R. W. Lunday, Alva Connell Sr., Alva Connell Jr., G. H. McDonnall, W. D. Robinson, T. J. Devereaux, J. M. Morris, W. P. Riddell.

After issuing a call to the physicians of Texas inviting them to meet in Houston on April 15, 1869 for the purpose of organizing, or rather re-organizing the State association, the Harris County association adjourned and never held another meeting until resurrected in 1904, since which date it has been one of the largest and most useful county associations in the State. The State Medical Association, however, was formed April 15, 1869 in the parlors of the Hutchins House.

If the early lawyers of Houston had any association they have left no record of the fact. There were great lawyers then and they set a standard of professional ethics and courtesy which, be it said to the credit of those who followed them, has never been lowered. From the earliest date the bar of Houston has always been great and influential. Among the big men when Houston was in its swaddling clothes were such men as Archibald Wynn, a criminal lawyer of marked ability; Peter W. Gray, W. P. Hamblen, E. A. Palmer, A. N. Jordan, J. W. Henderson, Benjamin F. Tankersley, Gus Tompkins, A. P. Thompson, A. S. Richardson and C. B. Sebin. The mere mention of these names is sufficient to show the high standing of the Houston bar at the very beginning.

During and after the close of the war there were many very brilliant and able lawyers who came to Houston. Among the most distinguished of these was Hon. Charles Stewart, D. U. Barziza, John H. Manley, Frank Spencer, George Goldthwaite, E. P. Hamblen, W. H. Crank, Judge Wilson, James Masterson, C. Anson Jones, son of the last President of the

Republic of Texas; W. A. Carrington, F. F. Chew, J. C. Hutchinson, Judge James Baker, W. B. Botts and others of equal prominence. As all know, these were men of the greatest probity and honor and would have reflected honor on any bar.

When the first amended constitution of Texas was adopted, it created a criminal district court for Harris and Galveston Counties. Judge Gustave Cook was appointed presiding judge and held the position for fourteen years. His successors on the bench have been C. L. Cleveland, E. D. Cavin, J. K. P. Gillaspie, E. R. Campbell and C. W. Robinson.

The following were the officers of the Eleventh District Court from its organization to the present day:

> 1837 to 1842—Benjamin C. Franklin, Judge; James S. Holman, Clerk; John W. Moore, Sheriff
>
> 1842 to 1849—Richard Morris, Judge; F. R. Lubbock, Clerk; M. T. Rogers, Sheriff
>
> 1849 to 1854—C. W. Buckley, Judge; F. R. Lubbock, Clerk; David Russell, Sheriff
>
> 1854 to 1862—Peter W. Gray, Judge
>
> 1862 to 1866—James A. Baker, Judge; W. B. Walker, Clerk; B. P. Lanham, Sheriff

From 1866 to 1869, during Reconstruction, there were no elections but the members of the bar selected George R. Scott, C. B. Sabin and P. W. Gray to act as judge of the court.

> 1869 to 1870—George R. Scott, Judge
>
> 1870 to 1892—James R. Masterson, Judge
>
> 1892 to 1896—S. H. Brashear, Judge
>
> 1896 to 1900—John G. Tod, Judge
>
> 1900 to date—Charles E. Ashe, Judge

The following is a complete list of the sheriffs of Harris County since the organization of the county to 1912:

> 1837-42—John W. Moore
>
> 1842-49—M. T. Rodgers

1849-54—David Russell

1854-58—Thomas Hogan

1858-62—M. M. Grimes

1862-66—B. P. Lanham

(Note: In 1866 John Proudfoot was elected sheriff but after holding office for a short time he disappeared. Mr. I. C. Lord, who was city marshal at the time, was appointed to act as sheriff until an election could be held. Another regular election was held and A. B. Hall was elected.)

1866-73—A. B. Hall

1873-76—S. S. Ashe

1876-82—Cornelius Noble

1882-86—John J. Fant

1886-94—George Ellis

1894-96—Fred Erichson

1896 to date—A. R. Anderson

The Fifty-first District Court was organized in 1897, and since then has had but three judges, the most recent of which are:
      1902 to 1911—Judge Wm. P. Hamblen.
      1911 to date—Judge William Masterson.
      (Judge Hamblen died in office and Judge
      Masterson was appointed to succeed him.)

The Sixty-first District Court was organized in February of 1903, and has had but one presiding judge since its organization, Judge N. G. Kittrell.

The Harris County Court was created by the Legislature in 1867. John Brasher was elected county judge and served until 1869. His successor was Judge M. N. Brewster, who was put in office by the Republican reconstructionists. Judge Brewster was ousted by the Democrats in 1867 and Judge C. Anson Jones was elected. He served until his death in 1882. Judge E. P. Hamblen was elected in 1882 and served until 1884. Judge W. C. Andrews was elected in 1884 and served until 1892. Judge Andrews was a candidate for re-election in 1892, but died just before the election. On the death of Judge Andrews, Judge John G. Tod was placed on the ticket and was elected. In 1896, Judge W. N. Shaw was elected and remained in office for two years, being succeeded by Judge E. H. Vasmer in 1898. Judge Vasmer held office for four years and was followed by Judge Blake Dupree in 1902. Judge Dupree held office for two terms and was succeeded by Judge A. E. Amerman, the present incumbent.

The Corporation Court for Houston was created by act of the Legislature in 1899. Before the creation of this court, the city had a somewhat similar court. The presiding judge was sometimes the mayor, sometimes a recorder and at other times a justice of the peace. The method was so unsatisfactory that the present court was created to avoid all confusion. The first election to provide a judge for the new court was held soon after its creation. Judge A. R. Railey was elected and served until 1902, when he was defeated by Judge Marmion. When the form of the city government was changed, Judge Marmion was elected as one of the commissioners and Judge John H. Kirlicks was appointed to fill his unexpired term. He has held office ever since, much to the satisfaction of everybody except the evil-doers.

The Houston Bar Association was organized in 1870. Judge Peter W. Gray was its first president, Judge George Golthwaite its vice president and Col. Thomas J. Whitfield, recording secretary, N. P. Turner, corresponding secretary and W. C. Watson, treasurer. The Association was not numerically strong at the beginning, but it was strong in every other way, for among its members were some of the greatest lawyers in the country. Today the Association is strong in every way and compares favorably with similar associations anywhere. L. J. Bryan is president; Thomas H. Botts, secretary and Chester H. Bryan is treasurer. The Association has a membership of several hundred.

Before the invasion of Texas by Santa Anna, there was a Mr. Gray who had a printing office consisting of a few fonts of type, a dilapidated press and a few other necessary things at Brazoria. From time to time he published a little news sheet, but made no effort to issue a regular newspaper. About the same time there was a little paper published at Nacogdoches, but it was spasmodic, irregular and not entitled to be considered a newspaper. With these two exceptions there was not a paper published in Texas prior to the Texas Revolution, nor while the Texans were striving to bring about concerted action against Mexico, except that established by the Borden Brothers, Gail and Thomas, at Columbia on October 10,1835. The Bordens had the greatest trouble getting not only material, but editors and printers, but finally they succeeded, and on the date named, issued the *Telegraph and Register.* Under the name of the *Telegraph* was destined to become and remain for years, the leading newspaper of Texas.

The *Telegraph and Register* was issued on the very day that the Texans, under Fannin, stormed and took Goliad, and as things began to happen with startling rapidity after that, there was no lack of sensational news for the paper. The paper was of the greatest assistance to the cause of the Texans, for it did much to concentrate public opinion and to keep the people informed about current events—information obtainable in no other way.

The paper was published regularly from October, 1835, until late in March, 1836, when the Bordens, learning that Houston had fallen back before Santa Anna and had crossed the Brazos at San Felipe, decided to fall back themselves and take their newspaper plant to a safer location. With great difficulty they managed to move everything to Harrisburg and had an issue of the *Telegraph* all ready for the press when Santa Anna's soldiers showed up, burned their building and threw their press into the bayou.

Instead of being discouraged, the Bordens ordered a new outfit from Cincinnati, and, sometime in August, 1836, resumed the publication of the *Telegraph* in Columbia, where the Texas Congress met two months later. Gail Borden had been appointed collector of customs at Galveston and it was necessary for him to make his home there. So he retired from the *Telegraph* and since his brother Tom wished to leave also, they sold the paper to Mr. Jacob Cruger and Dr. Francis Moore, who moved it to Houston and issued the first number here on May 2, 1837. Dr. Moore was chief editor of the *Telegraph* until 1853, when Harry H. Allen became editor and proprietor. In 1856, he sold the paper to Mr. E. H. Cushing, one of the most gifted writers and able newspapermen the state has ever had.

Ten years later, in 1866, Mr. Cushing sold the *Telegraph* to Col. C. C. Gillespie, who was a strong and forcible writer but rather a poor editor. Col. Gillespie employed Mr. J. E. Carnes as editorial writer and between the two, the *Telegraph* soon became the leading literary paper of the state. Too much attention was paid to fine writing and too little to news, so the paper lost ground and was about on its last legs when Col. Gillespie sold it to General Webb, who published it regularly until 1873, when the financial panic of that year killed it.

The next year Mr. A. C. Gray revived it and, under his able management, it soon became the leading paper of the state again. In its first issue under his management, April 16, 1874, Mr. Gray said:

> *The Houston Telegraph* is an old and familiar friend to very many in and out of Texas who will hail its reappearance as the return of an old, a much loved and greatly lamented companion. Founded in the days of the Republic, it was true to the government and to the people, and, by its efforts, accomplished perhaps as much as any other instrumentality in calling attention to and developing the resources of this great commonwealth. Under the control and guidance of such men as Gail Borden, Dr. Francis Moore, Henry Allen, E. H. Cushing and others, it has reared for itself an imperishable monument, by its fidelity to the law, good government and general progress.
>
> It is with no ordinary satisfaction, and we trust a pardonable pride, that the present managing editor and proprietor refers to his past connection with and present relation to the office of the *Telegraph*. Twenty-eight years ago, when a mere boy, he entered it as an apprentice. By patient toil and proper pride in his chosen profession he became its business manager during its most prosperous period. And when, under the financial panic of 1873, it was forced to suspend and ceased to make its daily appearance, he mourned it as if a friend had fallen. Since then it has been his ambition to call the slumbering Ajax to the field again and bid it battle with renewed energy for constitutional government, Democratic principles and the general weal.

Mr. Gray made a magnificent fight to reinstate the *Telegraph* in the front ranks of Texas journals. From a literary and politically influential point of view he was successful, but the financial strain became too great. In 1878 the *Telegraph* was forced to cease publication and its pages were closed forever.

In the early fifties a Mr. Cruger (not the Cruger who was associated with Dr. Moore on the *Telegraph* when it was established in Houston) began the publication of a tri-weekly paper called *The Morning Star*. This appears to have been quite an ambitious and prominent paper, judging by the incomplete files of it now in the Carnegie Library.

It seems that everybody wanted to start a newspaper in Houston after the war, for between 1865 and 1880 there were no less than twenty-one that had appeared, splashed about in the troubled waters of journalism and then sunk beneath the waves to rise no more. Some of them were worthy and deserving papers, but the majority of them were catch penny affairs that were started on a shoestring, merely to get hold of a little cash from a confiding public.

An exception was the *Houston Age*, owned later by Mr. Fourmy, the Directory man at present associated with Mr. Morrison. The *Age* became famous under the editorial management of Major Dan McGary, and also through the caustic articles contributed by Col. Dick Westcott during heated political campaigns, and all campaigns were heated during the existence of the *Age*.

In 1880, Mr. Gail Johnson, a grandson of Mr. Gail Borden, the founder of the old *Telegraph*, established the *Houston Post*. This paper had ample financial backing and an able, well-organized editorial and business force. It was a bright, newsy paper and soon secured a strong foothold in Houston and throughout the state as well. There is no question that it would have ultimately become one of the leading papers of the state but for a fatal error committed by Judge Johnson, the father of Mr. Gail Johnson. The Judge was an ardent Republican and conceived an idea that he could make the *Post* a power in politics by supporting a candidate against the regular nominee of the Democratic party.

The Judge lost sight of the fact that Texas had so recently emerged from the Reconstruction, scalawag rule that had cursed the state, and that the average citizen associated the name "Republican" with all that was despicable and contemptible. Judge John Ireland was the regular Democratic nominee and he was opposed by Col. Wash Jones, who ran as an independent candidate. The *Post* supported Jones, and did so in such a masterly manner as to attract attention and cause a demand for the paper. The circulation increased rapidly and continued to increase until the day of election. Then Ireland was triumphantly elected and the bubble burst. The circulation dropped off more rapidly than it had increased. The paper had lots of money behind it, however, and continued its career just as though nothing had occurred to mar the serenity of its course.

Mr. Gail Johnson had grown disgusted and had disposed of his interest to his father, who in 1883 sold the *Post* to a syndicate of Houston capitalists, who had conceived the idea of converting it into a great Democratic State paper. They secured the services of Mr. Hardenbrook, an experienced newspaperman, and placed him in full charge, supplying him with plenty of money and giving him a free hand to do as he chose. Hardenbrook brought Mr. Tobe Mitchell from St. Louis and placed him in charge of the editorial room. Hardenbrook and Mitchell spent money freely and soon made the *Post* one of the leading papers of the South. In eight or nine months they spent very nearly $300,000. Then the backers of the paper became alarmed and, one by one, withdrew. Then the crash came and the paper suspended publication suddenly.

The suspension of the *Post* left Houston without a morning paper and, to remedy the defect, Dr. S. O. Young (your humble author) organized a company composed of practical printers and newspapermen and began the publication of a morning paper which was called the *Houston Chronicle*. Mr. Baker, who now owned the *Post* plant, allowed the company to use it and also allowed them to use the large supply of paper the *Post* had on hand when it suspended, charging only for what was actually used at cost. The *Chronicle* was not a brilliant sheet, but it was an honest and fairly good paper. It was run strictly on the pay-as-you-go principle and at the end of its first year, it had an empty treasury but it did not owe a dollar to anyone.

After an existence of very nearly eighteen months Dr. Young, who had secured entire control of the *Chronicle*, merged it with the *Journal*, an afternoon paper owned by Professor Girardeau and Mr. J. L. Watson. The *Journal* ceased publication and the new morning paper was called the *Houston Daily Post*.

The first issue of the *Post* was on April 5, 1885. Effort was made to publish a more pretentious paper than the *Chronicle* had been, but that increased the expense so much so that serious complications arose. Professor Girardeau became disgusted and turned his back on journalism. Messrs. Young and Watson purchased his interest and continued the struggle. The loss to the paper of such a man as Professor Girardeau was a serious embarrassment. However, it was a blessing in disguise, for the gentlemen were enabled to secure Col. R. M. Johnston as editorial manager, and Colonel Johnston is one of the best and most practical newspapermen in the country.

In September of the same year, Dr. Young received a flattering offer from the *Galveston News* to become one of its editorial writers. He gave his interest in the *Post* to Messrs. Watson and Johnston and went to Galveston. This left Watson and Johnston sole proprietors of the *Post*. They managed to keep their heads above water for about a year and in 1886, they reorganized the *Post*, turning it into a stock company. Even after that the *Post* had up-hill sailing for a year or two, but finally the magnificent ability of Colonel Johnston as an editorial manager, backed by the absolute genius of Watson in the business office, began to tell and the *Post* became what it is today, one of the great newspapers of the Southwest.

Mr. W. H. Bailey, a bright young newspaperman, began the publication of an afternoon paper called the *Herald*. This was a regular live wire and was fully charged all the time. Mr. Bailey believed in telling the truth all the time regardless of whom the truth might be about and he did so in every issue of the *Herald*. No one was too high and prominent to escape criticism and censure if he deserved them. Bailey played no favorites, but went after wrong-doers wherever discovered. The result was almost continual warfare for the first few months of the *Herald's* existence, and, what was more to the editor's satisfaction, an immense circulation for the paper. Subscriptions and advertisements poured in and the *Herald* became one of the leading papers in South Texas.

After a red-hot existence of eighteen years the *Herald* was finally sold to Mr. M. E. Foster, who had organized the *Houston Chronicle* and who bought the plant and good will of the *Herald*. The *Houston Chronicle* began publication on October 14, 1901, and it is no exaggeration to say that it was a success from its very first issue. Its editor and proprietor, Mr. M. E. Foster, was no novice, having been managing editor of the *Houston Post* and having had large experience and training. He has made the *Chronicle* one of the leading state papers and its influence is great both in Houston and throughout the state.

On May 18, 1880, a number of Texas editors assembled in the parlor of the Hutchins House and organized the Texas Press Association. For four years the Association met in Houston and then determined to meet each year in a different city. From a mere handful of members at the beginning, the Association has grown to be one of the largest and most important in the South and its annual meetings are looked forward to with pleasurable anticipation by the members for they are always most profitable and enjoyable.

Mr. T. W. House, Sr., Mr. W. J. Hutchins, Mr. Cornelius Ennis and others of the early merchants carried on banking affairs of their own in connection with their cotton and mercantile businesses, extending credit to customers. In 1854, Mr. B. A. Shepherd opened an independent bank, engaging exclusively in the banking business. This was the first bank in Houston and Mr. Shepherd was the first genuine banker.

In 1873 Mr. Hutchins ceased banking activities and devoted himself solely to his wholesale business. Mr. House reversed Mr. Hutchins' process in part, for while he did not close out his cotton and wholesale business, he separated them from his banking activities and gave the latter more of his attention. When Mr. House died in 1881, his oldest son, T. W. House, Jr., bought the interests of his brothers in the bank and devoted his whole time to its affairs. House's bank soon became one of the greatest financial institutions in the state. During the great panic of 1907, due to many complications and circumstances, it was forced to close its doors.

The City Bank of Houston began business November 1, 1870, with a capital stock of $250,000. It did business for fifteen years, but in 1885 was forced to suspend payment and went into the hands of a receiver. The Houston Savings Bank, organized in 1874, suspended payment and closed its doors in 1886. The public lost very little money by the failure of this bank or by that of the City Bank, which had occurred the year before.

The First National Bank was organized in 1866 by Mr. B. A. Shepherd and Mr. T. M. Bagby, the latter being its first president. On the death of Mr. Bagby, Mr. Shepherd became president and when he died his son-in-law, Mr. A. S. Root, succeeded him. A few years ago Mr. Root died and Mr. O. L. Cochran, another son-in-law of Mr. Shepherd, became and is still president.

This bank is one of the strongest institutions in the country. Its original capital was $100,000. In 1906 this was increased to $500,000. In 1909 the stock was again doubled and in 1912 it was increased to $2,000,000. Its business has also shown a phenomenal growth, having about doubled in three years. September 1, 1909, its deposits were $4,764,967. September 1, 1910, the deposits had grown to $6,421,938. Four months later, January 7, 1911, they were $7,953,096. Just two months later, March 7, 1911, they were $8,432,907. On April 18, 1912, deposits were slightly under $9,000,000, or to be exact, $8,973,999.80.

The home of this bank is one of the handsomest buildings in the city. It is only eight stories high, but it has an immense floor space, larger than any bank in the South. It has a fine frontage on Main Street and runs back for more than half a block on Franklin Avenue. In addition to this, it has an ell that extends from the Franklin side far back towards the middle of the block. The entire first, or ground floor is used by the bank while the other seven stories are used as offices. The building is of reinforced concrete, steel structure and is fireproof in every way. It has its own water supply, derived from a large artesian well. It also has its own heating and electric light plant. There are three large and rapid elevators, and the building is equipped from top to bottom with every device that contributes to the comfort and convenience of its tenants.

It was exactly twenty years after the organization of the First National Bank before another was organized. This was the Commercial National Bank, organized in 1886, with a capital stock of $500,000. This bank did an immense business and had large deposits. It was recently merged with the South Texas National Bank.

The Houston National was the third national bank organized in Houston. It was chartered in 1889, but in 1909 obtained a new charter under the name of the Houston National Exchange Bank. This bank has a most extraordinary record. Its capital stock is only $200,000, while its surplus and undivided profits amount to three-fourths of its capital stock. It has deposits of very nearly four million dollars. The officers of the Houston National Exchange Bank are Joseph F. Meyer, president; M. M. Graves, vice president; Henry S. Fox, Jr., active vice president; Joseph W. Hertford, cashier; F. F. Dearing and W. B. Hilliard, assistant cashiers.

The South Texas National Bank was the fourth national bank organized in Houston. It obtained its charter in 1890. On March 2, 1912, the South Texas National Bank absorbed the Texas Commercial National Bank. The new bank thus formed became the South Texas Commercial National Bank, with a capital of $1,000,000. Nineteen days after the consolidation the deposits of the new bank were $11,000,000, while the capital and surplus amounted to nearly $2,000,000.

The home of this bank is one of the finest and, architecturally, most beautiful buildings in the South. The front of the building is perfectly plain, but is of the purest marble. There are four columns supporting the main pediment, each turned from a solid slab of marble, the shafts of each being twenty-two feet long. The interior of the building is more beautiful than its exterior. Only the finest marble and ornamental bronze were used in the interior finish and the result is most pleasing. The high arched ceiling is an attractive feature. Only the very best artists and superior workers were employed in finishing this building and the results obtained by them speak volumes for their taste and skill.

The following are the officers of the South Texas Commercial National Bank: Chairman of the board, Charles Dillingham; president, W. B. Chew; active vice president and cashier, B. D. Harris; vice presidents, James A. Baker, John M. Dorrance, J. E. McAshan, Thornwell Fay and Judge T. J. Freeman. Assistant cashiers, August De Zavalla, P. J. Evershade, Paul G. Taylor.

There are twenty-five directors, being the directors of the two consolidated banks. They are James A. Baker, F. A. Heitmann, Conrad Bering, O. T. Holt, R. Lee Blaffer, R. S. Lovett, Horace Booth, H. F. McGregor, Chester H. Bryan, J. E. McAshan, W. B. Chew, C. H. Markham, James D. Dawson, J. V. Neuhaus, Charles Dillingham, Edwin B. Parker, John M. Dorrance, S. C. Red, Thornwell Fay, Daniel Ripley, Thomas J. Freeman, Cleveland Sewall, B. D. Harris, J. J. Settegast, Jr .

Houston's fifth national bank was the Union National Bank, organized in 1905. This bank represents three original banks. The Union Bank and Trust Company was chartered in 1905. In 1908, it absorbed the Merchants National Bank. When this was done the bank took its present name and was chartered as the Union National Bank with a capital of $1,000,000. This bank is one of the strongest banks in the South and does an immense business. The twelve-story steel, reinforced concrete, granite and brick building of this bank is one of the finest and most attractive buildings in the city. There are twelve stories above ground and an immense basement. The basement and ground floor are used exclusively by the bank, while the other stories are devoted to modern offices. The basement is fitted up as elegantly as other parts of the building and, besides the huge vaults, contains private rooms for the patrons of the bank. There are safety vaults and store rooms for the safe keeping of bulky valuables.

The building is entirely independent of all outside utilities, having its own artesian water supply, its own heating and electric light plant and its

own chilled air system for use in the summer. There are several large elevators in the building, making access to every floor an easy thing. Including
the ground the building cost almost exactly $1,000,000. The officers of the
Union National Bank are: J. S. Rice, president; T. C. Dunn, George Ham-
men, W. T. Carter, Abe Levy, J. M. Rockwell, Jesse H. Jones and C. G.
Pillot, vice presidents; DeWitt C. Dunn, cashier; D. W. Cooley and H. B.
Finch, assistant cashiers.

Houston's youngest national bank, the Lumbermans National, seems to
have been something of an absorber and consolidator itself. It was organized
and chartered in 1907 with a capital of $400,000. In 1909, it absorbed the
National City Bank, and the next year the American National Bank and
Trust Company liquidated and turned over its business to the Lumbermans
Bank. This bank is one of the strong financial institutions of Houston and
of South Texas, and does an immense business. The officers of the Lumbermans National Bank are S. F. Carter, president; Guy M. Bryan, active vice
president; H. M. Garwood and W. D. Cleveland, vice presidents; Lynn P.
Talley, cashier; M. S. Murray and H. M. Wilkens, assistant cashiers.

The fact that Houston is the real financial center of the State is shown by
the report of the Treasury Department in Washington issued February 20,
1912. In the report the standing of six leading cities is given and Houston
occupies first place with a wide margin over her nearest competitor, Dallas.

	Loans & Discounts	Lawful Reserves	Individual Deposits
Houston	$22,628,110	$3,728,112	$22,425,250
Dallas	$17,221,605	$2,021,996	$17,556,376
Fort Worth	$12,277,281	$1,277,660	$10,237,269
San Antonio	$9,073,658	$1,716,011	$9,105,007
Waco	$5,832,276	$711,567	$5,113,521
Galveston	$3,901,517	$764,253	$3,609,664

The foregoing pages tell of Houston's financial strength, but they tell only
one-half of the story. Banks represent the commercial and business life of
a community, their condition giving in concise form the extent and volume
of trade in a way that can be understood by all. In the very nature of things,
banks, no matter how great and strong, cannot add to the physical and ma-

terial growth of a community except indirectly. Banks prosper by lending money for short periods on commercial paper and similar securities. Their collateral must be such as can be easily turned into cash on short notice. Lands, mortgages, vendors lien notes and such things, considered gilt edge securities the world over, are not so considered by banks. The law even goes so far as to prohibit national banks taking land as security for loans.

It is for the purpose of handling just such business as the banks cannot or will not handle, that trust companies are formed. There is an indirect community of interest between the banks and trust companies, but there are no conflicting interests. One represents the financial and trade conditions of the community while the other represents the material growth, expansion and development of the community. No bank is willing to undertake to do the many things that modern business methods demand shall be done. Such things are entirely without the province of banks. It is for the purpose of doing these things that trust companies have been formed. The trust companies perform a dual duty. They care for and conserve estates placed in their charge, and they also afford a source from which may be obtained long-term loans. Usually these loans are made for the purpose of improving and developing intrinsically valuable property with the property itself taken as security for payment of the debt. The length of the loan, the rate of interest paid by the borrower and the absolute security afforded by the property held as collateral make such a transaction a safe and sure investment for the trust company. The reasonable interest paid by the borrower and the long time given him in which to pay back the loan make the transaction a very advantageous one for the borrower.

The wonderful growth of Houston during the last seven or eight years has led to the formation of trust companies here and Houston now has several of the strongest in the South. The oldest trust company in Texas was organized in Houston thirty-seven years ago, in 1875. The history of those dark and stormy days would lead one to think that large financial schemes would have no place in them, and yet the Houston Land and Trust Company was chartered during the darkest days of the city. It was originally chartered as a land and trust company and did only a small and unimportant business for years. In 1889 it was reorganized and took out a new charter which enabled it to do a regular trust and mortgage business. It is now one of the most important institutions of its kind in the country and does an immense and highly profitable business. Its business is strictly that of a trust company and in no way does it encroach on the business done by banks. The following was the condition of this company at the close of business, March 31, 1912:

Capital stock......................................	$250,000.00
Surplus...	$340,000.00
Undivided profits...............................	$2,980.00
Time certificates of deposit................	$1,313,364.44
Accrued interest payable....................	$13,063.66
Estate and trust account.....................	$104,827.27
Dividend #36, payable 5/1/1912........	$7,500.00
	$2,031,735.37

The officers of Houston Land and Trust are O. L. Cochran, president; R. E. Paine, vice president; P. B. Timpson, vice president; W. S. Patton, secretary and treasurer; O. R. Weyrich, assistant secretary.

The Southern Trust Company was organized in 1909 and began business in January, 1910. Its capital stock was $500,000 but this was almost immediately increased to $800,000. The success of this company has been phenomenal. It is only a little over two years old and yet it has earned over half a million dollars and has paid large dividends since its organization. Following is the statement of this company at the close of business April 18, 1912:

Capital stock......................................	$800,000.00
Surplus...	$400,000.00
Undivided profits...............................	$168,278.21
Trust funds...	$6,466.10
Reserved for taxes, 1912.....................	$4,500.00
Bills payable and rediscounts..............	$140,000.00
Certificates of deposit........................	$177,300.00
Accounts payable...............................	$2,438.28
	$1,698,982.59

The officers of the Southern Trust Company are James L. Autry, president; Travis Holland, vice president; J. W. Powers, Jr., secretary; Beverly W. Ward, assistant secretary; Ernest Carroll, treasurer.

The Texas Trust Company was organized in 1909 with a capital stock of $500,000. It at once established for itself a reputation for soundness and conservatism, which made at once towards its success. The company was in active operation for slightly over two years and during that time paid dividends of 10 per cent and accumulated a surplus of very nearly a quarter of a million dollars. On September 1, 1911, the Texas Trust Company consolidated with the Bankers' Trust Company, thus making the latter one of the greatest trust companies in the South.

The Bankers' Trust Company was chartered in 1909 with a capital stock of $500,000, and a paid in surplus of $25,000. The capital stock was soon increased to $1,000,000. The volume of business done by this company was very great and its success was phenomenal. September 1, 1911, the Bankers' Trust Company absorbed the Texas Trust Company, at the same time increasing its capital stock to $2,000,000. This company transacts a general trust business and is fully equipped in all its departments to meet the financial requirements of its patrons. It takes charge of real and personal estates, and acts as executor, administrator, receiver and trustee. Following is the statement of this company, issued at the close of business April 18, 1912:

Capital stock	$2,000,000.00
Surplus and profits	$881,638.23
Reserved for taxes	$12,000.00
Demand deposits	$44,102.35
Certificates of deposit	$723,496.21
Cashier's checks	$4,302.00
Trust funds	$900,992.46
Rediscounts	$12,973.35
	$4,579,504.35

The officers of the Bankers' Trust Company are Jesse H. Jones, chairman of the board; J. S. Rice, president; Tom M. Taylor, N. E. Meador, J. M. Rockwell, James A. Baker, A. M. Levy, W. T. Carter, C. G. Pillot and J. W. Link, vice presidents; C. M. Malone, secretary; F. J. Heyne, treasurer and cashier; Burke Baker, bond officer; William Malone, real estate officer; Andrews, Ball & Streetman, counsel.

The American Trust Company is a young affair, being only about a year old. It was organized in 1911 with a capital stock of $500,000. This company has banking privileges and intends on taking full advantage of them. Its business at present is both bank and trust business and it bids fair to be one of the strong financial institutions of Houston, both as a bank and as a trust company. Its officers are J. D. Hefley, president; J. E. Duff, vice president; N. B. Sligh, treasurer.

The Commonwealth Trust Company is Houston's latest trust company. It has just been organized and has not yet opened its doors for business. Its capital stock of $500,000 has been over-subscribed. Its charter is one of wide scope and gives it large privileges and an ample field of operation. The charter is that of the First State Bank of Hillsboro, Texas. Mr. W. E. Richards, the president of the present trust company, purchased the Hillsboro charter and at once organized The Commonwealth Trust Company. The officers of the company are W. E. Richards, president; Exile Burkitt, active vice president; Horace Booth, Geo. W. Riddle, W. R. Allison, Monta J. Moore, W. H. Gill, H. H. Simmons, John H. Foster, John S. Callaway and R. E. Burt, directors.

The Continental Trust Company is now in process of organization here in Houston. This is to be one of the greatest and most powerful trust companies in the country. The capital stock of the company will be $1,000,000, while there will also be a paid-in surplus of $1,000,000. The prospectus of this company gives so clear an idea of the functions of a trust company, and particularly of the objects of the present company, that the following liberal extract is taken from it:

> The Continental Trust Company (without banking privileges) of Houston, Texas, has been organized to assist in supplying the urgent demand for a place of sufficient magnitude and strength to which application may be made for absolutely good first mortgage or vendor's lien loans; where persons seeking investments may expect to find good securities in amounts commensurate with their respective means available for employment; being a medium where the borrower and investor come together; also where reliable information concerning relative values of property may be obtained with a view of creating closer relations with Eastern and foreign connections to the end of filling a distinct need incident to the up-building of a country already demonstrated to be resourceful and rapidly increasing in wealth.

Practically every city in Texas is experiencing a large demand for gilt-edge first mortgage and vendor's lien loans, and trust companies in Texas, which are only a few in number, are unable to supply but a small percentage of such demand...The powers which the company will exercise are those of the soundest institutions of this character, omitting banking functions, and especially the receipt of deposits subject to check. It will act chiefly as intermediary between the investor and the borrower, between capital and those who need capital to develop the resources of Texas. Its profits will be derived from expert service which it will offer the investor, together with the assurance of its large financial responsibility in placing and safeguarding funds; and to those needing capital, by furnishing a market for securities and rendering assistance necessary to place them in such form as will make them marketable.

Mr. S. F. Carter, president of the Lumbermans National Bank; Hon. Jonathan Lane, Mr. John H. Thompson, vice president and general manager of the Guarantee Life Insurance Company of Houston; Mr. James F. Sadler, Jr., and other business associates of these gentlemen are prominent in organizing this company, so it is quite evident that its success is assured.

CHAPTER VII:
GOD'S HOUSE ON THE BAYOU

When the Allens laid out Houston they set aside the quarter of a block on the northwest corner of Capitol and Main "for church purposes." The gift was to no denomination or sect, but was to all. A year or two later there was a small building erected on one of the lots and all denominations had the use of it. After the State House was built, religious services were held in one of its halls.

Legend says that the first religious service ever held in Houston was under the spreading branches of a tree that grew on Market Square, in 1837, but the fact remains that the first authentic evangelical service was that which occurred in 1836. The fact is a matter of record that Rev. Mr. Morrell, an itinerant Baptist preacher who came to Texas before San Jacinto, preached in Houston in 1836.

It is rather singular that with all the "hard cases" that were in Houston in the early days, and the consequent necessity for taking precautions for controlling them, the first vigilance committee formed in Houston should have been composed entirely of preachers and that the object of the committee should have been to guard the public against being imposed on by fraudulent preachers. Such was the case and the Preachers' Vigilance Committee was formed in May of 1837. There is no record of their stomping out any frauds, or of anything else they did. No doubt their very existence warned away frauds and thus accomplished what they desired without further exertion on their part.

The first church to secure a permanent foothold in Houston was the Methodist, which perfected an organization in 1837. That year the Allens donated to the Methodist brethren the half block on the north side of Texas Avenue between Travis and Milam Streets.

The establishment of Methodism here was almost entirely the work of one individual, the late honored and revered Charles Shearn. Mr. Shearn was a most earnest and devout Christian who devoted his life to the advancement of his church. He brought from New Orleans, at his personal expense, a minister of the gospel, gave him a home in his own house, and was mainly responsible for the establishment, growth and influence of the Methodist church here. In later years he gave largely, both in time and money, to the church cause and after the war he built, almost entirely with his own money, the church on Texas Avenue, afterwards torn down when the site was sold.

The valuable property on Texas Avenue was disposed of, and the congregation, now flush with money, was determined to build an imposing edifice. They put up a magnificent building on Main Street and so far forgot their old benefactor, in the days of their prosperity, that his name was dropped entirely. Shearn Church thus became the First Methodist Church. The writer is not a member of the Methodist church, and probably it is a bit of impertinence for him to express an opinion on the subject, but the temptation is simply too strong to resist. The dropping of the name of the good old saint who did so much for the church and who, unaided and almost alone, placed it on its feet and guided it on the way to prosperity, was an act by the side of which the proverbial ingratitude of republics sinks into insignificance.

The First Presbyterian Church was organized in the Senate chamber of the Capitol building in 1838. Though a church organization was perfected in 1838, no effort was made to erect a church building until 1843. One reason for the delay was, no doubt, the fact that the Allens had stipulated that all churches should have free use of the site on Capitol and Main until they secured building sites of their own, when the property should revert to the Presbyterians for their sole use. Although, by 1843, all the various churches did not have permanent homes of their own, most of them were making active efforts to secure them, so the Presbyterians determined to build. Early in the year a canvass was made, funds secured, and by the end of the year the First Presbyterian church was erected on Main Street near the corner of Capitol. It was a large frame building, facing Main Street, and was used by the congregation for many years until it was destroyed by fire in 1859.

When the congregation erected a new building they used brick and faced the church on Capitol Street. Services were held there until, in 1879, the building cracked badly and was declared to be unsafe. The building was torn down and restored, thus making it safe. The congregation moved into their restored building early in 1880. The first sermon was preached by their new pastor, Rev. E. D. Junkin, who in addition to being a most eloquent and Christian gentleman, had the distinction of being the brother-in-law of the famous Confederate General Stonewall Jackson. Dr. Junkin's successor was Rev. Dr. Wm. Hayne Leavell. Dr. Leavell resigned in 1906 and was succeeded by the Rev. Dr. Wm. States Jacobs, the present pastor.

The Presbyterians have had fewer pastors than any of the other churches, yet few as they have had, they have lost two by sea tragedies. In 1858 Rev. Mr. Ruthvan was lost at sea. He was going from Galveston to New Orleans on the ill-fated *Nautilus*, which was lost in a great storm that swept the gulf. All the passengers and crew were lost with the exception of a negro deck hand, who clung to a bale of cotton and was picked up by a passing vessel a day or two later. In 1866, Rev. Dr. Castleton and his wife took passage out of Galveston in a sailing vessel. From that day to this not a word has been heard from them, nor has a trace of the vessel ever been found.

The Episcopal church was organized in 1839, and had a fairly good congregation at the very start, since there were thirty-nine adherents of that denomination present at the initial meeting. The early services were conducted by laymen and an occasional itinerant minister, until 1845, when the members adopted a constitution, took the name of Christ Church and determined to erect a house of worship. The cornerstone for the new building was laid in 1846 and the building was consecrated by Bishop Freeman, Bishop of Louisiana, May 9, 1847. There was no regular pastor of Christ Church for several years, but services were held regularly, lay members and an occasional minister officiating.

The old church was torn down and another erected on its site in 1859. In 1876 that building was torn down to make place for a third church, which in turn was demolished in 1893, when the cornerstone of the present beautiful building was laid. Christ Church runs the Methodist a close race in the rapid change of pastors, for up to 1892 there had been no less than fifteen regular pastors. That year, however, something like permanency was established and Rev. Dr. Henry D. Aves took charge of the affairs of the church, both spiritual and temporal. Its great prosperity dates from his installation in office and during the years of his incumbency the most marvelous growth and expansion were shown. Dr. Aves became Bishop of Mexico and was succeeded by Rev. Dr. Peter Gray Sears, who has shown himself to be a worthy successor.

The First Baptist Church of Houston was organized April 10, 1841. The history of this church is interesting, for unlike that of the others, its inception was the result of the untiring efforts of two Christian women, Mrs. C. M. Fuller and Mrs. Piety L. Hadley. Soon after the organization of the church, these ladies undertook to buy ground and erect a church building. They had no money and met with small encouragement even from their fellow church members and members of their own families. Someone, as a joke, gave them a rawboned mule. This they fattened and sold, thus securing a nucleus for a building fund. They then gave a fair where homemade useful articles were sold. The fair and the mule brought them in $450. Then they gave another fair, larger than the other, and secured an additional $900.

With this money they purchased the lots on the corner of Texas Avenue and Travis Street, where the Milby Hotel now stands. During all their labors these ladies had the untiring assistance of good old Brother Pilgrim, a pious and devout Christian gentleman. After purchasing the lots, the ladies wrote to Rev. William Tryan and asked him to come and take charge of the church, which numbered seventeen members. Dr. Tryan accepted the call, came to Houston, and it was through his effort that sufficient money was obtained to build the first Baptist church, which stood for many years on the southeast corner of Texas Avenue and Travis Street. In 1883 the property was sold and a new church was erected in 1883-84. This church was destroyed by the great storm in 1900 and another was erected on the corner of Fannin and Walker in 1903. Rev. Dr. J. L. Gross is the present pastor of this church.

There were Catholic missionaries here in the very early days of Houston's existence, but no effort was made to establish a regularly organized church and to erect a building until 1841, when a French priest, Rev. Father Querat, purchased the quarter block on the south side of Franklin Avenue and Caroline Street. Through his efforts sufficient money was obtained to put up a small wooden building and to build another for a schoolhouse and home for the priest. For many years this little church was used and not until 1869 was an effort made to secure larger quarters. In 1869 the old church property was sold and a block of ground on Texas Avenue and Crawford Street was purchased. In 1871 the new church was completed and has been occupied ever since. The handsome brick building known as the Church of the Annunciation, and is one of the most beautiful churches in the city. Father Hennessy was pastor at the time and has been such all these years, honored and respected by both Catholics and Protestants. The whole block is used by the church, the church edifice occupying the northwest side, while the remainder is given over to elegant school and priest houses.

The first German Lutheran church was organized in Houston either in 1851 or 1852. This tardy organization is somewhat difficult to understand, since there were so many Germans among the early citizens of Houston. In 1853 the church purchased the northwest corner of the block on Texas Avenue and Milam Street and erected a very large and imposing frame building on the corner lot. Rev. Mr. Braun was the pastor, and he also conducted a fine German and English school, using the church building for that purpose. Among the members of this church were some of the most prominent and useful German citizens of Houston. About 1875 a second Lutheran church was built on Louisiana between Prairie and Preston. Some years later both the first and second sites were sold and new churches erected elsewhere, one on Texas Avenue and Caroline Street and the other on Washington and Young Avenue.

From the earliest days of Houston's existence until in the early sixties, the Hebrew congregation in this city was kept intact through the personal exertions of Father Levy, as the venerable rabbi was called. He was a man of great force of character and was honored and respected by everybody irrespective of creed or belief. After his death the office was filled by a most worthy successor, Rabbi Samuel Raphael. Rabbi Raphael had a strenuous time during the continuance of the war between the states, but through his fine executive ability and enthusiastic zeal he managed to keep his congregation together and the return of peace found it stronger than ever. Rabbi Raphael was a profound scholar, an eloquent speaker and a man of great personal magnetism. No man, Jew or Gentile, has ever stood higher in this community than he.

It was five years after the close of the war before an effort was made to secure a suitable house of worship by this congregation. In 1869 a building committee was appointed and in 1870, the cornerstone was laid for the first Synagogue, which was located on Franklin Avenue. Two sons of Rabbi Raphael, Benjamin and Mose, were prominent in the work of building this first house of worship for the congregation their father had done so much for spiritually.

The cornerstone for the Young Men's Christian Association was laid October 17,1907, and the building was formally opened June 21, 1908. The building is one of the finest in the city.

Though it is said the first Christians in Houston were forced to hold religious services under the wide-spreading branches of a tree that grew on Market Square, their descendants are better provided for and today, by actual count, there are sixty-six houses of worship in this city, representing all shades of faith and belief. Houston is rapidly becoming a city of churches. Following is a list of the churches and chapels:

Methodist

Epworth Methodist Church; Harrisburg Methodist Episcopal Church; Grace Church, Houston Heights; McKee St. Methodist Church; First Methodist Church; Trinity Methodist Church; Bering Memorial Church; Washington Avenue Methodist Church; First Methodist Church of Houston Heights; McAshan Methodist; St. Paul's Methodist Church; Tabernacle Methodist Church; Brunner Avenue Methodist Church and Ebernezer German Methodist Church.

Presbyterian

First Presbyterian Church; First Presbyterian Church of Houston Heights; Hardy Street Presbyterian Church; Woodland Heights Presbyterian Church; Third Presbyterian Church; Oak Lawn Presbyterian Church; Second Presbyterian Church; Central Presbyterian Church; Westminister Presbyterian Church; Park Street Chapel; Market Street Chapel; Hutchins Street Chapel; Hyde Park Chapel and Blodgett Mission.

Episcopal

Christ Church; St. Mary's Episcopal Church; Trinity Church; St. John's Church and Clemens Memorial Church.

Baptist

First Baptist Church; Lee Avenue Baptist Church; Magnolia Baptist Church; Brunner Baptist Church; Calvary Baptist Church; Tabernacle Baptist Church; Emanuel Baptist Church; Bishop Street Baptist Church; Tuam Avenue Baptist Church ans Liberty Avenue Baptist Church.

Catholic

Church of the Annunciation; Sacred Heart Church; St. Joseph's Church; Church of the Blessed Sacrament and St. Patrick's Church.

Christian Church

Houston Heights Christian Church; Central Christian Church; Second Christian Church.

Apostolic Faith
Clark Street Mission; Brunner Tabernacle.

Lutheran
Trinity Evangelical Lutheran Church and First German Evangelical Lutheran Church.

Christian Science
First Church of Christ Scientist.

Congregational
First Congregational Church.

Evangelical Association
The Oak Lawn Church.

Church of Christ
First Church of Christ.

Spiritualist
The Spiritualists have a large society in Houston and hold regular meetings every Sunday.

The founding of Houston closely followed the Texas revolution, so it is not surprising to learn that there was a strong martial spirit among its citizens and that they should be willing and eager to embark in military movements that included active or prospectively active service. Governor Lubbock mentions in his memoirs that there were two military companies in Houston in the very early days. One of these, to which he belonged, saw service against the Indians, but there is nothing to show that the other had active service. These companies were what would be called state troops today.

In the early fifties there were two military companies here. One was the Washington Light Guards which held at that time very much the same place that the Houston Light Guard holds today. The other was the Milam Rifles organized after the Washington Light Guards had been in service for some time, and organized for the purpose of taking away from the Washington Light Guards the honors they had won, which were principally the smiles and admiration of the ladies. The two companies were about socially equal and there was intense rivalry between them, which occasionally led to personal collisions between the individual members.

On one occasion, during a target contest between the two companies on San Jacinto Day, there came near being something of a general riot because a lieutenant of one company and a private of the other went to war on their own account over a disputed score.

When the war broke out, instead of entering the Confederate Army as organizations, these two companies disbanded and the individual members joined new companies that were organized. The great bulk of the members of the Washington Light Guards joined the Bayou City Guards which afterwards earned such glory in the Army of Northern Virginia under Lee, known officially as Company A, 5th Texas Regiment, Hood's Brigade. In fact so many of the old company joined the Bayou City Guards that it was practically the old company itself.

Other members of both companies joined a cavalry company raised by the late Major Ike Stafford for service on the Rio Grande, which was the very first company to leave for the front at the breaking out of the war.

The Captain of the Washington Light Guards, Captain Edwards, raised still another company of infantry, while Captain Ed Riordan took some of the members of the Milam Rifles and with them as a nucleus formed a splendid company of infantry. It is doubtful if there was a single member of either of the two original companies who did not volunteer in some of the companies that left Houston in 1861.

At that time there was a boys' military company here, something on the order of the High School Cadets of today. This company was commanded by Captain W. M. Stafford, now of Galveston. When the war broke out, Captain Stafford and most of the older boys entered the Confederate Army. Captain Stafford was made a lieutenant in an artillery company and rose soon after to the rank of captain. He was, perhaps, the youngest captain in command of a battery in the Confederate service.

Another company that distinguished itself during the war was the Houston Turners, composed almost, if not entirely, of members of the Turnverein association. This company was organized and commanded by Captain E. B. H. Schneider and saw much active service, giving a good account of itself on several bloody fields.

The Confederate Grays was a fine infantry company from Houston that saw much active service, first at Shiloh under Johnston and afterwards in the campaign in Mississippi and at Vicksburg. After the capture of Vicksburg they were exchanged and transferred to this side of the river.

When the war began, it was looked on as a joke and there was much joking at the enthusiastic eagerness of the young men to get to the front. The Bayou City Guards was christened "The kid glove gentry," and when the company was ordered to Camp Van Dorn, below Harrisburg, for the purpose of being mustered into the service, preparatory to going to Virginia, Mr. T. W. House, Sr., sent them a big box of white kid gloves. The members put them on their bayonets and marched up Main Street with them thus displayed. Afterwards when the accomplishments of this company in the Army of Northern Virginia began to be known and bragged about, Mr. House was very proud of the "Kid glove gentry," and told frequently of how he had fitted them out for war with kid gloves.

After four years of actual warfare there was not much martial spirit left in the young men who returned home after the surrender. Consequently, there was no talk of organizing a company of play soldiers and the average returned veteran would shy at the sight of a sword or musket. However, there was a new crop of young men coming to the front and in 1873 some of these got together and organized the Houston Light Guard, a military company destined to shed as much honor and fame on Houston during peace times as the others had done during war.

The Houston Light Guard was organized April 21, 1873. Captain Fairfax Gray, a member of the United States Navy before the war and a distinguished officer in the Confederate Army, was the first captain of the company. For some reason the members soon lost interest and the organization practically ceased to exist. After the first meeting, none were held until late in the fall of the same year, when some of the most zealous of the young men got together and determined to reorganize the company.

This they did, electing J. R. Coffin captain. From that meeting dates the success of the Light Guard. Captain Coffin began regular drills and soon had the company in such form as to make a creditable showing as soldiers. The boys purchased uniforms, which were Confederate gray, and appeared in them for the first time in the great carnival of King Comus in February, 1874.

Four months later, when the May Volksfest was held, the Light Guard entered their first competitive drill, meeting four companies from outside points. Entering was all they did for they got no prize, but did get experience. The next year under Captain Joe Rice they won their first prize at the Austin drill, a sword valued at $500.

About that time there seems to have been a general revival of the martial spirit throughout the country and each city strove to secure a crack military company. All over the South and in many of the Northern and Western cities military companies were formed. While there was lots of pleasure and sport in indulging in this fad, it was very expensive and the heaviest expense fell on the individual members. Each company paid for its own travel expenses, its uniforms and everything, except its guns which were furnished by the State government. Interstate drills became all the rage and in 1881 the Houston Light Guard entered its first one at New Orleans where it competed against some of the crack companies of the South. The Light Guard took fourth prize, $500.

Their next appearance was in 1882 at the interstate drill that was held at Nashville, Tenn. There were five companies competing and the Light Guard took fourth prize again. However, they had the satisfaction of beating the Lawrence Rifles, a company that had come all the way from Boston, Mass. Beating that Boston company gave them the only bit of satisfaction they had.

However, the Light Guard were as strong in defeat as they afterwards proved themselves to be in the hour of victory. Captain Thomas Scurry was their commander and he determined to make them world-beaters, and did so before he completed his work. In the face of two or more failures they became more determined than ever and they were loyally backed by the businessmen of Houston.

In 1884 the businessmen raised a large sum of money to be used as prizes and to pay other expenses, and issued invitations to all the military companies in the United States to come to Houston for a great interstate drill. A number of crack companies promptly accepted the invitation. The War Department at Washington appointed three army officers to attend the drill, act as judges and make a report of results to the Department. Mr. H. Baldwin Rice was appointed manager of the drill, which took place at the Fairgrounds, where now stands the Fairgrounds Addition. The drill lasted a week. The first prize was $5,000. From that sum the prizes were reduced so that the last prize was only about one-quarter of that amount.

There was a state as well as an interstate drill held at the same time. In the interstate drill were such companies as the Treadway Rifles of St. Louis; the Columbus Guards of Columbus, Ga.; the Montgomery Greys of Montgomery, Ala.; the Washington Guards of Galveston, and the Houston Light Guard. The Houston Light Guard put up one of the most perfect drills that had ever been witnessed. They took first prize easily, as the following report of the army officers who were judges shows. The totals were as follows:

Houston Light Guard, 2.66; Treadway Rifles, 2.55; Columbus Guards, 2.35; Mobile Rifles, 2.29; Montgomery Greys, 2.28; Washington Guards, 1.95. A perfect drill would have given 3.00, the maximum score. To show how perfectly the Light Guard drilled, the following extract from the report of the judges is given:

> *Houston Light Guard*—It is observed that the inspection was nearly perfect. The appearance of the men in their dress, arms and accoutrements and their neatness, exceeded anything we have seen anywhere—each man like a color man at the United States Military Academy at West Point. Captain Scurry had not proceeded far in the programme when, while wheeling his company from column of twos, improperly, the company was placed in a position

from which it was almost impossible to extricate it, except as done, exhibiting great presence of mind on the captain's part. Captain Scurry's appreciation of the programme and its requirements was superior to that of the other commanders.

The ground was laid out with the view to testing the length and cadence of the step in quick and double time. A company marching as contemplated in the method applied would take the following number of steps in quick and double time, and in the time specified. In quick time, 284 steps in 2 minutes and 35 seconds; in double time, 284 steps in one minute and 26 seconds. The Houston Light Guard made the following record: In quick time, 283 steps in 2 minutes and 35 seconds; in double time, 1 minute and 27. Aside from all practice in this particular, the result was almost phenomenal. Captain Scurry was the only one who marched upon the flag with guide to the left as directed by the judges.

The Houston Light Guard generously offered to turn over the $5,000 first prize to the visiting companies to help pay their expenses, but the offer was refused with thanks, of course.

During 1885 the Houston Light Guard, under the able leadership of Captain Scurry, won three first prizes in interstate contests. These footed up $12,000. The first was at Mobile, Alabama, in May and the second a few days later in New Orleans. The third was in Philadelphia in July at the great drill that was held in Fairmount Park. In this drill and encampment nearly every section of the country was represented. There were seventy-five companies there, about one-half of them entering the interstate contest. The Houston Light Guard was an easy winner, the judges stating that there was enough room between their score and that of their nearest competitor to place three or four companies.

From Philadelphia the company went to New York, where they were royally entertained by the famous New York regiments. It is only an act of justice to give here the names of the officers and men who made the Houston Light Guard "world-beaters." They were:

Captain, Thos. Scurry;
1st Lieutenant, F. A. Reichardt;
2nd Lieutenant, T. H. Franklin;
3rd Lieutenant, Spencer Hutchins;

Quartermaster, W. A. Childress;
Surgeon, Dr. S. O. Young;
1st Sergeant, George L. Price;
2nd Sergeant, R. A. Scurry;
1st Corporal, H. D. Taylor;
2nd Corporal, W. K. Mendenhall;
3rd Corporal, George N. Torrey.

Privates—Byers, Barnett, Bates, Bull, Byres, Cook, Dealy, Foss, Golihart, Hodgson, Hutchins, Heyer, Reynaud, Swanson, Johnson, Journey, Wilson, R. Kattman, E. Kattman, Lewis, Mahoney, Mitchell, McKeever, Powell, Randolph, Steel, Sawyer, Sharpe, Tyler, Taft, Taylor, Torrey, Wisby. Perpetual drummer, John Sessums (colored).

The next great victory of the Light Guard was at Galveston in 1886, where they took the first prize, a purse of $4,500, in competition with such companies as the Montgomery True Blues, San Antonio Rifles, Branch Guards of St. Louis, Company F, Louisville Legion and Belknap Rifles of San Antonio. That drill of the Light Guard was the most perfect ever witnessed in the United States and excited widespread wonder and admiration among military men and the general public.

The Light Guard went to Austin in 1888 and took first prize, $5,000, in competition with some of the crack companies in the U.S. The next year Galveston had another great interstate drill and, in order to not bluff off other companies, the Galveston people barred the Houston Light Guard, thus paying them the highest compliment they ever received. Galveston gave the Light Guard a special prize of $500 for an exhibition drill.

The Houston Light Guard showed that they were not merely fancy soldiers when the war with Spain began. They volunteered promptly and, under command of Captain George McCormick, went to the front. They saw service in Florida and Cuba. When peace negotiations began, Captain McCormick returned home and R. A. Scurry became captain of the company, returning home with it soon after. The Light Guard owns its armory, the handsomest in the state. It was paid for partly with money won as prizes and partly by issuing bonds. The property, in the business section of the city, has become extremely valuable and could be disposed of today at many times its cost to the company.

The following are the captains who have commanded the Houston Light Guard from its organization to the present day: Fairfax Gray, John Coffin, Joe S. Rice, George Price, James S. Baker, Jr., Thomas Scurry, F. A. Reichardt, George McCormick, R. A. Scurry, C. Hutchinson, Milby Porter and Dallas J. Mathews, the present able captain.

Troop A has always been the crack troop of cavalry of the Texas National Guards. This is a Houston company and during the war with Spain was part of the First Texas Cavalry, United States Volunteers.

The Jeff Miller Rifles, which belonged to the Second Infantry regiment, was also a noted company, that saw service during the skirmish with Spain.

While there was quite a large sawmill, a gristmill, blacksmith shop and lumberyard at Harrisburg, established there by Mr. Robert Wilson, father of the late Mr. Jas. T. D. Wilson, who came to Texas in 1828, it would not be exactly fair to claim these as the first Houston manufacturing enterprises. The first strictly Houston concern in the manufacturing line, if a sawmill falls under that head, was the old sawmill that stood just about where the Milam Street bridge crosses Buffalo Bayou. That mill was built in the early forties.

Mr. Elim Stockbridge built a cornmeal mill at the foot of Texas Avenue in 1844. The *Morning Star* was greatly pleased with this evidence of progress and gave quite a glowing account of the motive power which was three oxen on a treadmill.

During the same year Mr. N. T. Davis erected the first compress in Houston. The *Morning Star*, speaking of this compress in its issue of March 11, 1844, says:

> A few days ago we visited the cotton compress lately erected in this city by Mr. N. T. Davis, and were agreeably surprised to find that the machine used for compressing cotton bales admirably answers the purposes for which it was constructed. With the aid of only two hands, Mr. Davis can compress a bale of 500 pounds into a space only 22 inches square in 15 minutes. The facility with which the work is done is truly surprising.

Since the best modern compress can turn out a 500-pound bale compressed into a space of 22 cubic feet, it is evident that the editor of the *Star* got his notes mixed when he wrote of "22 square inches."

In 1845 there was a rope-walk on the block now owned by the Houston Turnverein. It was used for manufacturing rope until about 1853 or 54. The first iron foundry was established in Houston in 1851 by Mr. Alex McGowan on the north side of Buffalo Bayou and on the banks of White Oak Bayou. For the first year or two its principal work was in making kettles for the sugar plantations near here and in constructing light machinery for farm and plantation use. However, after the Houston & Texas Central road began operation, the work of the foundry increased and it was kept busy doing repair work for the road. For several years this foundry was the largest and best in Texas and did an immense amount of all kinds of foundry work. Even during the war it was enabled to continue a regular foundry business, something that others were not able or willing to do.

About 1858 or 59, one of the best and most expert foundrymen in the business came here from the North. This was Mr. Cushman, the owner and manager of Cushman's Foundry, which was located on the south side of the west end of Preston Avenue bridge. Mr. Cushman put up extensive buildings and established suitable machinery for doing all kinds of pattern-making and foundry work. About the time he got everything going smoothly, the war came on and as his workmen volunteered almost to a man, in the Confederate Army. He was left with an expensive plant on his hands and no labor to use it. He struggled along in a haphazard way for awhile and then converted his plant into an arsenal and began manufacturing cannon, shells and such things for the Confederate government. The commander of this department detailed skilled mechanics to do the work and, before long, Cushman's Foundry became one of the most important concerns in the State. After the war Mr. Cushman restored his plant to its original use and did a large foundry business for many years, finally disposing of the plant.

Perhaps the most successful manufacturing enterprise to grow from an insignificant beginning is the Dickson Car Wheel Works. When Mr. Dickson first announced that he was going to manufacture car wheels here he was laughed at and certain defeat was predicted. He persisted, however, and today the Dickson Car Wheel Works are among the largest and most profitable establishments of that character in the South. There is a steady and constantly growing demand for their output.

The first artificial ice made in Houston was at a plant established by Dr. Pearl, who was associated with two young Englishmen. These gentlemen established an ice-making plant and also a meat packery on the Bayou below the city in 1869. Lack of experience, being rather in advance of the times and other causes combined to frustrate their designs and after a year or two of hopeless struggle the plant proved a failure and went out of business in 1873.

During 1875, Mr. E. W. Taylor and one or two associates bought some of the abandoned machinery of the Pearl plant and established a regular packery. The next year Mr. Geiselman established another packery, and both of them did a good business for some years. Transportation facilities were unsatisfactory and that limited the field of operation of the two plants to such an extent that both voluntarily went out of business. Not until 1894 did Houston come to the front as a packing house center. That year the Houston Packing Company's plant was established here. This is the largest independent packing house in the United States and does a business of about $4,000,000 annually.

Both the Swift and Armour companies maintain branches here and own their own buildings. Every large packing house in the United States has a branch office or agency in Houston, induced to come here by Houston's admirable facilities for receiving and distributing their products.

Since the packing house part of the old Pearl plant was, in a measure, resurrected through the efforts of Mr. Taylor and his associates, one would have supposed that attention would have been given to ice-making also. That was not true, however, for it was not until 1880 that a successful ice manufacturing plant was established. That was the Central Ice Company, organized by Mr. Hugh Hamilton. The first machinery was a dilapidated and abandoned ice machine. This is today one of the largest and most successful plants in the state. The American Brewing Company is another large and flourishing concern. It was chartered in 1894 and its principal owner is Mr. A. Busch of St. Louis.

Today Houston has a number of large ice-making plants. Chief among them are the Houston Packing Company, the Henke Artesian Ice and Refrigerating Company, the Crystal Ice and Fuel Company and the Irvin Ice Factory.

Shortly after the close of the war, one or two attempts were made to establish cotton mills here. Not until 1872 was the movement successful. In that year the City Cotton Mills were erected in the Second Ward. Mr. B. A. Shepherd was the principal stockholder, owning slightly more than half of the stock. The mill was just beginning to do a good business, when, in August, 1875, it was destroyed by fire. The loss was complete, being $200,000, with no insurance.

A few years later Mr. E. H. Cushing and Mr. James F. Dumble started another cotton mill out at Eureka, five miles from Houston on the Houston & Texas Central Railroad, but after a struggling existence of a year or two, they were forced to abandon the undertaking.

From that time until 1903 no further attempt was made to build cotton or textile mills here. However, in 1903, the Oriental Textile Mills were established, and this institution now ranks among the largest and most successful textile mills in the United States.

At the close of the war there were several small wagon and vehicle manufacturing concerns established here, and there were also one or two planing mills and sash factories. The planing mills and sash factories of Bering & Cortes and of Henry House were the principal ones, and both did an immense business. As remarked, the manufacture of wagons, while one of the earliest of Houston's manufacturing enterprises, was never carried on extensively until a year or two ago, when in 1910, the Eller Wagon Works were established here. This concern does an immense business and manufactures heavy trucks, oil-tank wagons and such things, which are distributed over the state.

Aside from having several skillful cabinetmakers who did fine but limited work, no attention was paid to the manufacture of furniture on a large scale until in 1904, when the Myers-Spalti Company established their plant here. This is one of the largest and most prosperous plants of its kind in the country. The firm makes anything and everything in the way of furniture. They employ only the best and most expert workmen. They have branch offices in all the leading markets, and the amount of their business is immense.

A fact not generally known is that Houston has the only piano and organ manufacturing plant in the South. It was established here in 1909 and is now doing a good and lucrative business. The work turned out by them beings of the highest order of excellence.

Houston's standing and importance in the nation as a manufacturing point is demonstrated by the U.S. Census Report. Following are the figures for Houston, for 1909, the year when the figures were taken by the government:

Number of establishments, 249; capital invested, $16,594,000; cost of material used, $14,321,000; salaries and wages, $4,254,000; miscellaneous expenses, $1,942,000; value of products, $23,016,000; value added by manufacture, $8,695,000; number of salaried officers and clerks, 725; average number of wage earners, 5338; total number of steam laundries, 9; capital invested in laundries, $270,000; cost of material used, $74,000; salaries and wages, $256,000; miscellaneous expenses, $129,000; value of products, $500,000; number of salaried officers and clerks, 34; average number of wage earners, 422.

When the government figures were taken in 1909, comparison was made with those of 1904 to show percentage of increase and decrease. The comparisons for Houston are as follows:

Increase in cost of material used, 88 per cent; increase in capital invested, 87 per cent; increase in number of salaried officers and clerks, 75 per cent; increase in miscellaneous expenses, 72 per cent; increase in value of products, 70 per cent; increase in value added by manufacture, 46 per cent; increase in salaries and wages, 24 per cent; increase in number of establishments, 19 per cent; increase in average number of wage earners employed during the year, 6 per cent.

In many ways Houston is an ideal point for manufacturing enterprises. An inexhaustible supply of the purest artesian water can be obtained anywhere in or for miles around the city, while the question of fuel is almost as easily solved, since Houston is just on the edge of the great oil field and is connected by pipelines with all the fields as far north as Oklahoma. Water can be had at the small cost of sinking a well, while there is an abundance of the best and cheapest fuel. When to these advantages is added the superb transportation facilities possessed by Houston, it is surprising that there are not a hundred-fold more great manufacturing enterprises here than there are.

Perhaps no city in the United States had among its early settlers so many prominent and distinguished men as had Houston. As a rule, new cities as well as new countries are settled by pioneers who are distinguished more for their brawn and muscle than for their culture and intelligence. Hard work, requiring strength and endurance, counts for more in a new country than courtly manners and scientific ability. These latter belong rather to the children of pioneers than to the pioneers themselves. Houston affords a striking exception to this rule, for among her early settlers were some of the greatest, most prominent and intellectual men in America. This was as true of the foreign element as of the native-born Americans. In fact the latter, as a whole, contrasted rather unfavorably with the distinguished Germans who were among the first settlers. While the Americans excelled naturally in statecraft and in the legal and medical professions, being far more accustomed to the needs, requirements and customs of this country than their foreign friends and associates, the latter contributed more largely to the arts, sciences and general literature. Thus, between the two, Houston was placed on a most advantageous plane at the very beginning.

It must not be supposed that the learned professions, the arts or anything that related to literature occupied the stage to the exclusion of everything else, for that was far from true. There were lots of typical pioneers, rough men, but all men; and in addition to these there were typical "bad men" and toughs. These latter were in a woeful minority and were too few and insignificant to stamp their individuality on the community.

While Houston and Galveston have always been strong business rivals and have never failed to give each other commercial black eyes when opportunity presented, the people of both cities have always been the best of friends in a social way and have done much good for each other. The first literary society, lyceum or whatever it was called, in Texas was located in Galveston in the early forties. While nominally a Galveston institution, this society was loyally supported by Houstonians who contributed regularly to the monthly entertainments that were given.

In 1848 the Houston Lyceum was chartered. Almost before it was born, it went to sleep and did not wake until 1854. That year it was revived and showed considerable animation for awhile but soon lapsed into innocuous desuetude. At that time 382 volumes had been gotten together and a bookcase had been purchased.

For a short time considerable interest was taken in the affairs of the Lyceum by the gentlemen having its management in hand, but they soon grew weary and the Lyceum was allowed to die again. During the war nothing was, or could be, done, but at the close of the war an attempt was made to revive interest in it. This effort met with only partial success. Spasmodic attempts were made to establish the Lyceum firmly on its feet, but it was not until 1895 that such an attempt was crowned with success.

In that year Mrs. Looscan, president of the Ladies Reading Club, brought that Club to the assistance of the Lyceum. Every member of the Club became a member of the Lyceum and the books were removed to a room in the Mason building. Through the efforts of these ladies, the city officials were induced to give official recognition to the Lyceum in 1899 and to make an appropriation of $200 monthly for its support.

The next year Mr. Carnegie gave $50,000 for a library building fund, providing the city would donate a suitable building site. The conditions were complied with and the present library building was formally opened to the public in March, 1904. In 1900 the Houston Lyceum and Carnegie Association was chartered and took the place of the old Houston Lyceum. About the same time Mr. N. S. Meldrum endowed the children's department with $6,000 as a memorial to Norma Meldrum.

Miss Julia Ideson, the librarian, stated in her report for 1904 that there had been 59,751 books withdrawn from the library for home use. At that time there were between eight and nine thousand volumes in the library. In her report for the municipal year ending February 29, 1912, Miss Ideson says, "The circulation from the main library amounted to 102,580 volumes, an increase of more than 8,000 volumes over the circulation of last year. In addition to the above 5,177 books have been distributed through the other distributing agencies." On May 1, 1911, there were 31,678 volumes in the library. During the year that just closed there was a net gain of 3,657 volumes bringing the total number of volumes in the library May 1, 1912, to 35,426.

The officers of the Houston Lyceum and Carnegie Library Association are: Mr. E. L. Dennis, president; Mrs. H. F. Ring, vice-president; Mrs. I. S. Meyer, secretary; Mrs. E. N. Gray, treasurer; Mrs. E. Raphael, corresponding secretary, and Miss Julia Ideson, librarian.

The Ladies Reading Club, organized in 1885 by Mrs. M. Looscan and Mrs. C. M. Lombardi, is the oldest and largest of Houston's purely literary clubs. The Ladies Shakespeare Club was organized in 1890 with Mesdames E. Raphael, I. G. Gerson, I. Blandin, Blanche Booker and Misses C. R. Redwood, Lydia Adkisson and Mary Light as charter members. This club has kept its organization and has been in active existence since its formation. Another Shakespeare Club was organized in 1904 by Mrs. A. G. Howell, Mrs. J. W. Lockett and Mrs. J. W. Carter. This club is very active and great interest is taken by its members in the work they have outlined for themselves.

Perhaps the most interesting of the women's clubs in Houston is the Current Literature Club, which was organized in 1899 by Mrs. Si Packard. The club was originally organized for the purpose of reading current novels and light literature, but members soon grew ambitious and more substantial books were taken up and discussed, until today the club represents through its members the cultured literary taste of Houston.

The Houston Pen Womens' Association was organized in 1906 by eighteen ladies who met at the residence of Mrs. William Christian for the purpose of forming an association composed of ladies engaged in newspaper and literary work. Mrs. Elizabeth Strong Tracy was chosen as the first president and Mrs. Dancey as first secretary. The membership consists of historians, poets, authors, journalists and newspaper workers. The association has been wonderfully successful, showing a consistent growth and influence ever since the day of its organization.

A Chapter of the Daughters of the American Revolution was organized in Houston in 1899 by Mrs. Seabrook W. Sydnor, who had been appointed regent by the general organization. The chapter took the name of Lady Washington Chapter. The organization has been in active operation since its organization and has accomplished a great deal in the way of patriotic work.

San Jacinto Chapter No. 2, Daughters of the Republic of Texas, was organized in 1901. The chapter has accomplished a wonderful amount of valuable work, in perpetuating the memory of those who fought for Texas' independence, and has collected valuable historical data. This chapter has taken under its care San Jacinto battlefield and has marked with suitable monuments and tablets, historical points and localities associated with early Texas history.

Robert E. Lee Chapter, 186, United Daughters of the Confederacy, was organized in 1897 and Oran M. Roberts Chapter, 440, United Daughters of the Confederacy, was organized in 1901. Each chapter has a large membership and their meetings are always largely attended. Since their organization they have accomplished much good, both in the way of collecting and preserving historical data and in looking after indigent and disabled Confederate veterans.

There are a great many charitable, musical and literary associations in Houston, nearly every one organized and kept alive by the ladies. Nearly all the societies, in the beginning, had meeting places of their own, but since the completion of the Library building nearly all of them meet in the elegant quarters provided for that purpose by the Library Association.

The Labor associations of Houston are numerous and thoroughly organized. The following facts are taken from a statement published by Mr. Max Andrew, editor of the Labor Journal:

The total number of industrial workers in Houston is 25,000, graded as follows: Men, 15,000; women, 6,000; children fifteen years and under, 4,000. Organized: Men, 55 per cent; women, 2 per cent. Of the skilled trades, 85 per cent are organized and 15 per cent unorganized.

During the last ten years the hours of labor have been decreased, all along the line, from ten hours to eight hours. During the last ten years there has been an average increase in wages of 25 per cent. However, against that increase is placed the increased cost of living which amounts to 40 per cent.

The total number of organized men and women in Houston is 8,250. The plumbers, printers, brickmasons, plasterers, stonecutters and marble cutters are the best organized of any of the crafts. All trades limit the number of apprentices. This has done much towards maintaining a living wage for the journeyman. Public sentiment and feeling towards union labor in this city and community is very favorable and all important work is done by union labor.

Since the general public has only a vague idea of labor matters and of the conditions that prevail in labor circles, the following extracts are taken from Mr. Andrew's article, as matters of useful information. The following are the working conditions that prevail in various branches of labor, both organized and unorganized:

In the packing houses 500 men, women and children are employed. Wages, for men, $1.50 to $2.00 per day; for women, 75 cents to $2.00 per day; for children, 50 cents to $1.00 per day. No Sunday work. Little opportunity for training or educational advancement. Employees not organized.

In the railroad shops and yards, there are about 4,000 employed. About 25 per cent of laborers work on Sundays. Conditions very good for training and educational advancement. Average wage for all employees about $2.50 per day. Ninety per cent of workers organized.

In the cotton-oil mills and compresses there are about 1,500 employed. Wages of men, $1.50 to $2.50 per day; women, $1.00 to $1.25 per day; children, 50 cents to 75 cents per day. Work covers only six months of the year. No opportunity for training or educational advancement. Conditions are far in advance of those found in other Southern States.

In the sawmills and factories the number of employees is 500. Wages for skilled men, $2.50 to $3.00 per day; unskilled men, 75 cents to $1.75 per day; women, 50 cents to $1.00 per day; children, 25 cents to 75 cents per day. Little opportunity for training or educational advancement. About 10 per cent organized.

In the general stores there are about 3,000 employed. Wages for men, $5.00 to $18.00 per week; women, $3.50 to $10 per week; children, $1.50 to $5.00 per week. Conditions are deplorable. Not one in a thousand of the employees has the slightest chance for training or educational advancement. Unless the general public interferes, Houston will soon parallel the large cities where young womanhood is sacrificed at the altar of greed and avarice. This labor is unorganized.

There are about 500 employed at the breweries. Working conditions are exceptionably good. Wages range from $2.00 to $5.00 per day; hours of labor, eight per day. The breweries operate 24 hours per day, labor being divided into three shifts of eight hours each. Employees thoroughly organized. All workmen in the breweries, where steadily employed, must join the Brewers Union.

There are about 5,000 common laborers in Houston. Wages, for men $1.25 to $2.00 per day; women, 50 cents to $1.25 per day; children, 25 cents to $1.00 per day. Only about 10 per cent of these laborers are organized.

There are about 3,000 employed in the industrial crafts. That is in addition to those working in railroad shops, mills, etc.

Carpenters and Joiners—Approximately 75% organized. Wages, union, $4.00 per day; non-union, $3.50 per day. Educational and training conditions are fine. No Sunday work. Steady employment the entire year round.

Plasterers—Conditions are good. 90 per cent organized. Wages, for union men, $6.00 per day; for non-union men, $3.50 per day. No Sunday work.

Sheetmetal Workers—Steady work the whole year. Wages, union men, $3.50 to $4.50 per day. Non-union men, lower. About 90 per cent of the craft organized.

Brickmasons—Conditions are fine. Wages, union men, $6.00 to $7.00 per day; non-union men, $3.00 to $4.00 per day. About 95 per cent organized.

Machinists—Steady work all the year. Wages, union men, $3.80 per day; non-union men, $2.50 per day.

Theatrical Stage Employees—Conditions reasonably good. Wages range from $15.00 to $25.00 per week. Every day work, including Sunday.

Blacksmiths—About 65 per cent organized. Wages, union men, $3.80 per day; non-union men, $2.50 per day.

Lathers—Steady employment. Wages, union men, $4.00 to $6.00 per day; non-union men, $2.50 per day.

Printers—Thoroughly organized. Wages, $3.50 to $8.00 per day, according to men and position. About 75 per cent of printers are homeowners.

Pressmen—Thoroughly organized. Wages, $3.50 per day. There are also many homeowners among the pressmen.

Bookbinders—Thoroughly organized. Work eight hours per day. Wages, $4.00 per day.

Electrical Workers—About 80 per cent organized. Wages, $3.50 to $4.50 per day. All members at work.

Bartenders—About 80 per cent organized. Wages $15.00 to $21.00 per week.

Tailors—Poorly organized. Hours of labor, ten hours per day. Wages, $2.00 to $3.00 per day, mostly in piece work.

Coopers—Thoroughly organized. Average wages, $2.85 to $4.00 per day. Hours of labor, eight hours per day.

Bridge and Structural Iron Workers—Organized 100 per cent. Hours of labor, eight. Wages, $3.50 to $4.50 per day. Plenty of work. Duties most hazardous.

Boiler makers—About 90 per cent organized. Wages, $3.50 to $5.00 per day for union men; non-union men, scale lower.

Marble Workers—Thoroughly organized. Wages, $4.00 to $6.00 per day. Work eight hours a day.

Journeyman Barbers—Both white and negroes organized. Conditions above the average. No Sunday work.

Elevator Constructors—Thoroughly organized. All employed at present. No Sunday work. Wages $4.00 per day.

Pattern Makers—Well organized. Work nine hours a day. Wages 50 cents per hour.

Garment Workers—This is the only organized craft of women workers. Membership about 200 strong. Work, eight hours a day. Wages, $9.00

to $18.00 per week. No Sunday labor. Sanitary conditions exceptionally good.

Horseshoers—Organized about 75 per cent. Wages, $2.50 to $3.50 per day. Work eight hours a day.

Stationary Engineers—Organized about 80%. Average wages about $3.00 to $4.00 per day.

Painters, Decorators and Paperhangers—Organized about 80 per cent. Work eight hours per day. Wages, $3.50 to $4.00 per day.

Plumbers—Thoroughly organized. Work eight hours a day. Wages $6.00. The union has many educational features to perfect the skill of its members.

CHAPTER XII:
COMMERCE, COTTON, RICE AND TIMBER

Unquestionably the first commercial organization in Texas was the old Chamber of Commerce organized in Houston April 5, 1840, with Mr. Perkins as president. Unfortunately this association has left nothing but a name, for there is no record of work done by it, though it is fair to presume that it accomplished some of the objects for which it was formed.

Not for thirty-four years was another attempt made to form a commercial body in this city. On May 16, 1874, a number of the prominent businessmen of Houston met in one of the parlors of the Hutchins House and organized the Houston Board of Trade and Cotton Exchange. Mr. C. S. Longcope was elected president, Mr. Wm. J. Hutchins, vice-president and Mr. George W. Kidd, secretary.

The new organization went actively to work. Perkins Hall, used also as a theatre at times, was leased. Mr. Kidd purchased some small blackboards and with no other furniture or fixings, the Exchange was officially declared open and ready for business. At that time telegraph tolls were very high, in fact they were prohibitive so far as the new exchange was concerned. The amount of commercial news and quotations received by the exchange in a full working day was about equal to that now received in a few minutes, even on dull days. Mr. Kidd helped out the quotations by using the scant commercial report received by the *Houston Telegraph*, of which paper he was also commercial editor.

Conditions such as these prevailed for the first three years of the Exchange's existence, or until 1877. In that year businessmen appear to have recognized the great values of the Exchange and rallied to its support. Something like a reorganization took place within the Exchange. A new charter was obtained and the name of the organization was changed to the Houston Cotton Exchange and Board of Trade. New rules and regulations were adopted, the initiation fee was increased and provision was made for a regular and permanent income through fees and dues, for the support of the Exchange. From that moment the course of the exchange has been upward, until today no commercial body in the South stands higher in every way than the Houston Cotton Exchange and Board of Trade.

Not content with caring for the large and constantly growing cotton business of Houston, the Exchange was always found in the front ranks working for the good and advancement of the city. For a number of years the Exchange has had among its standing committees one whose special duty it is to look after the welfare of the ship channel. When the present Chamber of Commerce was formed, the Cotton Exchange turned over an immense amount of work to it that before that was tended to by the Exchange. It retained its interest in the ship channel, however, and while working in perfect harmony with the Chamber of Commerce and all other Houston organizations, it is still found working most zealously.

In 1883 the members of the Exchange determined to build a home of their own. Ground was purchased, plans adopted and on November 15, 1884, the new building was turned over to the Exchange by the contractors. It was a very handsome, though small, building and answered every purpose for which it had been constructed for many years. In later years it was remodeled. Additional stories were added and today the Exchange building is one of the most attractive and valuable buildings in the city.

There is no cotton exchange in the South more prosperous Houston's Exchange. When it was first organized a membership cost but $1 a month. A certificate of membership now costs $2,000 and is difficult to secure one at even that price. Annual dues on each certificate are $50, while provision is made for fees and other dues to maintain the exchange.

The following gentleman have served as president of the Exchange since its organization:

C. S. Longcope	1874-75	Wm. D. Cleveland	1884-91
Wm. D. Cleveland	1875-76	Wm. Read	1891-92
George L. Porter	1876-77	H. W. Garrow	1892-1902
H. R. Percy	1877-78	Wm. D. Cleveland	1902-05
S. K. McIlhenny	1878-79	W. E. Andrews	1905-06
Wm. V. R. Watson	1879-80	H. R. Percy	1877-78
A. H. Lea	1880-81	W. O. Ansley	1906-07
S. K. McIlhenny	1881-82	E. W. Taylor	1907-08
S. A. McAshan	1882-84	A. L. Nelms	1908-12

Mr. George W. Kidd, the first secretary of the Exchange, served actively until 1898 when he became secretary emeritus. He was succeeded by Mr. B. W. Martin who resigned to accept a more lucrative position and was succeeded in turn by Mr. B. R. Warner. Mr. Warner, after serving from

1899 to 1903, resigned to return to newspaper work in New Orleans. In 1904 Mr. W. J. DeTreville was elected secretary and served until June, 1910, when, on his death, Mr. J. F. Burwell, the present efficient secretary was elected.

With its immense lumber, oil, rice and manufacturing interests Houston long ago passed that point in its progress where its prosperity depended on any single commodity or industry. Like other commercial centers, Houston for some years counted heavily on its cotton receipts for its prosperity, but does so no longer. The modern Houston merchants are not indifferent to the great value of the cotton business, however. They are anxious to get all of it possible, and with the object of doing so, they have left nothing undone to make this the most attractive market and concentrating point in the South. They have constructed large compresses and cotton warehouses and now have some of the largest and most conveniently situated buildings of that kind on this continent.

The great fire which occurred in the Fifth Ward early this year destroyed three of Houston's fine compresses. There are three large ones left and two are being constructed on so great a scale that when completed in time to handle the coming crop, Houston will have the finest facilities for handling and caring for cotton in the South.

The presses destroyed were the Cleveland, the Standard and the Southern, their combined capacity of presses being 3,000 bales daily and their storage capacity about 100,000 bales. The Cleveland and the Merchants have combined and plans are now being perfected for the erection of the finest and largest compress and warehouse in the world. The storage capacity will be limited only by the restrictions of the insurance companies. They are unwilling to insure so great an amount of cotton as the company could care for. It is certain that the storage capacity of the new press will not be less than 300,000 bales. The company owns something like seventy acres of land on the ship channel and therefore will not be restricted by want of space. Captain W. D. Cleveland is the head of the new company.

Houston already has in the Magnolia Warehouse and Storage Company one of the best equipped, largest and most powerful presses in the country. Every compress and warehouse in Houston is located either on the banks of the bayou or on a railroad and all of them have rail connection. The result is that drayage, a costly feature in handling cotton, is entirely eliminated and the business is conducted economically and expeditiously. Last season there were shipped down the bayou about 400,000 bales of cotton. As each bale represented a saving to the owner of 12 1/2 cents because there was no drayage, it is evident that the shipments represented about $50,000 in savings. No other cotton market in the world can or does do business so cheaply.

The history of Houston's cotton business is of more than passing interest since in its entirety it represents every phase of the evolution of the world's cotton trade. As already noted in these pages, in the early days all cotton raised in the state was brought here by ox-wagons for marketing. The Houston merchants bought the cotton both with cash and groceries and goods. It was a most satisfactory method of doing business and both the farmer and merchant profited by the transaction. After the merchant had accumulated a sufficient number of bales to warrant it, he shipped the cotton down the bayou to Galveston to be placed on chartered vessels, to be shipped to Liverpool or other foreign markets. Since there was no way of knowing how prices were ruling in the foreign markets, the merchant guarded against possible loss by discounting his last information materially and paying from seven to ten dollars per bale less for the cotton than he estimated it to be worth. This was fair since there was always serious danger of a heavy decline in prices before the cotton could arrive on the other side.

After the railroads were built in Texas, Galveston became the great cotton market of the state and every bale raised in Texas was shipped there. One thing that helped build up Galveston was the fact that there were no such things as through bills of lading and rail rates favored the port. In 1874, J. H. Blake & Co. established their firm in Houston and soon evolved a plan for overcoming the disadvantages under which Houston was placed. By an arrangement made with the Houston & Texas Central and the International Railroads this firm was enabled to buy cotton in the interior, bring it to Houston and then ship it out again either by rail or by water. Under this arrangement Messrs. Blake & Co. made the first shipment of cotton from an interior point to a foreign market on a through bill of lading in 1874. This was the first shipment of the kind ever made. That method of doing business soon placed Houston, if not on an equal footing, at least on nearly such with Galveston and saved this market from utter extinction.

Then the system of buying and selling future contracts was established. This was perhaps the greatest advance that could possibly have been made towards stability of the cotton market, and the establishment of something like uniform prices all over the world. The system was very simple. Cotton was purchased on this side only when prices in Liverpool were favorable for such purchases. The cost of freight, insurance, commission and other charges were added to the price paid for the cotton and then, if Liverpool prices were sufficiently high to warrant doing so, the cotton was bought and future contracts sold in Liverpool by cable. In that way every possible chance of loss was eliminated from the transaction. When the cotton arrived on the other side the future contract was closed out; the difference in the price of the contract and the price of the actual cotton equaled each other.

The next great change that took place was more radical and far-reaching. In their effort to do away with middlemen, the spinners on the other side established buying agencies of their own on this side. These, in turn, established sub-agencies all over the country, so that the producer of cotton instead of having to seek a market, found one right at his door. There was such competition between the buyers that the highest prices possible were paid in order to get the cotton. Every crossroad and little town in the state became a center of information about prices and the farmer could learn every morning the quotation of that day both in American and foreign markets.

It soon became evident that it would be necessary to provide some place where large quantities of cotton could be concentrated for inspection, classification and arranging for final shipment. The Houston cotton men realized that a radical change in the method of marketing cotton was about to take place and they began at once to prepare themselves to care for this concentrated cotton. Old warehouses and compresses were enlarged and new ones erected. The storing capacity of the city was materially increased and when the work was finished, Houston was most thoroughly equipped to meet all demands that could be made on her.

Another thing that was done, which shows the great forethought of the Houston merchants, was reducing all local charges to the lowest point possible. No attempt was made to make money directly from the compresses and warehouses, as such, but these were used very much as so much capital, to attract and keep the cotton business here. It is a fact that cannot be disputed that today Houston's local charges on a bale of cotton are from 25 cents to 30 cents per bale cheaper than are those in any other cotton market in the South. Now when to this saving in local charges is added the further saving of from 10 cents to 12 cents through the absence of drayage, it is readily seen why so much cotton is shipped here and why Houston stands so prominently forward as a great cotton market.

Mention has been made of the Chamber of Commerce that was organized in Houston in 1840, but the present magnificent body of that name has no direct nor indirect connection with that early body. The Chamber of Commerce of today is for today and looks more to future accomplishments than to traditions of the past.

The immediate forerunner of the Chamber of Commerce was the Houston Business League, which was organized in 1895 by about forty gentlemen who sought to form an association that would look after the best interests of Houston. Col. R. M. Johnston, editor of the *Houston Post*, and Mr. W. W. Dexter, at present editor and proprietor of the *Bankers' Journal*, were prime movers in the organization and did much to insure its success. The constitution adopted declared the following to be the object of the association:

> The object of the Houston Business League is to promote immigration, to create and extend and foster the trade, commerce and manufacturing interests of Houston; to secure and build up transportation lines; to secure reasonable and equitable transportation rates; to build up and maintain the value of our real estate, progressive, efficient and economical administration of our municipal government, to collect, preserve and disseminate information in relation to our commercial, financial and industrial affairs and to unite, as far as possible, our people in one representative body.

The following gentlemen were chosen as the first officers of the new organization: J. M. Cotton, president; Ed Kiam, first vice president; J. C. Bering, second vice president; E. T. Heiner, third vice president; W. W. Dexter, secretary; Guy H. Harcourt, treasurer.

After serving for only a short time, Secretary Dexter resigned and Mr. George P. Brown was chosen as his successor. The election of Mr. Brown was a most fortunate thing for the Business League, since he brought to its service splendid executive and administrative talent and a wonderful amount of energy and zeal. Under Mr. Brown's administration the Business League forged rapidly to the front. A large number of manufacturing and industrial plants were secured for Houston, the Floral Festival and

No-Tsu-Oh associations were formed and the name of the city was placed permanently on the map of the country.

In 1910 the Business League was enlarged and a necessary reorganization took place. The name Business League was dropped and the organization became the Houston Chamber of Commerce. Mr. Adolph Boldt was secretary at the time and it was largely due to him that the scope of the association's objects and energy were enlarged. He recognized the magnitude of the field and the Chamber of Commerce was organized to fill every part of it.

In the Chamber of Commerce there is a general association, but all the details of practical work are in the hands of special committees who have absolute authority and freedom of action, being responsible only to the general association. These committees are called bureaus. There is, for instance, the Traffic Bureau, to which is referred all matters relating to freight rates, rate discriminations and questions of that kind. There is a Convention Bureau which looks after securing conventions to meet in Houston and looks after the entertainment of strangers who come to such conventions. There is a Publicity Bureau, an Industrial Bureau, which looks after securing manufacturing and industrial concerns for Houston, and a number of other important bureaus.

It is obvious how thoroughly organized the Chamber of Commerce is. One of the most pleasing features connected with the organization is the perfect harmony that exists between it and other organizations working either directly or indirectly towards accomplishing the same ends. The citizens attest their faith in the Chamber of Commerce by giving it the most loyal support, and it is today one of the strongest and most efficient organizations of its kind in the South. Its officers are: Adolph Boldt, secretary; C. G. Roussel, assistant secretary; C. C. Oden, traffic manager; Jerome H. Farbar, director of publicity. There are of course a great many businessmen who are heads of committees and good workers too, but the gentlemen named are the real workers and the ones who accomplish things.

The average citizen does not know how much good has been accomplished for Houston by the Chamber of Commerce, nor how much good is being planned for the future. It is a working body and it does not confine its labors to union hours of an eight hour day, but puts in every waking hour of the entire twenty-four. A vast amount of valuable information has been collected, and preserved in such form as to be immediately available.

Houston is today the home of vast commercial and manufacturing enterprises, most of them having come here during the last six or eight years. It is, for instance, the largest lumber market in the Southwest and one of the largest in the world. That does not mean that there are extensive mills and manufacturing plants here, but it does mean that about all the lumber made in Texas is controlled and handled by Houston firms, which are the greatest in the South. There are over 250 sawmills in Texas, Louisiana and Arkansas controlled and represented through offices located here. The following are the big Houston firms and the capacity of their plants:

Kirby Lumber Company, manufacturers, 400,000,000 feet.
Long-Bell Lumber Company, manufacturers, 500,000,000 feet.
West Lumber Company, manufacturers, 175,000,000 feet.
W. H. Norris Lumber Company, wholesalers, 100,000,000 feet.
Vaughan Lumber Company, wholesalers, 100,000,000 feet.
Continental Lumber and Tie Company, wholesalers, 100,000,000 feet.
Trinity River Lumber Company, manufacturers, 60,000,000 feet.
Central Coal and Coke Company, manufacturers, 50,000,000 feet.
W. T. Carter & Brother, manufacturers, 50,000,000 feet.
Carter Lumber Company, manufacturers, 40,000,000 feet.
W. R. Pickering Lumber Company, manufacturers, 50,000,000 feet.
Sabine Lumber Company, manufacturers, 40,000,000 feet.
Ray & Mihils, wholesalers, 40,000,000 feet.
Carter-Kelly Lumber Company, manufacturers, 30,000,000 feet.
Big Tree Lumber Co., manufacturers & wholesalers, 30,000,000 feet.
C. R. Cummings & Co., manufacturers, 25,000,000 feet.
J. S. and W. M. Rice, manufacturers, 25,000,000 feet.
Gebhart-Williams-Fenet, manufacturers, 25,000,000 feet.
Bland & Fisher, manufacturers, 25,000,000 feet.
J. C. Hill Lumber Company, manufacturers, 20,000,000 feet.
L. B. Manefee Lumber Company, manufacturers, 20,000,000 feet.
R. W. Wier Lumber Company, manufacturers, 20,000,000 feet.
Alf. Bennett Lumber Co., manufacturers & wholesalers, 20,000,000 ft.
R. C. Miller Lumber Company, manufacturers, 20,000,000 feet.
Bush Brothers, manufacturers, 15,000,000 feet.
Southern Pinery Tie & Lumber Co., manufacturers & wholesalers, 10,000,000 feet.

The foregoing foot up within a fraction of two billion feet of lumber annually controlled by Houston firms.

Houston is the recognized center of all that relates to handling, refining, exporting and financing the output of the Texas oil fields and is rapidly assuming the same relation to the oil fields of Oklahoma. An idea of the importance of Houston in this respect may be formed from the fact that there are five large oil refineries here, thirteen oil dealers and thirty-nine producers and exporters, twenty-three of the latter being large concerns. Houston has the largest independent oil company in the United States, the Texas Company, with a capital of $86,000,000. Pipelines from all the Texas fields and from Oklahoma converge at Houston and additional lines, to cost in the neighborhood of $7,000,000, are being constructed.

Houston naturally holds first place as a rice market, since it has every possible advantage. Aside from the physical aspect, there is something of a sentimental side to the question, since it was a Houston man who first pointed out the possibilities of rice culture here and who actually undertook steps to develop it. The late J. R. Morris, as early as the middle seventies, organized a company and took out a charter for the purpose of cultivating rice in all that territory lying between Houston and the San Jacinto River. He had a survey made which demonstrated that Houston is about twenty-eight feet lower than some near point on the San Jacinto River from which he proposed to start his canal. He wanted to deflect the water from the river and use it in irrigating the prairie lands and to utilize the surplus in running machinery at the mouth of White Oak Bayou, at the foot of Main Street.

For some reason nothing was ever done by Mr. Morris and his associates, but attention was drawn to the possibilities of rice culture, which has resulted in its becoming one of the large and rapidly growing industries of Texas. At the time of Mr. Morris' death it is doubtful if there was as much as an acre of ground in Texas devoted to the cultivation of rice. Today rice holds third place in point of importance among the crops of the state. Harris County alone has 30,000 acres, while there are 253,560 acres in all, of which about 200,000 acres are tributary to Houston.

Houston has five rice mills with a daily capacity of 7,600 bags, while the capacity of all the mills in the state is 25,200 bags. The annual production averages about two and a quarter million bags, and Houston handles about three-fourths of it.

Including the railroad shop workers there are several thousand wage earners in Houston employed all the year round to whom is paid something
like $8,500,000 annually. This is not for one year, but is for every year and
therefore it is not surprising that Houston should be known as the best
retail town in Texas. There are over twelve hundred retail dealers who,
according to an estimate made by the Chamber of Commerce based on
almost complete returns, do an annual business of $55,000,000.

The wholesale business of Houston is very great, estimated by the Chamber of Commerce at $90,000,000 annually. The leading articles and the
amount of business done in each are as follows:

machinery, $3,000,000
hardware, $4,000,000
lumber, $35,000,000
petroleum products, $1,000,000
drugs and chemicals, $4,000,000
paints and glass, $1,000,000
furniture, $1,400,000
dry goods, $1,750,000
liquors, $1,250,000
beer and ice, $2,500,000
groceries, $8,000,000
produce, $4,600,000
sugar and molasses, $2,000,000
tobacco, $1,250,000
packing house products, $3,750,000

When to these is added the business done in building material, paving material, electrical supplies and other things, it becomes apparent that the estimate of $90,000,000 must be under rather than above the actual figures.

Not counting the railroads, trust companies and banks, there are 376 incorporated companies doing business in Houston, the combined capital of
which is $145,943,900. There are, of course, thousands of individuals and
numerous unincorporated companies doing business in addition to these,
which shows the magnitude of Houston as a trade center.

In the early days the Houston merchants and property owners who wished
to insure against fire loss were compelled to send to New Orleans for their
policies, for there were no local insurance agents here. These conditions

prevailed until 1858, when Mr. John Dickinson established the first agency in Houston, representing a New Orleans firm. Just about the time Mr. Dickinson got his office working satisfactorily and began doing a lucrative business, the war broke out and knocked his business into a cocked hat.

In 1868 the first local insurance company was organized in Houston. This was the Planters' Fire Insurance Company, which did a good business until 1880, when a disastrous cotton fire occurred, causing such heavy losses to the company that it went into voluntary liquidation.

In 1895 the Houston Fire and Marine Insurance Company was organized. This company did a good business for several years, but through the innocent purchase of a lot of bogus bonds, it was forced to suspend and go out of business a few years ago.

The Guarantee Life Insurance Company was the first life insurance company organized in Houston. It was organized in 1906 with a capital stock of $100,000 and prospered from the very beginning. It does an immense business and has over $13,000,000 insurance in force. The officers of the Guarantee are Jonathan Lane, president; John H. Thompson, vice president and Charles Boedeker, secretary-treasurer.

The Great Southern Life Insurance Company is, in some respects, a wonderful organization. It was organized in 1909 and though it is less than three years old, it has done and is still doing, an immense business. It has a capital of $500,000 and a surplus of $500,000 and outstanding insurance of over ten million dollars. Among its policyholders is one who is insured for $100,000, the largest policy ever written in Texas for one person. The officers of the Great Southern are J. S. Rice, president; O. S. Carlton, C. G. Pillot, J. S. Cullinan and P. H. McFadden of Beaumont, vice presidents; J. T. Scott, treasurer and Louis St. J. Thomas, secretary.

The *Houston Telegraph* of March 18, 1853, mentions the fact that some of the material for the telegraph line between Houston and Galveston had been received at the latter place. At that time the land part of the line had been constructed, but the two-mile stretch across the bay at Virginia Point was causing a great deal of trouble. Modern submarine cables were unknown at that time and many substitutes for them were suggested and tried. Finally the difficulty was overcome by using ordinary iron wire covered with gutta percha, which was warranted by its maker to last for one year and which cost $350 per mile. But before the problem was solved, the land part of the line grew old and fell down, so that it was not until 1858 that an actual working line was constructed between the two cities, this being the first telegraph line constructed in Texas. It was not a great financial undertaking, since the cost of the entire fifty miles including the two miles of bay, was only $6,200, of which the Houston people contributed $3,000.

Having constructed the Galveston-Houston line successfully, the owners formed a company called the Star State Telegraph Company and built a line along the Texas and New Orleans railroad which was being constructed about that time. When the war occurred, the company had its line completed to Orange in East Texas. As an item of interest, it may be stated here that when the Texas ports were blockaded during the war it was almost impossible to get sulfuric acid with which the batteries of those days were operated, and that telegraphing would have been impossible had not some genius found that the acid water from Sour Lake made an admirable substitute for sulfuric acid. The telegraph batteries were charged with Sour Lake water and all difficulty disappeared.

Soon after the close of the war, the Star State Company was absorbed by the Southwestern Telegraph Company which then covered most of the Southern States. Mr. D. P. Shepherd, who is possibly the oldest telegraph operator in this country and is said to have been the first operator in the world to take a message by ear, was placed in charge of the new telegraph company with headquarters in Houston.

In 1867 the Southwestern was absorbed by the Western Union Telegraph Company, the latter company gaining control of all the telegraph lines in the United States. The Western Union remained master of the field until late in 1910, when it, in turn, was absorbed by the Southwestern Telegraph and Telephone Company, the largest corporation of its kind in the world.

The first manager of the Western Union in Houston was Mr. Merrit Harris, who died during the great yellow fever epidemic of 1867 and was succeeded by Col. Phil Fall, who has the distinction of being the oldest operator in actual service in this country.

The Postal Telegraph Company opened its office in Houston during July, 1898. The establishment was merely on a small scale, but by strict attention to business has managed to build up an immense business and has made itself a formidable competitor of the Southwestern Telegraph and Telephone Company in the local field. The Postal aims at promptness and dispatch, and has thus earned an enviable reputation.

In the latter part of 1910 the Mackey Telegraph and Cable Company established its chief office in Houston, thus making Houston the great telegraph center of the state. All the companies have direct cable connection with all parts of the world, but the Mackey company has facilities possessed by no other company. The cable business out of Houston is immense and the general telegraphing done by all the Houston lines amounts to very near four million messages each year and is constantly increasing.

In the late seventies, the latest in communication invention arrived in Houston in the form of a telephone. The *Houston Telegram* of June 18, 1878 reports:

> Mr. J. W. Stacey, the efficient manager of the Western Union Telegraph office in this city, has procured a telephone of the latest improved construction, which he will put up for use during the military encampment of the volunteers of the State next week. The line will run from the Fair Grounds to Mr. G. W. Baldwin's library room in the Telegram building and everybody wishing to have the pleasure of conversing with a friend a mile distant will have an opportunity. Our friends from the country and many in the city who are skeptical about the truthful working of the wonderful instrument, will have an opportunity to test it to their satisfaction. To many of them it will be quite a curiosity, and we expect to see its capacity fully tried. Mr. Stacey will make a trial test today and will have the apparatus in perfect working order by the end of the week.

During the fall of the same year, Mr. Pendarvis, who was telegraph operator for the Morgan Transportation Company, connected his office in Houston with the office in Clinton, ten miles away and for a time had direct telephone connection between the two. Commenting on this innovation the *Houston Telegram* stated that unquestionably when the great convenience of the telephone was appreciated they would be installed in railroad depots, business houses and, perhaps, residences. This prediction has come true in a much greater degree than the *Telegram* supposed possible.

It was not until 1880 that a telephone exchange was established in Houston. Two years later Mr. G. W. Foster took charge of the exchange and it was largely through his efforts and the hearty and valuable assistance of his wife that the telephone business in Texas attained such huge proportions in so short a time. Mr. Foster is still an active man in the company and fills one of the higher offices. The local company has just completed its own skyscraper at a cost of about $1,000,000, and has equipment for caring for 20,000 subscribers with out making further additions to its plant.

Houston's long distance telephone system is very complete, with twelve circuits to Galveston, seven to Beaumont, three to San Antonio, three to Dallas and one each to Fort Worth and Corpus Christi. Each of these direct circuits has branch circuits reaching all parts of the state.

In addition to the old telephone company there is an automatic telephone company also operating in Houston. This company owns its own home, an elegant building on Rusk Avenue near the Federal building.

There are two wireless telegraph companies operating in Houston. One is a strictly private affair owned by the Texas Company. This company has 2,700 miles of private wires in Texas, Oklahoma and Kansas. It uses these wires for business purposes, but keeps its wireless plant always in readiness for use in case of failure of its wires. The company owns similar outfits at Beaumont and in Oklahoma.

The other company, the Texas Wireless Telegraph-Telephone, is the only one engaged in public and commercial business. The company has perfectly equipped stations at Houston, San Antonio, Victoria, Fredericksburg, Waco and Fort Worth. It is distinctly a home company, for all of its stock is owned by Texans, and its officers and managers are all Texans.

The Houston Electric Light Company was organized in 1882, by Mr. E. Raphael. Its first officers were: E. Raphael, president; D. F. Stuart, secretary. The board of trustees were: A. Grosebeck, B. A. Botts, F. A. Rice,

E. P. Hill, D. F. Stuart, J. C. Hutcherson, G. L. Porter and E. Raphael. At that time, only the old Brush carbon lights were used. Mr. Raphael exhibited the first incandescent lamp ever seen in Houston in August, 1883. The great merit of the incandescent lamp was recognized at once and Mr. Raphael secured a contract to equip the Howard Oil Mill plant with them. This was the first installation of incandescent electric lights in a building in Texas. Mr. Raphael and his associates conducted the business for a year or so and then sold their plant to the Houston Gas Company. That company organized the present electric light company in 1894.

CHAPTER XIV:
MR. RICE AND HIS INSTITUTE

Among the very early settlers in the new town of Houston was Mr. Wm. M. Rice, who was destined to impress his name indelibly on this, his adopted home. Mr. Rice was a remarkable man. He began his mercantile life in a modest way, but by strict attention to every detail of his business he was soon able to extend his field of operation. His success was assured from the beginning, and, his money-making instinct, or faculty, largely developed, he soon became one of the best known and most prosperous merchants of the city.

Much has been said and written about Mr. Rice. Some things absolutely true and some largely imaginative. Those who knew him are aware of the fact that he would not have appreciated some of the latter. Mr. Rice was intensely practical, and cared little for the applause of the crowd. He was a successful merchant, a king of finance and nothing more. He was absolutely honest and just, and what was more to the point, he was as just to himself as he was to others. If he made a contract he carried out every detail and he required those who made the other side to do the same. If he owed money he paid every cent of the debt and those who owed him money were required to settle in full. He was merely an ordinary merchant and businessman, though a remarkably successful one.

Had the early friends and associates of Mr. Rice been asked to select one of their number who would make a princely donation towards the cause of education, the chances are ten to one that Mr. Rice would never have been selected. If he ever gave a thought to art, science or literature no one knew of it. The first intimation that he took the least interest in educational matters was given some time during the middle eighties when the city was endeavoring to raise money to purchase what was known as Academy Square and the old building that stood on it, for the purpose of turning it into a high school. The property had been owned by a company but had passed into the hands of a private citizen and the city wanted to buy it. Mr. Rice was living in New York at the time, but was paying an annual visit to Houston when the purchase matter came up.

Mr. E. Raphael, who was very close to Mr. Rice, and who looked after some of his Houston interests for him, was requested by a committee of citizens to ask Mr. Rice for a subscription to the fund. Mr. Raphael did so and was met by a prompt refusal. Mr. Rice stated that it was the duty of the city and not of individuals to care for such things as public schools. Then he surprised Mr. Raphael by telling him that he was thinking of a plan by which he hoped to establish a great educational institution here. A few months later he took into his confidence a few gentlemen and, after a thorough discussion of his plans, an organization was formed and, in 1891, a charter was applied for and granted. The terms of the charter were most liberal and the trustees were given wide latitude for the future organization of a great nonpolitical, non-sectarian institution of technical learning to be dedicated to the advancement of letters, science and art, to be located in the adopted home of Mr. Rice. As a nucleus for the endowment fund, Mr. Rice placed in the hands of the trustees an interest-bearing note for $200,000.

The original trustees were the following named gentlemen: Mr. Rice, himself; his brother, Mr. F. A. Rice, Mr. A. S. Richardson, Mr. James A. Baker, Mr. J. E. McAshan, Mr. E. Raphael and Mr. C. M. Lombardi. Under the terms of the charter this board is made self-perpetuating and its members are elected for life. Since its organization vacancies have been filled by the selection of the following: Mr. Wm. M. Rice, Jr., a nephew of Mr. Rice, Mr. B. B. Rice and Dr. E. O. Lovett.

Having taken the first step, Mr. Rice became infatuated with the idea he had conceived, and from time to time, transferred to the trustees large interests and then, by his will, left the bulk of his large fortune to the institute. Mr. Rice was murdered in New York in 1900 and there was a long fight in court over his will.

When the trustees finally came into possession of the full resources of the foundation, which then amounted to approximately ten million dollars, they invited Dr. Edgar Odell Lovett, Professor at Princeton University, to assist them in formulating and executing the educational programme of the Institute. The President thereupon undertook a year's journey of study which extended from England to Japan. Upon the completion of this preliminary investigation by Dr. Lovett, a most suitable site of three hundred acres was secured. To Messrs. Cram, Goodhue and Ferguson of Boston was committed the task of designing a general architectural plan consistent with the programme which had been adopted for the Institute.

In 1911, on the seventy-fifth anniversary of Texan Independence, the cornerstone of the Administration Building was laid by the trustees. This building, together with the first wing of the Engineering Quadrangle, the

Mechanical Laboratory and Power House, and the first Residential Hall for Men, is rapidly nearing completion. The initial building schedule also includes special laboratories for instruction and investigation in physics, chemistry, and biology, and in the application of these sciences to the arts of industry and commerce. In the preparation of these preliminary laboratory plans the Institute has enjoyed the cooperation of an advisory committee consisting of Professor Ames, director of the physical laboratory of Johns Hopkins University; Professor Conklin, director of the biological laboratory of Princeton University; Professor Richards, chairman of the department of chemistry, Harvard University; and Professor Stratton, director of the National Bureau of Standards.

The academic work of the Institute will begin this autumn on the 23rd day of September. A few days later the formal opening will be observed with appropriate ceremonies of inauguration and dedication, on October 10th, 11th, and 12th, 1912. Distinguished scholars and scientists from a number of foreign seats of learning have consented to participate in the proceedings of the Institute's first academic festival by preparing lectures in the fundamental sciences of mathematics, physics, chemistry, and biology, and in the liberal humanities of philosophy, history, letters, and art.

The initial staff of the Institute will be organized in a faculty of science and a faculty of letters. Of those who have been selected for positions under the direction of the faculty of science it is possible to announce the following elections, in alphabetical order:

Philip Heckman Arbuckle, B. A. (Chicago), of Georgetown, Texas; Director of Athletics at Southwestern University; to be Instructor in Athletics.

Percy John Daniell, M. A. (Cambridge), of Liverpool, England; Senior Wrangler and Rayleigh Prizeman of the University of Cambridge; Lecturer in Mathematics at the University of Liverpool; to be Research Associate in Applied Mathematics.

William Franklin Edwards, B. Sc. (Michigan), of Houston, Texas; formerly Instructor in the University of Michigan, and later President of the University of Washington; to be Lecturer in Chemistry.

Griffith Conrad Evans, Ph. D. (Harvard), of Rome, Italy; Sheldon Fellow of Harvard University ; to be Asst. Professor of Pure Mathematics.

Julian Sorrell Huxley, M. A. (Oxford), of Oxford, England; Newdigate Prizeman of the University of Oxford; Lecturer in Biology at Balliol College, and Inter-collegiate Lecturer in Oxford University; to be Research Associate in Biology.

Francis Ellis Johnson, B. A., E. E. (Wisconsin), of Houston, Texas; recently with the British Columbia Electric Railway Company; to be Instructor in Electrical Engineering.

Edgar Odell Lovett, Ph. D. (Virginia and Leipsic), LL. D. (Drake and Tulane), of Houston, Texas; formerly Professor of Mathematics in Princeton University, and later Head of the Department of Astronomy in the same institution; President of the Institute; to be Professor of Mathematics.

William Ward Watkin, B. Sc. (Pennsylvania), Architect, of Houston, Texas; to be Instructor in Architectural Engineering.

Harold Albert Wilson, F. R. S., D. Sc. (Cambridge), of Montreal, Canada; Fellow of Trinity College, Cambridge University; formerly Professor in King's College, London; Research Professor in McGill University; to be Professor of Physics.

There is being constituted a faculty of letters in which will be developed facilities for elementary and advanced courses in the so-called humanities, thereby enabling the Institute to offer both the advantages of a liberal general education and those of special and professional training. For these faculties of science and letters the best available instructors and investigators are being sought in the hope of assembling in Houston a group of unusually able scientists and scholars through whose productive work the new university should speedily take a place of considerable importance among the established institutions of the country.

The subjects in which instruction will be provided as rapidly as possible are mathematics, physics, chemistry, biology, engineering, architecture, ancient languages, modern languages, history and politics, philosophy and psychology, economics and sociology, and art and archaeology. The programmes of study are being so arranged as to offer a variety of courses leading after four years of undergraduate work to bachelor's degrees in arts, in science, in letters, and in their applications to the several fields of engineering, domestic arts, and other regions of applied science. Extensive general courses in the various domains of scientific knowledge will be available but in the main, the programmes will consist of subjects carefully coordinated and calling for considerable concentration of study. For the advanced degrees, Master of Arts, Doctor of Philosophy, and Doctor of Engineering, every facility will be afforded properly qualified graduate students to undertake lines of study and research under the direction of the Institute's resident and visiting professors.

Candidates for admission to the Institute who present satisfactory testimonials as to their character will be accepted either upon successful examination in the entrance subjects or by certificate of graduation from an accredited public or private high school.

There will be no charge for tuition and no fees for registration or examination in the Institute. A small deposit will be required to cover possible breakage in the laboratories and losses from the libraries; the balance from this contingent fee is, of course, returnable at the close of the session.

Rooms in the Residential Hall, for men, completely furnished exclusive of linen, together with table board at the Institute Commons, will be available for from eighteen to twenty dollars per month of four weeks. For both single and double rooms the rental will be uniform without regard to their location, and they will be let in the order of applications received. Diagrams showing the floor plans will be sent on request to anyone who may be interested. Accommodations for the residence of young women on the university grounds will not be offered during the coming year. The Residential Hall for Men is of absolutely fireproof construction, heated by steam, lighted by electricity, cleaned by vacuum apparatus, and equipped with the most approved forms of sanitary plumbing, providing adequate bathing facilities on every floor.

The general plan for the improvement of the site of the Institute calls for a number of playing and exhibition fields in the vicinity of the residential groups. In fact the wide expanse of the campus affords abundant space for every variety of physical exercise. A determined effort will be made to systematize and make general a sane devotion to outdoor sports in climatic conditions, which render athletics and open-air gymnastics profitably possible the whole year round. The daily timetable of each student will include a definite period under the instructor in athletics. Similarly, with a view to developing every student in the manly art of self-defense in oratory and disputation there have been appointed, in the South Tower of the first Residential Hall for Men, halls for two literary and debating societies, whose activities should supplement the work of certain chairs under the faculty of letters.

www.ingramcontent.com/pod-product-compliance
Lightning Source LLC
Chambersburg PA
CBHW020336100426

42812CB00029B/3147/J